Pernicious:

The Neo-Confederate Campaign against Social Justice in America

Edward H. Sebesta

Copyright Edward H. Sebesta 2009 Anti-Confederate flag in Black & White

Third American Revolution Press

Dallas, Texas

Edward H. Sebesta is an independent researcher of the neo-Confederate movement. He has been published by university presses and peer reviewed academic journals as well as *Black Commentator* and elsewhere on the neo-Confederate movement. He is also an activist fighting neo-Confederacy.

The publisher can be contacted through the web page www.templeofdemocracy.com. Given the nature of the groups that the author researches including a mailing address would be inadvisable.

Third American Revolution Press

www.templeofdemocracy.com

Copyright © 2016 Edward H. Sebesta

All rights reserved.

ISBN: 978-1537732541
ISBN-13: 1537732544

To Steven, whose love and support has helped make this book possible.

Book and websites by Edward H. Sebesta

Books

Neo-Confederacy: A Critical Introduction, edited by Euan Hague, Heidi Beirich, and Edward H. Sebesta, University of Texas Press, 2008. The University of Texas Press web page for the book is at http://utpress.utexas.edu/index.php/books/hagneo.

Co-editor of *The Confederate and Neo-Confederate Reader: The 'Great Truth' About the 'Lost Cause'* Edited by James Loewen and Edward H. Sebesta, Univ. Press of Mississippi 2010. (http://www.upress.state.ms.us/books/1338). The title is ironic, the 'Great Truth' is that the Confederacy was about white supremacy and is a reference to Confederate Vice-President Alexander H. Stephens's speech explaining that the Confederacy was about white supremacy which Stephens claims is the "Great Truth."

Web Sites

www.citizenscouncils.com has the entire newspaper run of the White Citizens Councils from 1955 to 1961 as a historical research resource and also to show that Confederate symbols have always been about racism and white supremacy by mainstream elements of society.

www.confederatepastpresent.org is a source of additional historical reference material that didn't have room in the book, *The Confederate and Neo-Confederate Reader: The 'Great Truth' About the 'Lost Cause.'*

www.templeofdemocracy.com is a web page which has the author's curriculum vitae and has links to many of the articles that he has had published in peer reviewed academic journals and at *Black Commentator*. It also has links to other anti-Confederate web resources.

Forthcoming Books and by the Author

Prelude to Texas Secession: In a recent opinion poll in August 2016 three out of five supporters of Donald Trump for president said that they supported Texas secession if Hillary Clinton is elected president. The Texas secession movement didn't come out of nowhere. This book details the prevalence of secessionist and neo-Confederate ideas in Texas conservatism.

The Neo-Confederate Nationalist Intelligentsia: Every nationalist movement has its intelligentsia and the neo-Confederate movement is no exception. This book details the writings and contributions of Richard M. Weaver, M.E. Bradford, John Shelton Reed, Eugene Genovese, and numerous other academics who wrote for the *Southern Partisan* magazine in developing neo-Confederate thought.

Collected Black Commentator Articles, 2011-2015: This is a collection of articles written for *Black Commentator*, an online publication. It includes a lengthy four-part expose of the Museum of the Confederacy in Richmond, Virginia; a proposal to screen out supporters of the Confederacy from juries; a dossier of the racism and extremism of the Sons of Confederate Veterans; an autobiographical account of the authors 25 year struggle against neo-Confederacy in 2015; and other articles.

Collected Touchstone Articles: This collection includes: A review of former Texas U.S. Senator Phil Gramm and Texas U.S. Representative Dick Armey's interview in *Southern Partisan*; a review of a *Chronicles*' article "From the Alamo to Kosovo: The Anti-Muslim-Hispanic Movement in Texas;" a report on a neo-Confederate speech by former Texas A&M president Frank Vandiver; and a review of Ann Coulter's article in the *Confederate Veteran* magazine defending the Confederacy.

CONTENTS

	Foreword	ix
	Acknowledgments	xi
	Preface	xiii
1	Introduction	1
2	Soft Power	7
3	The Geography of Politics	11
4	Poisoning White People and Teaching that African American Lives Don't Matter	31
5	Fighting Neo-Confederacy	35
6	What Is Neo-Confederacy and Who Are the Neo-Confederates?	41
7	Neo-Confederate Organizations	51
8	Against Equality and Democracy	57
9	Against Public Schools	75
10	Violence and Insurrection	93
11	Division by Prejudice	117
12	Division by Prejudice: African Americans	163
13	Enablers: Banal White Nationalism	193

FOREWORD

14	American History Textbooks	231
15	Conclusion	259
	Epilog	261
	Five Recommended History Books	262
	An Anti-Confederate Flag	263
	About the Author	267
	Index	269
	Footnotes	276

FOREWORD

In 1999, I delivered a brief presentation to colleagues at the annual conference of the Royal Geographical Society-Institute of British Geographers which outlined some of my recently completed Ph.D. research. I had spent four years exploring American interpretations of Scotland and Scottish nationality and, for reasons too convoluted to explain here at length, British newspapers had become interested in my comments. The London *Times*, the *Guardian* and others described some of the connections I had advanced in my lecture between understandings of whiteness and Scottishness evident in U.S. popular culture. Wire services picked up the story and papers in cities such as San Francisco, Atlanta and Memphis, reproduced it. It was in one of these American imprints that Edward Sebesta read about my presentation. A few weeks later, a package of photocopies arrived at my office. Edward had sent me an envelope filled with articles from publications with strident titles like *Southern Patriot*, *Southern Partisan*, and *The South Was Right!* These pieces outlined the positions of authors who had in the mid-1990s coalesced around a new nationalist organization, the League of the South. Its leaders maintained that they were ethnically of Celtic descent, as was the culture of the American South. My interest was piqued. After all, I was studying how Americans understood Scotland and these claims of Celtic identity as a foundational rationale for a contemporary nationalist movement were both intriguing and confusing. Who were these people who were proposing this Celtic thesis to advance a new ethnic nationalism in the USA? How much influence did these authors really have? Was this League of the South going to become as politically influential as the equally new, and also supposedly Celtic-descended Lega Nord in Italy? What else did these authors believe?

I contacted Edward and asked for more information. It seems only a short time ago, but in 1999 the internet was still a relatively new phenomenon (no-one had posted anything on Facebook, let alone used YouTube or Twitter – none of these companies existed!). As Edward knew more about going online than I did, his searches generated more packages of printouts and photocopies containing articles by people I now understood to be neo-Confederate activists. Consistently in these writings, authors saw current events through the lens of the Nineteenth Century Confederacy and, of more concern, understood these interpretations as the basis for political action. One photocopy that I remember most starkly was a review of Mel Gibson's 1995 Scottish blockbuster *Braveheart*, penned by League of the South director Clyde Wilson: "Imagine the film of our *Braveheart*: The Life of General Nathan Bedford Forrest." I'd never heard of Forrest, but soon discovered his role in a Civil War massacre at Fort Pillow and connections to the establishment of the Ku Klux Klan in the years following the end of the hostilities. If Forrest was worth celebrating as a role model, I wondered, what other political positions would neo-Confederates consider?

Such was my entry into the world of neo-Confederacy. I read the decade-long scholarly debate over McWhiney's "Celtic thesis" which, although ultimately discrediting it academically, did little to stem its popular appeal in the post-*Braveheart* glow of the late-1990s. I dug through nineteenth century theological justifications for slavery to try to understand why neo-Confederate authors would reprint and praise these obscure, long-forgotten texts. I scoured the shelves of used book stores and libraries to track down books by neo-Confederate authors, and recognized their names on programs for conferences about nationalism and secession in the post-Cold War United States. I learned a new lexicon as neo-Confederate articles fulminated against "activist judges," "political correctness," and "multiculturalism." These people were not just historians arguing over the meaning of the past; they were drawing from the past to plot out an alternative future, one in which an independent Confederation of Southern States would exist, within which, the League of the South's President, Michael Hill explained, "a European population, especially Anglo-Celts, ...must be preserved as the dominant majority."

About two years later, in summer 2001, I drove to Texas because one of the founders of the League of the South, Grady McWhiney (1928-2006), was scheduled to speak at a Scottish Highland Games. With around forty others, I attended McWhiney's presentation, during which the elderly professor of history read excerpts from his book *Cracker Culture: Celtic Ways in the Old South* as bagpipers played outside. It was also on this trip that I first met Edward Sebesta. We have since worked together, most substantively on our collection *Neo-Confederacy: A critical introduction* (University of Texas, 2008). Sebesta's understanding of neo-Confederacy is unparalleled, and with this depth of knowledge, he has demonstrated how blithely and widely accepted are neo-Confederate readings of the past. Neo-Confederate assessments supportive of the Confederacy appear in textbooks, on monuments, in military awards, in public ceremonies, and in the discourse of countless politicians, past and present. Consequently, neo-Confederate attitudes perniciously shape the present and will likely continue to distort the future of American politics unless, as Sebesta demands in this book, they are continuously and robustly challenged.

Euan Hague,   9/26/2016

ACKNOWLEDGMENTS

I would like to thank Charles "Chaz" A. Todd Jr. for the assistance he has given me from 2012 to 2015 in my efforts to learn how to effectively communicate the relevance of the neo-Confederate movement to the concerns of the general public. He spent many hours in discussing the issues and giving feedback, reviewing presentations, working on storyboards, giving computer support, and giving technical assistance in presentations. Most importantly he has always understood the importance of this topic and has given encouragement for my efforts.

I would like to thank Michael Phillip professor of history at Collin College for his many hours in reviewing, editing and providing feedback on all the chapters and also for his encouragement. This was critical in making this book possible. Any mistakes in the book are my own.

I would also like to thank Dr. Euan Hague of DePaul University for his assistance in obtaining academic materials for my research and having spent some time discussing the relevance of my research to public concerns. Also, for the Foreword for this book.

PREFACE

I wrote this book to mobilize people to oppose the pernicious neo-Confederate movement and to explain the very real negative impact that the neo-Confederate movement has and has had regarding the everyday issues of people's lives such as health care, economic equality, democracy, and social equality.

Generally the importance of defeating the neo-Confederate movement is not understood. Some think it is about arguing over 19th century history. Others see that they are a reactionary group with a contemporary agenda, but that they are of minor importance.

The fact is that the issue is about a struggle for the future of the United States of America is generally not understood at all. Instead it is often thought that it is some struggle over historical memory with only esoteric impacts.

The neo-Confederates use methods of misrepresenting history to manipulate popular memory to defeat social justice. This is what makes this movement so pernicious is that they use methods that the public doesn't recognize as such and thus their agenda often moves along unhindered.

In reviewing the geography of the ratification of the Nineteenth Amendment giving women the vote, and the geography of the defeat of the Equal Rights Amendment for women in this book it will becomes apparent that having a region identified with the Confederacy has had huge impact on America's social progress.

PREFACE

The neo-Confederate movement will continue to undermine and block efforts to achieve social progress and an egalitarian society unless it is defeated.

So this book was written to explain the following: Who the neo-Confederates are, their impact, what they are trying to do and why it is important that they be opposed.

Or more specifically as outlined here:

1. Explain what the neo-Confederate movement is.

2. Explain that the issue just isn't about debating 19th century history but is a contest for the future of our nation. It is about real everyday issues.

3. Explain the three means by which they accomplish a reactionary agenda in the United States.

   3.1. Creating a Confederate cultural consciousness in particular in the South, but also across the nation.

   3.2. Using their positions in the establishment to advance their reactionary agenda.

   3.3. Having neo-Confederate groups to campaign directly for their political agenda.

4. Discuss and document the tremendous impact it has had on our national history.

5. Describe and document their agenda against democracy and human rights.

6. Provide the information to discredit them and thus defeat them.

7. Make people aware that the neo-Confederates have enablers.

I have omitted many topics about the neo-Confederates to focus on immediate issues and keep this book from becoming too long. In particular I didn't discuss the defenses of slavery that the neo-Confederate movement is publishing and how pro-slavery books from before the Civil War are being republished.

The book generally doesn't go back in time more than 20 years and focuses more on the neo-Confederate movement of the 21st century.

In discussing some issues I focused on giving enough examples of the neo-Confederate agenda so that the neo-Confederates could not deny that an element was a part of their agenda. In the chapter on the neo-Confederate agenda for African Americans I focused on three serious issues to review them more in depth rather than cover all possible matters related to this topic. However, readers will note that in writing about one topic elsewhere in the book, in the examples given, there will be more than one prejudice or bigotry which can include racist hostility against African Americans.

Also, the book doesn't supply critiques of neo-Confederate assertions about history. Though neo-Confederates misrepresent history to advance their agenda, debating their historical claims detracts from focusing on what they are trying to achieve and have achieved in subverting efforts to achieve social justice. These arguments over history obscure why neo-Confederates use historical claims, that is to get places and people to have a Confederate identity and how this results in the undermining of social justice. Arguing over which Civil War generals owned slaves is of little interest today and doesn't explain something much more important and relevant to the present: such as how neo-Confederates delayed women getting the vote and how they helped defeat the Equal Rights Amendment resulting in the present day situation for women.

Since this is intended primarily to be an e-book in some cases I have rather lengthy quotes. I ask that the reader read them. The lengthy quotes often allow the reader to have a more immediate sense of what the author is communicating. One can only fully appreciate the sheer arrogance and extremism of neo-Confederate writing by reading longer passages of such works.

Regarding the book I have adopted new approaches which I consider appropriate for an e-book. The footnotes are not condensed. There is no use of "Ibid." to refer to the same source. This is done to make the footnotes easier to use and the person doesn't have to do any process of deduction to know the source. There is no ink or paper involved so the footnotes don't need to be condensed. The result is that in the paper version of this book will have some additional pages, but footnote ease of use I think justifies it.

Finally, though I will often introduce an abbreviation for a group, I will still spell out the group's name in different chapters and sections. Some of this is rhetorical, but also I don't want the reader to have to have to go back through the book to find where the abbreviation was first defined.

The e-book format was adopted to allow this book to reach the general public rapidly without the delays of academic publishing.

PREFACE

Also, utilizing new methods available with the Internet I am crowd sourcing the copy editing of this book. Editing was done but we hope to hear from readers to make corrections for the 2nd edition.

The neo-Confederate movement needs to be recognized for what it is: an often unacknowledged force poisoning American politics and it needs to be opposed, stopped, and utterly defeated.

This book is the first step.

Edward H. Sebesta   9/17/2016

1 INTRODUCTION

Fighting neo-Confederacy isn't about haggling over history, it is a fight for the future of the nation. It is about the issues of the day. It is about a pernicious movement that has retarded and held back our nation, which is against social justice in the present, and strives to lead our nation into a dark reactionary future and has real prospects of doing so.

The neo-Confederate push a reactionary agenda in three ways:

- One, by what their organizations do directly in politics for specific reactionary issues.

- Two, by what individual neo-Confederates do in their individual roles in the conservative establishment where they advance the neo-Confederate agenda.

- Three, by the organizations' actions to maintain a Confederate self-identified region of the United States.

An Example: Health Care and neo-Confederacy

The Abbeville Institute, a neo-Confederate organization, advocates opposing "Obamacare" (Affordable Health Care Act) by nullification, a concept in which a state can unilaterally declare a federal law unconstitutional and void. This is an organization in which their ads claim "… have the resources of more than a hundred academics in all fields of learning." Indeed its members are university and college professors from all parts off the nation. Its founder and president is professor of philosophy emeritus of the prestigious Emory University. They are not marginal individuals, they are persons in the establishment.

INTRODUCTION

The neo-Confederate Abbeville Institute (www.abbevilleinstitute.com) has run the same full page ads headlined, "Compatriots! Learn About the Abbeville Institute," in the *Confederate Veteran*, the official publication of the Sons of Confederate Veterans (SCV), nine times starting in 2013 and continuing to 2015. The ads want the SCV membership to know that their scholars opposed the Affordable Health Care Act. The ad states:

> Abbeville scholars are asked for advice on public policy. Three of us testified before State House committees in framing bills nullifying Obamacare as an unconstitutional intrusion into the state's reserved powers. We had some influence in the bills passed last term by the Oklahoma and South Carolina House. … Abbeville scholars were asked to speak before the Liberty Caucus in the House of Representatives in Washington on state nullification.

Opposition to the Affordable Health Care Act is the primary reason given in the ad to support the institute. The ad solicits the SCV membership to give funds for student scholarships to attend their summer school sessions because:

> The United States is in the grip of a culture war. These wars take no prisoners. They are won by ideas. It is imperative we educate our youth at the college and graduate school level.

The next generation of neo-Confederates are being trained.

Fighting culture wars, opposing "Obamacare," and supporting nullification is what the Abbeville Institute felt would appeal to the membership of the SCV in asking for donations. The Abbeville Institute sees its task as fighting for a reactionary agenda concerning important contemporary issues and believes that this is what would appeal to the SCV members. The Civil War[*], Robert E. Lee, Jefferson Davis, the Confederate soldier, or anything about the Confederacy aren't even mentioned in an ad appearing in a magazine titled *Confederate Veteran* of the Sons of Confederate Veterans. Instead it is about fighting a culture war in the here and now and fighting over health care in the here and now. In calling the SCV members "Compatriots" they assert that their agenda is one in which the Sons of Confederate Veterans, the descendants of Confederate

---

[*] Neo-Confederates do not use and dislike the term "Civil War," but use instead "War Between the States," "War of Southern Independence," "War of Northern Aggression," etc. Refusal to use the term "Civil War" is a fairly good identifier of someone who is a neo-Confederate. Interestingly enough, in the *U.S. Congressional Record*, the term used for the Civil War in indexing was "War of the Rebellion" for many decades until it was changed to "Civil War."

soldiers are partners in, that is "compatriots," implying that their agenda is Confederate.

The ad also mentions that members of the Abbeville Institute have contributed essays for every issue of the *Confederate Veteran* over the last three years. Further, the ad mentions that the Abbeville Institute also helps the Stephen D. Lee Institute, an educational organization of the SCV, conduct its conferences. The Abbeville Institute's assertion that the SCV members are "compatriots" is supported by the joint record of the two organizations working together.

This example is given to show that neo-Confederacy is **not** about haggling over the past. The neo-Confederate agenda is about important contemporary issues. It is about seizing the future. The agenda of the neo-Confederates isn't limited to "culture wars" and health care, it is against public schools, against civil rights and a long list of minorities, voting rights, environmentalism, immigration, green energy, democracy, feminism, concern over global warming, and just about anything progressive, which might be considered liberal, and any social justice movement. The *Confederate Veteran* in 2015 and 2016 has carried editorials apparently against the Black Lives Matter movement, though not specifically by name, by Thomas Strain, SCV Lt. Commander-in-Chief, who in 2016 was elected SCV Commander-in-Chief.

The neo-Confederate hostility against minorities includes racial and ethnic minorities including Eastern and Southern Europeans, Unitarians, Muslims, Jews, Lesbian, Gay, Bi, and Trans (LGBT) and just about anyone that isn't a Christian member of the religious right and a reactionary patriarchal white heterosexual male.

Also, the Abbeville Institute isn't composed of socially or economically marginal persons, they are professors, school instructors, and others in the academic world. As will be detailed in this book neo-Confederates are persons in the establishment, persons in positions of real influence. They have the venues to advance their agenda, they have been doing so and are doing so. They are changing America, and changing it for the worse.

Though the Abbeville Institute wishes to emphasize their influence by mentioning their testimony before committees and claims of influence with legislatures, it has to be asked why any state house committees would even have hearings on nullification in the first place on any issue and then would even invite Abbeville Institute scholars to testify as experts or even think they are experts. It has to be asked why they wouldn't be considered crackpots.

INTRODUCTION

As for the Liberty Caucus in the U.S. House of Representative, what year are they living in, 2016? 1861? Or 1832?† Again why would there be any elected representatives of the U.S. House would even take seriously talk of nullification or consider the Abbeville Institute as experts instead of crackpots.

The neo-Confederates have some direct influence in politics as when they testify before a state committee or a U.S. Congressional group. But it has to be asked why there would even be a state house committee and even be any U.S. Representatives that would even consider nullification seriously and not as craziness and would even consider the Abbeville Institute scholars as experts instead of crackpots.

They are taken seriously because the neo-Confederates have, largely unnoticed, deeply shaped the consciousness of American society and particularly the broader conservative movement. Whether they are conscious of it or not, members of Congress and state legislatures have been fed the Neo-Confederate worldview for years to the point that the extremism of the Abbeville Institute has become normalized.

In this book it will be discussed where the neo-Confederates have direct influence, but it is the indirect influence of the neo-Confederates in support of their reactionary agenda which is much more important and pernicious and which will also be discussed. Focusing on the usual means of political influence misses where they have a tremendously toxic impact.

The Abbeville Institute has a few hundred members, and the Sons of Confederate Veterans roughly 30,000 members. The indirect influence isn't limited to the number of their members. What the SCV along with other neo-Confederate groups do is define in the popular mind, particularly in the South, that the Confederacy is the South's heroic past, that the Civil War was about states' rights and excessive federal government power and the Confederacy was the force for states' rights. All that an opponent of a specific political measure needs to do to oppose a measure is to state that a certain measure is against states' rights or leads to excessive federal power, and without the Confederacy even being mentioned. Or conversely a supporter of a measure can insist that a measure is in support of states' rights or less federal power. The public can connect a specific issue by themselves, on their own, as being against or for the values of a heroic Confederacy which fought for states' rights and against federal power. The public can also see a measure as being for or against these values without even consciously thinking of the Confederacy specifically. Confederate values often lurk in the background, consciously or not, when political debates center on local control and whether federal power has lurched

---

† The Nullification Crisis was in 1832. The Civil War started in 1861.

out of control. The supposedly heroic Confederate past, provides roles models for those fearing they are up against an out-of-control government in Washington, D.C.

The Abbeville Institute in this ad is accomplishing two tasks. One is making sure that a connection is made in the minds in the SCV membership between the Confederacy and opposition to the Affordable Health Care Act of which the membership is already predisposed to make that connection and provide arguments to SCV members grounded in a historical narrative of the Confederacy and their definition of the South. With the prior shaping of historical memory in the South to embrace the Confederacy and therefore adopt its reactionary values, the additional actions of the Abbeville Institute and other neo-Confederate groups, are just enhancements of a process that has already occurred and will continue to occur. Two, they are communicating to the SCV membership that they have the same values regarding the Affordable Health Care Act as the members and the Abbeville's campaign against this Act is a Confederate campaign.

We live in a society that over the decades has become one of increasing economic inequality and inequality of opportunity. Voting rights are currently under siege across the country. The middle class is eroding away while elites grow richer, and everyday people face increasingly grim economic prospects. We face living in one big economic plantation. It might be considered that when a major portion of the nation believes in plantation fantasies they are disposed towards accepting inequality in society.

In the Abbeville Institute ad there is the offer to donors contributing over $100.00 to get a free signed copy of *Rethinking the American Union for the 21st Century*, a book of essays by Abbeville Institute members. If the neo-Confederate movement isn't stopped we might end up living in their rethought American Union, a 21st Century nightmare Confederate States of America.[1]

The Abbeville Institute isn't the only group with a modern agenda looking back to the Confederacy. Greg Eanes gave a speech printed in a booklet titled, *Enduring Principles: Remarks Delivered at the 50th Anniversary of the United Daughters of the Confederacy Massing of the Flags in Honor of Confederate President Jefferson Davis*. In this speech which has the usual assertions about the Civil War being about states' rights he argues that the debates over issues in the 19th century apply to issues today such as: "accountability of the Federal Reserve"; "the waste of millions of your Federal tax dollars for green energy"; abortion; and the legalization of marijuana which he feels causes "lawlessness and safety issues." Neo-Confederates see the present and future through lenses of the Confederate past.[2]

INTRODUCTION

This book is about the pernicious neo-Confederate efforts to pervert and distort the history of the United States of America as a form of soft power to poison people's thinking in order to block social justice in America. It is about who they are, what they believe, what methods they use and the real concrete impact on our society.

It *isn't* about being negative about the South, but to free these states from the prison house of the Confederacy.

It *isn't* about arguing over 19th century history, even though neo-Confederate are distorting history to achieve their goals. There will be some reference to history, but it won't be the focus of this book.

The book is about a contest over the future of the United States of America and the real danger of America having a very dark future.

2 SOFT POWER

Before discussing the who, what, when, and how of the neo-Confederate movement, we need to understand their means of soft power how they shape society and that further requires discussing how society can thus be shaped by soft power. Very concrete examples will be given to show that neo-Confederacy has had serious consequences for the entire nation. Also, what will be explained is what can be accomplished by fighting the neo-Confederate movement, how defeating the neo-Confederate movement could have a revolutionary impact on the struggle for social justice.

At one level human rights or equality fail to advance and can even regress because of specific votes by a legislatures, state or federal, in the passage or the repeal of a law relating to economic policy, labor law, housing, and voting, as well as Supreme Court decisions such as the recent decision undermining the Voting Rights Act.

However, it has to be asked if at a deeper level there isn't a mentality, a thinking, a consciousness, created by a soft power strategy which undermines support for human rights and equality leading to these specific political actions undermining social justice. This worldview might not be held by most of the general public but it doesn't necessarily need to be in order to be effective in blocking progress, it just needs to be held by a significant fraction of people geographically concentrated or persons strategically placed. It has to be asked why with our democratically elected legislatures and chief executives there is enough popular support for politicians who are constructing our increasingly unequal and unjust society.

As in the example above, the Abbeville Institute testified for nullification of the Affordable Healthcare Act and surprisingly there was actually in any state let alone two states a legislative body that took them seriously. What creates the social environment, the underlying mentality, consciousness for that social environment that there would be elected officials who would take neo-Confederates seriously and a public that would elect such officials? This is where the soft-power of the neo-Confederates come in.

Of the means and methods of creating, shaping and structuring society often people think of the numerous and obvious ways in which these things are done. There are elections and campaigning, legislatures and their debates and actions in creating the law, the work of lobbyists, media coverage, political activities, social activism, and protests. There is a direct connection and obvious connection between these actions and the resulting change in policy, law, education, and other elements of which society is constructed.

What is often overlooked are the forms of soft power, the subtle means by which our thinking is shaped, means that can be so subtle that we are often unaware that our thinking has been shaped by it. Our attitudes, biases, pre-conceptions, values, and beliefs from which we form opinions about what society should be, our thoughts on how we should judge things, what policies we should support, what actions we should take can result from cultural, social, and governmental activities that don't appear to be related to these things.

Soft power is additionally very powerful since we often are not aware of it, because it is indirect, because it is often the unrecognized precursor shaping people's thinking which we should understand includes ourselves. With soft power shaping people's thinking they will develop opinions which they view as coming from within, which they will act upon, and which will support one type of society and be opposed to other social and political ideas.

Distorting and perverting the historical record to misinform people, to infuse them with false historical memories, is a strategy of soft power that is often very powerful indeed.

American history has had notable milestones in freedom and equality. There are no longer any property qualifications to vote in any state. There has been the Emancipation Proclamation and the Thirteenth Amendment abolishing slavery, the Fourteenth Amendment making African Americans citizens, the Fifteenth Amendment giving Americans the right to vote regardless of race, the Nineteenth Amendment giving women the right to vote, the landmark Supreme Court decisions integrating the schools and civil rights legislation of the 1960s. There has been the Supreme Court decision affirming the principles of what was called "one-man, one vote," (which should be understood as including women), which means state legislative districts are apportioned by population and not acres of land.

On the other hand the United States didn't ratify the proposed Equal Rights Amendment (ERA) making women equal to men under the Constitution. The United States gave women the vote only after over two dozen other nations had already done so. We were a follower and not a leader on this. The Supreme Court rulings integrating the schools and the civil rights legislation came about 100 years after the Civil War, after years of Jim Crow segregation, and the terrorism of groups like the Red Shirts and the Ku Klux Klan. Other examples could be given.

SOFT POWER

3 THE GEOGRAPHY OF POLITICS

Soft power can seem to be abstract, esoteric, vaporous, vague, and insubstantial. However, if you look as the geography of politics it becomes concrete and visible. Consider the maps on the following pages.

THE GEOGRAPHY OF POLITICS

Compare this map of the Confederate States of America to the maps which follow.

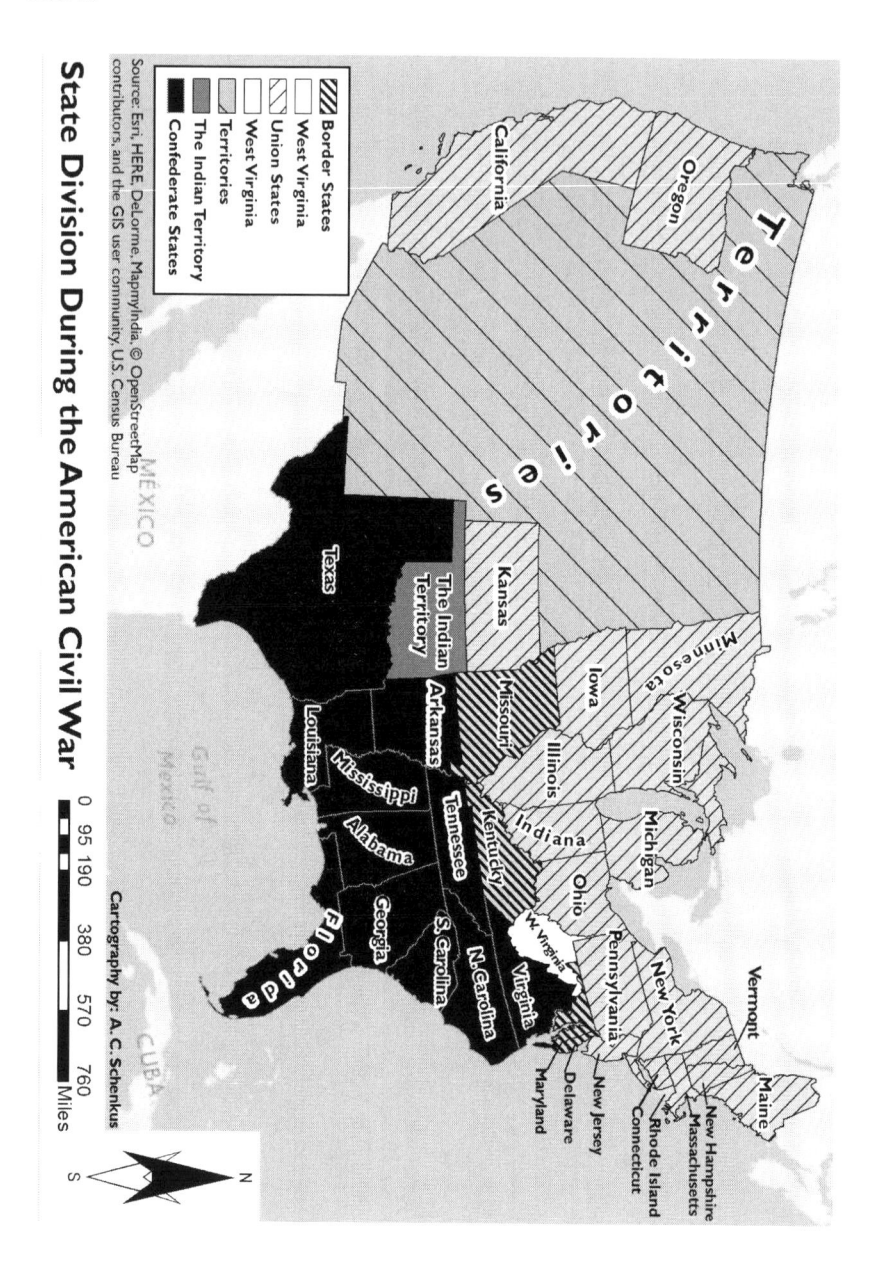

To this map of the ratification of the Nineteenth Amendment

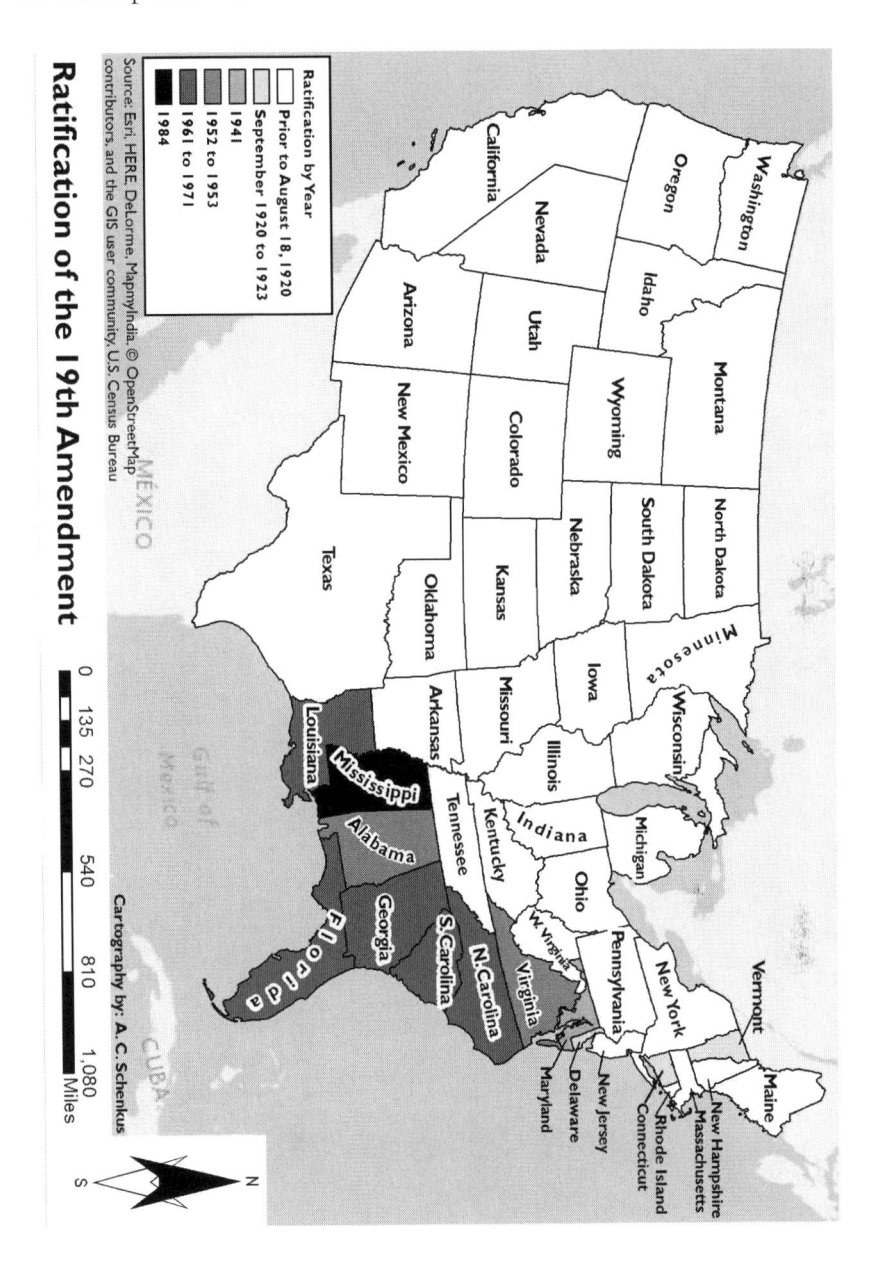

THE GEOGRAPHY OF POLITICS

And to this map for the ratification of the Twenty-Fourth Amendment ending the poll tax.

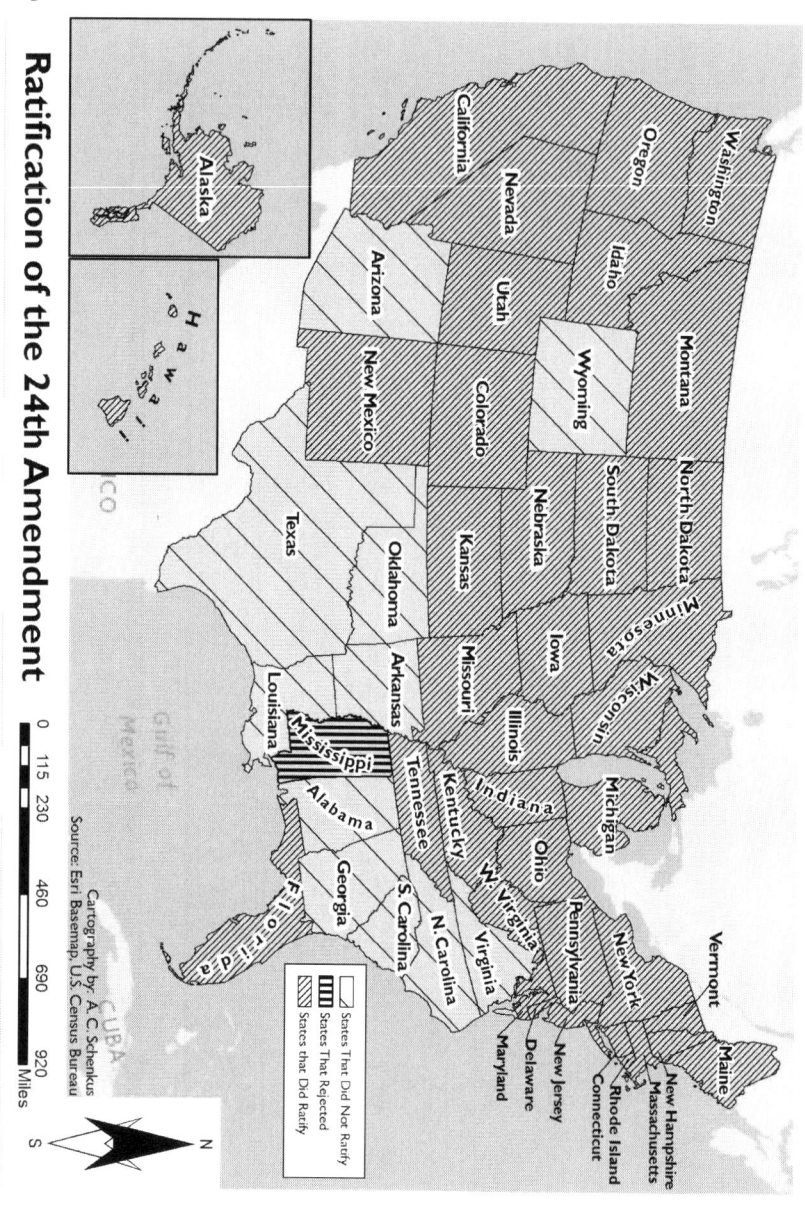

And to this map of the failure to ratify the Equal Rights Amendment.

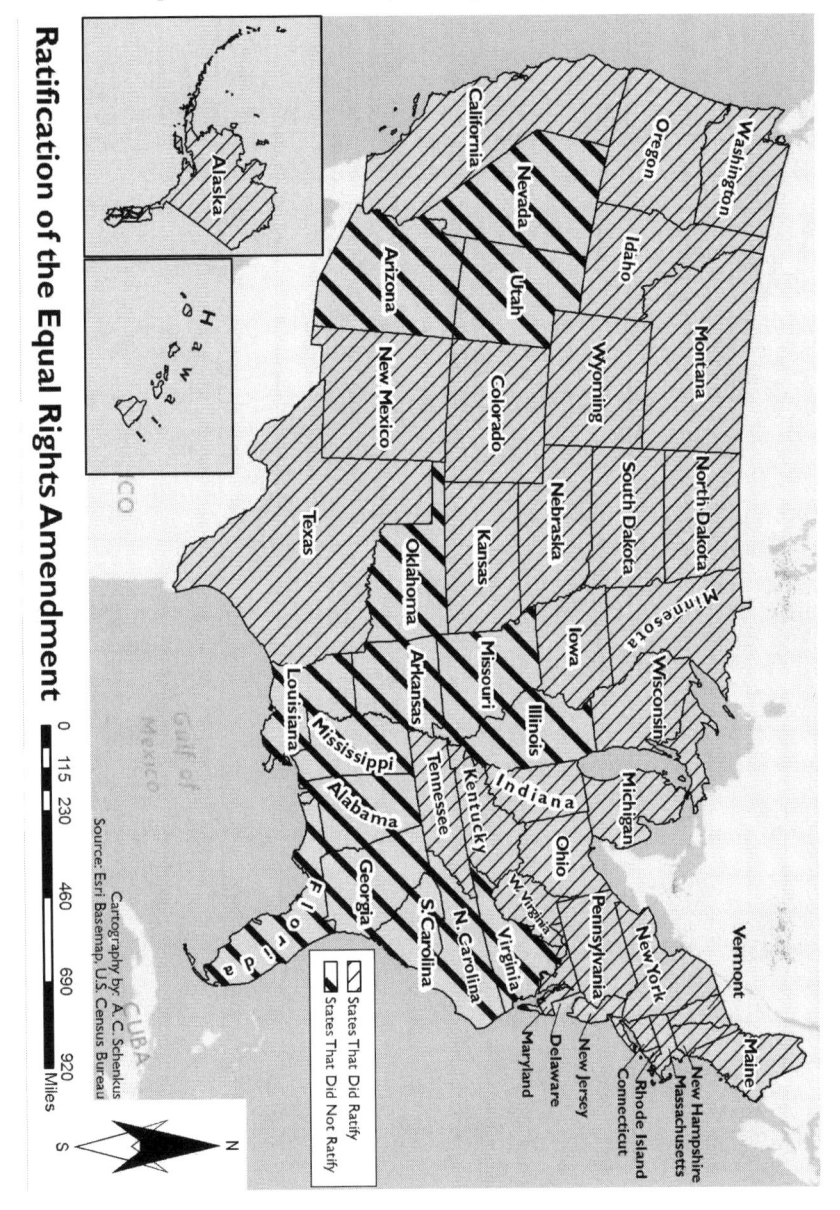

Looking at the maps you can see Confederacies. Not exactly the same states as the Confederacy, or the same states in each example, but all are approximations of the Confederacy.

In the ratification of the Nineteenth Amendment you can see that the 19th Amendment is only ratified by the near unanimous support of states outside the former Confederate states and a couple of former Confederate states. The United States, a nation which prides itself on being at the forefront of freedom and democracy, wasn't a leader on giving women the right to vote (women's suffrage) but a late follower. A couple dozen nations had already given women the vote. The movement to give women the vote started before the Civil War in 1848. An amendment to the Constitution to give women the vote was first submitted to Congress in 1878 by U.S. Senator Aaron A. Sargent. What would have been the impact on women's lives if it had been passed even 20 years earlier than it was, in 1899 instead of 1919? Women voting in one generation would have led to further progress in the lives of people in the next generation on issues of gender. What would have been the impact on the world if the United States had given women the vote in 1900 instead of 1920?

Similarly ratifying the Twenty-Fourth Amendment, banning the poll tax as a requirement for voting, was successful due to the nearly unanimous support outside the former Confederate states and with the support of just a few of the former Confederate states.

Outside the former Confederate states, 33 out of 38 states ratified the Equal Rights Amendment (ERA) to the Constitution which would have banned discrimination based on gender. Support from states outside the former Old Confederacy was at more than a 6 to 1, greatly exceeding the 3/4th majority necessary to ratify an amendment to the Constitution. Yet the ERA, became a rusting wreck left on the way side of history passing out of the public's memory. Phyllis Schlafly, a conservative leader who led the effort to defeat the ratification of the ERA was interviewed by the neo-Confederate magazine *Southern Partisan* in 1982 the morning after her victory celebration of the defeat of the ERA. The role of the "South" is discussed.

> **PARTISAN**: But don't you agree that without the conservative thinking people of the southeastern United States, your job would have been much harder in this ten year battle?
>
> **SCHLAFLY**: That's right, we could not have won without the South, no question about it. The South has provided about ten of the fifteen states that went against ERA.
>
> **PARTISAN**: So the South really sort of put the icing on the cake?
>
> **SCHLAFLY**: We are very grateful for the Southern opposition to ERA – we could not have won without you.[3]

Schlafly is quite correct that without this reactionary region of the nation, the South, the ERA would have easily passed with states to spare.

This geographical "Confederate" oppositions to progressive ideas has had very concrete, very real effects. It is not vaporous, esoteric, abstract, but has been a crushing reality on the hopes of American women going back generations. For other issues, the human rights of other groups, examples could be given where the opposition to social justice is geographically located in a latter day Confederacy, issues where there are real serious impacts. It is important that we know and understand the origins of these Confederacies that block or crush our hopes for justice and equality.

But why would the opposition to these measures of social justice be geographically grouped into these latter day Confederacies? It is not enough to just say it is because the South thinks this way or that, because this doesn't answer the question. That only leads to another question, why is the South like this? What forms and shapes thinking in this region?

The values people have are often shaped by what is called a civil religion. "Civil religion" refers to the public history that is generally believed in and the heroes that are publically held up for admiration in a place, state, region or nation. This necessarily involves teaching of values. In teaching us that a figure in history is a hero, their deeds and beliefs are necessarily defined as heroic and we adopt beliefs which provide a framework within which the hero's actions and beliefs are heroic.

Public history, the official narrative of what happened incorporates values both explicitly stated and implied and we being taught this history, in the schools and elsewhere, absorb these values. Depending what you are taught about the American Revolution, your opinion of whether the American founders were heroic champions of freedom or radical trouble-making insurrectionists will likely determined which slogan, "Taxation Without Representation" or "God, King and Country," represents your values and that would in turn shape your opinion on other political questions.

History is like the wooden preforms used when concrete is poured in construction. When we come across a highway structure we see the concrete, but not the wooded preforms which have been removed. We do not think of them, yet is the preforms that shaped the structure.

Major religions, themselves very powerful belief systems, have stories, historical narratives to use the academic term, to describe origins, what happened, why things are the way they are, and to claim authority.

THE GEOGRAPHY OF POLITICS

What is called the South, has its own civil religion separate from the rest of nation. It has towns, roads, cities, counties, highways, streets, buildings, schools, forests, and parks named after Confederate leaders and thus define the landscape as a Confederate.

Monuments to Confederate leaders abound in the South racializing the landscape, and defining the South as a Confederate place. There are churches that have Confederate stain glass and symbols making these sacred spaces Confederate spaces and the Confederacy being worth being honored in a sacred space.

The Mississippi state flag incorporates the Confederate battle flag. The current Georgia state flag is the one Georgia state adopted right after it seceded and is a Confederate flag. Other state flags contain Confederate elements. Cities often have Confederate symbols incorporated into their official seals and flags. Maryland has a neo-Confederate state song. States issue Confederate license plates giving the Confederacy an implied endorsement.

Time itself is marked by one or more Confederate holidays in many former Confederate states, and cities, counties, and states declare April to be "Confederate Heritage Month." When states and local government adopt holidays to honor the Confederate States of America, use Confederate symbols, and mark off months and days to celebrate the Confederate past, these governments are self-identified as being Confederate.

Over generations people in the South have been taught what is called the Lost Cause interpretation of history. Briefly summarized, this collection of distortions and misrepresentations of the past, depicts slaves as having been largely happy in bondage, their owners as benevolent, the Confederate national effort as having been a heroic struggle for states' rights and a proper understanding of the Constitution, and that Reconstruction was a horrible mistake resulting in, to use the Lost Cause terminology, "negro misrule."

This massive effort just described, marking both time and space as Confederate, affects people's beliefs. We end up with a metaphysical Confederacy and those persons living in the American South thus become trapped in this metaphysical Confederacy.

One of the more obvious effects of this metaphysical Confederacy is on people's attitudes towards secession.

An April 2011 CNN Opinion Research Poll,[4] which included questions regarding the Civil War, asked individuals whether they sympathized more with the Union or the Confederacy. In the South 38% said that they were more sympathetic to the Confederacy (Sampling error +/- 6%). The data isn't further broken down further by race. I think it would be reasonable to assume that African Americans in the South are much less likely than whites to identify with the Confederacy, hence the percentages of whites who do is significantly higher than 38%. In April 2011 The Pew Research Center released polling results of the attitudes towards the Civil War. [5] According to the poll was 64% of whites in the former Confederate states considered themselves Southerners. Additionally of those whites identified as Southerners, 52% thought it was appropriate for politicians to praise Confederate leaders. This means that 33.3% of whites in the former Confederate states feel that it is appropriate for politicians to praise Confederate leaders (0.64 X 0.52 = 33.28). The Pew Center results corroborate the CNN poll and suggest that there is a large fraction of white Southerners who have very positive feelings towards the Confederacy. Possibly it is higher than represented in the polls since some individuals might not want to admit to admiring the Confederacy to a stranger.

Public Policy Polling released Dec. 2012 found that Georgia Republicans were upset with President Obama's re-election and that 47% of them supported the idea of secession.[6]

In 2014 the Public Policy Polling asked Mississippian, "If there were another Civil War today, would you side with the Confederate States of America or the United States of America?" The poll found that 29% of all Mississippians would back a new Confederacy and 21% were not sure, for a total of 50%. The poll also found that only 2% of African American Mississippians would support the Confederacy so the secessionist sentiment is among white Southerners must be much higher than 50%.[7]

Most troubling are the Public Policy Polling Jan. 2013 results for Texas. There was a surprising level of support for secession: 47% of those who call themselves very conservative, 35% of Republicans, and 7% of Democrats. Unlike other states, Texas has the Texas Nationalist Movement (TNM), (http://www.thetnm.org/) which is beginning to make some significant progress. As a recent *Washington Post* April 19, 2016 article headline read, "The Texas secession debate is getting kind of real."[8]

The TNM tried and failed to get a secession measure on the 2015 Republican Primary ballot by collecting enough signatures for the measure. This can be done under Texas law. They did however, have support from Tanya Robertson, a member of the State Republican Executive Committee (SREC). It appears she was able to get it out of the SREC resolution committee for a vote on whether a secession measure would appear on the Republican primary ballot by the 60-member SREC at their December 2015 meeting.[9] The resolution was defeated by roughly two to one, but what was really interesting is that the SREC refused to have a roll call vote on the measure. First there was a voice vote and then after complaints, they then had SREC members stand to indicate their vote. This was done so quickly that it was hard to determine how anyone voted. The TNM took photos of the voting and later published a record of how people voted based on the pictures, but even so they couldn't determine how all the committee members voted on the secession ballot proposal.

It was surprising that even one-third of the SREC, a body governing a supposedly mainstream political party, was willing to vote for the measure. What was alarming is that the SREC members who voted against it were afraid to have a roll call vote and be counted as having voted against secession.[10] However, even with that defeat, or perhaps embolden by it, when the Republican Party had their county conventions the TNM managed to get some county conventions to pass their resolution. The TNM claimed 20 counties out of 270 Republican Party county conventions passed the resolution, but the *Houston Chronicle* reported that they could only confirm 10 county conventions had passed the resolution.[11] At the Texas State Republican Party convention May 2016 in Dallas, Texas the GOP platform committee voted down the secession platform item by only 16 to 14, with one member abstaining.[12] For a supposedly mainstream political party you would think the vote would easily be 31 to 0.

The TNM doesn't appear to discuss the Confederacy and instead focuses on the referencing the secession of Texas from Mexico as a heroic narrative. Texas' history of twice seceding, once from Mexico and then from the United States might be why secession sentiments have moved further along in Texas then in other states. The Texas public, as well as many outside of Texas, are largely unaware that slavery was a major factor driving Texas secession from Mexico. However, having a state with Confederate monuments and names and a state holiday for those who attempted to secede by a violent insurrection legitimizes secession.

The memorialization of the Confederacy undoubtedly makes secession appear to be a legitimate political option among some Southern voters today. This should be of serious concern for those who care about the integrity of the United States as a nation.

Modern secession sentiment is reviewed here because it can be quantifiably measured by polls and is fairly obviously and directly derived from the history of the Confederate states' secession. It demonstrates that historical memory does shape contemporary values in a concrete measurable way.

The other Confederacies shown in the maps shown earlier are resulting from a reactionary culture formed out of a society shaped by a neo-Confederate understanding of history, but not in a way that is so directly measureable or always so obviously derived from a specific Confederate historical events like secession. The fact that they are geographical Confederacies is a strong clue that they are created by a neo-Confederate understanding of history and ideas derived from this history.

To understand how these neo-Confederate distortions of history work to create these latter day Confederacies we can trace the connections several ways.

We have to think about what type of consciousness would find acceptable as heroes persons that fought to preserve slavery and white supremacy and who if they were successful would have shattered the United States of American, discredited the republican form of democracy, and romanticized plantation life. A person honoring the Confederacy would have to have a set of values that would not really care that much about or be at odds with human rights, democracy, equality, and in particular not find African Americans to have real human worth. Otherwise how would you find the Confederacy and its leaders acceptable? These type of values would be the basis for other values and beliefs that would be in opposed or unsympathetic to social justice. The neo-Confederate distortions of history thus create a framework of thinking that is in opposition to social justice.

The neo-Confederate distortions are in support of a reactionary system which in turn has its own historical consequences and further reactionary developments that seem to have no remote connection to the Civil War or the Confederacy. These developments can then in themselves be extensions to Confederate history and these extensions together reach to the present.

These surprising connections can be excavated through historical research and review of neo-Confederate writings. For example, women's suffrage and the Confederacy may seem totally unrelated to us living in the 21st century, but study of the opposition to the ratification of the Nineteenth Amendment in the South in the South reveals the surprising link.

Neo-Confederate history sees the Civil War and Reconstruction as the two phases of one long conflict. The Neo-Confederate historical distortions of Reconstruction are to support white supremacy. Neo-Confederates portray Reconstruction as a time, to use their terms, of "negro misrule." The neo-Confederates denounce the Fifteenth Amendment. Neo-Confederates see the Ku Klux Klan and the Red Shirts, organizations of violent men, as saviors of the South, white womanhood and white supremacy with their violent terrorist campaigns to overturn Reconstruction. This historical idea asserts that a patriarchy of violent white men was needed to save white women. Also, neo-Confederates portray the Confederate armies as fighting for states' rights making later claims of states' rights to block federal actions for justice seem heroic. These two Lost Cause ideas are instrumental in Southern conservative opposition to the 19th Amendment.

Kenneth R. Johnson in his article, "White Racial Attitudes as a Factor in the Arguments Against the Nineteenth Amendment," in the academic journal *Phylon*, repeatedly gives examples that Southern elected officials saw the ratification of the Nineteenth Amendment as leading to the federal government enforcing the Fifteenth Amendment which gave African Americans the right to vote. Johnson states that these officials denounced the purposed ratification of the 19th Amendment as a "double ratification." Johnson explains that there was concern in the South that the Nineteenth Amendment might result in African Americans getting the vote, since it would authorize women voting including African American women voting and the South might not be able to prevent African American women from voting without federal intervention. If African American women could vote then it would surely follow that African American men would be able to vote.

Johnson describes the hysterical fear of Southern legislators:

> This condition led Senator Ellison D. Smith, Democrat of South Carolina, to announce that the South had always considered the Fifteenth Amendment a crime against civilization and that a vote for the proposed amendment as the same as a vote to ratify the Fifteenth Amendment. He protested against adding another amendment to the organic law which would permit "an alien and ignorant race to be turned loose upon us."[13]

Elizabeth Gillespie McRae in her article, "Caretakers of Southern Civilization: Georgia Women and the Anti-Suffrage Campaign," described the campaigns of two Lost Cause leaders, Dolly Blount Lamar, who was a president of the United Daughters of the Confederacy, and Mildred Rutherford the Historian General of the United Daughters of the Confederacy for many years, against the ratification of the Nineteenth Amendment. McRae explains, "Images of Reconstruction were central to the anti-suffrage political strategy. Schooled in lessons of southern history, anti-suffragists repeatedly referred to a chaotic time in the remembered white past to address the uncertainty and insecurity of the present." These same lessons about Reconstruction were what the United Daughters of the Confederacy historically insured were taught in the schools.

Dolly Blount Lamar gave an anti-suffrage speech to the Georgia state legislature. McRae writes, "Lamar claimed that the 'foul fiend of carpetbaggery' cloaked in women's clothes would descend on Georgia and recruit modern-day scalawags. Like the despicable Fifteenth Amendment and the Lodge bill, the proposed suffrage amendment represented the most recent attempt by the federal government to infringe on states' rights."[14] Scalawag is a neo-Confederate term for Southerners who don't support white supremacy, southern nationalism, or neo-Confederacy. It is used specifically in histories of Reconstruction in reference to white southerners who were members of the Republican Party. Neo-Confederates consider them traitors and the terms synonymous. The Lodge bill also known as the Federal Election Bill was legislation drafted by U.S. House Representative Henry Cabot Lodge of Massachusetts and submitted in 1890, would have authorized federal government supervision of elections to enable African American men to vote which would have directly threatened white supremacy in the former Confederate state.

Even in the late 20th century neo-Confederates condemned the Nineteenth Amendment. Ellen Campbell in 1983 in the *Southern Partisan*, in "Trampled Ground," argues that the state legislature of Mississippi argument of states' rights to define who can vote in rejecting the Nineteenth Amendment in 1920 was correct. (Mississippi would ratify in 1984.) Campbell also writes:

> Efforts by unknowing or – knowing, as the case may be – persons to serve some social cause by the process of amending the Constitution has served nothing else than to damage (perhaps irreparably) the form of government created by the framers of the Constitution. Four Constitutional Amendments can be accused of doing just that: the Fifteenth Amendment (1870) prohibiting the abridgment of the right to vote because of race; the Nineteenth Amendment (1920) prohibiting abridgment of the right to vote because of sex; the Twenty-Fourth Amendment (1964) taking away the voting qualification of the poll tax; the Twenty-Sixth vote because of age (18 years or older).[15]

This opposition to the 19th Amendment is part of a larger anti-democratic view of the Constitution.

In summary opposition to the 19th Amendment comes out of the Lost Cause in four ways.

1. A general cultural environment in which justice is not valued.

2. A Lost Cause interpretation of Reconstruction which provides a framework to oppose the Nineteenth Amendment as another Reconstruction amendment.

3. A neo-Confederate general theory of the Constitution which in general is against amendments to further social justice.

4. Lost Cause historical narratives in general and those of Reconstruction in particular supporting a system of white supremacy. Systems where one group of people oppress another will always feel threatened by any discussion of social justice or granting any specific class of people rights especially by outside authorities.

The opposition to the Nineteenth Amendment in the South clearly illustrates how through different channels the Lost Cause distortions of the historical record can work directly and indirectly to block social justice. Directly in this case in the references to Reconstruction. Indirectly in that the Lost Cause understanding of history supports a reactionary understanding of the Constitution which in turn is used to oppose the Nineteenth Amendment and any expansion of voting rights by the federal government. Also, indirectly the Lost Cause in its support for white supremacy has a consequent historical development which is a reactionary society which will feel threatened by the discussion of social justice.

I think more work needs to be done to see other Confederacies in the geography of politics. I encourage the reader to start considering the geography of politics in regards to all political questions. However, as praise for the Confederacy becomes national in reactionary politics and neo-Confederate ideology spreads across the nation it may be harder to see Confederacies on maps, because neo-Confederacy has gone national.

The neo-Confederates misrepresent the past to control the present and direct the future.[16]

The effectiveness of having a section of the nation set aside as a reactionary fortress for a reactionary agenda by having its own anti-democratic civil religion is shown by looking at the simple arithmetic involved. You can see in the following graphs that there is a big leverage.

For purposes of argument imagine that 25%, one-quarter, of the nation is reserved as a reactionary fortress as shown by the lower bar, which is divided into quarters, and the reactionary fortress illustrated by Confederate flags shown in the illustration below.

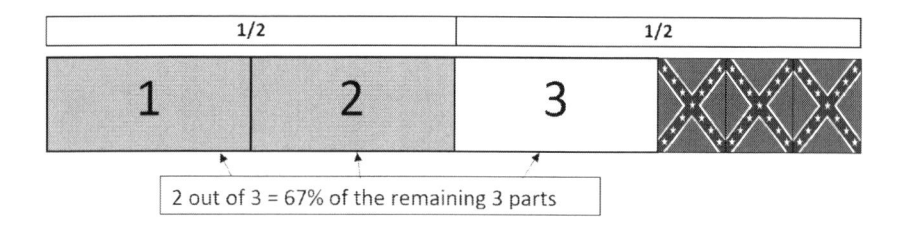

1/2		1/2	
1	2	3	

2 out of 3 = 67% of the remaining 3 parts

To get the support of half, 50%, for some, progressive law or proposal you will need to get two-thirds of the rest of the country outside this reactionary fortress. To get support for progressive legislation, as shown above you have to get two (filled with gray) of the three remaining boxes representing quarters of the population, that is $2/3^{rd}$ support, 67%, of the population outside the neo-Confederate stronghold, a very high majority to succeed.

If you need a 2/3rd majority to confirm a federal judge or ambassador or to send out a proposed Constitutional amendment to the states for ratification or some other action requiring a 2/3rd majority, and if the reactionary region is against it, you will need 8/9th, 89%, support for the measure outside the reactionary region. That is 8 gray boxes out of the 9 boxes with numbers shown above each box representing a twelfth of the population. This would be a very high barrier to get over. See bar above which it has been divided into twelfths. ($3/12^{th} = 1/4$; $4/12^{th} = 1/3$).

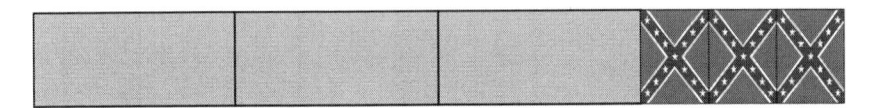

Finally if you are attempting to get a Constitutional amendment ratified and the reactionary region is against you will need all the support outside the region, that is 100%, all three of the gray quarters shown in the bar above, or hope for a couple states to fall loose from the reactionary region. You will face a tremendous obstacle. The 19th Amendment to the Constitution managed to overcome this obstacle, the ERA didn't.

Neo-Confederates have always conceived the South as being as a neo-Confederate bulwark against change and the anchor or base for a national reactionary force against social justice. The *Southern Partisan* sold a t-shirt in 1996 making this point graphically very clear. The front has the Republican Party elephant logo filled with the Confederate Battle flag with the motto, "Lincoln's Worst Nightmare," emblazoned above.

THE GEOGRAPHY OF POLITICS

LINCOLN'S WORST NIGHTMARE!

And on the back of the t-shirt was the statement, "A States' Rights Republican Party Based in Dixie," surrounded by 13 state flags that the *Southern Partisan* claimed for the South, with the "X" in Dixie a Confederate battle flag. With the Confederate battle flag "X" in Dixie the South is equated to the Confederacy. Note that this t-shirt claims two more states than actually seceded in 1861.

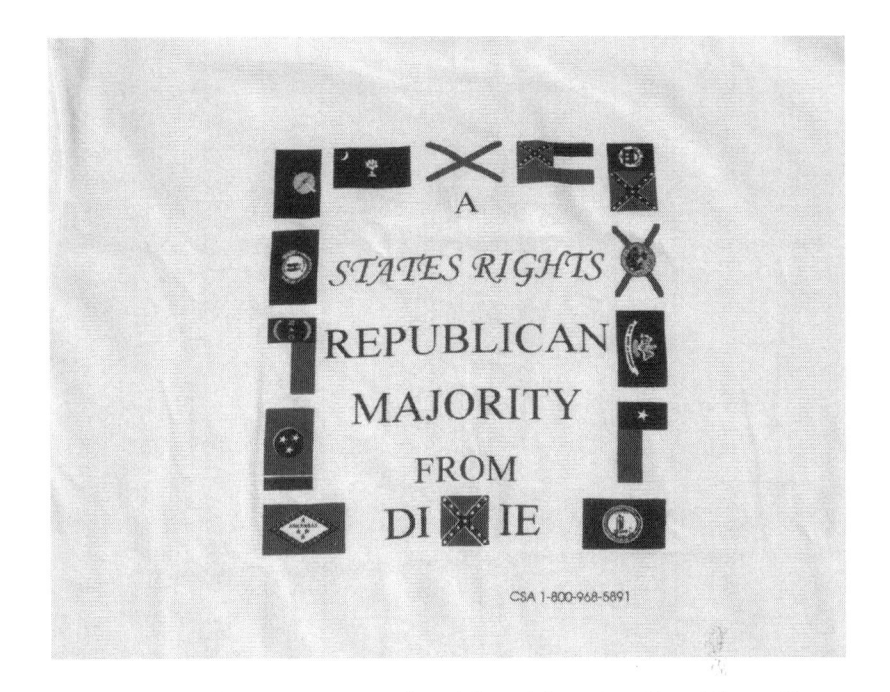

A STATES RIGHTS REPUBLICAN MAJORITY FROM DIXIE

CSA 1-800-968-5891

The *Southern Partisan* very well might claim the Republican Party as Confederate. The contributors to the *Southern Partisan* and those interviewed by it were not marginal individuals. Religious right leaders interviewed by the *Southern Partisan* were evangelical broadcasters Jerry Falwell,[17] and Pat Robertson,[18] and Donald A. Wildmon, the founder of the American Family Association.[19] Elected officials were: Virginia U.S. Senator Henry Flood Jr.,[20] then U.S. House Rep. Phil Gramm (later Texas U.S. Senator),[21] North Carolina U.S. Senator Jesse Helms,[22] U.S. House Rep. Trent Lott (later Mississippi U.S. Senator0,[23] Texas U.S. House Rep. Dick Armey,[24] Mississippi U.S. Senator Thad Cochran,[25] Missouri U.S. Senator John Ashcroft,[26] and South Carolina U.S. House Rep. Lindsey Graham (later U.S. Senator).[27] Numerous other prominent conservatives, celebrities, current and former Reagan administration officials were contributors or interviewed.

With the Spring/Summer 1981 *Southern Partisan* issue the editor was political consultant Richard M. Quinn who had run Ronald Reagan's presidential campaign in South Carolina, and associate editor Richard T. Hines who later in 2000 enabled George W. Bush to beat John McCain in the South Carolina presidential primary. McCain's campaign in the 2000 South Carolina presidential primary was also ran by Quinn.

Another example on how the South is conceived as a Confederate bulwark against social justice is an address, "A Long Farewell to Union: The Southern Valedictories, 1860-1861," by M.E. Bradford, a central figure in the neo-

Confederate movement in the period roughly from 1960s to his death in 1993, given during the national bicentennial observances. The address was originally given on Jefferson Davis's birthday June 3, 1986 at the Arlington National Cemetery. *Southern Partisan* later published the speech in 1988, and it appeared in *Against the Barbarians*, a book published in 1992. In the address Bradford reviews the farewell speeches in the U.S. Senate by senators from seceding states just before the Civil War.[28] The *Southern Partisan* article mentions that Bradford was the National Historian of the Sons of Confederate Veterans (SCV).

In this essay the seceding U.S. senators' speeches are held to be worth studying since they express a true understanding of the U.S. Constitution which is applicable to present day political controversies.

Referring to contemporary bicentennial observations of the adoption of the constitution Bradford writes that they are, "dramatically colored by exchanges and disputes concerning the origins, true meaning … " of the constitution. Bradford argues that it was hopefully "the right time" to "… [be] appreciating the importance of those even more heated discussions of the Constitution which occurred … during the 'great secession winter' of 1860-1861," because "… the relation between the current arguments and those of one hundred twenty-five years ago are direct and unmistakable."

Bradford sees the opportunity for a national reactionary alliance based on neo-Confederate ideology. Referring to the "North" and "West" he writes that there is an opportunity for "our countrymen from North and West" who he feels are ready "to penetrate the curtain," of what Bradford feels is a northern mythology of the Civil War, thus adopt a neo-Confederate perspective of the Civil War, to "discover there how prescient the Southern forefathers were in predicting to what would happen once they had departed from the protections of 'the Union as it was, the Constitution as it is.'"

Neo-Confederates see neo-Confederacy as a method to block progress or at least keep it out of the South under the guise of "states' rights" or some other formula which they define as southern conservatism. Neo-Confederates build upon the general cultural attitudes derived from these historical distortions, which predisposes people to a system of beliefs of which they call Southern conservatism starting with the Confederacy but extended into the future into the present day and expanded to encompass all issues. Persons who believe in the Lost Cause view of history will be predisposed to believe in this Southern conservatism.

Reactionaries outside the South have realized that though their agenda might not be getting the necessary support outside the South to block justice, such as the ERA, within the South there is enough backing to compensate for the lack of support outside the South, enough for their agenda to succeed. This is called the Southern strategy, which became a term in politics in the 1970s, but probably was understood much earlier by those interested in blocking justice. If you have an agenda to undermine civil rights, to block economic justice for working people, you might not have enough support outside the South to have a chance, but with Southern conservatism you may well be in a commanding position to advance your agenda or and if not in a commanding position, still be able to stall or retard the progress of social justice.

It has to be considered what the United States of America would be like without this ongoing opposition to social justice. What nation would we live in without these Confederacies? It would be a radically different nation, though the neo-Confederates would retort that it would simply be a radical nation. Let's tear down the neo-Confederacy and find out. Help Southern states escape the prison house of the Confederacy.

Finally, if we don't deal with neo-Confederacy we can expect to continue to live in "Lincoln's worst nightmare." We can continue to see this engine of injustice hobble or defeat efforts for justice for decades if not for generations and longer to come.

THE GEOGRAPHY OF POLITICS

4 POISONING WHITE PEOPLE AND TEACHING THAT AFRICAN AMERICAN LIVES DON'T MATTER

Every Confederate monument whispers, "Civil Rights may be the slogan of the day, but white supremacy is for the ages." A monument that glorifies an individual or groups of people that fought for a nation created to preserve slavery and white supremacy can't be anything but an endorsement of those values. Monuments are messengers sent by one group in one generation to the living and to generations yet unborn.

The fact that such monuments are still standing shows that the human worth of African Americans isn't really taken very seriously in the community where the monument stands, otherwise it would be have been taken down. It shows a priority in society's values. It is foolish to think that white people at some level are not getting the monument's message. Confederate monuments poison white people with racism.

The arguments about Confederate monuments or flags often revolve around how they are insensitive and hurt the feelings of African Americans. This is paternalistic and attempts to make the issue an emotional issue and to avoid the real issues involved. African Americans intellectually, rationally, see the issue of a racialized landscape and how society devalues them as a human being.

British journalist of Barbadian descent, Gary Younge, understood this in Richmond, Virginia, while walking among a series of one hundred year old statues depicting Confederate leaders:

> I turned around to walk back up Monument Avenue, feeling angry and confused… I had spent about an hour walking along a road in which four

men who fought to enslave me… have been honoured and exalted. I resented the fact that on the way to work every day, black people have to look at that. Imagine how black children must feel when they learn that the people who have been raised and praised up the road are the same ones who tried to keep their great-great-grandparents in chains.[29]

Viewing a landscape in which you are literally monumentally devalued by society probably elicits an emotion of anger. Arguments against Confederate monuments often are framed in terms of it hurting African American feelings as if it was an emotional response by African Americans and not a response based on critical thinking by African Americans. Younge wasn't having hurt feelings. He saw that the monuments represent the dominating values of Richmond devaluing the human worth of African Americans.

A recent event, (April 2016), the decision to remove a Confederate monument from the University of Louisville, provoked the usual white paternalistic reasons for the change. Louisville Mayor Greg Fisher issued a statement, "This monument represents our history – a painful part of our nation's history for many – and it's best moved to a new location."[30]

It seems though that many people in Louisville can't say that the Confederacy was not a good thing, excepting Professor Ricky L. Jones, chair of the Pan-African Studies at the Univ. of Louisville who had written an editorial against the memorial. Jones is dismissive of the paternalistic rationalizations for removing the monument including the mayor's, even ridiculing the excuses. An article in the *Louisville Courier-Journal* covering Mayor Fischer's decision reported Jones' views on the matter:

> Jones said that **whatever motivated the decision**, he is elated the monument will no longer be on campus. He said generations of U of L students, faculty and staff have opposed the statue's existence.
>
> "Let's see the Confederacy for what it is, not some lost cause, it was a war about slavery," Jones said, "And that is fundamentally inhuman, ***so if that's a part of Kentucky history, place it in a part of Kentucky where people still have those beliefs***." [emphasis added by author.]

The mayor's statement was ridiculous. The neo-Confederates tear it to shreds in their statements quoted in the same article.[31] A lot of history is sad or painful and should be remembered. The problem with history that is painful is that often it isn't remembered because it is painful. The issue with the Confederate statue at the University of Louisville is that the Confederacy is exalted, as Professor Jones says, not that it is painful. There is a difference between a Hitler Highway and a Holocaust memorial.[32] There would be a difference between a memorial to the victims of slavery and a Confederate monument glorifying a Confederate leader.

By avoiding judging the Confederacy, contemporary leaders avoid confronting the white supremacist message of these monuments and these monuments do their work until the end. Even after their removal the damage continues because they were taken down not in condemnation, white supremacy of the Confederacy acknowledged, but because, supposedly, someone's sensitive feelings got hurt.

There are consequences of this argument also. The feelings argument doesn't provide a basis to continue to remove Confederate monuments. In 2015 a state commission voted 7-2 to keep the Jefferson Davis statue in the Kentucky capitol rotunda. When the argument to remove a monument is just about feelings you find all sorts of people have feelings and can make sad faces for Confederate "heritage" on television. One protestor had a sign "Jeff Davis Statue Matters." The opinion polls showed that 73% of Kentuckians thought the statue should remain, and only 17% wanted it removed. Both the mayor of Louisville and the state commission can probably read polls.[33]

In particular naming schools after Confederate leaders is vicious. Often in the South a school named after a Confederate leader will be nearly all minority students. It communicates to African American children that they aren't really valued as human beings by society and it communicates to white students the same thing. Both have obvious negative effects. It doesn't inspire African American students to study and is instead a disincentive. If society sends them to school named after those who fought for white supremacy what opportunities can they expect in that society?

Confederate monuments need to come down because they teach white supremacy to the public and devalue African American lives. The instruction to society that Black lives really don't matter is literally monumental and we can observe the results.

POISONING WHITE PEOPLE

5 FIGHTING NEO-CONFEDERACY

To first step in bringing down the metaphysical Confederacy and is to eliminate what sustains it. All the places that are named after Confederate leaders need to be renamed, and holidays in honor of the Confederacy eliminated, Confederate history months need to stop being observed, monuments to the Confederacy or Confederates moved out of places of public honor, and state flags should be redesigned. Public officials need to stop praising the Confederacy and neo-Confederate groups. Other actions by government that valorizes the Confederacy needs to end.

To get support for this and to reduce support for the Confederacy it would be good if American public history text books stopped accommodating pro-Confederate sentiments by distorting the history of slavery, abolition, and the Civil War. These textbooks need to stop misrepresenting Reconstruction which was tragic only because it ended with the violent overthrow of America's first multiracial democracy and not because during its brief time African Americans has some political rights.

However, efforts to move Confederate monuments, or to get the government to give up Confederate symbols, and otherwise stop supporting valorization of the Confederacy are often defeated or have had only very modest success. Neo-Confederates are organized and they are not marginal members of society. An effort to move a monument will soon face the opposition of the Sons of Confederate Veterans, the United Daughters of the Confederacy, and other neo-Confederate groups and so-called "heritage coalitions." They will argue for the Confederacy and they have been doing so for generations. They have arguments that have been developed over generations, they will apply political pressure, and threaten electoral defeat to public officials that they see as being against the Confederacy. Additionally there were threats to the careers or businesses of those they see as threats to the neo-Confederate cause.

Witness the fact that the city of New Orleans at this time (4/30/16) is having trouble hiring any firm to move Confederate statues because of death threats.[34] Neo-Confederates will have the sympathy and support of a large fraction of the public. In a CBS News/New York Times Poll conducted July 14-19, 2015 right after the Charleston church massacre by Dylann Roof, the poll found that nationally 57% of whites and 21% of African Americans thought the Confederate battle flag was more a symbol of Southern pride than racism. In a 2026 Louisiana State University poll, 88% of whites in Louisiana and 47% of African Americans opposed removing the Confederate statues in New Orleans.[35] Neo-Confederates can shape public opinion because they have material resources. They are often members of the middle and upper classes. They frequently will get support from local institutions, professors, and historians[36].

These groups defending so-called "Southern heritage" present themselves as nostalgic defenders of history and appeal to sentimental feelings about the past. They consider the issue of great importance and with their neo-Confederate ideology realize that these monuments are instrumental to maintaining a reactionary South. They devote time and energy to defending the Confederacy and will do so over an extended period of time.

In contrast, the opponents of the Confederacy have limited support. Persons might support getting rid of the Confederate monument or changing of the state flag, and they might be glad that someone else, not them is attempting to do something about it. However, they won't consider getting too involved since they don't see it as something that has a real material or concrete importance like housing, education, health, the environment, or social justice. The issue will seem to them haggling over history.

So active opponents of the Confederacy will be limited in numbers. They often have just organized ad hoc as will be their arguments. They won't have much information on their opposition, much experience in arguing over the history of the Civil War or the Confederacy. They often don't have experience on campaigning on this issue. The often lack a network to mobilize. They don't plan to campaign on this issue for years to come. They often limit their scope to a particular monument or school name or state flag, and not neo-Confederacy in general. They expect the struggle to last for just a few months. They often have little or no comprehension that there is a neo-Confederate movement or what is really at stake let alone inform the public about the existence of the neo-Confederate movement. They may see the struggle as an argument over the past rather than challenging the neo-Confederate movement.

After being defeated they will be demoralized and give up. In 2015 this started to change somewhat, there has been a lot of successes, and now there isn't always defeat at the end of the campaign, but it remains to be seen how long the effect of the Charleston massacre – in which a man who embraced Confederate battle flags and rhapsodized about a fake mythic antebellum past before slaughtering the members of a black church – lasts. A recent (3/13/16) *New York Times* article, "Momentum to Remove Confederate Symbols Slows or Stops," described how there are attempts in state legislatures to pass bills that prevent local officials from removing local Confederate monuments.[37] Although a lot of progress has been made the fight isn't over.

This books seeks to provide the basis for a successful movement to de-Confederate the South. This book seeks to explain what the neo-Confederate movement is about. Who the neo-Confederates are, what are their goals, and reveal their methods. Also the enablers of the neo-Confederate movement will be identified.

If the public knew what the real agenda is of neo-Confederate movement was and what their real reasons were behind their defense of the Confederacy, the neo-Confederates would have no credibility in their "heritage not hate" defense of the Confederacy. The sentimental nostalgia given in public forums would be seen for the sham it is. If the public knew what the neo-Confederate movement was about they would want to see action against what sustains the neo-Confederate movement, such as Confederate names for places, Confederate monuments, and Confederate symbols on flags and seals. They would want to make sure that the neo-Confederate don't have cultural or political influence. They would criticize those who enabled the neo-Confederate movement and thus institutions would be less likely to enable this movement. This would go a long way to defeating neo-Confederacy.

If the public knew about the agenda of the neo-Confederate movement and how it is advanced, they would see it as involving concrete relevant issues, and understand how often it stands in the way of progress and they would give defeating neo-Confederacy and the infrastructure that supports it a higher priority in their politics.

Bringing down the infrastructure of Confederate glorification and the anti-egalitarian culture it supports would lead to the defeat of the neo-Confederate movement and the oppressive politics it so successfully promotes.

Fighting the monuments and the ideas they represent also helps the public recognize neo-Confederacy when they see it and mobilizes them for a more progressive contemporary politics.

A major benefit of fighting neo-Confederacy is that it will bring to the surface people's racial attitudes and identify those who are sympathetic to the Confederacy. The racism in society will be highlighted and made more visible.

There are additional benefits when the public is aware of what neo-Confederacy is about,

When we can more clearly see neo-Confederacy and recognize what it represents, we won't tolerate racially-biased neo-Confederates on juries. Those who imagine African Americans were happy slaves won't be that concerned over a false conviction and incarceration of an African American defendant in the present. Increased awareness of this movement will make it less likely that we would elect neo-Confederates to public office or appoint them to positions of public trust.

The scope of this book is limited to explaining what the neo-Confederate movement is and what it isn't, and who the neo-Confederates are, what they believe, and what they advocate for society. In addition, there are the following resources online which an opponent of Confederate glorification will find very useful.

In refuting the historical distortions of the neo-Confederates I recommend the ironically titled, *The Confederate and Neo-Confederate Reader: The Great 'Truth' About the Lost Cause*, edited by Edward H. Sebesta and James Loewen, published by the University Press of Mississippi and the online resource www.confederatepastpresent.org which also has abundant helpful additional material. Both use the Confederates and neo-Confederates own words regarding what the Confederacy was about and what the neo-Confederacy has been about, white supremacy.

For a very academic analysis of neo-Confederacy there is *Neo-Confederacy: A Critical Introduction*, edited by Euan Hague, Edward H. Sebesta and Heidi Beirich, University of Texas Press.

Additionally one of the central arguments of the neo-Confederates is that the Confederate battle flag isn't racist, but has a bad image because the Ku Klux Klan misappropriated it in the 1950s and 60s. You can go to www.citizenscouncils.com and see how mainstream Southern society in the 1950s perceived the meaning of the Confederate flag as supporting white supremacy.

UCLA professor David Hayes-Bautista has written a very interesting history book *Cinco de Mayo: An American Holiday*, which shows the origins of Cinco de Mayo as an anti-Confederate holiday in California. At the early Cinco de Mayo celebrations portraits of Abraham Lincoln and Benito Juarez were carried together.

As you read this book and find out what neo-Confederates believe and how they are not marginal but part of the establishment and how influential they are you will be alarmed.

6 WHAT IS NEO-CONFEDERACY AND WHO ARE THE NEO-CONFEDERATES?

What

What is neo-Confederacy? Who are the neo-Confederates? "Neo" is from ancient Greek meaning "new." Neo-Confederates are new Confederates. Neo-Confederacy is a reactionary belief system which has at its center beliefs and historical narratives (tales) of the Civil War, Reconstruction, the antebellum South, and slavery. The United States of America is held to have taken the wrong direction in history as a result of the defeat of the Confederacy.

Neo-Confederacy is based on their interpretations of these historical periods and events related to the Civil War and Reconstruction and additionally the thinking of Confederate leaders, pro-slavery theologians, antebellum (before the Civil War) pro-slavery politicians (such as John C. Calhoun).

Built upon this base, neo-Confederacy is also a continuing and developing ideology with a series of intellectuals such as the early 20th century Southern Agrarians, 20th century conservative philosopher Richard M. Weaver, and M.E. Bradford who are understood by neo-Confederates as continuing this ideology, though often under the label of "traditional Southerners" or "Southern conservatives." These neo-Confederate intellectuals not only seek to defend the neo-Confederate understanding of the past and further develop and explain it, but also apply it to current issues and by doing so extend it into the present and bring it into the future.

In short, it is an ongoing developing current of thought, but a stream which has as its head waters the original Confederacy and the plantation slave South.

To support their understanding of the Civil War and their overall ideology they have expanded their historical interpretations backward in time to the American colonial era. In particular, the American Revolution, and the origins of the American Constitution, are interpreted to defend the Confederacy and its ideology. Additionally, this understanding of the American Constitution and American Revolution is also used to support neo-Confederate understanding of the rest of American history and is used to support neo-Confederate positions regarding current affairs.

In speaking to the public, neo-Confederates groups largely discuss the Confederacy and don't discuss Reconstruction much if at all. If they did give their true opinions about Reconstruction and the Ku Klux Klan, it would quickly discredit their movement and their slogan "Heritage Not Hate." Very importantly the neo-Confederates see the Civil War and Reconstruction as two phases in one long conflict. Groups like the Sons of Confederate Veterans (SCV) and the United Daughters of the Confederacy, however, do extensively focus on interpreting Reconstruction and holding up the Ku Klux Klan and other violent white terrorist groups of Reconstruction as Confederate heroes. The UDC has a museum, Oakley Park, in South Carolina which they call a shrine for the Red Shirts, a violent white supremacist groups that overthrew Reconstruction in 1876.[38] The Sons of Confederate Veteran sells books and videos praising the Ku Klux Klan as saviors of the South during Reconstruction.

Neo-Confederates portray Reconstruction, as a disastrous time in which allegedly incompetent and ignorant African Americans gained the right to vote in the South and elected corrupt and oppressive men to public office. This historical distortion has been a key element for racist white people in the South to justify denying African Americans their rights as citizens and to deny their human rights. Unfortunately this historical distortion became nationally accepted thus nationalizing support for the denial of citizenship rights for African Americans. Whites hostile to the 1950s and 1960s Civil Rights movement would refer to it as Reconstruction II.

Neo-Confederates are also separatist Southern nationalists who define the South as being Confederate and the region as a victim of ongoing abuse and oppression from before the Civil War to the present. A true Southerner is held to be a person who is pro-Confederate and understands the South as a continuation of the Confederacy. Neo-Confederates advocate the use of the term "Confederate Americans" as an ethnic group. In the April 2016 issue of the *Confederate Veteran*, the official publication of the Sons of Confederate Veterans (SCV), SCV Chaplain-in-Chief Ray L. Parker, in defending the Confederacy, states, "As Confederate Americans we honor our Southern Heritage."[39]

Before discussing the following example the author wishes to state that it is to the author fairly obvious that it is about the Black Lives Matter movement. However, the writing is curious in that it omits mentioning Black Lives Matter and African Americans and it might be that the Sons of Confederate Veterans would argue that it was about something else.

An example of neo-Confederate thinking illustrating how an understanding of the past shapes views of current events are two editorials of then SCV Lt. Commander-in-Chief Thomas V. Strain, (elected in 2016 as the SCV Commander-in-Chief), which appears to the author to be commenting on civil unrest over police shootings of African Americans in recent issues of the *Confederate Veterans* magazine. Strain seems to be condemning the Black Lives Matter movement, though not by name. He opens his March/April 2015 editorial "Courage," as follows:

> Compatriots, The United States are enduring some very troubling times currently. We have young men with no guidance attacking law-abiding citizens and law enforcement officers in the streets of this country. Moreover, when the officers do what is necessary in many cases to remedy the situation and protect the innocent, they are being called murderers.

Strain further in his editorial comments, "This is not a black-and-white issue: it is a right-versus wrong issue," and condemns the African American leadership of the protests stating, "To make matters worse, a certain group of self-appointed leaders, who wish to prosper from the very people they claim to be helping, don't speak of peace, and instead call for riots and more violent acts." Strain resents that those who condemn the protestors "are automatically labeled a racist." He doesn't specify the race of the leadership of these protests, but it seems to be in reference to those leading protests against police shootings. He doesn't specifically mention that the leadership is African American.

Regarding why this editorial about which appears to be about protests about recent police shootings was appearing in a publication for an organization that presents itself to the public as merely historical, Strain explains:

> You are probably wondering what this has to do with the Sons of Confederate Veterans, and the answer is a simple one. Reconstruction is where the very seeds were planted for such situations and in those years is found the root causes of where much of this began. Once all power was usurped from the States and transferred to a central government which would later take the form of a "direct democracy," it was to be expected this same government would use the power of its vast centralized offices to create a form of dependency — in return for votes, of course.

Strain continues to explain that "dependency" causes its recipients to be moral failures and how Reconstruction oppressed Southerners and that Southerners continued to be oppressed and that it "never truly ended and is continued today with Political Correctness."

In the July/Aug. 2015 issue of the *Confederate Veteran* in his editorial "Continue the Fight," Strain references "my article a few months ago," stating:

> All across the country we have had people rioting and looting because something happened to an individual whom they didn't even know.

Strain further explains that there are "'professional rioters,' involved in the protests, and further states, "I found that this is an actual profession for some people in this country." Strain sees this as a "direct result of the deterioration of the family and Christian values in our country today," and states that children are growing up without respect for authority and gives as one cause the lack of prayer in the public schools.[40]

Strain also states that he thinks "some of these murders could be avoided, and excessive force is used in some cases, in most it is due to the lack of trust and total disregard to the laws and authority figures, as well as a disrespect for the lives, property and rights of other individuals."

With the election of Strain as their leader, the Sons of Confederate Veterans appear to be continuing to campaign against the Black Lives Matter movement, again not by name. Strain issued on July 21, 2016 General Order 2016-01, Law Enforcement Appreciation Day. The opening of this general order declares:

> Whereas, with the current vicious and despicable attacks being waged against the law enforcement officers around the country today, and

The general order asks that, "Camps, Brigades, and Divisions are hereby highly encouraged to show their support to their local law enforcement on this day …"[41]

In his first article in the *Confederate Veteran*, Sept./Oct. 2016 as Commander-in-Chief he refers to General Order 2016-01. He states he was "propelled" to issue it after the murder of five Dallas police officers "as they were protecting a group who were protesting the recent killings of two men – one in Louisiana and the second in Minnesota," and "… many other acts aimed towards law enforcement officers all across the country."[42]

Besides not using the phrase "Black Lives Matter" or some variant, Strain's writing appears to be a little vague to the author. Unless the author missed it, there doesn't appear to be any reference to the city of Ferguson, Missouri, there is no specific*reference that these protests are over the shootings of African Americans by police officers, or that it involves shootings by police officers, or reference to African Americans at all. A hypothetical reader uninformed about current events might possibly not recognize that this is about the Black Lives Matter protests. It is the author's interpretation that it is.

These articles and what appears to be an anti-Black Lives Matter campaign, again Strain never refers to them by name, is a typical example how neo-Confederates relate contemporary issues to their understanding of history and how they see the nation as having gone in the wrong direction since the Civil War. Clearly these neo-Confederate groups often have a larger agenda then nostalgic historical remembrance.

As a side note, H. Rondel Rumburg, former Chaplain-in-Chief of the Sons of Confederate Veterans, and editor of the *Chaplains' Corps Chronicles of the Sons of Confederate Veterans* published in 2015 "Confederate Flags Matter: The Christian Influence on the Flags."[43] The book is offered for sale in the July/August 2016 *Confederate Veteran* in the SCV sales section, "Confederate Gifts from GHQ."[44] I think the title can be seen as a disrespectful appropriation of the slogan "Black Lives Matter."

There are other reactionary movements with similar agendas to the neo-Confederate movement, such as the neo-Reactionary movement who call themselves the "Dark Enlightenment," and the paleoconservatives, and paleolibertarians. Often members of these movements incorporate neo-Confederate elements in their thinking and there isn't a hard and fast boundary between them. A neo-Confederate view of American history might also be grafted onto a larger reactionary view of world history.

Similarly there isn't a boundary separating neo-Confederates from more explicitly racist organizations.

WHO

When you mention racists people often immediately conjure up the stereotypical images of some belligerent raging individuals spewing forth racial slurs and loudly proclaiming white supremacy. Perhaps they will be wearing strange clothing. They are frequently marginal persons in society both economically and socially and not in positions of influence.

Neo-Confederates in contrast are rarely if ever belligerent. They never, in public, or at least not in front of the media, use racial slurs or openly embrace white supremacy. They seek to be charming. They are educated. They are not marginal individuals, but inside the establishment. They are professors, columnists, persons on the mastheads of academic journals, authors of best-selling books, officials in presidential administrations, and they hold numerous other influential positions in society.

An example of the polished neo-Confederate elite can be found at the Abbeville Institute (www.abbevilleinstitute.org) referred to in an earlier chapter. The Institute is an organization of academics headed up by philosophy professor emeritus of Emory University Donald Livingston. Until 2013 they had listed scholars affiliated with the group and many of them are or were academics at colleges and universities. At the website you would have seen listed Thomas Di Lorenzo, professor of economics at Loyola University in Baltimore; Marshall DeRosa, professor of constitutional law at Florida Atlantic University; Paul Gottfried, professor of Intellectual History at Elizabethtown College in Pennsylvania; David Bradshaw, professor of philosophy at University of Kentucky; James Rembert, professor of literature at The Citadel; William Wilson, professor of religious studies and associate dean at University of Virginia; and 46 other professors at other institutions of higher learning. [45] *Southern Partisan* magazine had numerous contributors who were academics at some institution of higher learning. (See end notes to see Abbeville Institute list of scholars at www.archive.org.)

Others influence public opinion in venues outside of higher education . Regnery Press (www.regnery.com) publishes the Politically Incorrect Guide (PIG) series on topics such as American history, the American Constitution, the American presidents, global warming etc. Regnery's publications have proven to be very popular with conservatives, some are *New York Times* best-sellers.[46] You can easily find these books in mainstream book stores such as Barnes & Nobles. Neo-Confederates are the authors of several of these books.

Thomas E. Woods, Jr. graduated with a Ph.D. from Columbia University in New York, a prestigious ivy league school. He is a Senior Fellow at the Ludwig von Mises Institute,[47] a libertarian organization that supports secession and other neo-Confederate ideas, was a member of the League of the South and a contributor to its journal *Southern Patriot*,[48] and was a contributor to *Southern Partisan* magazine and *Chronicles* magazine, two journals of neo-Confederate opinion. He was listed on the Abbeville Institute as an associated scholar,[49] and even now (4/27/2016) appears on the Abbeville Institute on their webpage "Selected Books and DVD Videos by Abbeville Scholars."[50] In one *Southern Partisan* article,[51] "Sitting Amongst the Ruins: The South vs. The Enlightenment," he condemns the 18th century Enlightenment as being against Southern values and in another *Southern Partisan* article, "Christendom's Last Stand," he argues that the Civil War was a theological war between an orthodox Christian South and a heretical North.[52]

Woods' web site gives a lengthy listing of his writings and the publications and books he has contributed to, but the site doesn't mention any of his neo-Confederate writing.[53] He is the author of the *Politically Incorrect Guide to American History*, which was a *New York Times* best-seller. The book doesn't mention his involvement with neo-Confederate publications and organizations. The person purchasing his book won't have any knowledge that the author is a neo-Confederate scholar, the only hint being that the book has a Confederate soldier on the cover.

The Politically Incorrect Guide to American History teaches the American conservative movement American history from a neo-Confederate perspective. This is an example how neo-Confederacy is expanding beyond the land of Confederate monuments and going national.

Brion McClanahan, who serves as an instructor at Chattahoochee Valley Community College in Alabama,[54] is the author of *The Politically Incorrect Guide to the Founding Fathers*, *The Politically Incorrect Guide to Real American Heroes*, (Underline in the original title) and *The Founding Fathers Guide to the Constitution* all published by Regnery Press. What the PIG books don't tell you is that he was listed as the editor of the *Abbeville Review*, on the Abbeville Institute website until recently and is a frequent contributor of articles to the website.[55] He is also a contributor to www.lewrockwell.com with articles such as, "Lincolnites Are Crazed Warmongers," "Secede," and "Secede!" among others.[56] A visit to his website http://www.brionmcclanahan.com/ shows that he is a part of the conservative establishment.[57] He was also a contributor to *Southern Partisan*.[58]

Kevin R. Gutzman, professor of history at Western Connecticut State University,[59] is the author of *The Politically Incorrect Guide to the Constitution*. He is listed on the Abbeville Institute web page of "Selected Books and DVD Videos by Abbeville Scholars." He was a contributor of about 20 book reviews and articles to *Southern Partisan*. In his book review of *Taming the Storm: The Life and Times of Judge Frank M. Johnson, Jr. and the South's Fight Over Civil Rights*, by Jack Bass, a book about the heroic life of Judge Johnson and his support for Civil Rights, Gutzman condemns Johnson stating:

> All in all, while Bass thinks Johnson a heroic moderate, he shows him to be a lonely old authoritarian whose life is an example of the over-centralization of the USA, following the European examples, began to indulge in the 1930s.
>
> God willing, there will be fewer such "heroes" in the future. [60]

This is the person teaching the American conservative movement about the Constitution.

He was on the Abbeville Institutes listing of Associated Scholars.[61] He is also a contributor to www.lewrockwell.com, where he has an article attacking the Supreme Courts historic 1954 decision *Brown vs. Board of Education*.[62] The very conservative *Claremont Book Review*, had a review of his PIG book on the Constitution titled "Whistling Dixie," which the reviewer called the book "bizarre."[63] Visiting his website http://www.kevingutzman.com/ you can see that he is not marginal and is part of the conservative establishment. He is an author who can get his books reviewed in the *Wall Street Journal* and other prestigious publications.[64]

H.W. Crocker III is the author of the *Politically Incorrect Guide to the Civil War*, and the *Politically Incorrect Guide to the British Empire*, and was an Associate Editor of *Southern Partisan* and contributor to the magazine.[65] He is a contributor to *National Review*,[66] the conservative Catholic *Crisis Magazine*,[67] and *The American Spectator*.[68] The American Spectator has posted online his article, "How Would Jefferson Davis Vote?"[69] He is the Vice-President and Executive Editor of Regnery Publishing.[70] He is the author of a neo-Confederate management book, *Robert E. Lee on Leadership: Executive Lessons in Character, Courage, and Vision*, published by Three Rivers Press of the Crown Publishing Group, a division of Penguin Random House.[71]

In regard to the numerous neo-Confederate professors, (very often with some exceptions), the students don't know about their ideology. Women and minority students sign up or are assigned to classes taught by neo-Confederates. Students should Google their professors and with the terms "Confederate," or "agrarian" and see what they come up with. The author has seen no indication that the universities care at all about this.

The Abbeville Institute and the PIG book series are mentioned to show that neo-Confederates don't fit the stereotype of fringe political figures, or economically marginal individuals. They have real avenues of influence. Highly influential neo-Confederates include or have included Pat Buchanan, contributor and at one time senior editor of *Southern Partisan* magazine; Joe Sobran, former senior editor at *National Review* who was a contributor to *Southern Partisan*; Samuel Francis, columnist for conservative newspaper *Washington Times*, who was a contributor to *Southern Partisan*; and Russell Kirk, author of *The Conservative Mind*, columnist for *National Review*, and a leading conservative figure in the 20th century, who was on the masthead of *Southern Partisan* as a senior advisor and was a contributor. To list all the conservatives of some note and their neo-Confederate resumes would be a book-sized directory itself and a substantial project. Perhaps if there was an institute formed for research on the neo-Confederates this could be done and made available online.

These neo-Confederate authors, columnists, and politicians are able to shape the consciousness of America since not very many people know that there is a neo-Confederate movement let alone know that these authors are neo-Confederates. If the public was aware of the neo-Confederate movement and that these authors were neo-Confederates the impact of these authors would be far less and their agenda supporting inequality would be greatly impeded.

Regnery Press, (http://www.regnery.com/), is a one of the leading conservative publishers and was founded in 1947. With these books American conservatives are learning about American history, the Constitution, the Civil War, the American founding and American heroes from neo-Confederate intellectuals. We should not be surprised that we one day awaken and find that the United States has become a new Confederate States of America. And, if we think inequality is bad now, it will be nothing compared to this nightmare new Confederate States of America.

7 NEO-CONFEDERATE ORGANIZATIONS

The neo-Confederates are organized with web sites, email lists, Facebook pages, twitter accounts, blogs, and print periodicals. They have conferences, classes, and national conventions. Several of these groups have substantial buildings for their headquarters. They have financial resources. They have kept the Southern landscape in the South Confederate for generations.

Some organizations incorporate extensive parts of neo-Confederate ideology into their agenda but might have additional significant elements in their ideology that are not neo-Confederate. Sometimes the neo-Confederate agenda is attached to a larger reactionary interpretation of world history supporting a more global reactionary agenda. All neo-Confederate groups don't have the same ideas and within a neo-Confederate group there can be a range of beliefs. Neo-Confederate organizations can have different focuses in supporting neo-Confederacy and this focus can change over time. They also vary in how forthcoming they are about the elements of their neo-Confederate agenda.

The United Daughters of the Confederacy (UDC), established in 1985, is the oldest organization of this sort now existing. Its membership is restricted to those who are descendants of those who served in the Confederate services. Their publication is *UDC Magazine* and has a circulation of 6,600 as of 2015.[72] Membership is not known. In the early 20th century the UDC praised the Ku Klux Klan enthusiastically and openly, and in the 1950s their magazine ran a series of articles attacking civil rights and the Supreme Court decision *Brown vs. Board of Education* integrating schools. However, in the late 20th century and in the 21st century the *UDC Magazine* articles don't openly express opposition to civil rights. They still praise what could be reasonably called racist books, and praise the Red Shirts, a violent white supremacist organization of

Reconstruction.[73] They have an impressive headquarters building in Richmond, Virginia.

The United Daughters of the Confederacy supervises the Children of the Confederacy (CofC) to instruct the next generation in neo-Confederate ideology. A 1960 article by an 8th grade member is gleeful over the murderous slaughter of African American soldiers during Reconstruction.[74]

The Sons of Confederate Veterans (SCV) originally known as the United Sons of Confederate Veterans was organized in 1896. The name was changed because members were according to scholar Gaines, "Horrified that people might confuse the abbreviation on their badge, USCV, with United States Colored Volunteers, in 1908 the Sons dropped *United* from their name."[75] They are also a descendant's organization. They have an associate membership for those who are not descendant's but wish to support the SCV. In addition, there is a women's support group the Order of the Confederate Rose, membership of which is not limited to descendants. Their publication is the *Confederate Veteran*, named after the original *Confederate Veteran* magazine of 1893 to 1930. On the table of contents page there is a disclaimer that, "The opinions expressed by the authors of signed articles reflect the personal views of the writers and are not necessarily a statement of SCV policy."[76] Circulation figures are not publically known. In 2012 SCV Lt. Commander-in-Chief Charles Kelly Barrow stated that the group had over 30,000 members.[77] The SCV Educational Political Action Committee published the *Southern Mercury* from 2003 to 2008. This publication also had a disclaimer, "The opinions expressed by the authors of signed articles the personal views of the writers and are not necessarily a statement of FPAC policy."[78] That publication had articles which were very frank in their racial attitudes, attacks on civil rights, minorities, and it contained hysterical screeds such as one claiming that Lincoln was a communist and another predicting cities might be devastated by race riots if Barack Obama wasn't elected.[79] Publication was stopped officially due to the lack of funds, but perhaps the realization that it was documenting what Confederate "heritage" was really about was a factor as well. They have a plantation house, Elms Spring, for a headquarters in Columbia, Tennessee.

The SCV runs the Sam Davis Youth Camps to instruct the next generation on neo-Confederate ideology. In its print ads starting in 2003 and currently online at the camp web-page, the group says that the reason for starting the class is that surveys had shown more students know that "'Snoop Doggy Dog' is rapper" then know James Madison is considered the father of the Constitution, and that more students who knew about the cartoon *Beavis & Butthead* than knew "that George Washington's Farewell Address warned against establishing permanent alliances with foreign governments." However, the real purpose of the camps is revealed in an article describing a contest for the students at the first camp in 2003 with the theme, "Why My State Should Secede."[80] In encouraging families to send their children to this camp Ron G. Wilson, SCV Commander-in-Chief, tells families that the students will be instructed on the "TRUTH" on the topics such as slavery, pro-slavery theologians R.L. Dabney, Benjamin Morgan Palmer, and supposed "Theological differences" between the Confederacy and Union which made the Civil War a religious conflict. The same issue has an article by the John Weaver, SCV Chaplain-in-Chief, and who was an instructor at this first youth camp explaining this idea that the Civil War was clash between a heretical "North" and a Christian South.[81]

Organizations formed in the late 20th and early 21st century are the League of the South organized in 1994[82] and the Abbeville Institute started in 2002.[83]

The League of the South (LOS) was important in the neo-Confederate movement from 1994 to about 2001, but had an abrupt decline when LOS leader Michael Hill issued a press release that the 9/11/2001 terror attack on the World Trade Center was a punishment for American for its misbehavior, in particular U.S. – NATO bombings in Serbia, "… [T]hat judgement is visited upon nations who use their own vast powers unjustly." The League of the South also published the essay, "Why Should God Bless America?" by Wayne Carlson which argued that God had punished America for its sins.[84] The organization is just a remnant now, but it is useful to observe to find out what neo-Confederates truly believe and what their real agenda is. The LOS openly spells out its reactionary and racist beliefs while other neo-Confederate organizations are not so open about their beliefs and agenda. (leagueofthesouth.com and https://www.facebook.com/leagueofthesouth/)[85].

The League of the South Institute seemed to become inactive not too long thereafter Hill's press release and Carlson's essay. The Abbeville Institute (www.abbevilleinstitute.org) was started by Donald Livingston who was previously the director of the League of the South Institute, with many of the same scholars and professors who had been in the League of the South Institute affiliating with the Abbeville Institute.[86] They advocate Southern nationalism. They see white Southerners as a separate people, distinct from the American mainstream. They take care not to express blatantly racist opinions, but will praise rabid neo-Confederate books and their authors.[87] They have conferences and classes. Donald Livingston is professor emeritus of Emory University in Georgia.

The Council of Conservative Citizens (www.cofcc.org) is the organization which inspired Dylann Roof to massacre African Americans at a church in Charleston, South Carolina. Several of its leaders have passed away, but it is still active. At one time they were heavily connected with the Republican Party, but due to materials supplied to the *Washington Post* and other media by Edward H. Sebesta, the Republican Party disconnected from the organization.[88] They were a successor organization to the White Citizens Council, an anti-civil rights group in the mid-20th century called by some the "uptown Klan," because of the surface respectability of its members. Its publication is *The Citizen Informer*.

The Ludwig von Mises Institute, (LvMI), (www.mises.org) was founded in 1982.[89] It is the libertarian branch of the neo-Confederate movement, along with the web site www.lewrockwell.com founded by Lew Rockwell, (founder and CEO of the LvMI) and Burton S. Blumert. Hating Abraham Lincoln is one of its particular focuses. The group rejects any and all civil rights legislation and supports secession. It has multiple publications.

The *Southern Partisan* was the major magazine of the neo-Confederate movement from its founding in 1979 to about 2004 when it started to be very irregularly and infrequently published with one last issue appearing in 2008. It experience declined after it was revealed that U.S. Senator John McCain's South Carolina presidential campaign manager was Richard Quinn, the editor of the magazine. Edward H. Sebesta supplied numerous media outlets with information about the publication and later when Sebesta pointed out to mainstream journalists U.S. Senator Trent Lott's interview in *Southern Partisan* where Lott described the Republican Party as the party of Jefferson Davis's descendants.[90] After that no one no prominent figure or anyone who hoped to achieve prominence would appear in it. It was notable for the numerous conservative leaders, religious right leaders, elected Republican officials, and numerous professors who gave interviews to it, or who contributed articles to it. Many essays that appeared in Southern Partisan are now online at the Abbeville Institute web site.

However, one individual deserves special mention, the late Willard Scott formerly of the *Today Show*, who gave an interview to the *Southern Partisan* in 1984.[91] It should give people pause to think what *Today Show* co-host Bryant Gumbel had to deal with on the program's set where he shared screen time with a neo-Confederate and what Scott's Confederate uniforms on the show were about.

Thomas Fleming was editor of *Chronicles* from 1985 to 2015. He proposed the organization of the Southern League in *Chronicles* magazine,[92] which later changed its name to League of the South (LOS). He was a founding board member of the LOS[93] and at one time *Chronicles* ran ads in the LS *Southern Patriot* stating that all the editors of the magazine were LOS members.[94] It still has prominent neo-Confederate contributors such as Clyde N. Wilson, a founding board member of the League of the South and who contributed to *Southern Partisan* magazine as well authoring an online series of articles for the Abbeville Institute. William J. Watkins Jr., former contributor to *Southern Partisan* magazine writes for *Chronicles* as well.[95] The magazine still defends the Confederacy with the August 2015 issue featuring multiple articles defending the Confederate battle flag. The issue had a Confederate battle flag on the cover in response to the massive rejection of the Confederacy after the massacre in Charleston, SC by Dylann Roof.[96] The current editor, Chilton Williamson Jr., recently published a 2015 *Chronicles* anti-immigration article, "The Revenge of the Confederacy," tracing supposed immigration problems back to the Union victory over the Confederacy.[97] The Rockford institute publishes and sells neo-Confederate books. Their latest book, published in 2015, edited by Clyde N. Wilson, is "Life, Literature, & Lincoln," a compilation of neo-Confederate Thomas Landess Jr.'s writings, including as the title indicates, his attacks on Lincoln.[98] Another major work was the two volume set, published in 2010, "Chronicles of the South," which consisted of articles mostly by neo-Confederates that have been published in *Chronicles* magazine, an anthology also edited by Clyde N. Wilson.[99] Even so, the magazine can't be called a neo-Confederate magazine since its scope is larger than that. It would call itself a paleoconservative magazine and it is, which includes in its scope neo-Confederacy. There isn't a boundary between these two movements. *Chronicles* magazine is a publication for those raging against the present and this rage includes a neo-Confederate ideology along with other reactionary ideologies.

Neo-Confederates aren't confined to neo-Confederate groups. You find some contributors to *Southern Partisan* and *Chronicles* at *American Renaissance*, (www.amren.com) a white supremacist publication as well as at Virginia Dare (www.vdare.com). There isn't a clear boundary between the neo-Confederate movement and white supremacist groups, but neo-Confederates would generally avoid groups that fit the public stereotype of racist extremists and usually avoid language and behavior that fit those stereotypes.

As noted earlier neo-Confederates are often paleoconservatives and these groups overlap. The publication *American Conservative* is a paleoconservative magazine, but the number of neo-Confederate contributors is notable and there are neo-Confederate articles in it. David Gordon, in the article "Southern Cross," portrays M.E. Bradford, a founder of the modern neo-Confederate movement, campaigner for segregationist Alabama governor George Wallace, and life-long enemy of civil rights legislation, as a hero, explaining and praising Bradford's writings against equality, and claiming that Bradford was a victim of neoconservative lies.[100] The author, who has read all of Bradford's books, can assure the reader that Bradford wasn't misrepresented and is as bad as the neoconservatives claimed, if not worse. The author has authored an unpublished manuscript on Bradford about 100-plus pages long.

The major neo-Confederate groups and magazines have been described, but there are other minor groups.

In a lot of cases when the prominent neo-Confederate groups don't want to directly oppose an effort to remove a Confederate monument or flag they will organize a "heritage" coalition which allows them to have defend a Confederate monument or symbol without their organization's deeper agenda being brought up.

The extent of neo-Confederacy can't be measured by the membership of these groups and circulation figures of their publications alone. The book, *The South Was Right!* published by neo-Confederate Pelican Publishing, has had a 120,000 copies sold and is still in print and has had 13 printings since the 2nd edition was published in 1994. The book can be found in most major books stores in the Civil War section in all parts of the nation.

8 AGAINST EQUALITY AND DEMOCRACY

The central focus of the neo-Confederate movement is opposition to democratic values. Racism, homophobia, antifeminism, and other prejudices are tools in a tool box to achieve their anti-democratic goals.

As mentioned earlier in the book, *The South Was Right!*, 2nd edition, by James Ronald Kennedy and Walter Donald Kennedy, has sold over 120,000 copies since it was published by Pelican Press in Gretna, Louisiana in 1994. The Kennedys maintain a website www.kennedytwins.com in which they promote their series of books, some of which are as *Was Jefferson Davis Right?*, *Myths of American Slavery*, (which defends Southern slavery as biblical), and *Rekilling Lincoln*.

The SCV offered for sale, *The South Was Right!*, in their 2004-2005, 2005-2006, 2008-2009, 2009-2010, 201-2012, and 2015-2016 merchandise catalogs, online store, and (starting in 2001) in their magazine *Confederate Veteran*.[101] It was also offered it for sale in the SCV Merchandise Catalog 2013-2014 which was an insert in the Sept/Oct. 2013 *Confederate Veteran*.[102]

The Kennedys were the speakers on the topic of "Heritage" at the 2015 Sons of Confederate Veterans national convention in Richmond. In 2008 SCV Lt. Commander-in-Chief R. Michael Givens, (later SCV Commander-in-Chief), in his regular column "Report of the Lt. Commander-in-Chief," in discussing the need of educating the SCV membership informs his readers, "In each issue of *Confederate Veteran*, I will supply you with a few books that will be helpful to this end." The number one book on his list is *The South Was Right!*[103]

In a chapter titled, "Equality of Opportunity" the Kennedy's propose four major restrictions on who should be allowed to vote. Major restrictions on who is allowed to vote would seem to contradict the principle of equality, but in the neo-Confederate worldview, words often mean something very different of what the general public think they mean. The Kennedys quote 19th century British philosopher John Stuart Mill to justify restrictions emphasizing on voting that Mills is a "non-Southern and non-racist source."

These are the qualifications which the Kennedy brothers propose.

1. "The first requirement is that all who would seek the privilege must be able to read, to write, and to demonstrate certain elementary knowledge of history, geography, and mathematics."

2. "The second requirement is that being a taxpayer should be a prerequisite to voting."

The Kennedy brothers further explain that "an indirect tax or easy tax" such as "a sales tax or payroll tax" such as the federal income tax doesn't meet this requirement, but only a direct tax payment would qualify.

3. "The third requirement is that those who support their existence with relief (i.e., welfare, public housing, etc.) should not be allowed to vote."

They also state, "Mill would also deny the privilege of voting to those who take advantage of bankruptcy …"

Under the Kennedy system if there were poor or non-existent schools and you and your family suffered from the want of a good education you might not be able to vote for better schools and a better system of public education because you couldn't pass the education qualification test.

They are unclear on what constitutes "elementary knowledge" of history, geography, and mathematics and what they define as being sufficiently able to read and write to qualify for voting. This literacy requirement is dangerously broad since it could be define to be very demanding and greatly restricting voting. Those who lived in areas where there wasn't sufficient funds for education might not be able to vote. Those who got a poor or marginal educational opportunities because their parents had a marginal or poor economic position in society and thus lived in a poor neighborhood with poor schools might not be able to vote. This provision alone could be used to undermine democracy and create an underclass of non-voters going on indefinitely for generations.

As the chapter on neo-Confederates and public schools will explain, neo-Confederates are hostile to public education, so if the neo-Confederates had influence it very likely might be that you or your children would not have an opportunity for a good education at a public school since there might not be any public schools, and you would have to try to give your children a private school education with what funds you could afford. Given that neo-Confederates believe in inequality you might very little funds for your children's education.

The only direct tax that most Americans pay is the property tax by those who are well off enough to own property. A great portion of Americans would likely find that they couldn't vote. Also, with this system individuals might be heavily taxed through sales taxes and income taxes, and indirectly taxes on those who provide essential services but they still would not qualify as voters. Renters would not be able to vote even though they are playing the landlord's property tax through their rent. The Kennedy brothers in their book defended the poll tax that had existed in some Southern states and was outlawed later by the Twenty-Fourth Amendment to the Constitution in 1964. So if neo-Confederates were in charge it might be that you would have to pay for voting after you pay for your children's private education in a society of economic inequality.

The use of the abbreviation "etc." in the Kennedys third requirement for voting, that the individual can't be the benefit of any public relief, should be noted. The vagueness of the "etc." is a trap door through which many voters could fall. "Relief" could be defined very broadly. If poor economic policy meant you lost your job and were receiving unemployment, you are getting "relief" to "support" your "existence." In a neo-Confederate society, supposing there still were unemployment benefits, you wouldn't be allowed to vote for candidates who want to change economic policy. If an unequal society meant that often you needed assistance because of government economic policies you wouldn't be allowed to vote to change those policies. Those who found difficulty in finding work because they were members of a group discriminated against could find that they were less likely to vote since they were economically disadvantaged. Those who were differently abled and perhaps needing assistance at some time would find then they would not be able to vote.

The forth requirement would mean that if poor economic policy resulted in the bankruptcy of your business or personal bankruptcy you would not be able to vote to change economic policy. In an unequal society economic bankruptcy might be a much more significant hazard in general and in particular even more so to the economically disadvantaged.

It has to be considered that even a partial implementation of these restrictions, or even a partial implementation of one of these restrictions could have a great impact. First, by directly disqualifying some of the less affluent and poor segments of society from voting. Even the disqualification of a few percent of the electorate would shift a lot of elections in a reactionary direction.

Secondly, by changing who is allowed to vote, there would be a shift in the elections of the choices of candidates to a choice between one candidate for the affluent and another candidate for the affluent or the even more affluent, leaving the non-affluent voter and the poor voter, even if he or she can qualify for voting, little incentive to vote since neither of candidates are concerned with their needs.

This would support a feedback loop of greater and greater voting restrictions. With a partial implementation of these restrictions you could with your new, narrower set of qualified voters get could get more of these restrictions implemented and then with this yet even further restricted set of voters even yet more restrictions on suffrage, probably more. As the Kennedy brothers explain.

> The sovereign community, through its representatives within each state, is the only authoritative source for establishing acceptable qualification for voting. The only restraint that can legitimately be placed upon the sovereign community is that it must maintain a Republican form of government within its state.

They reference Article 5, Section 4 of the U.S. Constitution as for the requirement that the government be republican.

The Kennedy restrictions alone would probably disqualify the majority of American adults from voting or at least nearly a majority.

The Kennedy brothers then explain:

> Some will protest that we are "repealing" the Voting Rights Act; this is not true! You do not repeal a fraud; you correct it. You not recall a tyrant; you remove him. The same is true with the so-called Voting Rights Act. The Voting Rights Act as with all other Reconstruction legislation (see Chapter VI) must be annulled to restore the balance of power between the federal and state governments. These Reconstruction acts violate the principle of the consent of the governed within each of the sovereign communities of the South…

However, the Kennedy brother's concern about the "consent of the governed" doesn't preclude them from denying a large fraction of the public from voting, in particular the less affluent and poor, on who might govern them, precluding them by these restrictions from giving any consent.

The condemnation of the Voting Rights Act as "Reconstruction legislation" again shows how contemporary issues are related by neo-Confederates to the Civil War and Reconstruction.

Though the Kennedy brothers are careful to reference John Stuart Mill who they emphasis is "non-Southern and non-racist" their real agenda is suggested by their past history of campaigning against civil rights legislation in the 1960s.

Michael Hill, president of the League of the South, reviewed two of the Kennedy books in *Chronicles* magazine in an article titled, "The Good Kennedys," that included a biographical background of the authors and a history of the origin of the book *The South Was Right!*[104] As Hill explains, the book, originates from the Kennedy brothers activism against Civil Rights in the 1960s. Hill writes:

> As teenagers in the 1960s, the Kennedys came to regard the defense of the South from its detractors as a "spiritual duty." When the civil rights activists stepped up their attacks on Southern traditions, especially states' rights, James and Walter volunteered to serve Mississippi gubernatorial candidate Ross Barnett and the "unpledged electors" movement. Both cast their first vote in a national election for Democratic candidate George Wallace in 1968. ...
>
> As Lyndon Johnson and the civil rights movement continued to dismantle the Constitution, the Kennedys contemplated a book project to defend the founding principles of the Old American Republic.

In summary, *The South Was Right!* is an anti-civil rights book originating from their opposition against civil rights. Both the 1st edition and 2nd edition were praised in book reviews in the *Confederate Veteran*.

Historically voter restrictions in the former Confederate states such as poll taxes and literacy tests excluded whites as well as African Americans. Though the percentage of African Americans excluded was higher than that of whites, in terms of total numbers more whites than African Americans were denied the right to vote by these laws. These restrictions posed by the Kennedys would very likely selectively disenfranchise African Americans more than whites, but the intent of them is to apply to persons of any race. These proposed restriction do double duty to create both race and class hierarchy.

When first released in 1991 the Kennedy book received a favorable review in the *Confederate Veteran*, with James N. Vogler Jr., writing:

> As you probably have guessed by the title this is not your usual diatribe of why the South lost the War. It is, instead an attempt by the authors to

attain several goals, including exploding many misconceptions about our region; the War; Reconstruction; and the "New South." They also want to instill a renewed pride in being Southern and show us the way to reclaim that which we have lost over the last 125 years.

… At the conclusion, the authors outline how we as Southerners must renew our regional pride, and elect legislatures who will represent all of our best interests.[105]

When the 2nd edition came out Vogler, acknowledging the wide impact of this book wrote this review in 1994:

In 1991, Ron and Don Kennedy first released *The South Was Right*, and many of us have not looked at the War Between the States the same way since. …

I found this new, expanded volume to be excellent reading. The new additions definitely add to what already was a most interesting and thought-provoking book. [106]

This is one of the major founding books of the modern neo-Confederate movement, it has had over 120,000 readers, and has been endorsed enthusiastically by book reviews in the *Confederate Veteran*, and it is a book dedicated to destroying American democracy. This isn't the only example where neo-Confederates are campaigning against democracy.

The SCV has offered this book for sale in at least six merchandise catalogs, online, and in their magazine *Confederate Veteran* starting in 2001.[107]

More recently two books condemning democracy have been published: *Democracy, The God That Failed: The Economics and Politics of Monarchy, Democracy, and Natural Order*, by Hans-Hermann Hoppe, Transaction Press, in 2001; and *After Tocqueville: The Promise and Failure of Democracy* by Chilton Williamson Jr., Intercollegiate Studies Institute Books, the publishing arm of the Intercollegiate Studies Institute (ISI), in 2012.[108] ISI also supports and funds the conservative university student newspapers across the nation.

Hans-Hermann Hoppe is professor emeritus of economics at the University of Nevada Las Vegas, and he is a Distinguished Senior Fellow of the Ludwig von Mises Institute, Auburn, Alabama, founder and president of The Property and Freedom Society, and the former editor of the *Journal of Libertarian Studies: An Interdisciplinary Quarterly Review*.[109] Transaction Press is at Rutgers Univ. in New Jersey and has published several neo-Confederate books. Again, neo-Confederates are in the establishment. Also, neo-Confederacy is not confined to the South.

The Ludwig von Mises Institute published a volume, *Property, Freedom & Society: Essays in Honor of Hans-Hermann Hoppe*, in 2009 presenting it to him in a private ceremony.

The book argues that the end of monarchy, what he characterizes as privately owned government, and the rise of democracy, what he calls "public owned government," had led to the decline of Western civilization, what he calls "decivilization."

> Rather, it is only when a government is *publically* owned (under democratic-republican rule) that the decivilizing effects of government can be expected to be strong enough to actually halt the civilizing process or even to alter its direction and bring about an opposite tendency toward decivilization: capital consumption, shrinking planning horizons and provisions, and a progressive infantilization and brutalization of social life. [Italics in original.][110]

The book regards American history from a neo-Confederate view. The Civil War is referred to as the "American War for Southern Independence."[111] One example is in the chapter condemning democracy as leading to "decivilization" Hoppe gives a states' rights view of the Civil War:

> The U.S. had been founded as a republic, and the democratic principle in particular, inherent in the idea of a republic, had only recently been carried to victory as the result of the violent defeat and devastation of the secessionist Confederacy by the centralist Union government.[112]

So Union victory led to "decivilization."

Hoppe explains that the purpose of his book is to delegitimize democracy for the purpose of eliminating it.

> And just as monarchy was once accepted as legitimate but is today considered to be an unthinkable solution to the current social crisis, it is not inconceivable that the idea of democratic rule might someday be regarded as morally illegitimate and unthinkable. Such a delegitimization is a necessary precondition to avoiding ultimate social catastrophe.[113]

Hoppe's doesn't propose a restoration of Monarchy, but instead the institution of what he calls an "anarcho-capitalist society." He is "convinced that such a society is the only social order that can be defended as just," where there is no government.

He introduces this idea in his chapter "On Free Immigration and Forced Integration" where he introduces the concept, but doesn't want to explain in the chapter why he thinks it is just, but instead "employ it as a conceptual benchmark, because this will help explain the fundamental misconception of most contemporary free immigration advocates." The reasons for Hoppe's hostility towards democracy become apparent.

In Hoppe's just society, "All land is privately owned, including all streets, rivers, airports, harbors, and so on. The property can be restricted in multiple ways including, "no buildings more than four stories high, no sale or rent to Jews, Germans, Catholics, homosexuals, Haitians, families without or without children, or smokers for example."

Further, "under this scenario no such thing as freedom of immigration exists," and when immigrants were admitted it would be only to a specific private property and there would be no "freedom to move around" and "There will be as much immigration or nonimmigration, inclusivity or exclusivity, desegregation or segregation, nondiscrimination or discrimination based on racial, ethnic, linguistic, religious, cultural or whatever other grounds as individual owners or associations of individual owners allow."[114]

Hoppe's complains that in a democracy there is egalitarianism and this results in "the forcing of masses of inferior immigrants onto domestic property owners," and as the best example of bad immigration policy of a democracy, Hoppe writes, "… the United States immigration laws of 1965 eliminated previous 'quality' concerns and the explicit preference for *European* immigrants, replacing them with a policy of almost complete nondiscrimination (multiculturalism)." [Emphasis in the original.]

Hoppe also complains that egalitarian sentiments will also lead democratic rulers to want to pass non-discrimination laws and "Thus it is hardly surprising that the so-called 'civil-rights' legislation in the United States, which outlawed domestic discrimination on the basis of color, race, national origin, religion, gender, age, sexual orientation, disability, etc. and which thereby mandated forced integration coincided with the adoption of a nondiscriminatory immigration policy; i.e., mandated *inter*national desegregation (forced integration.) [Emphasis in the original.][115]

In another chapter, "On Free Trade and Restricted Immigration," Hoppe complains that public parks, roads, and buildings allow immigrants to "cross every domestic resident's path, and move into virtually any neighborhood."[116]

Hoppe sees "'natural' forces of repulsion or enmity arising from the differences between and even within the races" as a problem his system of anarcho-capitalism will solve through separation of groups.[117] Public streets are again a problem "… whereon everyone may proceed wherever he wants – all forms of ethnic, tribal, or racial tensions and animosities will be stimulated."[118]

Hoppe also believes that defense and policing should be done by private insurance companies. Instead of prisons Hoppe states, "Indeed, in cooperation with one another, insurers would want to expel known criminals not just from their immediate neighborhood but from civilization altogether into the wilderness or open frontier of the Amazon jungle, the Sahara, or the polar regions."[119]

In the conclusion of the book, Hoppe points out the failure of the Confederacy to secede and so advocates adopting the model of a medieval Europe divided into hundreds of states and to be like this model do a "piecemeal withdrawal" of cities to "create a U.S. punctuated by a large and increasing number of territorially disconnected free cities…" that could act in concert defeat the government and break up the United States.[120] Though exactly how this might be done isn't made clear in the book. The Texas secessionists are probably thinking of how to do this, but as the Malheur Refuge events in 2015 – in which armed anti-government militants for a time occupied a national wildlife refuge in Oregon – shows, it is likely through violence or threats of violence.

To the author the argumentation used in the book is astonishingly deficient and reading this book is like falling into a vortex of madness and it is astonishing is that a publisher that claims to publish books on critical thinking released this book. This is what lurks at Rutgers University.

Neo-Confederates embraced this book.

Joe Sobran, former Senior Editor of the *National Review*, in his *Southern Partisan* column, "The Sobran View" in 2002 enthusiastically praised the book and equated living in a democracy with slavery. Sobran also argued that the Civil War "established the fatal principle that no state could withdraw, for any reason. So that the states and the people lost their ultimate defense against Federal tyranny."[121]

Marco Bassani, professor of political theory at the University of Milan, had a lengthy 2003 *Southern Partisan* book review, "Democracy: An Indictment That Will Not Wash Away." Bassani explains how Hoppe sees monarchy as being better than democracy which breaks down civilization, that private insurance companies should provide police protection, that secession is a good thing, and that the U.S. should be broken up into many small states. Bassani recommends that Hoppe's book should be read along with Pat Buchanan's book *Decline of the West*.

The book review is also interesting in what it omits. Whereas Hoppe is fairly open about being against civil rights and wanting to discriminate, in particular against immigrants because they aren't European, Bassani's book review doesn't mention civil rights at all and only briefly discusses Hoppe's ideas about immigration in a very oblique manner obscuring that this is about discrimination and antipathy to non-European groups. A neo-Confederate reader would understand what Bassani was stating, but the casual reader or a reporter wouldn't and it could be plausibly denied if criticized. Neo-Confederate racism is often under the table.[122] Bassani is a contributor to publications of the Mises Institute.[123]

Thomas Fleming, founder of the League of the South, founding editor of *Southern Partisan* magazine, and editor of *Chronicles* for 30 years, opens his review with the statement, "Hans-Hermann Hoppe may be the most brilliant and original classical liberal alive today." "Classical liberal" is a term used by paleoconservatives for a reactionary belief system and they aren't liberal in any modern understanding of the word "liberal." The review concludes with the statement, "… any conservative or libertarian with the slightest interest in political history should buy this book."

One interesting thing about the review is that Fleming is not happy with Hoppe's criticism of Pat Buchanan and Hoppe's accusing some conservatives of "national socialism." Fleming comments, "I have heard him refer to criminals, gypsies, and 'other human garbage'; even in this book, he concludes that proletarian consumers are more or less subhuman beasts." But Fleming defends Hoppe as a "sentimental German monarchist."[124] *Chronicles* magazine has waged an ongoing campaign against democracy over the years.

Chilton Williamson's started as the Literary Editor at *National Review* in 1976, later was Senior Editor, and left *National Review* to be an editor at *Chronicles* in 1989.[125] He is currently the Editor of *Chronicles*. His book, *After Tocqueville: The Promise and Failure of Democracy*, is a long fearful railing and wailing with arms flailing against the modern world.

Alexis de Tocqueville visited the United States in the 19th century and published *De La Démocratie en Amérique*, (Democracy in America) in two volumes in 1835 and 1840. Francis Fukuyama in 1992 published, *End of History and the Last Man*, proclaiming that democracy, with the fall of the Soviet Union, had triumphed and was the end point of history. Williamson's book is partially a rebuttal of Fukuyama and partially Williamson's assessment of present day democracy and its prospects in relation to Tocqueville's assessment of American democracy. The book is a condemnation of democracy and a rebuttal of Fukuyama and Tocqueville's writings are referenced to attack contemporary democracy.

Williamson writes, "The ultimate definition of democracy, I believe is that it is a false religion – a proposition I shall consider at length further in this book."[126] Elsewhere he declares, "Modern democracies are morally relativist and inherently atheistic societies, devoid of absolute principles and prepared to set popular will (however that may be determined) above even their supposed commitment to pragmatism."[127] In yet another condemnation by Williamson, he quotes reactionary Claude Polin, "Polin concludes that democracy is the only form of government suited to the mentality of modern man. 'The good to be satisfied in a democracy, not the common good but the private one, has two faces: vanity and greed, the two breasts upon which democracy feeds.'"[128]

In his chapter "What is Democracy?" Williamson stands against universal suffrage stating that politicians before the extension of suffrage "knew their classical political theory, for which it was axiomatic that to give the lower classes a voice in politics was actually to give them shouting rights to dispossess the higher ones. Ultimately, academic theory and popular politics compelled the political class to retreat from what it recognized to be both political common sense and a bulwark of civilization by giving in to the demands of the mob…"[129] This is an opinion which Williamson makes clear that he shares in commenting on the welfare state, in which he states "The great question for democracy is, If the proletarian is deemed incompetent to assume charge of his own life, how can he be expected to have a responsible voice in running the state? No politician, democratic or otherwise, honestly believes that he can be."[130] Elsewhere Williamson comments that the voter who was poor or without property was a threat that might "employ his vote as a highway man holds a knife to the throats of citizens wealthier than himself."[131]

Williamson concludes this chapter claiming that democracies lack an ability to critique themselves "short of a catastrophe" and "Nor is there agreement on the proposition that democracy guarantees efficiency in modern capitalist societies." Then he states, "In the end, democracy may be best understood as a means rather than an end – a means that, in a pinch, should be sacrificed to those conditions and amenities of life we call civilization."[132] Given that the book makes it clear that he feels that one way or another that democracy is headed towards catastrophe, he is advocating democracy's termination in case of a crisis, or much less than a crisis, when the democratic state is in a "pinch." This is a call for reactionaries to start thinking about the overthrow of democracy when the opportunity arises.

Williamson has a chapter, "The Business of Aristocracies" in which he argues that landed aristocracies are a necessity for civilization. He attacks meritocracy as uncultured and the end of aristocracies in Western civilization as having "regrettable results" pointing out that the decline of Great Britain "as a world power and as a civilization" coincided with the decline of its aristocracy.[133]

In the chapter, "Christianity the Vital Spot," he asserts, "democracy is a creation of the Christian West that conceived and nurtured it. Democracy depends on, if not Christianity itself, then at a least a moral and philosophical bent of Christian origin or affinity."[134] He also states, "Democracy being a false religion, is therefore the natural and inevitable enemy of true religion and a friend to the various other false or substitute religions, many also of a political nature as well. Among these is advanced liberalism, modern democracy's alter ego."[135]

In reading Williamson's book it becomes clear that his hostility to democracy is motivated by his hostility to contemporary democratic American life with its "advanced liberalism." Democracy allows the development of opinions and views that he abhors.

In the book's opening chapter, "From Tocqueville to Fukuyama," Williamson comments, "No modern reader who considers Tocqueville's 'main causes tending to maintain a democratic republic in the United States' can fail to notice that not one of the conditions he mentions persists today, including the religious faith of the American public, which is everywhere under assault by real or virtual secularists…" He then references the opinions of Pat Buchanan and Kirkpatrick Sale, both neo-Confederates, that the necessary conditions to maintaining a democratic republic aren't there stating, "Moreover, they maintain that American society is being progressively undone by the decay of religious belief and by moral rot, by cultural illiteracy and incoherence by public indifference to serious issues of public concern, and by the decline in educational standards."[136]

Williamson states, "The Left today places Western culture, rationality, the rule of constitutional law, free markets, the white race, the human male, sexual morality, the family, 'patriarchy,' intermediate social institutions, moral restraint, and religious authority at the top of its list of idols for destruction." Williamson further asserts, "By succumbing to the Left in the guise of 'advanced' liberalism, modern democracies have surrendered to a pseudopolitical movement that attacks more less forthrightly both democracy's root and the soil in which the tree grows."[137] Thus Williamson argues that democracy enables the attack on religion, the white race, men, and Western culture.

Williamson sees multiculturalism as a disease "which has infected the cultural mainstream of the West …" and asserts that its supporters respect religions of non-Western cultures, but "… are united, however, in their hatred of Christianity …"[138]

Williamson chapter, "Democracy and Modern Man," sees, "Among the gravest threats to the Western democratic nations is the transformation – and in some countries, such as the United States, almost the replacement – of the original population." He states that there are two major forces driving this "replacement," one of which "... profound demographic change, an ethnic and racial alteration of the Western democratic republics." The other force is that the residents of these republics have become modern and believe in ideas that are modern and not reactionary.

Williamson claims that the American Founders, George Washington, John Adams, Thomas Jefferson, and Alexander Hamilton believed that an ethnically homogenous population was a good thing and immigration would have a negative impact and that Hamilton warned that immigration would produce "a heterogeneous compound."

Williamson writes, "Against their wishes and advice, the heterogeneous compound proved to be the American future. The arrival of millions of starving Irish peasants during the potato famine of 1845-1850 and then after the War between the States, successive waves of immigrants from central, eastern, and southern Europe – encouraged by American industry demanding vast supplies of cheap labor – transformed a demographically and culturally unified society into its opposite... immigration resumed in 1930s after the Nazis came to power in Germany. Since the passage of the Immigration Act of 1965, the flow of immigrants to America from the Third World (Mexico especially) has been literally uncontrolled."[139]

Williamson declares that "the folkways of Mexico are an amalgam of Spanish and Indian cruelty."[140] And he fears that "twelve to twenty million immigrants, the majority of them Mexican" present a danger to the territoriality of the United States stating, "Although the spirit of Reconquista is limited to a minority of the Mexican immigrant community, mainly in California and Texas, the Mexican government covertly but strongly encourages it."[141]

The infamous anti-immigration speech of former British secretary of state for health, J. Enoch Powell in 1968 is discussed as being prophetic.[142] Williamson sees Muslims as a menace and quotes Christie Davies that "Gradually, Britain will become part of the Muslim world, with all its innate backwardness, leaving the modern world to be divided between the fiercely Christian Americans and the secular Chinese."[143] Referring to Jean Raspail's notorious novel, *The Camp of the Saints*, he goes on to discuss how he sees Muslims over running Europe which he states is "the intraplanetary equivalent of H.G. Well's *War of the Worlds*."[144] Being compared to bug eyed aliens with tentacles from outer space shows just how alien Williamson perceives Muslims to be.

Williamson attacks Supreme Court decisions and support for civil rights, "After the World War that immediately followed the first era of progressive jurisprudence, issues of civil and human rights moved to the legal and political foreground in Western democracies – especially the United States, where what is now called 'rights talk' has since become a type of mania." Williamson explains that the judiciary has focused on rights issues which has had the negative effects that, "encourage and reward a sense of individual rights over social obligation, intransigency over compromise, emotion over reason, intemperance over calmness, and moral absoluteness over compromise."[145] Williamson mentions the historic Supreme Court decision in *Brown vs. Board of Education* in his chapter "Three Against Democracy" as part of his historical narrative on how the constitution has been subverted by Supreme Court justices.[146]

There are other notable reactionary sentiments here and there in the book such as his statement, "What may easily lead to a loss of freedom in President Obama's insistence that the justices he nominates must possess 'the empathy to understand what it's like to be poor, or African American, or gay, or disabled, or old.'"[147] Another quote, "This is not the place to consider the liberalizing, the democratizing, and ultimately demoralizing effects of Vatican II on the Roman Catholic Church, none of them beneficial and some of them catastrophic. (Had it not been for the Second Vatican Council, the priestly pedophile crisis might have been avoided …)."[148]

Williamson's book, *After Tocqueville*, is about his fear that there is a coming United States where straight white Christian middle and upper class men are not privileged over others and the others are not subordinated. This he feels is a disaster for the United States. He will be willing to assist and to terminate democracy if the opportunity arises, in order to save the country.

The more subtle and perhaps more powerful strategy is the effort to convince the reader that democracy is inevitably going to crumble and likely soon. This might incline those who are still supportive of democracy to give up, if they think that democracy's prospects are hopeless. For those who are the enemies of democracy already this book is encouraging that their goal is realizable, likely soon, so they might conclude that they should keep up their efforts against it.

The book incorporates a neo-Confederate understanding of American history. The Civil War is referred to as the "War Between the States," the neo-Confederate name for the Civil War incorporating their states' rights understanding of the Civil War and to obscure that it was a rebellion.[149] Williamson gives a neo-Confederate view of 19th century American history citing neo-Confederate leader Clyde Wilson as an authority. Williamson sees the Civil War and Reconstruction as destroying the Constitution. He writes, "After 1865, the hegemony of the Grand Old Party had four great consequences. First, owing to the postwar constitutional amendments, the states, which for Jefferson had been 'the best bulwarks of our liberties,' had ceased to be subsovereignties within the federal system, endowed with the authority to defend their citizens against encroachments by the newly empowered federal government."[150] The Reconstruction amendments were the

13th to abolish slavery, the 14th to make the freed African Americans citizens, and the 15th to guarantee the freed slaves the right to vote. The legal rhetoric about the American constitution avoids discussing that the real issue is about African Americans.

The dust jacket for the book has the endorsement of Donald Livingston, head of the Abbeville Institute. The book was favorably reviewed when it came out by William Murchison in 2012 in *Chronicles* magazine in an issue with the cover theme, "The Failure of Democracy." The issue contains multiple articles attacking democracy. Murchison was a longtime columnist for the *Dallas Morning News*, a contributor to *Southern Partisan* magazine and at one point was a board member of the Texas League of the South. Murchison points out many of Williamson's key points against democracy, but with the more pungent statements omitted such as Williamson's assertion that Mexican folkways were an amalgam of Spanish and Indian cruelty. What is interesting is that Murchison's book review focuses on how the book applies to 2012 presidential candidate Mitt Romney's "secretly recorded comments concerning the 47 percent of Americans to whom Romney imputed intractability in their commitment to the existing democratic order, under which they pay no income taxes."[151] Murchison discusses how "… thirst – sometimes outright lust – for other people's property is an element of modern democracy," echoing Williamson's characterization of the poor voter as a "highway man holding a knife."

In 2012 in the *Confederate Veteran* Boyd D. Cathey's essay, "The Land We Love: Southern Tradition and Our Future," attacks the American democratic idea. The article appropriately enough has a picture of Oak Alley Plantation in Louisiana for its illustration.

The article starts out with Cathey discussing the *Charge of the Sons of Confederate Veterans* by Gen. Stephen D. Lee, which calls on the members of the SCV to honor the Confederate veteran. Cathey quotes Lee's *Charge* saying that "the perpetuation of those principles which he loved and which you love also, and those ideals which made him glorious and which you also cherish." Cathey then asks, "What were those 'principles' General Lee refer to?"

In the article Cathey is argues that democratic equality is in opposition to the principles of the Confederate soldier and so the purpose of the *Charge of the Sons of Confederate Veterans*, which is held to be the very purpose of the SCV, is defined by Cathey as being an opposition to civil rights legislation.

The title also utilizes Southern nationalism. The title declares that Boyd's ideas in this article are the "Southern Tradition" and implies that if you love the South you will believe in the principles and ideas that Boyd is arguing make up the Southern tradition. .

Cathey recommends Richard M. Weaver's book, *The Southern Tradition at Bay*, Weaver's Ph.D. dissertation posthumously published in 1968 for readers who want to learn about what he calls "Southern Philosophy."

In *The Southern Tradition at Bay* Weaver enthusiastically praises a hierarchical South. In a section titled "The Feudal System," the antebellum South is claimed by Weaver to be a feudal system based on the plantation and the plantation's resulting social values which he enthusiastically praises. Weaver writes, "A fine glimpse of a feudal paradise which survived until 1865 is given by Mrs. Virginia Clay in "A Belle of the Fifties." Weaver sees the slaveholders forming a knightly class of aristocrats.

Weaver, argues that the Confederate soldiers were divided into a lower class and an aristocratic leadership. He quotes various historical sources to claim that the "common" Confederate soldier was a sort of beast, "long hair, dirty, tobacco-stained, and ignorant." Another source is quoted referring to their "brutishness." In contrast the soldier from aristocratic classes is held to be the best fighters and the sum of all virtues. Weaver argues that as a consequence of what he claims was a recognized superiority of the aristocratic Confederate leader in the Civil War Southern society came to accept a class based social order.[152]

Cathey also recommends the book, *Remembering Who We Are: Observations of a Southern Conservative*, by M.E. Bradford. In reading Cathey's comments on the book you might get some romantic agrarian traditional impression about Bradford's book.

The author is working on a short book length manuscript about M.E. Bradford and has read this book closely and can testify that the book's dust jacket very ably and accurately summarizes this book in these few sentences.

> The United States was not founded, Bradford argues, with the idea of creating a society dedicated to either justice or equality, and all attempts to turn America in that direction have resulted in a perversion of the nation's true origins in the struggle for liberty from oppression of a remote and sometimes hostile government. Discussing some of those attempts, several of the pieces in the collection examine recent efforts by the federal government to impose a single vision on the diversity of America, to transform the nation from a land of liberty to one that promotes equality.[153]

In naming the three basic principles of "Southern republicanism," that is what Cathey alleges to be the political philosophy of the South, he writes:

> Thirdly, Southern republicanism is anti-egalitarian. … Participation in government was not based on the modern concept of "one man, one vote."
>
> Our ancestors believed in limited suffrage, and throughout our history favored age, race, se and educational qualifications for exercising the franchise. Egalitarianism for them was a leveling view of society which meant an enforced standardization and the same rights for all, and they rejected this outright.

Cathey seeks to minimize slavery and race. In discussing both he writes:

> Most significantly, in both slavery and post-slavery times it was not so much race, but rather a desire to preserve the social order – hierarchy and balance in society – which motivated most thinking Southerners.[154]

After Tocqueville isn't specifically a neo-Confederate book, it is rather an anti-democratic book with a neo-Confederate historical understanding, written by a neo-Confederate, but for any reactionary opponent of democracy. *The South Was Right!* is a neo-Confederate book by neo-Confederates for an audience of persons who support the Confederacy. *Democracy, The God That Failed*, is a radical libertarian book with a neo-Confederate historical understanding and advances secession by an author who is a member of the Ludwig von Mises Institute, which has a neo-Confederate agenda. *Democracy, The God That Failed*, is embraced and praised in *Southern Partisan*. Boyd D. Cathey in the *Confederate Veteran* is making a neo-Confederate argument that modern democracy is anti-Southern referencing earlier anti-democratic neo-Confederates. Through different means the neo-Confederate movement is engaged in the anti-democratic movement through the production and promotion of its own anti-democratic ideas and in the support for anti-democratic ideas generated outside of the neo-Confederate movement.

The neo-Confederate movement is anti-democratic, but it is only a part of a larger anti-democratic movement. The neo-Confederate movement drawing on popular support for the Confederacy can channel anti-democratic ideas to supporters of the Confederacy and the popular support for the Confederacy can be channeled into the anti-democratic movement.

The relation of the neo-Confederate anti-democratic beliefs to their numerous prejudices against many groups and their civil rights isn't necessarily simple.

1. The neo-Confederate support for numerous divisive prejudices could be seen as a tool box to divide the public into segments set against each other so they can advance their anti-democratic agenda. A society that is divided against itself is easy prey for those hostile to democracy.

2. Neo-Confederates also realize that democracy at some point or another has led to subordinated groups obtaining rights as citizens and not remaining subordinated. Undermining democracy and its ideas of equality preserves and supports a discriminatory society.

3. Division of people into segments where some are subordinated or super-ordinated relative to other segments, a hierarchy of any type, is anti-democratic in itself. When you can divide one way, why can't you divide another way? Anti-democratic thinking inevitably arises out of a discriminatory society in which the more privileged groups, in order to support their privilege, find further segments of society to be denied full citizenship.

These elements can't be ordered in a chain in which one causes the other. All are processes working together simultaneously and mutually supporting each other to undermine democracy and support discrimination. However, it should be understood that the hostility towards democracy isn't only in service of their prejudice against minorities. They want to subordinate everyone.

A society that is anti-democratic is not going to be supportive of equality of educational opportunity. A lack of public schools would support inequality as some individuals would be likely to afford for themselves or their children better private schools, others worse schools and perhaps some would not be able to afford any schools. With education being unequal, economic outcomes would be unequal. As voters, (if they were allowed to vote), the disadvantaged would be less able to use the ballot to advance their interests.

Elimination of public schools would aid discrimination as people would not go to a common school and would be less likely to socialize with people different then themselves. Education works against prejudice.

So the anti-public school ideas of the neo-Confederates are intertwined with their agenda of prejudice and hostility towards democracy.

This book discusses neo-Confederate hostility to democracy and egalitarianism first, their hostility to public schools second, and then their numerous hostilities towards minorities of many types. This order is not to suggest that the relationship of these items is that one leads to another in this order. They all are being advanced at the same time and each objective supports the other. Also, neo-Confederate activities in regards to all three issues don't neatly divide into categories so some of the items discussed will involve more than one element. There isn't a real dividing line between discrimination and being anti-democratic. As you disfranchise groups you are destroying democracy for the disfranchised group.

9 AGAINST PUBLIC SCHOOLS

Neo-Confederate opposition to public education, free public schools provided by the government by school districts, uses two different historical narratives, stories, to justify this extremist position.

One narrative comes from the Confederate Christian nationalist movement which sees the Civil War as a theological conflict, a holy war, between a heretical "North" and a Christian Orthodox South[155] and which includes the opposition to public schools by Robert Lewis Dabney. The other narrative sees the effort to provide public schools in the South after the Civil War as a conspiracy to oppress the South and destroy its culture.

Robert Lewis Dabney (1820-1898) was a pro-slavery Presbyterian theologian at the Union Theological Seminary who served as Confederate General Thomas Jonathan "Stonewall" Jackson's army chaplain during the Civil War. Dabney wrote a popular biography of Jackson after the war. He is considered a hero in the neo-Confederate movement[156] and is a major historical figure and hero in the Confederate Christian nationalist movement. Dabney was a post war defender of slavery in his book *A Defense of Virginia and through her of the South*. He claimed that the bible sanctioned slavery and that it was a good thing for persons of any race he considered "depraved."[157] This book will not review the growing amount of pro-slavery literature being published and republished, but neo-Confederate ideology sees slavery as being possibly applicable to anyone.

Dabney's racism is blistering. This chapter will focus not on Dabney's white supremacist views, but on neo-Confederate use of Dabney's opposition to public education in their campaign against public schools though often these two things are intermixed in his writing. (Although it is interesting that neo-Confederates who claim to not be racist see Dabney as a hero.)

AGAINST PUBLIC SCHOOLS

In the original texts I quote "Negro" was not capitalized and I wish to have the texts as exactly like they were with bold face and italics as they were used so that neo-Confederates can't claim that I have tampered with the text.

Dabney was opposed to public schools in general and in particular for African Americans. In 1876 he wrote a lengthy article, "The Negro and the Common School," submitted to the *Planter and Famer* periodical and later republished in 1897 in his 4 volume work "Discussions." In the article Dabney states that schools for African Americans "made my blood boil with indignation." He opens his letter to the editor which a general condemnation of public education and how he is pleased to see it condemned in the publication *Planter and Farmer.*

> **Dr. L. R. Dickinson, Editor Planter and Farmer.—Dear Sir:** I have read the essays of "Civis" in your December, January and February numbers with profound interest, and with general approbation. Concurring fully with him in the opposition to the whole theory of primary education by the State, I also feel the force of his views concerning the negro and the common school. For some years I have had strong convictions of the falsehood and deadly tendencies of the Yankee theory of popular State education; and I confess that the influence which prevented my lifting up my voice against it was, simply, the belief that so puny a voice could effect nothing against the prevalent "craze" which has infected the country on this subject. You may conceive, therefore, the satisfaction with which I saw "Civis" take up the cause of truth in the columns of the **Religious Herald**, and subsequently in the **Planter and Farmer**, and my admiration for his moral courage, eloquence and invincible logic: With such champions, the cause of truth is not so hopeless as I feared. [Emphasis as it was in the original.]

Note, the "N" in "Negro" was not capitalized until sometime in the 20th century. Further, I have not changed spellings. Spellings have changed over time. The other is that I think that these differences in style and spelling offer a historical window to see into the past.

These quotations are also somewhat ample so there can be no claim that Dabney is quoted out of context and to give the reader a full measure of Dabney's shrill rancid racism, his vortex of hysteria, and yet this is just a sample from Dabney's essay. The reader needs to know and feel this so they appreciate the enormity of what the neo-Confederates are doing when they praise Dabney.

Also, 19th century writers are wordy and it is hard to do short quotes of them.

Dabney's opposition to public education of African Americans is that they are too stupid to learn anything and going to school is really a way to escape working. Dabney, evidently in response to an inquiry by the editor of the

Planter, writes, "But, you asked for my opinion of this fearful question of the negro in our common schools."

These are some extracts of Dabney's opinion.

> ... to raise these taxes to give a pretended education to the brats of the black paupers, who are loafing around their plantations, stealing a part of the scanty crops and stock their poor, struggling boys are able to raise. Not seldom has this pitiful sight made my blood boil with indignation, and then made my heart bleed with the thought

And this following extract again attacks the concept of public education in general as well as mocking African American's "wool on their head." Note also Dabney believes that African Americans shouldn't vote because they don't own property, a restriction that would apply to any race. Public education is condemned also because the non-slave states which had it, suppressed the Confederate insurrection.

> For, second: the pretended education which Virginia is now giving, at so heavy a cost, to the negroes, is, as a remedy for negro suffrage, utterly deceptive, farcical and dishonest. The tenor of the argument concedes, what every man, not a fool, knows to be true: that the negroes, as a body, are now glaringly unfit for the privilege of voting. What makes them unfit? Such things as these: The inexorable barrier of alien race, color, and natural character, between them and that other race which constitutes the bulk of Americans: a dense ignorance of the rights and duties of citizenship: an almost universal lack of that share in the *property* of the country, which alone can give responsibility, patriotic interest and independence to the voter: a general moral grade so deplorably low as to permit their being driven or bought like a herd .of sheep by the demagogue: a parasitical servility and dependency of nature, which characterizes the race everywhere, and in all ages: an almost total lack of real persevering aspirations: and last, an obstinate set of false traditions, which bind him as a mere serf to a party, which is the born enemy of every righteous interest of our State. Let the reader look at that list of ailments. Not an item can be disputed. Now, our political quacks propose to cure them, and that in such time as will save the Commonwealth before the infection becomes mortal. And how? By such an infusion of (not education, but) a *modicum* of the arts of reading, writing, and cyphering; which are at best uncertain means, only, for educating; and that, such a *modicum* as the kind of teachers and schools Virginia can now get, will infuse through the wool of such heads. Does any sane man really believe this remedy will do that vast work? Nay, verily, "Leviathan is not so tamed." Or, to return to the former trope, we may use the exclamation of John Randolph against a weak book, which was proposed to him, as an

antidote for the malignant ability of Bolingbroke's infidelity. "Venice treacle, and syrup, against *Arsenic*!" Whether this remedy will save us, may be settled by an argument of fact, unanswerable to every patriotic Virginian. The Yankees have had this "nostrum" of free school education, in full force, for two generations. Has it reared up among them, out of white people, a popular mass fit to enjoy universal suffrage? Did not this very system rear us that very generation, which, in its blind ignorance and brutal passion, has recently wrecked the institutions of America; has filled our country with destitution, woe and murder; and, with a stupid blindness, only equalled by its wickedness, has stripped its own Commonwealths, in order to wreak its mad spite on ours, of the whole safeguards for their own freedom and peace? *These are the fruits of* this Yankee system of State primary education, as working on a white race. Will it work better on a black race? I have not yet learned enough of that type of "intelligence" which this system seems to foster, to repudiate my Saviour's infallible maxim, "the tree is known by its fruits." The Yankee has bragged so much of his "intelligence," of his floods of books and oceans of newspapers, that some Southern people seem "dazed" by the clamor. Well; there may be "fussiness," there may be plenty of self-conceit, and flippancy; but I stand simply and firmly by this impregnable fact: This system has not given the Yankee true wisdom enough to prevent his destroying the country and himself. What mere self-delusion is it, to dream that it will give this quality to the negro?

And:

But, third: There are causes peculiar to the negro and the South, which leave us no hope that this so-called system of free schools will produce even as much fruit as in New England or New York. One is the fact which "Civic" has so boldly stated: The black race is an alien one on our soil; and nothing except his amalgamation with ours, or his subordination to ours, can prevent the rise of that instinctive antipathy of race, which, history shows, always arises between opposite races in proximity. Another cause is the natural indolence of the negro character, which finds precisely its desired pretext, in this pre-tended work of going to school. Still another is the universal disposition of the young negro to construe his "liberty" as meaning precisely, privilege of idleness. It was easy to see that the free school must needs produce the very result which it is usually producing, under such exceptional circumstances; not education, but discontent with, and unfitness for, the free negro's inevitable sphere and destiny—if he is to have any good destiny—manual labor. With such teachers, such parents as the negro parents, and such material, it was hopeless to expect any really beneficial knowledge of the literary arts to be diffused among this great mass of black children. The only thing the most of them really learn is a fatal confirmation in the notion that "freedom" means living without work, and a great enhancement of the determination to grasp that privilege. The one commanding and imperative necessity of the young negro at the end of the war, in the eyes of any sober philanthropist, was this: that he should be promptly made to learn some way to earn an honest living

Then Dabney gets to his real "fear" regarding the schools that it would lead to social equality, that there would be "amalgamation," that is interracial sexual relations in which white people in the South would be corrupted by a "sordid, alien taint" and eventually the whole nation would "putrify."

Again: Let us grant that free schools effect all that is claimed for the elevation of the negro; that he is actually fitted for all the dignities of the commonwealth, and for social equality. Then, will he not demand it? Of course. Here then, is my concluding dilemma. If these negro schools are to fail, they should be abolished without further waste. If they are to succeed, they only prepare the way for that abhorred fate, amalgamation. If the State School Board are working for anything, they are working for this; here is the goal of their plans. The most solemn and urgent duty now incumbent on the rulers of Virginia, is to devise measures to prevent the gradual but sure approach of this final disaster. The satanic artificers of our subjugation well knew the work which they designed to perpetrate: it is so to mingle that blood which flowed in the veins of our Washingtons, Lees, and Jacksons, and which consecrated the battle yields of the Confederacy, with this sordid, alien taint, that the bastard stream shall never again throb with independence enough to make a tyrant tremble. These men were taught by the instincts of their envy and malignity, but too infallibly, how the accursed work was to be done. They knew that political equality would prepare the way for social equality, and that, again for amalgamation. It is only our pride which hides the danger from our eyes. A friend from Virginia was conversing, in London, with an old English navy surgeon, who was intimately acquainted with the British West-India Islands. He assured the Virginian that the "reconstruction acts" tended directly to amalgamation, and would surely result in it if persevered in. "Never," exclaimed my Virginia friend, "In our case, our people's pride of race will effectually protect them from that last infamy." "Had ever any people," replied the ex-surgeon, "more pride of race than the English? Yet they are amalgamating in Jamaica. We have the teachings of forty years' experience in this matter; when your emancipation has become, like ours, forty years old, you will see." The Virginian was silenced. Even now, after ten years of the misery and shame of subjugation, one has only to open his eyes to see the crumbling away of the social barriers between the two races. The nearest and heaviest share of this curse of mixed blood will, of course, fall upon the conquered States themselves; but the revengeful mind will have the grim satisfaction of seeing the conquering States reap their sure and fearful retribution from the same cause. Eleven populous States, tainted with this poison of hybrid and corrupted blood, will be enough to complete the destruction of the white States to which they will be chained. The Yankee empire will then find itself, like a strong man with a cankerous limb, perishing by inches, in chronic and hideous agonies. The member which spreads its poison through the whole body can neither be healed nor amputated, all will putrify together.

The essay also has another section in which he condemns the white poor for wanting to send their children to public schools as being silly and motivated by envy.

> Luckless urchins:! what they needed was wholesome food and medicine, not books and confinement. The result of this blind disregard of times and differences, and abilities, is, that about the time famine and the sheriff are both knocking at the old lady's door, her children are sent back to her, in raging delirium from brain fever, either helpless, or rending each other in their phrensy.[158]

I leave it to the reader to conclude whether Dabney suffered from "brain fever" or "phrensy."

This isn't the only essay in which Dabney condemns public schools. Dabney also denounces them in a screed in the *Southern Plantar and Farmer* in 1879. The article combines opposition to public schools, with anti-immigration sentiment, religious bigotry, fear of an educated working class as a revolutionary threat, and racism all in one paragraph.

> This suggests a point against our present plan, whose formidable character is now making thoughtful men at the North, and in Britain, tremble. The Redeemer said, "He that is not with me is against me." There cannot be a moral neutrality. Man is born with an evil and ungodly tendency. Hence a non-religious training must be an anti-religious training. The more of this, the larger curse. But the American commonwealth has expressly pledged herself to a non-religious attitude. Hence, she cannot, by her State-action, endow or inculcate a particular religion. While the population of some States was homogenous, this radical difficulty was not seriously felt: the people of a Protestant State, like Connecticut, could quietly overstep the true history of their own constitution, in favor of Protestantism and there was nobody to protest. But now we have Papists, Unitarians, Chinese, Jews and Atheists by the myriads; and they will not acquiesce in the wielding of State-power, in which they have equal rights, for the partial advantage of a creed to which they are opposed. The result will be, that their protests will triumph, as they now do, in many States; and we shall

have a generation of practical atheists reared "on State account"; just as clear-sighted men in the North see they have on their hands there, rapidly preparing for them another sans-culotte revolution.[159] [A Sans-culotte was a lower class Parisian in the French Revolution in the 18th century. Papist is an anti-Catholic slur.]

Boyd Cathey in *Southern Partisan* in 1984 praises Dabney in a lengthy article, "Robert Lewis Dabney And The New South Creed." Cathey writes, "The tenets of the New South Creed Robert Dabney attacked – whether industrialism, monopoly, educational reform, or religious heresy – had existed in the South before the war." Otherwise Cathey doesn't discuss Dabney's ideas on education.[160] However, having praised Dabney, Cathey can lead the reader to Dabney.

Lloyd Sprinkle, interviewed in the *Southern Partisan* in 1994 by Christian Reconstructionist Byron Snapp, runs Sprinkle Publications in Harrisonburg, Virginia. Sprinkle started republishing Dabney's biography of Gen. Thomas Jackson (Stonewall) in 1975 and steadily added more publications of Dabney and other pro-slavery theologians and various Confederate books over the years. Though the interview doesn't mention Dabney's views about education, this interview would help publicize Sprinkle's publishing and so Dabney's books would become more distributed in the neo-Confederate movement.[161]

Clara Erath, in 1995 in the *UDC Magazine* of the United Daughters of the Confederacy, gives the mailing address of Sprinkle Publications, and mentions Confederate books for children.[162] Though not mentioning Dabney or Sprinkle Publications' other works, this would help make the neo-Confederate movement aware of this publishing house and by this help Sprinkles other books reach a wider audience.

However, by the 1990s neo-Confederates are more willing to openly attack public education.

In "R.L. Dabney, Confederate Prophet," by Collie Owens, in the 1995 *Southern Partisan*, Owens writes:

> One of Dabney's classic expositions is on "the falsehood and deadly tendencies of the Yankee theory of popular State education… Furthermore, forcing impressionable children to mingle with the morally impure would inevitably, given our sinful natures, tend toward corruption. … The purpose of the school would not be to educate but "to incalculate upon all the children … the malignant and lying creed of Radicalism."

Owens argues that Dabney foresaw all the things that contemporary reactionaries complain about in modern American life. In this article the rejection of the idea of public education itself is being communicated to the neo-Confederate movement in general. Owens was an assistant professor at Dekalb College and poetry editor of *The Chattahoochie Review*.[163]

Scott Whitten Williams in "Seven Reasons to Homeschool," in the League of the South publication, *Southern Patriot* in 1998 denounces public schools. As for parents who might want and need public schools to educate their children, Williams quotes Dabney, "Parents who remain too poor and callous to educate their own children are so because they are ignorant, indolent, unaspiring, and vicious." It doesn't occur to either Williams or Dabney that some parents have to work very long hours at poor wages and have neither the money nor the time to do homeschooling or afford the fees of a private school.[164]

Leslie Riley, in "Save the Children (and the South): Don't Send Them to Marx's Schools," in the 2001 *Southern Patriot*, wrote "The South's great theologian and prophet, R.L. Dabney, warned over 100 years ago about the dangers of the 'free state school system.'" The subtitle of the article is, "(Theft-funded, God-hating, South-hating, Leviathan/New-World-Order-promoting, government schools are our enemies' greatest weapon against us." The article asserts that public schools are not constitutional or biblical. Examples of Riley writing are, "Government schools were conceived, planned and implemented by atheistic, Marxist/Communist subversives in the 1800s …" In regard to the prohibition of school sponsored prayer, he writes, "The problem is not that unjust judges are in rebellion when they take prayer out of schools. They are doing what God-hating, unjust pagan judges do. The problem is not that the theft-funded, atheistic government schools are in rebellion. The problem is Christian parents (especially the fathers) are in rebellion." Riley was at the time the Mississippi State Chairman of the Constitution Party.[165]

The *Southern Mercury*, a publication of the educational political action committee of the Sons of Confederate Veterans, in 2004 ran an article by Boyd Cathey, "Robert Lewis Dabney and the New South Creed," which portrays Dabney as a heroic prophet of the future. Cathey in the 21st century openly attacks public education.

Cathey writes, "Dabney made periodic assaults on other new ideas. His running debate with Virginia's first superintendent of public instruction, William H. Ruffner, over state-supported schools, is a case in point." Cathey writes:

> Dabney began the controversy with his February, 1876, article, "The Negro and the Common School," in *Planter and Farmer* magazine, in which he clearly stated his opposition to the "Yankee theory" of free public education, especially for freedmen. For him the former slaves were in a real sense wards of the South to be guided slowly and paternally through difficult years of adjustment. To promise the Negro immediate rights and

an education that could never be his was wrong and insensible; only through an extended period of tutelage would the Negro advance in Southern society.

Cathey discusses Dabney's series of articles against public schools in the *Richmond Enquirer*:

> General and free education sought to impose an unnatural equality on all, he insisted. "Providence, social laws, and parental virtues and efforts, do inevitably legislate in favor of some classes of boys," he declared. "If the State undertakes to countervail that legislation of nature by leveling action, the attempt is wicked, mischievous, and futile."

Cathey also discusses Dabney's idea that working people don't need much formal education.

> Indeed, Dabney questioned "whether the use merely of letters is not education, but only one means of education, and not the only means." True education involved more than simply the use of letters. The laboring classes had traditionally found education through their various professions, a training of the "moral virtues by the fidelity and endurance" with which they earned their livelihood. The laboring man "ennobles his taste and sentiments by looking up to the superior who employs him. If to these influences you add the awakening, elevating, expanding force of Christian principles, you have given the laborer a true education...a hundred fold more true, more suitable, more useful, than the communication of certain literary arts, which he will almost necessarily disuse."

It is hard to imagine that none the leadership of the Sons of Confederate Veterans are aware of Robert Lewis Dabney's blistering racism.

The Ludwig von Mises Institute and the website www.lewrockwell.com also mention R.L. Dabney's opposition to public schools as part of their opposition to public schools as libertarians. *The Journal of Libertarian Studies* in 2006 published Barry D. Simpson's article "The Cultural Degradation of Universal Education: The Educational Views of Robert Lewis Dabney." This article is not only about education, but about attacking democracy, Simpson writes:

> This study introduces the ideas of Robert Lewis Dabney on universal education. The goal of presenting Dabney's views is to add to the discussion of natural order versus democracy. Hans-Hermann Hoppe's pioneering work in this field has given libertarians a reason to question the modern notions of democracy. The idea of democracy is carried to the masses in America through universal education. Thus, Dabney's insights

are of great importance to this area. Hoppe argues that democracy represents a backward step in the process of civilization. Dabney explains exactly how the degradation of culture is carried out through universal education.

Simpson summarizes Dabney's ideas as follows:

> Dabney offers several lines of argument against the statist view. First, he argues that the provision of universal education does not necessarily imply that people will be educated. Second, he argues that literacy does not necessarily imply an increase in the cultural awareness of the citizenry. Third, Dabney argues that the appropriate flow of culture is from the higher to the lower classes. Otherwise, a general debasement of culture follows, lowering the culture consciousness of all classes. Fourth, Dabney presents statistics on crime to support his view that universal education is not a blessing, but a bane to the cultural norms of a nation. Finally, Dabney argues that universal education is more problematic under democratic rule than under monarchy.[166]

Simpson's argument shows the employment of made up arguments that no one is making. There is no guarantee that a person offered any type of opportunity will accept it or act on it or effectively use it. However, there is going to be little or no education, when a person has little or no opportunities for an education, it will not be a matter of choice. No one said that literacy meant that a person necessarily would become more culturally aware, but without literacy a person can't read novels, essays, histories, poetry, religious works, book reviews, commentary on art or likely earn money to buy a book. Also, given that in 2006 the need for a literate, highly educated work force in the modern global world of technology should be self-evident and this article is a good example of the idiocy that passes for thinking at the Mises Institute.

The September 2003 issue of *Chronicles*, with the cover theme, "America's Classical Tradition: The Way Back to Educational Sanity," has two articles against public education of particular interest.

R.C. Sproul Jr.'s article, "The Heart's Own Instinct," is about conservative Presbyterian opposition to public education. The latter half of the article discusses Dabney. Sproul informs us that Dabney's book, *A Defense of Virginia and the South*, "is a careful examination of the justice of the Southern cause," but otherwise doesn't mention its contents defending slavery as being Biblical. The primary focus is discussing and quoting Dabney's opposition to public schools.[167]

The more sinister article is "Classical Education Redivivus," by Douglas Wilson about the Association of Classical and Christian Schools (ACCS).[168] He is the head of Christ Church in Moscow, Idaho.

Douglas Wilson is a neo-Confederate, one of the contributing editors of the neo-Confederate homeschooling book, *The War Between the States: America's Uncivil War* and the pamphlet, *Southern Slavery As It Was* with co-author Steve Wilkins, pastor of Auburn Avenue Church in Monroe, Louisiana, and founding board member of the League of the South. Southern Slavery As It Was earned some notoriety locally in Moscow, Idaho for defending antebellum slavery and arguing it was important to Biblically defend slavery so as to be able to Biblically denounce gays and Lesbians.[169]

Wilson's church publishes *Credenda Agenda*, and an issue published on or before 2001 had the cover theme, "Bad Moon Rising: The Coming Break-Up of These United States," with the title article by Wilson. In it Wilson sees the breakup of the Soviet Union and Yugoslavia, and the then-current potential separation of Quebec from the rest of Canada as portents of a coming wave of secession. He sees multiculturalism and the rising Hispanics populations as increasing forces that would break up the United States.[170] The Sixth Annual Credenda Agenda history conference in 2001, "Saints and Scoundrels," had Thomas "Stonewall" Jackson and R.L. Dabney as saints.[171]

In the Sept. 2003, *Chronicles* article, Wilson reports that the ACCS has 140 member schools in "about 40 states," and schools in Nigeria, Cambodia, Peru, New Zealand, France and Canada. That the last ACCS national conference had 700 educators and that "there are approximately 32,000 children being educated in member schools."

Wilson discusses that the ACCS churches can face adverse publicity.

> Another pitfall occurs when a school is struggling faithfully to implement this classical and Christian vision for education and finds itself under a mountain of bad publicity that it cannot afford. For example, our classical Christian school recently underwent a slanderous drubbing in the local press, which accused us of harboring affinities for white separatists because we teach about the War Between the States with a measure of honesty and do not make the Confederate armies out to have been made up of orcs and Klingons.

The criticism was of Douglas Wilson for his book defending slavery and the neo-Confederate writings in his churches publication. Douglas here reveals another aspect of neo-Confederate writing is that sometimes it is not very forthcoming.

The sinister part comes when Wilson imagines how his movement to end public schools will succeed.

> The most encouraging thing about what is happening is that parents have taken on what, in military terms, would be called a decisive point. In order to qualify as a decisive point, a contested battleground must meet two criteria —it must be both feasible and strategic. A targeted objective must matter to the enemy if you take it, and it must be possible to take. If cultural conservatives took New York City, that would certainly be strategic. It is not feasible, however. We could take Bovill, Idaho, in just a matter of days. That is feasible but not strategic; it would not matter if we did.

Wilson later explains further this "decisive point"

> When our local classical Christian school started 20 years ago, fewer than five percent of the local schoolchildren were being educated privately. Today, the figure is around 33 percent and growing. Within a few years, if God continues His kindness, we may see the local government schools become the choice of the minority.

> In doing this, we have stolen a page from the playbook of the liberals: Think globally; act locally.

It doesn't appear that Wilson has taken Moscow, Idaho, the location of the University of Idaho, yet. Visiting the Association of Classical and Christian Schools website it seems that they have a great many schools across America and these school may well share a hope to supplant the local public schools.

In a town, where even a large fraction of schools are private, it can be expected that there will be less support for funding public educations and which would lead to their underfunding which, in turn, would make the private schools relatively more desirable. This would support a feedback loop in which more students would go to private schools resulting in further underfunding of public schools driving more students to private schools which would end with a remnant of students for public schools for the children of those too poor for any private school. With the concept of charter schools funded by the state government, this process could be accelerated or started.

The neo-Confederate movement continues to be hostile against public schools. More recently a new approach to attacking public schools has started conceptualizing public schools as a conspiracy against the South which started as a Reconstruction measure but later destroyed education everywhere. Dabney is still respected in the neo-Confederate movement. This idea that the promotion of public education in the South as a conspiracy to oppress the

South during Reconstruction is an addition to neo-Confederate ideology against public schools and doesn't supersede or replace Dabney's thinking.

John Chodes in his articles and with his book, *Destroying the Republic: Jabez Curry and the Re-Education of the Old South*, has advanced these theories which have been broadly accepted in the neo-Confederate movement. He has gotten positive reviews in *Southern Partisan* (2007), and *Confederate Veteran* (2009) and at the Abbeville Institute website (2015).[172]

Jabez L.M. Curry, usually referred to as J.L.M. Curry, was a prominent Alabama resident who served in both the U.S. Congress before the Civil War, sat in the Alabama secession convention, in the Confederate Congress during the Civil War, and in the Confederate Army. After the Civil War he became a part of the effort to open public schools in the South and worked for the Peabody Fund a charity set up to support education in the South.[173]

The article "Origins of the Educational Nightmare," by Clyde Wilson published at the Abbeville Institute website in 2015 praises the book and writes, "The chapter on 'Reconstruction as Re-Education,' is alone worth the price of the book." This is because he feels that "The Marxist class/conflict perspective, with a Gramscian twist, is now 'mainstream' American history," and the book's chapter "shows that Reconstruction was more than a horror of military domination and economic exploitation. It was also a program of ideological and ethnic cleansing which continues to damage the American people in our own time."

Antonio Gramsci was an Italian Marxist theorist. Reactionaries of all sorts, including neo-Confederates, like to call anything they don't like as cultural Marxism which is held to have been invented by Gramsci. To neo-Confederates, America's first attempt at a multi-racial democracy, has always been a horror to them. During the 1950s and onward the White Citizens Council made numerous references to Reconstruction as a warning against civil rights. The website (www.citizenscouncils.com has the White Citizens Council newspaper from 1955 to 1961 and the reader is invited to visit it to see both how the historical memory of Reconstruction and the Confederacy is employed against civil rights.)

Wilson sees Curry as a traitor to the South for supporting public education in the South. He writes:

> How did the ex-Confederate Curry become an instrument for the undoing of his own principles and his own people? For doing the bidding of rich inveterate South-haters? It was not simply a case of a defeated Confederate making the best of a bad situation. Education is, of course, a good thing. The South was poor and needed money for education. But

why did a man like Curry buy the whole hog – not just education but universal, compulsory, "free," tax-supported schooling on a model dictated by the relentless Bostonian enemies of his blood?

Wilson concludes with the lesson to be learned from the book:

> It has long been an accepted article of faith among Americans that education is a good thing. That, indeed, it is a necessity for a free and self-governing people. But when and by whom was it determined that this desirable thing was to be universal, compulsory in attendance and tax support, "free," and devoted to inculcating government-coerced conformity? Destroying the Republic provides much of the answer to this vital question.[174]

The 2009 book review in *Confederate Veteran* by Cassie S. Barrow draws the same lessons seeing public schools as "vicious":

> Mr. Chodes states in his book. Two principles used by the Radical Republicans to completely overthrow the South's social, political and economic existence were "State Suicide" and "Conquered Province." Both were vicious plans to subjugate the South and both had universal education proposals.

Barrow further states

> "It appears that Jabez had no problem joining forces with those who were intent on exterminating Southern culture and Southern minds," per Mr. Chodes. Curry in 1881 became General Agent of the Peabody Education Board and a nationally prominent figure. This fund was used as a matching fund for communities starting public schools to entice the people to support a tax-supported school.

Barrow quotes Chodes that supporting public schools has been destructive:

> "By the 20th century, this plan had turned on itself and emptied out Northern children's minds as well. This transformed the US republic in the 21st Century into an emerging dictatorship," states Mr. Chodes on the back cover.

Barrow says that the book "is required reading for any educator or person working in the public school system."[175]

E. Ray Moore, Jr.'s, 2007 book review in the *Southern Partisan* sees Chodes' work as part of a larger body of writing against public schools all which he endorses, writing:

It joins the growing number of quality books on the history of the harm caused by state-sponsored public schools by notables such as 1991 New York Teacher of the Year John Taylor Gatto in *Underground History of American Education* (2001) and Dr. Andrew Couslon's *Market Education* (1999). Also, Dr. Bruce Short published *The Harsh Truth About Public Schools* in 2004, and the late Marlin Maddoux, a Christian talk show host, wrote *Public Education Against America*, published posthumously in 2006. The latter two books are primarily for the church audience.

Moore concludes with a call for the South to lead the way in ending public schools:

> John Chodes has written a critical book that can help with understanding first the history of the rise of state-sponsored public schools and then its damage; now remedial action can begin. The South, slow to adopt state education and only under coercion, could lead the way by rejecting that system and returning to the ideal model of private, religious, and home schools. The South would thus give herself a great gift and one as well to American culture and the world.[176]

John Chodes was a member of the League of the South, he was a scheduled speaker at their 2007 conference.[177] His earlier writings have claimed that during Reconstruction the Union Leagues in the South and not the Ku Klux Klan were the violent organizations and he defends the Ku Klux Klan.[178] He is the author along with Clyde Wilson of a 2016 book condemning the Union Leagues and defending the Ku Klux Klan.[179]

Chodes book starts out with Chapters devoted to Curry's early years before and during the Civil War and during Reconstruction. In the chapters he argues the usual neo-Confederate history of those periods and quotes "The South Was Right!" by James Ronald Kennedy and Walter Donald Kennedy that, "The Civil War and Reconstruction mark the end of the American constitutional Republic."[180] Chodes himself uses the term "War for Southern Independence."[181]

Chodes' book on Curry and the Peabody Institute is, as the reviewers claim, a book that argues that the promotion of public schools in the South was a Reconstruction measure to attack the South and then ultimately destroyed America. However there are some noteworthy items.

In the book a section titled, "The 14th Amendment: Nationalizing Justice Splits the Races," about the constitutional amendment which made African Americans citizens, Chodes denounces the amendment quoting racist president Andrew Johnson to assert that "… it discriminates against whites." Chodes also has a section titled, "The 15th Amendment Nationalizing Votes Splits Races," in which he denounces the constitutional amendment which guaranteed the right to vote regardless of race or color. Chodes quotes others including Curry to imply that African Americans weren't fit to vote and that universal suffrage is a bad idea, and that amending the constitution is somehow unconstitutional.[182]

Chodes also, in denouncing 19th century Henry W. Blair's education bill, condemns civil rights legislation in general. Chodes quotes a speech by Edwin Burritt Smith in 1888 to assert that the notorious Supreme Court ruling that held that the Civil Rights Act of 1875 to be unconstitutional was correct and that civil rights legislation is harmful to African Americans.

> … But the final and fatal objection to any measure of national aid for the benefit of the Negro race lies deeper still, and deeper than any mere consideration of public policy. I refer to the effects on the Negro himself. In the deeply significant language of the Supreme Court, in the opinion declaring the Civil Rights Act unconstitutional; 'When a man has emerged from slavery and by the aide of beneficial legislation, has shaken off the insuperable concomitants of that state, there must be some stage in the process of his elevation where he takes the rank of mere citizen and ceases to be the special favorite of the laws, and when his rights as a citizen or a man, are to be protected in the ordinary modes by which other men's rights are protected.' That man is not the best friend of the Negro, however excellent his intentions, who now seeks to have him treated as a special ward of the nation.[183]

By 1888 white supremacy had triumphed everywhere in the South with the overthrow of Reconstruction having been completed in 1876 and African Americans had very little of the rights of other citizens and the system of racial segregation was being constructed. This ruling by the Supreme Court is considered a disgrace in American history and was denounced by Supreme Court Justice John Marshal Harlan in his dissenting opinion.[184]

The book is a whirlwind of wild assertions and conspiracy theories. One section is titled, "The Freedman's Bureau as Marxist Government." The Bureau is held to be Marxist because in "Black Reconstruction in American," published in 1935, by W.E.B. DuBois who was a Marxist had done a Marxist analysis of the Freedman's Bureau and so retroactively in history the Bureau is made Marxist.[185]

The Morill Act which established America's system of land grant colleges is also held to be an anti-South measure since it was passed during the Civil War.[186] The Department of Agriculture and Agricultural Experiment stations are also held to be a part of a conspiracy. Educational nature training in 1897 in

New York State by the Agriculture Department is supposed to be retribution against the state for not being supportive of the Union cause during the Civil War. Chodes sees as sinister the Agricultural Department sending people to Europe to learn asking, "Why was it necessary to go to Europe to do the research? Was it to hide some aspect of it?" Chodes doesn't seem to realize that it wasn't until the 20th century and indeed until World War II and after that the United States was a technological leader in many technical fields. He also doesn't give any evidence that it was some type of Agriculture Department conspiracy, he just speculates that it might be.[187]

Training on science and nature is seen as some type of conspiracy against religion. Chodes writes, "Science which emphasized the observable objects of here and now, paralleled 'nature training' to reduce the impact of culture and religion's focus on tradition and bringing forth unobservable ideas from the past to the present."[188]

The book just seethes with conspiracy theories.

Public schools in America and the land grant system of colleges have given the public abundant opportunities to become educated. An educated public can read, can write, can think for itself, and communicate its thoughts to others. To those who are against democracy and wish to have what the public thinks dictated by a reactionary elite public schools are indeed a threat.

The neo-Confederates don't comprise the entire anti-public school movement. However, in defining public education as anti-Southern and Southern identity as being against public schools, they hope to mobilize white Southerners who identify with the Confederacy or have some sympathy towards the Confederacy or identify as Southern, to be against public schools and bring to a national anti-public school alliance a strategic block in opposition to public schools.

As explained earlier in this book if one section of the nation is entirely against a policy, you will need a super majority elsewhere to support the policy to get a simple national majority. If neo-Confederates get their way, public education could join the Equal Rights Amendment as a wreck left behind along the highway of American history.

…

10 VIOLENCE

The topics of violence and neo-Confederacy might bring to the public's mind of stereotypes of racists or racist groups such as the Ku Klux Klan spouting racist slurs and flying the Confederate battle flag. A person might think of individual extremists such as Dylann Roof who shot nine unarmed church goers to death at the Emanuel African Methodist Episcopal Church on June 17, 2015.[189]

Less well known is that when Timothy McVeigh blew up the Alfred P. Murrah Federal Building in Oklahoma City April 19, 1995 he was wearing a neo-Confederate T-shirt celebrating the assassination of Abraham Lincoln that was sold by *Southern Partisan* magazine.[190]

This chapter however doesn't seek to sort out the influences on these violent individuals, except to note that there were some. Instead this chapter describes the support for and glorification of violence by neo-Confederate groups going back to the early 20th century. This ideology of violence and extremism will very likely continue to have an influence on single violent individuals, but it is not the subject of this chapter.

The subject of this chapter is neo-Confederate ideologies and views supporting violence, in particular their support of violence that seeks to intimidate, to support insurrection, and terrorize communities.

In recounting some of the long history of these ideologies from early 20th century to the 21st century I wish to show that these ideologies of violence are not some isolated case, or some specific historical anomaly of one individual or group at a specific historical time and place, but an ongoing idea in neo-Confederate thinking, one with deep historical roots. I also want to outline the different neo-Confederate specific ideas regarding violence to show how they come together to form a systematic world view of violence. Finally, with all the evidence, the neo-Confederates will not be able to credibly deny that they have ideologies of violence though they certainly will try.

Since at least the 1980s there hasn't been any insurrection by any neo-Confederate group. They have not confronted law enforcement. However, there are more ways to support violence such as opposing anti-hate crime legislation, applauding gay bashers, denouncing efforts against police brutality, and criticizing the efforts of law enforcement acting against other insurrectionists and violent groups. Neo-Confederates also can hope that others act on their ideas.

Just because no neo-Confederate group itself has attempted violence, doesn't mean that they wouldn't in the future. These groups are not stupid. They know quite well that at some specific time it might be very unwise to act violently and that they have other options to advance their agenda. They also tend to see some catastrophic breakdown of the government or society coming in the future in which the government is discredited. Also, in a catastrophic breakdown of society they foresee their ideas dominating the mainstream of thinking. They think that this looming catastrophe will provide the environment in which their ideas can dominate mainstream thinking. In this apocalyptic future, the government will be incapacitated or powerless to stop any violent campaign. In the latter case their ideologies about violence could be given full vent. Alternatively they await the government to be discredited and the object of so much anger that there will be a revolution against it providing a scope in which they can act.

This should not be seen as being farfetched. Out in the Western states of the United States there has been violence directed at public officials in particular federal officials in charge of federal lands. The federal government was openly defied and is still defied at the Clive Bundy ranch (6/16/2016). More disturbing is that the Bundy's in both their insurrection at their ranch and in their occupation of the Malheur Refuge in Oregon had received the support of elected officials and enough popular support such the federal government was restrained in acting against them.

The boiling rage of a significant fraction of the public manifested in the 2016 presidential campaign is extraordinary. At some point it could be that a fraction of the public might be very angry over the changes in the United States, and also at the same time realize that their agenda has no chance in our democratic system. Americans may like to think that ethnic civil disorder is something that plaques other nations and regions but that it can't happen here. However, historically there has been the violence of the Ku Klux Klan and the Red Shirts in our history, and white race riots attacking the African American communities in the past such as Wilmington, North Carolina in 1898 and Tulsa, Oklahoma in 1921

There could very well be a point in the future in which neo-Confederates act on their ideologies of violence. A "lone wolf," a single individual acting by themselves in committing an act of violence, can be dealt with by law enforcement. More complicated would be how police deal with a single violent organization with a dozen or so members operating a planned and coordinated violent campaign of terror or several such organizations operating together, especially if they had some support in the general population.

The Confederacy itself was a violent insurrection led by slave owners over the results of a presidential election, that of Abraham Lincoln. Confederates feared that Lincoln's election would threaten slavery and white supremacy.[191] Neo-Confederate groups are organized to celebrate, praise and honor the Confederacy, its leaders and supporters and to justify them. They see their violent Confederate predecessors as role models.

Michael Andrew Grissom and Neo-Confederacy

Michael Andrew Grissom, a neo-Confederate free-lance writer, first book was *Southern by the Grace of God*, originally published by Rebel Press in 1988, then was picked up by neo-Confederate Pelican Publishing Company in Gretna, Louisiana, in 1988 and there have been eleven printings as of 2007, there may have been more printings and the book is still in print. It is distributed in mainstream bookstores.[192] He has since authored a series of books after this one.

This book is worth examining in detail for several reasons. It was, along with, *The South Was Right!* published a few years later by the Pelican Publishing Company, the two books that launched the modern radical neo-Confederate movement. It has been enthusiastically praised and has been supported by both the United Daughters of the Confederacy and the Sons of Confederate Veterans. As noted earlier it has sold many copies and is widely distributed. Grissom's writings as a whole are also worth reviewing, though not all of his books have sold as many copies. Other works by Grissom have been endorsed by neo-Confederate groups and they also reveal his thinking and his neo-Confederate ideology.

Again, I would point out that the lack of capitalization of "negro" is in the original. The effort to have "Negro" capitalized goes back to the early 20th century and was an accepted practice decades before Grissom's book was published. Grissom in refusing to capitalize "Negro" is making a statement.

Finally one reason to focus on Grissom's, *Southern by the Grace of God*, he has multiple elements of the neo-Confederate ideology relating to violence in just this one book and with the widespread praise of this book by the neo-Confederate movement, it is a good example of the movements ideologies relating to violence.

Grissom denounces emancipation as "the idea advocated by fanatic abolitionists, of freeing the slaves."[193] Grissom assesses Southern slavery as follows:

> There was a rudimentary misconception among northerners about slavery and the negro in general. Fiercely believing that slaves, who in the mild form of slavery practiced in the South would more fittingly have been called servants, were an unhappy lot just waiting for a chance to escape …[194]

Grissom has a chapter titled, "Reconstruction – Nightmare of the South." Quoting Thomas Dixon, it portrays African Americans as wild ignorant irresponsible savages in a time of misrule and corruption. The following are some typical texts:

> In North Carolina, burned plantations had resulted in roaming bands of negro bandits. In the northeastern part of that state, the crimes perpetrated by these hoodlums were particularly atrocious. They raided the unprotected countryside, burning houses and looting with near impunity. They entered the homes of defenseless ladies, forced them to entertain at the piano, cursed them, robbed them, stripped them of their clothing, and subjected them to indignities better left unprinted.[195]

> With a little prodding, the illiterate negro masses could be worked into a frenzy at most any time.[196]

Grissom defends the infamous Black Codes explaining that they were needed to get African Americans to work for wages.[197] The 14th Amendment, and 15th Amendment to the United States Constitution which, respectively, made African Americans citizens and gave African Americans the right to vote, are asserted by Grissom to be the cynical plans of the Republican Party to manipulate African Americans who he characterizes as ignorant. Grissom writes:

> … There were nearly 4,000,000 negroes in Dixie, most of whom could neither read nor write. Most of them had no comprehension of matters beyond the boundary of the plantation, this ignorance of affairs presenting a golden opportunity to the Republicans who could instruct them how to vote. Forbid white people to vote, and Negroes could be

manipulated into sending Republicans to Congress from every Southern state.[198]

Grissom refuses to recognize African Americans as citizens in the Reconstruction state constitutional conventions complaining:

> Every southern state was required to rewrite its constitution in a constitutional convention of delegates chosen in a statewide election of *all* adult males, *except those with disqualifications.* This meant that many ex-Confederates could not vote, and it meant that Negroes, even though they were not citizens, could vote. [Italics in the original][199]

Grissom devotes several pages portraying Louisiana's violent white supremacist groups, The Knights of the White Camellia and The White League, as heroes and saviors of Louisiana.[200] About the Knights of the White Camellia Grissom writes:

> With a negro police force in Shreveport who cared little for the safety of white citizens, the white men organized the Knights of the White Camellia. The Knights in Caddo parish declared "a white man's government or no government" and made night rides, breaking up political meetings in which scalawags and carpetbaggers were instructing and inflaming the gullible freemen.[201]

The Ku Klux Klan are especially held up as the saviors of the South. Grissom writes:

There were three requisite conditions for Republican power in the South: the negro vote, Republican control of the national government, and federal troops. Should any one of these supports be weakened or removed, Republican rule would collapse. The southerner had little control over troops or national politics, having himself been barred from voting, so he turned his efforts to the local scene, where the secret societies began to spring up in an effort to stop negro voting and run the carpetbaggers out of the South.

Grissom then writes of what he sees as the romance of the Ku Klux Klan, he recommends *The Clansman* by Thomas Dixon published in 1905 and the 1915 movie *The Birth of a Nation* which glorifies the Ku Klux Klan in Reconstruction and quotes Woodrow Wilson's praise of it, that it was "history written by lightning." This book and movie portray African Americans as beasts and glorifies their subjection by violence. [202]

Grissom captions an illustration of a hooded Klansman on a movie poster for D.W. Griffith's, *The Birth of a Nation*, as follows:

VIOLENCE

The original Ku Klux Klan (1866-1877) played a vital role in ridding the post-war South of brutal carpetbagger rule.

The Red Shirts in South Carolina, who violently established white supremacy in South Carolina are also praised by Grissom. [203]

In a short section in the book titled, "Papa and the KKK" Grissom portrays the Klan of the early 20th century as a benevolent patriotic organization that fought socialism and communism and did "*benevolent work among the poor.*" An example given of their patriotism was in a case of a sugar rationing violation in which "*they stopped the man and gave him a good beating.*"[204]

In another section, "The Hangin' At Ada," a lynching in Ada, Oklahoma, of a white man is praised as an example of civic spirit. Grissom quotes a newspaper, *Daily Oklahoman* that the lynching "was entirely justified in the eyes of God and man" and "those who took part in it have no reason today to be ashamed or conscience-stricken."[205]

Grissom has a chapter of recommended reading material with a list of books and periodicals. The white supremacist novels *The Clansman* and *The Leopard Spot's* by Thomas Dixon as well as his autobiography *Southern Horizons* are recommended.[206] The reader is strongly encouraged to read *Southern Partisan* and the *Citizen Informer*, the latter the official publication of the white supremacist Council of Conservative Citizens.

Grissom's book endorses white supremacist violent terror against African Americans explicitly. It has been praised by leading neo-Confederate organizations.

The United Daughters of the Confederacy helped launch the sales of the book by running an excerpt in their magazine in 1988 and announcing that the work would soon be published. The excerpt included an address where readers could order the book.[207] Retta D. Tindal, UDC Historian General (2010-2012) in a 2007 article, "Confederate Classics: For Research, Reference, or Refresher," enthusiastically recommends Grissom's book stating, "If you have a child or a grandchild or a UDC friend or any friend or family member who loves Confederate history, these books are sure to become their treasurers, too." *Southern by the Grace of God* is one of the books Tindal is referencing here.

Tindal informs the reader that *Southern By the Grace of God*, "is a primer of all things Confederate" and that:

> Mr. Grissom wrote this book for four reasons: to offer a firm understanding of our heritage, to instill pride in being Southern, to pursue

the elements that characterize the South, and to rally Southerners to defend and preserve their unique heritage.[208]

Being that Tindal considers this book a "treasure" she sees it as accomplishing these goals, which gives insight as to how she defines this "unique heritage."

In 2011 Tindal, as Historian General of the UDC published the General Historical Programs for Sept. 2011 to August 2013. These are a list of historical topics recommended for chapters for each month along with recommended books as references. For May 2012 the topic is Sam Davis, and one of the two books recommended is *Southern By the Grace of God* by Grissom. [209]

The UDC has also awarded Michael Andrew Grissom its Jefferson Davis medal, which is awarded "for outstanding contributions in furthering the study and preservation of Confederate history through historical research, writing, public speaking, and other points of special achievement."[210]

Other neo-Confederate publications gave Grissom's book their enthusiastic endorsement. In the 1989 *Confederate Veteran*, book editor James N. Vogler Jr. praises the book as follows:

> This is a 569-page love letter to the Southland and the author makes no bones about it. ... As the author reveals at the beginning of the book, if you want to read something negative about the South you had better pass this one up.[211]

In 1988 the *Southern Partisan* review commented:

> In attempting to turn the tide on twenty-five years of South bashing by mass media, liberals, and American history revisionists, Michael Grissom has produced the first modern Southern survival manual. ... *Southern by the Grace of God* is well written and very readable. [212]

The SCV started offering Grissom's *Southern by the Grace of God* for sale in *Confederate Veteran* in 2001 in the "Classic Southern Reprints," section with the notice, "Celebrates in photographs and text the enduring legacy of being a Southerner. Issues a clarion call for those who love the South to defend and maintain that heritage."[213] It is currently offered for sale by the SCV online with the notice, "The essential handbook for Southerners-proudly proclaims the traditions, the culture and the values that have long distinguished the South from the rest of the nation."[214] It was offered for sale in the SCV Merchandise Catalogs for 2004-2005, 2005-2006, 2008-2009, 2009-2010, 2011-2012, and 2015-2016 with the same book notice.[215] It was also offered for sale in the SCV Merchandise Catalog 2013-2014 which was an insert in the Sept/Oct. 2013 *Confederate Veteran* but without a caption.[216]

However, none of these ads or book reviews or articles mention the book's references to the Ku Klux Klan or any of Grissom's views about race, slavery, Reconstruction, or other white supremacist groups or Grissom's account of a lynching in Ada, Oklahoma. If a person was to pick up one of the neo-Confederate magazines or view an advertisement online none of these things would become evident. This is a key aspect of the neo-Confederate agenda. They are quite aware of the need to manage their image and it appears that often the communication of ideas that would injure their image is out of the general public's view.

Another Grissom book is, *When the South Was Southern*, which has a section of photographs of Ku Klux Klan robes. Grissom writes:

> The world knows the story of the Ku Klux Klan. Riding in the dark of night, southern men reclaimed the South from the black terror. Carpetbag rule was overthrown; civil law was reinstituted; and, negro rampage was summarily ended.[217]

The SCV offers for sale *When the South Was Southern* online currently (8/9/2016), and has sold it in their merchandise catalogs. It was sold in the SCV Merchandise Catalogs for 2005-2006, 2008-2009, 2009-2010, 2011-2012, and 2015-2016 with the same book notice.[218] It was also offered for sale in the SCV Merchandise Catalog 2013-2014 which was an insert in the Sept/Oct. 2013 *Confederate Veteran* but without a caption.[219]

KU KLUX KLAN AND RECONSTRUCTION VIOLENCE

While the SCV passes resolutions against the contemporary Ku Klux Klan, however, it has a long history of praising the Reconstruction-era Ku Klux Klan. When United Daughters of the Confederacy General Historian S.E.F. Rose first published her enthusiastic praise for the Ku Klux Klan in 1914 it was endorsed by the Sons of Confederate Veterans at their 1914 Jacksonville convention. Such SCV venerations of the Reconstruction Klan are not, however, only a century old.[220]

In Vol. 1 2001 issue of the *Confederate Veteran* in a section titled "Classic Southern Reprints," a video of the notorious film *Birth of a Nation*, which glorifies the Ku Klux Klan is for sale. The SCV notice for the book doesn't mention the Ku Klux Klan stating:

> … [D]irector D.W. Griffith recreates the human tragedy of the War Between the States and Reconstruction in the South after the downfall of the Confederacy. Filmed just fifty years after the end of the war, this epic

motion picture takes a controversial look at the birth of Lincoln's "new nation" out of the ashes of the Constitutional Republic.[221]

In the Volume Three 2001 *Confederate Veteran* ad for the video the notice is changed to read, "Relive history with this classic silent film from 1915, D.W. Griffith's masterpiece takes a controversial look at the birth of Lincoln's 'new nation' out of the ashes of the constitutional republic."[222] The idea that this film is historical instead of shrieking bigotry is laughable and calling it a "masterpiece" is an endorsement of the film.

The Volume Two 2002 *Confederate Veteran* laments that "Birth of a Nation," is "So demonized in today's politically correct climate that it is no longer shown publicly."[223]

It is also currently (6/18/2016) offered for sale online with the comment, "his silent film masterpiece made in 1915. An epic account of The War Between the States and Reconstruction. So Politically incorrect it hasn't been shown in years!"[224]

It was also offered for sale in the SCV Merchandise catalogs for 2004-2005, 2005-2006, 2008-2009, 2009-2010, 2011-2012, 2015-2016 with the comment, "An epic account of The War Between the States and Reconstruction. So Politically incorrect it hasn't been shown in years!"[225] It was also in the SCV Merchandise Catalog 2013-2014 which was an insert in the Sept/Oct. 2013 *Confederate Veteran* but without a caption.[226]

What seems to be the avoidance of actually mentioning that this film is about the Ku Klux Klan is, to the author, typical of how the SCV appears to seemingly promote the Reconstruction KKK as heroes. They praise a pro-Klan work, but at the same it is not apparent from their promotion of the video that film they promote is pro-Klan. The sales of the video stopped in the "Confederate Gifts" ad section of their magazine. Though in online ads and in the catalogs you do see the image of a Klansman on a horse on the DVD cover.

Clyde Wilson at the Abbeville Institute in his 2014 article, "Reconstruction: Violence and Dislocation," defends the Ku Klux Klan as being justified as a measure of self-defense of the South. He writes:

> In this situation, where the law was a travesty and the government was in the hands of the unscrupulous, Southerners reacted as free Americans have always done. They took matters into their own hands to restore genuine law and order. Sympathetic Northerners and visiting Europeans mostly agreed that the kind of resistance represented by the Ku Klux Klan and similar groups was necessary and right, at least in the beginning.

Southern actions, so viciously indicted by today's historians, were mostly defensive.[227]

Recently published in 2016 by a new neo-Confederate press, Shotwell Publishers, is *Washington's KKK: The Union League During Reconstruction*, by John Chodes with a forward by Clyde Wilson. This book argues that the Ku Klux Klan was organized to defend the South against who Chodes asserts were the real terrorists the Union Leagues. As Chodes states, "The Ku Klux Klan came into existence as a result of, and as a reaction to, the illegal, unconstitutional and criminal activities of the Union League."[228]

Another book which the SCV offers for sale, but the author hasn't seen offered online (last checked 8/10/2016) nor seen sold in the *Confederate Veteran*, but only sold in the SCV catalogs is *Invisible Empire: The Story of the Ku Klux Klan, 1866-1871*, by Stanley Horn. It was offered in five SCV Merchandise catalogs for 2004-2005, 2005-2006, 2008-2009, 2009-2010, and 2011-2012. From the text in the book for the catalog:

> Conceived in the minds of six former Confederates as a social club for their own amusement, this Klan was disbanded in 1871, after its purpose of countering post-war aggression against the Southern people by Carpetbaggers was fulfilled. Presented for research purposes.[229]

The Ku Klux Klan of Reconstruction in the SCV catalog is held to be the savior of the South and not a racist terrorist organization. It was also offered in the SCV Merchandise Catalog 2013-2014 which was an insert in the Sept/Oct. 2013 *Confederate Veteran* but without a caption.[230]

Red Shirts

The Red Shirts were a violent group that overthrew the Reconstruction government of South Carolina through violence and intimidation during the elections of 1876 ending multiracial democracy there. The United Daughters of the Confederacy (UDC) operates the museum Oakley Park, which in a 2001 *UDC Magazine article*, "Oakley Park: Only Shrine of its Kind," the author Donna Harris informs us that, "Today it stands as a shrine to the Red Shirt campaign of 1876."[231] The article gives briefly explains that the Red Shirts were a "… movement to redeem South Carolina from Radical rule."

However, when the UDC was raising funds for the building in the 1940s they were much more direct as to the reasons why they admired the Red Shirts.

The UDC South Carolina Division issued a publication, *United Daughters of the Confederacy, South Carolina Division: Golden Anniversary 1896-1946*. In it on page 13 is an article titled, "Oakley Park, Edgefield's Red Shirt Shrine." Oakley Park is an old Plantation house which the South Carolina UDC division had decided in October 1944 to restore. The importance of this house for restoration is stated in the article, "Oakley Park was the home of General Martin Witherspoon Gary, who with his Red Shirts, in 1876, did so much to restore white supremacy in South Carolina." The article also explains "The 'Red Shirts' were largely ex-Confederate soldiers under their one-time military commanders."[232] Thus the article explains why this violent white supremacist group is part of Confederate "heritage."

At the November 13, 1947 national convention of the UDC in Florida, the entire organization adopted the restoration of Oakley Park for a Red Shirt Shrine. A series of reports follow from 1948 to 1950 in the UDC Convention Minutes and articles in the UDC magazine on the progress of restoration until it is completed by Mrs. J. Frost Walker (Cornelia Walker).[233] In the *United Daughters of the Confederacy Magazine* there are reports that make clear the purpose of the Red Shirts were.

In the *United Daughters of the Confederacy Magazine*, March 1947, "General Wade Hampton," pp. 11-3, the author, Mrs. J.A. Yarbrough said:

> He devoted himself to the rehabilitation of his stricken State which was overrun by the Republican Party with Negroes holding high offices. Great as was his war service, his leadership in the trying days that followed was even greater. He was a member of a delegation sent by a taxpayers' convention to protest with the authorities in Washington against upholding the enemies of law, order and decency in Columbia. The appeal feel upon deaf ears.
>
> Exhausting every resource to secure peace and order, the white people of South Carolina determined to overthrow the government by a direct fight in 1876, and they selected as their leader, Wade Hampton. In convention at Columbia they nominated him for governor.
>
> The campaign was one of the most remarkable political struggles in the world's history. The famous Red Shirt campaign for the redemption of the State from outside and Negro rule is one of the great episodes of South Carolina history. Daily it seemed that a bloody conflict would ensue. The slightest error would have meant civil war. But Hampton kept the peace. His cool head, strategy and bravery gave his people the victory and once more South Carolina was under respectable rule. It was months, however, before the other party and the Federal troops were removed from the State and Governor Hampton was finally in full control.

In *United Daughters of the Confederacy Magazine*, May 1948, pp.16-7, Mrs. J. Frost Walker wrote:

> All whites over twenty-on years of age were required to take the 'iron-clad oath' before registering. This disenfranchised all the prominent whites and easily gave the ignorant negroes a majority.

According to the article by Caroline S. Coleman in the *United Daughters of the Confederacy Magazine*, Vol. 11 No. 7, July 1948, pp. 12-3.

> Carpetbaggers and scalawags flocked to the State from all parts of the nation, seeking rich plums and inciting hard feelings among the child-like Negroes who left alone would have turned to their own white folks as their best friends.

Similar praise of post-Civil War terrorism can be found in Mrs. J.R. Carson's[234] article in the *United Daughters of the Confederacy Magazine*, September 1948, pp. 6-8, "The Great Triumvirate of the Reconstruction Period in South Carolina." Carson also asserts that allowing African Americans to vote was a mistake.

> After the collapse of the Confederacy there was in South Carolina practically no civil authority; no organized State government, and no militia organization to afford protection of life and property. Garrisons of United States troops, many of them Negroes, former slaves, misled by passion, ignorance and evil counsellors, were stationed in the various towns and cities, and completely controlled the actions of citizens. Adventurers from without the State soon appeared to incite the Negroes to turn against their former owners, to become active in politics and to aspire to political office. Within a few years the control of the State government was rampant. Extravagance in the appropriation of public funds; dishonesty, disorder and a lawlessness reigned supreme, and for a decade the white population was helpless, and almost hopeless. Rancor towards the Southerners and philanthropy towards the Negroes combined to produce the measure known as Reconstruction, and this policy had the above disastrous results. No people in any time or anywhere faced so many difficult problems as did the people of South Carolina, and all of these at the same time. Social and economic, political and racial, all combined and interwoven, and upon the wise and proper solution of which depended not only white supremacy, but the very existence of the white race.

The *UDC Magazine* articles more recently have not included direct statements about white supremacy regarding the Red Shirts, as indicated in a 2013 article by Retta D. Tindal, Historian General of the UDC (2010-2012), "General Wade Hampton III," about a Confederate general who became governor of South Carolina when the Red Shirts overthrew Reconstruction in South Carolina. The essay entirely omits mention of the Red Shirts. Tindal instead states, "His reputation as spokesman for a conciliatory policy for the Negro in the South grew in the post war years." His opponent in the 1876 election for governor is called "a Maine carpetbagger." The Republicans in 1876 are "Radical" which continues the idea that only a "Radical" would not support white supremacy. Tindal concludes, "He was from that time on known as the man who brought South Carolina out of Reconstruction."[235]

The Sons of Confederate Veterans (SCV) has also advertised books for sale in which the Red Shirts are portrayed as Confederate heroes. The SCV advertised reprints of the 1935 book, *Hampton and His Red Shirts: South Carolina's Deliverance in 1876*, by Alfred B. Williams in a section, "Confederate Gifts from IHQ," (International Headquarters) in the *Confederate Veteran*. The book is praised as "a fascinating chronicle of how the people of South Carolina, let [sic] by former Confederate General Wade Hampton and his famous Red Shirts, rose up to free themselves form the intolerable and dangerous conditions of the Reconstruction period."[236] When the book is sold in the *Confederate Veteran* in 2009, the SCV is more oblique, stating "The story of the restoration of home rule in South Carolina following eleven years of reconstruction."[237]

Another book that the SCV also advertises in their 2015-2016 merchandise catalog and earlier catalogs is the 1927 book, as well as online is *Ousting the Carpetbagger from South Carolina*, by Henry L. Thompson.[238] Both these books on South Carolina and Reconstruction were also advertised in the SCV Merchandise Catalog 2013-2014 which was an insert in the Sept/Oct. 2013 *Confederate Veteran* but without captions.[239]

There are four important conclusions to be drawn from the history of neo-Confederate praise for the Red Shirts. One is that neo-Confederate groups see the Civil War and Reconstruction as one long conflict; two, that they comprehend the Red Shirts as part of the Confederate legacy to be honored; and three, they celebrate violent white terrorist as part of their Confederate "heritage."

The fourth important conclusion is how neo-Confederate ideology can embrace white supremacists, but not have it perceived by the public. Whereas almost all Americans know about the Ku Klux Klan, few know about the Red Shirts and other similar but more obscure violent groups during Reconstruction. So the groups have been somewhat more visible in their embrace of the Red Shirts, though there appears to be some efforts to obscure this since the neo-Confederate organizations know that the author has been tracking them and publishing results.

OPPOSITION TO HATE CRIME LEGISLATION AND SUPPORT OF BIAS VIOLENCE

Hate crime legislation is designed to stop bias violence by groups such as the Ku Klux Klan and similar groups as well as that committed by individuals. Hate crime legislation provides another defense against terror directed against individuals and groups based on who they are. Anti-hate crime legislation is directly counter to the neo-Confederate tradition of honoring violent white terrorists.

If a movement wanted a group to be the target of violence, they don't necessarily have to act themselves. An alternate strategy would be to devise means to render the law ineffectual in protecting targets of bias violence and opposing laws that would work against bias crimes. Further another strategy would be to applaud incidents of bias violence or otherwise defend perpetrators of that mayhem, whether committed by private individuals or individuals in government such as police.

Neo-Confederates oppose anti-hate crime legislation and otherwise support means by which bias crimes are enabled. It is a means of directing violence when more direct methods are not feasible.

The *Southern Partisan* in 1989 had an item in its "CSA Today" section about the notorious ruling of Judge Jack Hampton. A gay person was murdered in a park in Dallas and Hampton had given a lighter sentence. *Southern Partisan* reports:

> You may recall that Judge Hampton, in determining a murder sentence, had suggested that he'd taken in consideration the fact the victims were homosexuals soliciting sex, and therefore like prostitutes. The local "gay rights" activists went into a mad tarantella, demanding that Judge Hampton be removed …

The article approvingly reported that Hampton was cleared of charges.

> For a while it looked as if the city limits of San Francisco extended all the way to Dallas, but in the end everything turned out all right.

Southern Partisan mockingly dismisses the LGBT community outrage at Hampton being cleared of charges. They suggest that at the next election Judge Hampton would win the most votes and eventually he might end up on the Texas Supreme Court.[240]

However, the highest moral value of Dallas culture is real estate development and the greatest sin there is in Dallas is bad publicity and Hampton career didn't do well afterwards. He lost his bid for reelection as Criminal District Court judge in 1992.

The *Southern Partisan* in 1993 in its entry for Maryland in its "CSA Today" (Confederate States of America) section had this entry mockingly titled "Gay Ole Time" warns readers that hate crime legislation will result in gay men assaulting straight men, gays being a privileged group, and excessive punishments.

> Three men from Dundalk, a suburb tangent to Baltimore, were convicted of beating up gays outside a bar in Baltimore.

Southern Partisan comments:

> In Maryland, homosexuals are protected by politicians and coddled by the law. Crimes against these sensitive folk receive special handling. Ordinarily such incidents would have been punished by a fine and a night in jail. In this case, the punishments were beyond all reason.

The article then goes on to state that two of the assailants received prison time and quoted the lawyer for the gay bashers that it wasn't a hate crime, with hate crime in quotes, and that "one of the homosexuals grabbed his client's buttocks."[241]

The idea here is that hate crimes legislation would lead to gays sexually molesting straight men. The author some years ago wrote the Baltimore gay paper and this was a murderous attack with severe injury, not some drunken fisticuffs.

The *Southern Partisan* in 2000 in their "CSA Today" section in their entry for Tennessee mockingly describes a gay student group, Vanderbilt Lambda Association, float in the Vanderbilt University's homecoming parade being attacked by members of the Sigma Chi House fraternity who pelted it with rocks and mud. The spokesperson Carl Manalo's complaint that "I don't want this happening to anyone else, because it is the worst thing that ever happened to me," is mocked:

> Now there's a lucky fellow. Most people have worse things happen to them before they finish elementary school, (and without asking for it). Manalo should read Quentin Crisp's fascinating book on manners, in which the famous British homosexual apologizes to society for flaunting his homosexuality as a youth, saying he was self-centered and thoughtless of the sensitivities of others.[242]

In 2004 *Southern Partisan* in the "CSA Today" entry for Texas is gleeful that a pontoon boat rented by a gay and Lesbian group with 60 passengers capsized concluding with the statement that "Who says that inanimate objects such as boats don't have feelings like the rest of us?"[243]

At The Citadel, a military college in Charleston, South Carolina, on Oct. 23, 1986 five Citadel cadets wearing sheets and towels to resemble Ku Klux Klansmen burst into the barracks and went to the bed of African American freshman cadet Kevin Nesmith and lighting a paper cross and shouting racial slurs. His roommate was Michael Mendoza.

The Citadel didn't expel the students though that was the recommended punishment in their rule book. It wasn't, however, mandatory. Nesmith complained that "I feel that I have been made the villain when the villains remain at The Citadel," and he resigned. His brother Alonzo Nesmith was on the school's Board of Visitors and resigned saying the school was trying to "sweep it under the rug." There were protests of hundreds by African Americans against the school.[244]

The response of Matthew Sandal in "Criticus Essay: What Happened at the Citadel," in *Southern Partisan* in their 1986/87 double issue was to ridicule Kevin Nesmith, characterize the incident as a frivolous prank and the reaction overblown, and portrayed the students who harassed Kevin Nesmith as the victims.

Sandel characterizes it as a prank to motivate Nesmith because "His grades were poorer than they should have been and he didn't have the right attitude …" Sandel writes that the dean of students should have "told Nesmith and Mendoza they were a couple of crybabies …" Sandel writes, "First, no young man should go to a military school if he has delicate sensibilities." Sandel writes, "The punishment eventually imposed on the five offenders was beyond reason …"[245]

Not surprisingly the neo-Confederate movement opposes any legislation against hate crimes.

Paul Gottfried in his article, "Our American Cultural Revolution," published May 27, 2016, at the Abbeville Institute website, complains about student protests against prejudice and institutional racism and sees it deriving from civil rights legislation and anti-hate crimes legislation. Gottfried's broader complaint is about civil rights legislation in general. He writes:

> Now the kids and their instructors manufacture grievances as the action unfolds. Protestors are for or against the wearing of Hallowe'en costumes on campus, depending on which side can be used to humiliate gutless

administrators. They take offense at the name of any dead white man or denounce any form of lookism or micro-aggression, providing the resulting protest permits them to express outrage.

In the early 1960s such things did not happen, and for a self-evident reason. Sixty years ago we did not have a vast state apparatus fighting "discrimination," judging "hate crimes" and by implication "hate speech," and monitoring the treatment of protected minorities.

Gottfried, explains that he doesn't care about social justice or ending discrimination and sees efforts against discrimination as a means to expand the power of the state.

In regards to rape he writes:

> Woman students on our campuses are now encouraged by the state to accuse male students of rape; and those who have state power on their side are in a position to wreak havoc on those they accuse. Although felony laws protect women who have been physically assaulted in colleges and elsewhere, the Department of Education and other government agencies insist on more stringent guidelines. They mandate sensitivity training for faculty and staff and demand that university authorities give concentrated attention to well-rehearsed grievances. And the government, under both political parties, has created this Inquisition.[246]

In the early 21st century the book, *The South under Siege: 1830-2000*, by Frank Conner has gained prominence, acceptance and endorsement in the neo-Confederate movement. The following establishes this, before we discuss his views on hate crime legislation. Also, for a latter chapter on anti-Semitism in this book.

The Sons of Confederate Veterans have advertised it for sale in their magazine and merchandise catalogs, and a review in *Southern Mercury* recommended it. It is very clear what this book was about, so, for the author, it is hard to believe that the SCV didn't know or understand what the book was about.

Frank Conner ran a series of full page ads for the book in *Confederate Veteran* magazine starting in 2003. The July/August 2003 issue ad makes very clear the book's view point. One paragraph of the ad states.

> Ever since the 1830s, various groups of Northern liberals have been waging an ideological war against the white South, using black civil-rights as their main weapon against us. Their objectives are to discredit and destroy our society-and Southern Christianity along with it; and then to discredit Christianity in the US, and substitute

secular humanism for it as the official religion, to justify establishing a totalitarian-socialist government in America.

This ad was repeated in the Nov./Dec. 2003 *Confederate Veteran*. [247]

The South Under Siege was praised by Ann Rives Zappa in a review in the Sept./Oct. 2003 *Southern Mercury*, a publication of the Educational PAC (Political Action Committee) of the Sons of Confederate Veterans. She calls it "a masterful volume of work painstakingly researched" and that "Author Conner uses several chapters of *The South under Siege*, to detail the rise of powerful black political movements and the proliferation of our enemies. He covers policies and events created by liberals through the Supreme Court and Congress during the Fifties and Sixties to keep the South in subjugation."

In the Sept.-Oct. 2003 *Confederate Veteran* the full page ad lists some of the content.

> 7. How the white Southerners had to disenfranchise and segregate the blacks. …
>
> 9. How the liberals ran the black-civil-rights movement as a war against the white South.
>
> 10. How the liberals used the federal government to establish the first phase of Reconstruction II: the Civil Rights Act of 1964 and the Voting Rights Act of 1965 (still in force.)
>
> 11. How the liberals used the black activists and the news/entertainment media to establish the second phase of Reconstruction II, which is now destroying the white South.[248]

The March/April 2004 *Confederate Veteran* full page ad for the book omits mentioning civil rights legislation or African Americans, the book is about, "The fact is that various groups of Northern liberals have been waging an ideological war against the conservative Christian South at least since the 1830s …"[249] In the Sept./Oct. 2004 *Confederate Veteran* ad informs that reader that:

> The book chronicles the twists and turns in the ideological war which various groups of Northern liberals have been waging against the traditional white South for the past 170 years, in order to replace Christianity with secular humanism as the national religion, and to replace limited government with lockstep socialism in the US."

The May/April 2004 *Confederate Veteran* full page ad feels Southerners have been fooled:

> Those Southerners have been suckered into believing that states' rights is really racism; that a strong aversion to socialist government is really a complete disregard for the welfare of the blacks and other disadvantaged minorities ...[250]

It is hard for the author to believe that the Sons of Confederate Veterans at this time didn't know what this book, its racism, anti-Semitism, and conspiracy theorizing, was about.

In the next issue, July/August 2004 *Confederate Veteran* the book is first sold in the magazine by the Sons of Confederate Veterans themselves in their section titled, "Confederate Gifts from IHQ," with text explaining that it tells a true history how supposedly the South has been oppressed by the "North" and that it is "an excellent defense" against the history taught in "the government schools."[251]

The ad besides not mentioning the fact that the book is hostile to civil rights, also defines this book as a "Confederate Gift," that is it is part of Confederate "heritage."

The book is currently (6/24/2016) offered for sale online by the Sons of Confederate Veterans with the same comments as in the first SCV Confederate Veteran ad for the book.[252]

It has been offered for sale by the *Sons of Confederate Veterans Merchandise Catalogs* for 2004-2005, 2005-2006, 2008-2009, 2009-2010, 2011-2012, and 2015-2016 with the same endorsement.[253] It was also offered for sale in the 2013-2014 SCV Merchandise Catalog insert in the Sept.-Oct. 2013 *Confederate Veteran*.[254]

The SCV started to offer it for sale it more frequently again in the *Confederate Veteran* starting with July/August 2011, Sept./Oct. 2012, Sept./Oct. 2013, Jan./Feb. 2014, July/August 2014, Jan./Feb. 2015, May/June 2015 and since has stopped, probably because the author was sending documentation about the SCV selling this book to the media, synagogues, Christian denominations, and others in 2015.[255]

However, what really demonstrates the influence of Frank Conner in neo-Confederate circles and in the SCV was that he was selected to write a series of four articles for the *Southern Mercury* magazine of the Educational PAC of the SCV. These weren't just any articles. The *Southern Mercury* magazine had Conner define both the history of the South and also the purpose of the SCV and what direction it should take in the future. Each article also mentioned that he was the author of *The South under Siege* with contact information so the reader could purchase his book.

When the publication was launched Conner wrote the cover article, "Death of a Nation: The Almost Forgotten Body and South of the Confederate Veterans," for the first issue of *Southern Mercury*, July/Aug. 2003, in which he gives forth the neo-Confederate concept of Southern history, and calls for the SCV membership to be educated with a with that understanding. He is worried that "Some SCV members have actually accepted the beliefs of Northern liberalism (multiculturalism, et al.), and are helping the liberals to destroy the traditional Southerners as a people …"

Conner writes:

> Today the SCV should be a formidable instrument, successfully (and lawfully) defending the South's traditional belief system and way of life against the accelerating attacks by the liberals and black activists, who are bent on vilifying and suppressing every vestige of our heritage."

In the article Conner regrets that the SCV isn't currently this ideological force. [256]

In the next issue of the *Southern Mercury*, Sept./Oct. 2003, Conner writes "Where We Stand Now: And How We Got Here," where he gives his understanding of Southern history in the 20th century. Conner sees the civil rights movement of the 20th century as an attack on the South and to counter this attack Conner writes, "To do that, we must urgently reform the SCV, and convert it into a (lawful) effective fighting organization; and we must use it to fight."[257]

His Jan./Feb. 2004 *Southern Mercury* article, "The Enemy's Strategy," is a complaint that liberals and African Americans are attacking the "traditional South." [258]

However, of particular interest is his last article in the *Southern Mercury*, "Reorganizing the Sons of Confederate Veterans," in the May/June 2004 issue. In the article he calls for the reorganization of the SCV into a right wing ideological organization to fight culture wars. The individual members are to get training to fight culture wars to defend Confederate heritage which he defines is "the Protestant-based conservative belief system, and the set of values and way of life resulting from it, which were the essence of the Old South …"

Conner further explains in the article:

> It will teach each SCV member how and why a people possessed of that viewpoint would (and will) demand and get good (constitutional)

government, and maintain a moral society while enjoying maximum individual freedom of action and low taxation.[259]

This is largely the direction the SCV seems to have taken as it becomes more explicitly political in its publication *Confederate Veteran*.

Having established that Conner and his book are a significant influence in the SCV and the neo-Confederate movement we should become familiar with his view of hate crime legislation.

Conner's writing in the *Southern Mercury* didn't mention Judaism, Jews or Jewish culture. The book focuses heavily on just those things. Though one often hears that this or that writing is "frightening" to such an extent that the word is deadened in its impact when reading it or hearing it, "frightening" is truly the word to use here. However, that will be discussed later in a section devoted to anti-Semitism in the neo-Confederate movement. Here the focus will be on Conner's views on hate crimes. Every synagogue in the nation however should consider the risks to their security as well as that of any Jewish intellectual who isn't ultra-reactionary posed by the modern neo-Confederate movement. I am not however, suggesting that Conner would violently assault anyone, but other individuals might be inflamed by his writings.

In a section of one chapter, "The Liberal/Black Coalition Undertakes its Next Major Campaign: The Hate-Crime Laws." Conner explains:

> By the late 1980s, the black/liberal coalition's combination of attack campaigns in phase 2 had been so successful that the Jewish intellectuals/activists were ready to execute their master stroke: securing the enactment of comprehensive federal hate-crime laws.

This is in reference to what Conner sees as an attack on the South driven by "Jewish intellectuals." Conner claims:

> The real purpose of hate-crime legislation is to punish politically incorrect thoughts—initially, any dissent from liberalism's preachments re multiculturalism.

Conner references white supremacist Jared Taylor, publisher of the notorious *American Renaissance*, whose writings and books assert that African Americans are a menace to white people. Conner insists that hate-crime laws are meant to cover up the criminality of African Americans asserting:

> First, such laws can be used to conceal both the harsh fact that far more blacks commit crimes of violence against whites than vice versa, and the harsh fact that the percentage of young urban-black males who commit

violent crimes is now so high that many observers call into question the mental stability of the black race.

Conner recounts a history of anti-hate crime legislation claiming that these laws have an ulterior motive to protect Jews who have a fear of persecution in America:

> The hate-crime legislation that is ostensibly enacted to protect the blacks also provides equal protection to other designated "victim"-groups — including the Jews... the real purpose of the hate-crime laws is to protect the Northern Jewish activists ... against their fears of pogroms in America.

Conner sees anti-hate crime legislation leading to anti-hate speech legislation which Conner asserts is part of a long term deceptive campaign for political domination:

> It will be the culmination of a campaign begun by the Northern Jewish intellectuals in the 1920s ... And if the Northern Jewish intellectuals ... are given complete protection under law against whatever they may deem "hate speech," they will then be free to pursue any course of political action they may desire—and no one will dare question it. The Jews are perilously close to that point already.

Conner asks what might be the ultimate objective of this campaign and suggests that the momentum for hate crimes legislation is fed by a conspiracy led by Jews in the media:

> At this point we must ask ourselves two questions. First, why would the Jewish-controlled U.S. news media be so willing to distort the truth about racial violence so greatly, in order to obtain hate-crimes legislation?

As a possible answer Conner poses the question, "... are they the acts of a dangerously-paranoid people...?"

The author would like to point out that it isn't paranoia if some group is actually out to get you.

Besides arguing that hate-crime legislation is a secret Jewish conspiracy to dominate politics, this section of the book and other chapters in the book asserts in the most inflammatory language that there is a secret Jewish plot against the South. It is quite reasonable to be concerned that this book could lead some disturbed individual to commit an act of violence.

It also shows how the SCV efforts to offer for sale certain books could have a pernicious impact.

The ideology of violence is not just theoretical.

Recently on Dec. 17, 2015 the city council of New Orleans voted to remove Confederate statues and one monument that glorified violence in the overthrow of Reconstruction. As of the time of writing this chapter (6/25/2016) the city has not been able to get a contractor to submit a bid to remove the statues due to a campaign of intimidation and threats and the burning of one contractor's very expensive sports car. In one attempt to get contractors, the contractors requested that when and if they bid that they remain anonymous and be able do the work overnight due to threats.[260]

This should not surprise anyone that there would be a campaign of violence and intimidation. The ideology of terror is a core element of neo-Confederacy. The threats in New Orleans should also be understood as demonstrating how violence can be a tool in thwarting democracy. The path to undermining democracy can be done by voter suppression, but it also can be done through violence as it is being done in New Orleans right now and as it was done during Reconstruction.

VIOLENCE

11 DIVISION BY PREJUDICE

As mentioned earlier a small group of individuals desiring to direct society for the purpose of privileging themselves and dominating the general public would find it impossible to do so in a democratic society unless they executed some strategy to undermine democracy. Otherwise in a simple contest of numbers a small group would face the opposition of the rest of society whom this small group seeks to dominate.

There are several strategies available to accomplish this. However this chapter focuses on the neo-Confederate strategy of division by prejudice, in which the public is divided into groups and encouraged to be in conflict with each other and not united in support of democracy.

ANTI-FEMINISM

Mentioned earlier in this book was the *Southern Partisan* interview with Phyllis Schlafly over the defeat of the Equal Rights Amendment, and the *Southern Partisan* magazine article criticizing the passage of the 19th Amendment.

The neo-Confederate movement is opposed to feminism and denounces it relentlessly, but the author hasn't found an extended article devoted to systematically attacking just feminism besides R.L. Dabney's 19th century "Women's Rights Women."[261]

Often feminism is denounced along with other objects of neo-Confederate rage. For example, James Rutledge Roesch, the author of a recent online article (4/26/2016), "The Cause of Jackson is the Cause of Us All," posted online at the Abbeville Institute is enraged by the proposal to put abolitionist Harriet

Tubman on the front of the $20 bill and move Andrew Jackson to the back. Roesch argues that Tubman is historically unimportant, a "conductor on the mostly mythical Underground Railroad."

Abolitionists are denounced:

> Whatever the truth and justice of the cause for which abolitionists like Tubman fought, they were most certainly not conservatives in any sense of the word. Indeed, the abolitionists were the most fanatical Jacobins in American history, especially the militant wing to which Tubman belonged.

Feminism is also attacked. A Native American hero Wilma Mankiller is mocked along with the Black Lives Matter movement:

> Jackson was a famous war hero and a feared duelist, but he finally met his match at the hands of fainting-couch feminists who require trigger warnings when reading about history.

Roesch explains that he is consoled by the fact that Jackson won't be replaced by Mankiller or the "insufferable" Eleanor Roosevelt. Roesch also proclaims "Orange Lives Matter!" since he claims Jackson is "the sole Scotch-Irish figure" on American currency.

The theme of the article reveals itself later where we find out who the "Us" is in the title. Roesch writes that the American Left, which Roesch asserts has "glee" over the current redesign also has a plot to use immigration.

> As the Left's plot to elect a new electorate by disguising government-engineered mass-migration as mere 'immigration' populates America with people who admire Pancho Villa more than George Washington, can sing 'La Cucharacha' but not 'The Star-Spangled Banner,' and celebrate Cinco de Mayo over the Fourth of July, leftists have dropped all pretense and revealed their hate for America – specifically, white Americans and their history.

And in the conclusion Roesch sees the "politically correct charges" used against Jackson will be used against "other American heroes."[262]

Feminists are attacked as well as Hispanic immigrants, the American Left and abolitionists, as well as the Black Lives Matter movement, but the article itself is generally about white nationalism. It is like a lot of neo-Confederate writings, where a grab bag of different hostilities and prejudices are all thrown together.

Gottfried placement of the Fourth of July in opposition to Cinco de Mayo doesn't seem to make any sense. Cinco de Mayo is an American holiday started in California by Hispanics who supported the Union government and the Mexican resistance to the French invasion and were in opposition to the Confederacy and the French. It is only relatively recently that it is celebrated in Mexico for the benefit of American tourists. It is truly a home grown American patriotic holiday. I recommend to readers, *El Cinco de Mayo: An American Tradition*, by David E. Hayes-Bautista.

In "The Eternal 'Rebel Yell'," by Boyd Cathey published in 2015 online at the Abbeville Institute the struggled of the Confederate soldier is defined as a reactionary struggle against the modern movement for social justice including feminism.

> Once again, today, the call must go out for us to renew *their* struggle. This weary nation, eaten away by cancerous and alien philosophies—feminism, same sex ideology, egalitarianism, pseudo-"civil rights", "liberal democracy," statist centralization, and so on—will not survive as we have known it. [Italics in the original.][263]

In a 2000 interview with reactionary Marion Montgomery in *Southern Partisan* Montgomery argues that the world is God given and that "… the single parent family, hinges exactly the loss of an order of family in relation to givenness and a sense of tradition." The interviewer then comments, "So, in effect, the logical political extension of that, in a sense would be feminism, which is a revolt against God and the created order …" Montgomery replies "There is no question in my mind that the whole movement is a kind of dead end," and refers to it and deconstruction literary criticism as "destructive movements." This denunciation however is in passing in a general discussion of Southern literature and complaints about modern life.

The 1997 *Southern Partisan* interview, "Partisan Conversation: Elizabeth Fox Genovese," is focused on criticizing feminism. The article introduces Genovese as follows:

> Her call for a pro-family feminism and her redefinition of the term to include a role for men in society has wrankled [sic] the Feminist Industry as has her defense of the values of plantation women horrified the History Establishment.

Genovese's response to the interview questions are somewhat rambling and go off on tangents not related to the interviewer's question and it isn't quite clear sometimes what she is asserting.

The interview starts with a discussion of her efforts to keep two military academies, Virginia Military Institute (VMI), and The Citadel in South Carolina all-male including her court testimony on the VMI's behalf in the Shannon Faulkner case.

Genovese argues that the efforts to allow women at these schools are really attacks on men from less affluent families. *Southern Partisan* interviewer asks, "You said you weren't sure which the anti-VMI lawyers hated more, men or the South, What exactly did you mean by that?" Genovese doesn't answer the question. The *Southern Partisan* interviewer calls Shannon Faulkner's lawyers "carpetbaggers, riding in," and Genovese replied "They were bicoastal, Beltway DC Washingtonians, New Yorkers, and Californians." Feminists are criticized for their criticism of The Citadel's cadets' chivalry.

The interview then moves on to other issues. Genovese opposes abortion. She feels that mothers should not send their child to day care the first year after birth. Single motherhood is criticized, as is the depiction of the issue in the 1990s television show *Murphy Brown*, whose title character decided to have a child without getting married.

Genovese criticized universities that include what she calls "interest group education" naming, "Black Studies, Native American Studies, and Women's Studies," programs which she states are supported by persons "who like a very politicized curriculum" and Women's Studies, which she says, is inherently contradictory to the idea that gender is constructed.

Genovese wants to make divorce much more difficult so that married women don't have to work or have a career to fall back on for economic security in case of divorce.

Genovese states, "We certainly have a feminist *industry*," [italics in original]. She goes on to explain that women are impatient and should be content with the progress that has been made and women may not be in some professions because they don't want to be in them.

Genovese states, "Many people's lives have been so deeply rocked and destabilized," and that some men don't know what to do as a consequence. She claimed these are men who, "don't have codes to fall back on in their relationship to with women, who don't have clear guides about what their responsibilities are, and who may indeed feel they're losing out on opportunities and promotions because of women."

Genovese calls this situation with men, "A complicated morass, it defies talking about." However she does then talk about it stating, "For example, I don't know whether we're looking at an increase in rape, or an increase in reporting rape, or an increase in what we call rape."

Genovese explains she is against violence against women and rape, and then further states:

> At the same time, I'd probably be happier if young women did not feel themselves under pressure to go out and be sexually attractive to men in ambiguous situations because the message you're sending is that you want to be sexually attractive, then even if you don't want it, you may seem to invite more than you're ready to handle.[264]

The author half expected that Genovese in the interview was going to recommend that women blacken one or two front teeth.

Not to be overlooked are neo-Confederate Paul Gottfried's comments, previously mentioned, online at the Abbeville Institute that "Women students on our campus are now encouraged by the state to accuse male students of rape."

However, at this present time (6/26/2016) feminism is likely to be included in a laundry list of rage against social justice issues rather than subjected to a focused attack only on feminism.

ANTI-SEMITISM

To the casual observer the neo-Confederate movement would likely to seem not to be anti-Semitic. In the first issue of *Southern Mercury* Lewis Regenstein has a defense of the Confederate flag and relates the history of his great-grandfather Andrew Jackson Moses in the Civil War.[265] The Sons of Confederate Veterans sells online and in their book catalogs over the years the book, *The Jewish Confederates*, by Robert N. Rosen.[266]

However, the SCV's strong promotion of Frank Conner's intensely anti-Semitic book, *The South under Siege*, the prominence of Conner himself in the neo-Confederate movement (as described in the previous chapter on neo-Confederates and violence), and Conner's series of articles in *Southern Mercury* show not only how the SCV in its actions, effectively promotes anti-Semitic writing, intentionally or unintentionally, and how the anti-Semitism of this book isn't apparent in the SCV publications.

Compare these two passages. The first is from his Sept./Oct. 2003 *Southern Mercury*, article, "Where We Stand Now: And How We Got Here," Frank Conner states:

> Previously, anthropologists had routinely recorded the notable differences in IQ among the races; but at Columbia, a liberal cultural anthropologist named Franz Boas now changed all of that. He decreed that there were no

differences in IQ among the races, and the only biological differences between the blacks and white were of superficial nature. The liberals swiftly made it academically suicidal to challenge Boas' flat assertion. Meanwhile, the liberals in the media heaped special praise upon black athletes, musicians, singers, and writers – and treated them as typical of the black race. The liberals were creating a false image of the blacks in America as a highly competent people who were being held back by the prejudiced white southerners.[267]

Compare this to what he writes in his book, *The South under Siege*, on the same topic.

Until after the turn of the 20th century, anthropologists had routinely recorded genetic as well as cultural differences between races and ethnic groups – that being the whole point of anthropology. The highlighted differences among the races hand included those of intelligence. But as Kevin MacDonald points out in *The Culture of Critique*, a German-Jewish-immigrant named Franz Boas changed all that. At Columbia, Boas arbitrarily claimed that biological differences between races were miniscule – that environment alone shaped the behavior of the different races and ethnic groups (a la Rousseau). A number of other Jewish anthropologists swiftly adopted Boas' position; and soon the Jews dominated the field of cultural anthropology. As MacDonald points out, by 1915 the Jews had gained control of the American Anthropological Association; and by 1926 they were chairing the anthropology departments at all of the major universities.

Kevin MacDonald is a professor emeritus of psychology at California State University– Long Beach who has argued in several books that Jews deliberately undermine the societies in which they live as a survival strategy, and that as a groups they are opposed to Western values. He has written that Jewish support for immigration to the United States is part of their plan to subvert this country.[268]

In reading the *Southern Mercury* article and then examining Chapter 20 "Secular Humanism Wins," in *The South Under Siege*, you can see clearly that the *Mercury* article is a summary of a section of this chapter and the article in *Southern Mercury* substitutes "Northern liberals" for "Northern Jews." The *Southern Mercury* article doesn't reveal, at least to the author, Conner's anti-Semitism. Unless you managed to obtain a copy of Conner's book you would have no idea from the *Southern Mercury* review of the book or the advertisements in the *Confederate Veteran*, at least to the author, what the author considers, the anti-Semitism of this book.

In the book these two groups – "Northern Jews" and "Northern Liberal" – are referred to as separate and different. In a subsection titled, "To Gain Civil-Rights Protection Quietly for themselves, Northern Jewish Intellectuals Sponsor and Guide a Southern Black-Civil-Rights Movement During the Last Half of the 20th Century," Conner writes:

> The Northern liberals have been condemning the white South as the immoral discriminators against blacks since the 1830s. So the post-WWII white South – with its *de jure* segregation --- will make the perfect enemy in this case. The Northern Jewish intellectuals will portray the blacks as "black Jews" a brilliant and deserving race held back from success only by the straightjacket of Southern white discrimination.

Conner writes, "When we read between the lines of a number of texts written by, about, and for Jews, we see that their reasoning in the late 1940s ran more-or-less as follows:" Conner then asserts that "American Jews" are afraid to run a campaign "directly against the many anti-Semites among the Northern Gentiles, it could easily backfire, resulting in a marked increase in anti-Semitism. Some other strategy must be found."

This strategy Conner explains:

> First, by insisting that in business and social activities the overall society accept and respect and protect under the law the individual values and practices of each "victim" group – i.e., the blacks, the Hispanics, the American Indians, the Jews, militant women, and any other group that wants special status – the Jews then become merely one protected dissident group of many, instead of standing out all by themselves in lonely opposition to Gentile America.

Conner explains that this strategy will bring down the United States but the Jews don't care.

> ... The fact that if pluralism is implemented, it will Balkanize the U.S. – destroying both its stability and productivity – is of little concern to many Jews: they are fast on their feet; and they figure they don't owe the Gentiles anything.

There is another section with the title, "Northern Jews Wage All-Out Ideological Warfare Against the White South."

In the chapter Conner asserts that African Americans were incapable of a civil rights movement on their own, stating:

> Without the Northern Jewish intellectuals/activists to provide the funding, the guidance, and all-important media support, there would have been no 1960s Southern black-civil-rights movement.

Besides the directly stated racism in this book there are these indirect statements which imply that African Americans are too stupid to have run their own civil rights movement.

The chapter in its conclusion warns:

> Look well at the Northern Jewish intellectuals/activists, O South, for they – who by rights should have been your closest friends – are by their own choice your dedicated and deadliest enemy.

Conner concludes the chapter that he is going to examine the role of Jews in civil rights "in the following three chapters."[269]

It should be noted that the editor of *Southern Mercury* for this issue was Frank B. Powell III who is also the current (6/29/2016) editor of the *Confederate Veteran*.

"The South under Siege" was even rejected by major neo-Confederate publisher Pelican Publishing Company because of its content. The Sons of Confederate Veterans did not.

Sometimes an event will bring anti-Semitism to the surface. Thomas Fleming, founding board member of the League of the South, editor of *Chronicles* magazine for 30 years, and the person who came up with the idea of the League of the South, had this to say in 2006 upon the arrest of Mel Gibson and Gibson's reported drunken rage about Jews. Fleming is upset with *Los Angeles Times* reporter Zev Chafets article "Slurring More than His Words," when Chafets ridicules some of Gibson's statements.

In his column Fleming shares some of his thoughts regarding Jews stating:

> Whatever their role (minor) in the French Revolution, Jews were among the largest ethnic groups in the leadership of Marxist movements in Russia.

And:

> Liking or disliking the Jews one meets—or even liking or disliking them generally—is a matter of taste, preference, and upbringing. Most serious Christians, as a matter of preference and conviction, would rather spend time with other Christians. There would be something wrong with them if they did not … It is hard enough for Baptists to tolerate Lutherans and a

> bit too much to insist that they become matey with Jews who often despise their religion and their way of life

And:

> Theories of history are matters of fact and reason. The fact that so many troublemakers of the past 150 years have been of Jewish extraction—Marx, Freud, the Neoconservatives—is certainly no argument in their favor. Jewish "intellectuals" continue to be in the forefront of the movements that aim to destroy our religion and culture.

A little sectarian separatism is being thrown in for good measure.

Fleming emphasizes that, "Many Jews are fine and admirable people even if they reject my God, and many anti-Semites, Christian as well as pagan, are perfectly good people even if they allow their prejudices to overcome their religion."[270]

The League of the South (LOS) in its early years in the 1990s and 2000's didn't make anti-Semitic statements, in fact, in 1999, on a radio talk show League of the South President Michael Hill wanted members to know that Murray Rothbard, who Hill called a Jewish Libertarian, was a charter member.[271] However, as LOS President in 2016, Michael Hill has become very frank with his anti-Semitism.

In an article "Another Jew nominated to the US Supreme Court," posted on the LOS website, he laments that Merrick Garland has been nominated by President Barack Obama to the Supreme Court. Hill writes:

> If approved by the US Senate, Garland would be the fourth Jew on the highest court in the land. While Jews make up less than 2% of America's population, Garland's appointment would mean that they comprise 44% of the Supreme Court.[272]

In another article on their website, "What was World War II really about?" Hill states:

> … it was a war between Germany and International Jewry. Of course, the Bolshevik Revolution and subsequent Soviet governments were largely run by Jews (see earlier History Lessons). In other words, the former Czarist Russia had been taken over to be used as base of operations for worldwide Jewish interests via the spread of Communism into the rest of Europe (and eventually the world). Communism is a Jewish ideology and survival strategy.[273]

As of today (7/1/2016) the author can't provide any evidence of where this contemporary eruption of neo-Confederate anti-Semitism comes from. Was it always there and carefully hidden, only to come to the surface more recently, or was it a recent change or both?

The more immediate concern should be that an individual might believe in Frank Conner's assertion that Northern Jews are their deadliest enemy, that they have inflicted extensive damage on the South, and that such an individual might burst into a synagogue firing a weapon.

UNITARIANS

In 1998, Father Alister C. Anderson, SCV Chaplain-in-Chief, in the *Confederate Veteran*, in the "Chaplain's Comments" section, in his first column, gives forth six points of study for readers to pursue in next two years. One is as follows:

> Third: The major cause of the War for Southern Independence was ultimately theological. It was the great difference in the religious beliefs between the people of the North and South.

To support this assertion Anderson quotes a statement made by James Henley Thornwell in a speech which he finds in C. Gregg Singers' book *A Theological Interpretation of American History*[274]:

> The parties in this conflict are not merely abolitionists and slave holders – they are atheists, socialists, communists, red republicans and Jacobins on the one side and the friends of order and regulated freedom on the other. In one word, the world is the battleground, Christianity and atheism the combatants, and the progress of humanity is at stake.[275]

Another point for readers to learn is:

> Sixth: We should avoid referring to ourselves as Rebels. It was the Northern politicians who first called "our war" the "War of Rebellion." It was the radical Republicans who defined our ancestors as being Rebels. Our ancestors were loyal to the Constitution of the United States. It was the Northern socialists, communists, atheists, transcendentalists, abolitionists, rationalists, universalists, existentialists, utopians, materialists, Armenians [sic] and Unitarians who should be called Rebels.[276]

Armenians in this case doesn't refer to the nation of Armenia. Instead it a misspelling of Arminians and refers to a Protestant theology called Arminianism that rejects Calvinistic doctrines concerning predestination and whose leader was Jacob Arminius during the Protestant Reformation in Europe. Note that the Unitarians are specifically defined as usurpers of the Constitution.

Newly elected SCV Chaplain-in-Chief John Weaver, first *Confederate Veteran* "Chaplain's Comments," the official column of the SCV Chaplain-in-Chief, explains that the Civil War was a theological holy war.

> The war of Northern Aggression was indeed a war against Christianity. In his book, *A Theological Interpretation of American History*, C. Greg Singer states on page 83:
>
>> ... after 1830 there was a growing philosophical and theological cleavage between the North and South. While the North was becoming increasingly subject to radical influences, the South was becoming increasingly conservative in its outlook.

James Henley Thornwell quotation about the conflict is again quoted and Weaver explains that:

> When a section, a state, or a nation denies the authority, inspiration, and application of the Bible, it has set itself up for a cultural revolution with major consequences. The North did exactly this when it embraced Unitarianism, transcendentalism, and abolitionism.[277]

Weaver repeats the idea of the Civil War being a theological war and Unitarians being an element of the heretical North attacking the Christian South in a 2003 "Chaplain Comment's" column in the *Confederate Veteran*. Weaver contrasts a Christian South with an un-Christian North stating:

> The South has historically been known as the Bible belt. Why? Because it was the North that forsook Christianity, and went into transcendentalism, rationalism, and Unitarianism. The South clung tenaciously to the Word of God.[278]

C. Gregg Singers' book was originally published in 1964 by the Presbyterian and Reformed Publishing Co. during the Civil Rights movement, a second addition came out in 1981, and it is still in print. This idea of the Civil War being a theological Holy War or driven by theological differences has percolated in conservative religious circles and neo-Confederate ones.

In a Bob Jones University 1982 textbook, *United States History for Christian Schools*, a theological reason is mentioned in a list of the reasons for secession as follows: [279]

Religious Division – By 1860 the nation had already experienced division in its major denominations in its major denominational groups over issues of social reform, mainly slavery and suffrage. Baptists, Methodists, and others now became "Southern" or "Northern." Accompanying these divisions was a rise in Unitarianism, Catholicism, and Transcendentalism. Southern states, in what is even today called the "Bible Belt," saw themselves threatened by those holding these unbiblical beliefs, who were most numerous in the Northeast.

Neo-Confederate school text book *The War Between the States: America's Uncivil War*, edited by John J. Dwyer, George Grant, J. Steven Wilkins, Douglas Wilson, and Tom Spencer, also advances these ideas of a theological civil war with Unitarians being part of the heretical "North" against the South. This 685-page book is in its 3rd printing as of 2013. There is a Chapter 9, "Religion and Worldview I," about theological differences between "North" and South. In an attack on prominent 19th century revivalist Charles G. Finney in a special section, it opens with:

Both the abolitionist movement and later the Northern society that waged war against the South were powered with an engine rarely credited by historians for doing so – atheistic European rationalism. This potent philosophy collided with orthodox Christianity – in particular Calvinism – at nearly every point. For instance, rationalism fueled the Northern philosophical juggernauts of Deism and Unitarianism.

The section is a Calvinistic assessments of Finney's beliefs as a rejection of the Biblical truth and theologically in error and derived from rationalism concluding, "So rationalism, through both Christian and non-Christian philosophies, brought about the rejection of several pillars of Biblical distinctiveness."

Finney is condemned as enabling abolitionism. His beliefs supposedly helped cause the Civil War, "Charles Finney and his fellow revivalists succeeded in popularizing the concept of abolitionism among some in both the evangelical and mainstream circles, this is especially true in areas like western New York, Pennsylvania and Ohio, who would not otherwise be influenced by William Lloyd Garrison and his ilk. Indeed, theological differences became one of the great sources of the friction that led to war between North and South." Garrison was a leading 19th century abolitionist.

This attack on Finney isn't just an attack on Unitarianism. Finney was a major influence on American Christianity and his revivalism and thinking is a source of modern evangelicalism.

In the front page for Chapter 13, "Border States," is Thornwell's statement, previously quoted, about what the conflict was about.[280]

This book might be laughed at except it is in its 3rd printing. The primary editor John J. Dwyer was the editor of the religious newspaper, *Dallas Fort-Worth Heritage*, and has influence in conservative religious circles. The other editors of this book have some degree of prominence in reactionary religious circles.

Boyd D. Cathey, in his 2012 *Confederate Veteran* article, "The Land We Love: Southern Tradition and Our Future," reiterates the idea of the Civil War being theological. Boyd contrasts the "North" and South:

> In the South orthodox Trinitarian and Incarnational Christianity, in its various forms, has been and still is central to and pervasive in our society. ... While third and fourth generation Puritans of New York and Ohio began to veer into Unitarianism, transcendentalism, and heretical millenarian cults, the South's popular orthodoxy inhibited deviations and heterodoxy.

Boyd also sees this as a factor leading to the Civil War writing:

> Growing out of the reality of their religiously-grounded society, Southerners were – and still are – self-consciously "traditionalist." It was their defense of the legacy of their fathers – the customs, mores, usages, languages, and values they had inherited, as much as the economic warfare unleashed by the North – which propelled them to secession in 1860-1861.[281]

Most ominously was a book review in the Jan./Feb. 2016 *Confederate Veteran*, Boyd D. Cathey reviews "Cultures in Conflict: The Union Desecration of Southern Churches and Cemeteries," by Charles A. Jennings. The publisher given is Truth in History in Owasso, Oklahoma. This is the same publisher and city given for the book at the www.biblicalandsouthernstudies.com website.

Cathey's review states that in the book Jennings explains that "the Northern and Southern states were growing dramatically apart, not just politically and economically, but also religiously and culturally," and that "by the 1830s and 1840s, the South was becoming more conservative religiously and culturally, while in many areas of the North, the older Puritanism had evolved into Unitarianism and liberal evangelicalism."

Cathey then asks the question, "But how to explain the rage and sickening zeal of many Northern soldiers and the ravages they committed when they came South?" Cathey refers to the books forward written by Charles Baker stating:

> In his forward to the book, Dr. Charles Baker attributes this lapse into what was basically barbarism to the collapse of orthodox Puritanism and the increasing dominance of liberal Protestantism.

Cathey quotes Thornwell's statement about the true nature of the conflict as previously quoted in this chapter. The book thus makes the desecration of churches and cemeteries in the South, "barbarism," "ravages" done with "sickening zeal" due to the "collapse of orthodox Puritanism" which Cathey had also referred to as "the older Puritanism" having "evolved into Unitarianism and liberal evangelicalism."

The Truth in History web site currently (7/2/2016) has a web page article, "Jewish Hatred Against Jesus Christ." In another article, "The House of Israel and The House of Judah," asserts that the ancient Israelites weren't the ancestors of modern day Jews. Another article, "The Seventy Weeks of Daniel," explains the history of the persecutions of the Jews as the punishments by Jesus upon the Jews for their rejecting him and the destruction of Jerusalem by the Romans as another divine punishment.[282] At the Truth in History website Charles Jennings is listed as the contact person with the phone number matching the phone number in the *Confederate Veteran* review.[283] Also, earlier archived web pages at archive.org have Charles A. Jennings as the website author in the "About Us" description.[284]

Dr. Charles E. Baker was the Chaplain in Chief of the SCV in the early 1990s.[285]

The Truth in History website has listed this book on their website in the past and it can be found on archived web pages at archive.org. However, now you would not find it on the Truth in History website, but you will find it sold at the Biblical and Southern Studies website which was founded by Rondel Rumburg, past Chaplain-in-Chief of the SCV, and the editor of the *Chaplains' Corps Chronicles of the Sons of Confederate Veterans*, and is the editor of the 3rd edition "Chaplain's Handbook," for the Chaplains in the SCV.[286]

Boyd D. Cathey was on the Editorial Advisor Committee of *The Journal of Historical Review* of the Institute for Historical Review, according to an archived page from 2001.[287] According to Scott Miller, University Programs Coordinator at the United States Holocaust Memorial Museum in Washington, D.C., "The central institution of Holocaust denial in the United States is the Institute for Historical Review (IHR), located in southern California, and founded (with a deceptively scholarly name) by Willis Carto."[288]

The sale of this book as well as the book review could possibly introduce SCV members to the Truth of History publisher and possibly Truth of History's website's promotion of what could be characterized as virulent anti-Semitism without the book review referencing anything about Jewish people.

In regards to Unitarians, in being made historical villains whose religion resulted in "desecrations" and "ravages" done with "sickening zeal," it is entirely reasonable that someone might decide to avenge these alleged historical crimes with an act of violence.

MUSLIMS

The *Chaplains' Corps Chronicle of the Sons of Confederate Veterans*, Nov. 2006, has a short section, "Confederate view of Islam," to assert to the readers that there is, in fact, a Confederate view of Islam. The introduction to the section states, "Our Confederate compatriots saw the immense paganism and evil in false religions, and Islam was one of those that they viewed in such a way." The article then includes a set of quotes from pro-slavery theologians, with a note stating how each supported or fought for the Confederacy. R.L. Dabney states, "Mohammed extends the same hope to all his sinful follows." Girardeau is quoted, "Mohammedanism is the great apostasy of the East." Thornwell has a more lengthy attack, characterizing Islam as being swindle or racket, "Where it could not extort a blind credulity, it made the passions the vehicles of its doctrines; the timid it frightened to submission, the profligate it allured to acquiescence, and the heretic and skeptic it wheedled and cajoled by a partial patronage of their errors," and "its strongest attraction the license which it gave to voluptuous indulgences."

Someone might be critical of one religion or another. People make choices as to what religion they believe in and have opinions about others all the time. What is of interest here, however, is that condemnation of Islam is held to be a part of Confederate heritage.

In response to Minnesota Muslim Congressman Keith Ellison, an African American, taking his oath of office with a Koran owned by Thomas Jefferson, the *Southern Mercury* in 2007 ran an article by Ted Sampley titled "What Thomas Jefferson Learned From the Q'uran." The article is about the American war and victory over the Barbary Pirates in the early 19th century. Jefferson is supposed to have learned from his Koran that Islam is a danger, concluding, "Jefferson had been right. The 'medium of war' was the only way to put an end to the Muslim problem. Mr. Ellison was right about Jefferson. He was a 'visionary' wise enough to read and learn about the enemy from their own Muslim Holy Book."[289]

The current SCV Chaplain-in-Chief Ray Parker, Dean of the Master's Theological Research Institute of the MASTER'S International University of Divinity (The name of the university has "MASTER'S" in capitols.), has an editorial in the Feb. 2016 *Chaplain's Corps Chronicles of the Sons of Confederate Veterans* condemning "the culture of tolerance," asserting that those who are tolerant will get killed by Muslims as part of God's wrath against the tolerant.

> The great weakness of this culture of tolerance is that it denies the God of the Bible and falls under His wrath. Actually, Jesus Christ said, —He that believeth not the Son shall not see life; but the wrath of God abideth or remains on them. This culture has set itself up as judge and jury, but it will be destroyed by enemies from within. What enemies? Enemies they tolerate in their culture such as Islam! Why? ... They will be overwhelmed when they are lined up as cattle to be beheaded by their enemy for their moral decadence. When their protests cannot deter their enemy they will not know how to act. Why? They believe Islam is a peaceful religion...

Parker then discusses an act of terrorism in France. He criticizes the French who honored the dead with candles and flowers, rather than expressing hatred against Muslims. Parker rejects this stating, "Will flowers and candles protect you? Such reactions are the norm of a culture of tolerance. When such a radical Islamist goes to shoot you, just lift a flower in one hand and a candle in the other and all your problems are solved!"[290]

Parker revisits the topic of Muslims again in a June 2016 editorial *Chaplain's Corps Chronicles of the Sons of Confederate Veterans* discussing a defense of the Confederacy by Confederate Gen. D.H. Hill in the 19th century. Hill asserts that abolitionists were hypocrites. Then in reference to what I think is the massacre of church goers in Charleston by Dylann Roof Parker writes:

> But such hypocrisy has not ceased. For example, we are not supposed to judge Muslims by the myriads of atrocious acts (murders, beheadings, burnings, crucifixions, etc.) that they perform worldwide, but Confederate history, with its symbols, is supposed to be obliterated from history because of the action of one murderer who had a Confederate flag in his possession, but not a Confederate heart in his body.[291]

The Abbeville Institute also has articles which perceive Muslims as a menace. One example is Thomas Fleming who as former editor of *Chronicles* magazine ran a campaign of hysteria about Muslims in *Chronicles* for decades. His 2015 article at the Abbeville Institute, "From Under the Rubble: The Wearin' of the Cross," is a tirade against Muslims.

Fleming's article starts with a brief mention of "A Palestinian Muslim named – what else? – Muhammad kills five military men," and is upset that television ABC News focused on Muhammad's use of drugs. Fleming asserts that the murder was motivated by the Koran's teaching. Fleming writes:

As Srdja Trifkovic and others have shown beyond a shadow of a doubt, Islam is a religion of war, violence, and oppression. The only function of non-Muslims in their world is to pay taxes and endure oppression.

Srdja Trifkovic is a *Chronicles* writer and the author *of Sword of the Prophet: Politically Incorrect Guide to Islam*, and "*Defeating Jihad: How the war on terror may yet be won, in spite of ourselves.*

President Obama is portrayed as knowingly allowing Muslim immigration to make the United States an Islamic nation.

> What does it tell us, when we learn that under the Obama administration 400 thousand other potential Muhammads are arriving legally into the United States every year? ... He is getting the country he wants, a place where his Islamic friends and relations can be considered typical.

Muslim immigrants to the United States are held to be an instrument of terror like that of the French and Russian Revolutions, Nazi Germany and Maoist China by the ruling elite to oppress Americans .

> Our own regime has refined on their methods: Import dangerous people from Latin America and the Islamic world, fill their heads with nonsense about rights, and convince Americans that chaos and fear are normal, and they will surrender all that is left of their liberties to this new KKK–the KuKoranKlan.

And so on the article goes. The title is in reference to *Wearing of the Green* a poem by Dion Boucicault in reference to British oppression of the Irish. The implication is that Christians will be similarly oppressed. Fleming informs us that Dion Boucicault left Ireland to the United States. Fleming concludes the article with the question, "Where, now, would anyone go to escape cultural genocide?"[292]

In 2016 in a nation with anti-Muslim hysteria raging, these articles in SCV publications and elsewhere are just a few voices among many in a shrill cacophony. However, when presenting itself to the media, the SCV is usually perceived as a group with a sentimental interest in history that referenced as "heritage." The Abbeville Institute wishes to promote the romantic image of Southern cultural roots. These articles raise the question as to what the real agenda of the neo-Confederate organizations is.

HISPANICS AND IMMIGRATION

The *Southern Partisan* ran articles about immigration over the years in which immigration or immigrants, particularly Hispanic immigrants, are negatively portrayed.

In 2000 *Southern Partisan* editor, Christopher Sullivan, who in 2005 was Lt. Commander-in-Chief of the SCV, and in 2006 was Commander-in-Chief of the SCV, in his editorial, has an item, "Wild On New York," in which some Texas tourists were alleged to be sexually harassed by groups of young men attending the National Puerto Rican Parade. Sullivan quotes one of these tourists, "Is it normal to just turn the city over to those kind of people?" Sullivan alleges that crowds got out of control at the parade and the police failed to act because:

> In recent months the NYPD has come under attack for shooting people they shouldn't have. Some have even alleged that the police laid low during the parade in order to avoid the appearance of being too hard on the Puerto Ricans and other minorities. The unsurprising result was unbridled aggression.

Sullivan in this paragraph is asserting that Puerto Ricans have racist hostility towards whites and without being suppressed by the police, they will act with unrestrained aggression against whites. The media is alleged to be covering it up. Sullivan sees these Puerto Ricans as a consequence of the Union victory during the Civil War. He writes:

> Second, it is more than a little ironic that almost all of these attacks took place in a section of town known as Union Square. That's right, literally in the shadow of the statue of William Tecumseh Sherman ... we can see some of the fruits of his labors being played out.[293]

As usual with neo-Confederates, current issues are connected back to the Civil War.

Visiting the website of the SCV you will see "Education Committee Papers" including a category for "Hispanic Confederate Heritage," that includes a paper titled "Hispanic Heritage Month; Hispanics in Gray and Blue."[294]

In 2002, in the *Confederate Veteran*, in the section "Classic Southern Reprints," Patrick J. Buchanan's book, *The Death of the West: How Dying Populations and Immigrant Invasions Imperil our Country and Civilization* was offered for sale. The SCV caption for the book reads, "Bursting with facts, from which the reader can draw his own conclusions. Should be required reading for every American voter."[295] However, otherwise in the *Confederate Veteran* there wasn't commentary about immigration until sometime later in 2008.

The *Southern Mercury* on its masthead listed its publisher as, "Foundation for Preserving American Culture, Inc.," with the explanation that it is "An educational foundation of the Sons of Confederate Veterans, Inc." This is a publication to educate the members.

It is in this periodical that the SCV started publishing articles about immigration. In 2006 the *Southern Mercury* had an article, "The Tolerance Scam," by Michael W. Masters in which the concept of anti-racism itself is held to be a Marxist attack on Western Civilization. Masters describes immigrates as a menace. Of anti-racism, Masters writes:

> Using the wedge of anti-racism, cultural Marxists orchestrated judicial and legislative changes to society over the course of decades – e.g. Brown v. Board of Education in 1955, the Civil Rights Act of 1964, and the Immigration Reform Act of 1965. These supposedly noble triumphs quickly transmogrified into forced busing, the legalized reverse discrimination of affirmative action and an uncontrolled flood of culturally alien Third-World immigrants. The cultural Marxists relentlessly hammered away at Western cultural norms using the sledge of anti-racism as a battering ram to bring down the walls of traditional Western culture.

Masters claims that there is a double standard on racism and that minorities are unfairly exempted from being called racists. He informs the reader that "Black agitators openly call for the murder of whites and the rape and defilement of white women – indeed the genocidal extermination of the white race – with impunity." Mexican American organizations are held to be racist and working to break way a section of the United States to form the nation Aztlan.

Masters states, "But the worse is yet to come," and sees the destruction of Western culture in the United States with immigration. He wonders what will happen to the country when "Western people are no longer numerous enough to win elections?" Masters warns:

> A pattern of failure to sustain democratic forms of government is repeated all too often outside the West, from China and North Korea to Mexico and Latin America to the Middle East to almost uniformly bleak (and often murderous) landscape of post-colonial sub-Saharan Africa. Would America's current majority feel secure living in a country ruled by the liked of Idi Amin?

As an aside racists are always trying to portray Africa as a dangerous killing zone. Yet is it Europe that in about 50 short years had World War I, World War II, Hitler, Mussolini, and Stalin. It is Europe that has had gulags and concentration camps and the mass starvation of Ukrainians in the Holodomor.

Those who know Western history know that during World War II, modern Western modern democracy was in dire straits. Europe has demonstrated a pattern of failure to sustain democratic forms of government and the outcome of the 20th century might have been something else besides modern liberal democracy.

Masters sees a conspiracy behind the support for multiculturalism. Without mentioning the word "white" he essentially advocates a white nationalist politics against what he sees is a danger of non-white minorities, stating, "For too long the sword has hung over our head." That he would advocate such a politics is not surprising.[296] Michael W. Masters contributed articles to the *Citizen Informer* of the Council of Conservative Citizens and to *American Renaissance* a racist publication. The article in *Southern Mercury* appears to incorporate in shorter form two cover story articles which he contributed in 1995 to *American Renaissance*.[297]

In the April 2007 *Southern Mercury* are two articles about immigration. The longer article is "Immigration Around the World," by Lynda Sentell. Sentell poses the question, "why did immigration decrease in 72 countries between 1990 and 2005? Since 33 million of the 36 million total immigrations during this period occurred in industrial countries." She suggests that the answer lies in the review of the immigration policies and politics of the industrial Western nations and the article offers short reviews of these policies in each nation.

She claims that in each nation except the United States, elected officials and political leaders are taking strong stands against immigration.

She quotes Australian Federal Treasurer Peter Costello as warning immigrants "If those are not your values, if you want a country which has Sharia law or a theocratic state, then Australia is not for you." Sentell further writes, "Mr. Costello has raised the possibility of similar moves to deport people who are 'not comfortable with the way Australia is structured.'" In each of these nations Sentell describes a surging movement against immigrants and potential actions to restrict, reduce, or even expel immigrants. One such proposal she mentions is by Portuguese Prime Minister Jose Manuel of which Sentell writes, "Immigrant groups representing thousands of workers from Portugal's former colonies say this would lead to mass expulsions." Most of these nations invaded the world and this has been portrayed by the right as glorious. Now some people want to move to their country from former conquered lands and they are alarmed. Sentell fails to mention that Portugal's age of exploration was an effort to establish an international slave trade.

The review of policies in the United States doesn't mention any opposition to immigration, but focuses instead on the large number of immigrants entering the United States. Without stating a position on immigration, Sentell answers her introductory question, immigration is declining elsewhere besides the U.S. because of increasing opposition to immigration in the Western world. The U.S. is cast in contrast as having surging immigration and no significant opposition to immigration in contrast to these other nations.. The message is clear. The United States needs to become like the rest of the Western nations if it wants to reduce immigration and save its identity.

If the reader doesn't get the message, immediately following the article at the bottom of the page is a short item, "American Congressmen Speak Out on Immigration," quoting Rep. Tom Tancredo, Rep. Lamar Smith, Sen. John McCain, and Virgil Goode. It refers the reader to http://profiles.numbersusa.com for the voting records of members of Congress on immigration.[298]

In the same issue is an article, "The 'Sojourner' Argument: Scripture Texts Are Often Misused by Religious Communities to Advocate High Immigration," by Rev. Edwin Childress. It is reprinted from *The Social Contract* a publication in opposition to immigration.[299] The article is a Biblical refutation of a paper, "To Love the Sojourner," published by the United Methodist Church, which seeks to help immigrants. Childress states that the words "immigrant" and "immigration" are not in the Bible. He is according to *The Social Contract* the Deputy Director at NumbersUSA.com and a former United Methodist Church pastor.

Childress makes nominal statements of caring for refugees and helping immigrants come to the country, but he also makes it clear that refugees need to be returned, "Their temporary stay makes it possible for other refugees to sojourn here when necessary," and "Our ethic of caring requires that we not accept such a large number of annual immigrants that undermines the ability of workers to earn a decent living, harms the sustainability of the environment, and drains the best and brightest from their own nations where they can do the most good."[300]

He also indirectly argues for ethnic separatism. After describing the captivity of Israel in ancient Egypt and their return to the Holy Land. Childress writes, "God's intention all along was that Israel should remain so distinctive in Egypt that she would serve God's purposes in history. Is it still appropriate today to understand that nations possess a role in history and affairs of the world?"

Later that year in the August 2007 *Southern Mercury* had an article, "The North American Union May End Our Constitutional Republic," by Rev. Robert Slimp. The article opens with alarm that the U.S. Senate is debating a bill "which would grant amnesty to 12 to 20 million illegal aliens who are already in our country!"

The article asserts that U.S Rep. Ron Paul, R-Texas, "has proof of a secret meeting held in Waco, Texas" where a "North American Union" was planned and that it will be "become law by Presidential executive order or secret agreements." This alarms Slimp because this North American Union will end the border with Mexico, as he explains in the Glossary for the article, "Our Southern boarder will be that of Mexico and our northern border that of Canada's Artic north. There will be no need for borders because **anyone** can come and go freely." [Emphasis in original.]

Other assertions in the article is that The National Council of La Raza, a civil rights group, is a racist organization and, "they want to eventually start a new country in Texas, New Mexico, Arizona and California." Immigrants are alleged to not want to assimilate. According to the article "… many of those who cross our porous borders today have no desire to learn English or attend citizenship classes…"

A large part of the article is about a supposedly planned NAFTA (North American Free Trade Association) Superhighway and the need to stop it by having "Southerners" contact their representatives to stop it. Readers are urged to oppose certain legislation on immigration. Slimp writes, "If we are to avoid the loss of our sovereignty with the coming of the Superhighway, we must stop the Bush-Kennedy-McCain-Graham Immigration Bill in the Senate this summer!"

Slimp calls on members of neo-Confederate groups to fight, "Those of us in the Sons of Confederate Veterans, the United Daughters of the Confederacy, the League of the South, and other dedicated Neo-Confederates must continue to be very active and effective."

The article gives a link to congressional voting records on immigration at http://profiles.numberusa.com.[301]

What is interesting is that Slimp has the expectations that members of neo-Confederate groups would have an anti-immigration agenda.

An article, "San Francisco Promotes the Services for Illegal Immigrants," by Cecilia M. Vega which originally appeared in the *San Francisco Chronicle*, appeared in the 2008 *Southern Mercury*. It describes San Francisco's efforts to not enforce immigration laws and to have a campaign to inform the public of the policy. There is a quote from Mark Krikorian, executive director of the Center of Immigration Studies stating, "San Francisco clearly is going a step beyond most places in boasting [about] and advertising this. Most cities kind of almost apologize to their voters when they complain about it."[302]

What is of interest about all these articles is that an organization named Sons of Confederate Veterans has a publication with any articles at all about immigration policy. Why does a group dedicated to remembering the Confederate past have a position about immigration? Before the public, the SCV appears to be all about sentimental honoring of their ancestors and remembering history. In the *Southern Mercury* articles express a stridently anti-immigrant and anti-Hispanic hysteria.

In 2008 SCV Lt. Commander-in-Chief, and future SCV Commander-in-Chief, R. Michael Givens in his column "Report of the Lt. Commander-in-Chief" editorializes that the education of the membership is important and that he is going to be recommending to the SCV membership books to read. He then asks the question, "Why is this push so important?" He answers this question by telling that the South in danger and points to a *Newsweek* article "The End of the South," by Chris Dickey, son of James Dickey, who he calls a "scalawag" and an advocate of ideas that would destroy the South. Givens writes:

> What young Mr. Dickey is pressing is that if we would just give up our devotion to the past, we could be forgiven of our sins and embraced into the world of Marxist utopia. We could destroy all borders and make one North American nation from the Arctic Circle to the Panama Canal (Now, wouldn't that be grand). His article amounted to campaign propaganda for presidential candidate Barack Hussein Obama.

And:

> America has within her borders more than 20,000,000 illegal aliens. About 700,000 to 1,000,000 more cross our borders every year. I doubt that nary a one of these adventure-seeking nomads cares one iota for our Confederate and American heritage. All of our American institutions will be diluted right before our eyes.

Givens then assures readers that there is hope as long as the SCV has members who are dedicated to the *Charge of the SCV*. The *Charge of the SCV* is a formal statement of the purpose of the Sons of Confederate Veterans by former Gen. Stephen Dill Lee after whom they name their educational Stephen Dill Lee Institute. Confederate heritage and thus the purpose of the SCV is here defined as a position against immigration.[303]

Boyd C. Cathey in his 2012 *Confederate Veteran* article, "The Land We Love: Southern Tradition and Our Future," lists the means by which what he calls the "Second War of Northern Aggression," is being waged against the South for the purpose of "rejecting the principles and beliefs of our ancestors." One of these is "uncontrolled immigration polices favored by both political parties which dilute and submerge our native population."[304]

Chronicles magazine's campaign against immigration is endless. However a few articles stand out in their connection to the neo-Confederate movement and neo-Confederates embedded in the establishment.

John Shelton Reed has been called the Dean of Southern Studies and was one of the two founding co-editors of *Southern Cultures* periodical at the University of North Carolina. He was a founding writer for *Southern Partisan* who wrote articles for that publication under his own name and as J.R. Vanover. He wrote articles for *Chronicles* from 1982 to 1995.

John Shelton Reed in a 1989 *Chronicles* article, "Letter From the Lower Right: Allons, Enfants de la Patrie," is horrified by a multicultural Bastille Day Parade in Paris, France.

The article starts out Reed with having read an essay "Some Day in Old Charleston" by Donald Davidson who authored an essay about a parade in 1948 in which Davidson condemned drum majorettes. Reed explains that he originally didn't appreciate Davidson's essay. In seeing the 200th anniversary Bastille Day Parade in Paris produced by Jean-Paul Goude on television, Reed explains that he now appreciates why Davidson condemned the 1948 parade. Reed says Davidson's essay is about "perverting the beautiful" and that "I think I know what Davidson would have made of the French extravaganza." Donald Davidson was a Southern Agrarian and a racist crank, but I repeat myself. It is very likely that he would have condemned a multicultural Bastille Day parade. Reed is communicating to the reader that a condemnation is forthcoming.

Reed then goes on in his usual seemingly joking way to condemn the parade with various snide remarks. What really bothers Reed is the parade is "billed as The Festival of the Planet's Tribes" and has the theme of "the Rights of Man." What Reed then describes is the multiracial and multicultural nature of the parade which he sees as alien or repulsive. He notes in particular African floats, which he found particularly unappealing stating, "After all this the Florida A&M University marching band was downright homey as it moonwalked to James Brown's "I Feel Good." Which is to say that the parade was really so extreme such that it even made moonwalking by a marching band from an historically African American university homey. It is also interesting how he uses the Florida A&M University marching band as a reference point to explain how he found something really unappealing.

Reed comments on the parade:

> But the message it conveyed (to me at least) wasn't the upbeat, brotherly one Goude had in mind. The dim, smoky, pulsating scene pierced now and again by flashbulbs as if by lightning, the techno-primitivism, the

> Third World flavor—it was a lot like the New York subway at rush hour. (Sorry. Couldn't resist. Actually it was a nightmare vision straight out of Blade Runner, and it gave me the creeps.)

And:

> The African and Asian and Arab presence, as striking in the parade as it is these days on the streets of Paris, illustrated vividly France's colonial chickens coming home to roost.

This idiom of chickens coming home to roost means that a policy has resulted in something bad happening which to Reed is the presence of Africans, Asians, and Arabs in the parade and on the streets of Paris.

Reed then states that their presence "can be viewed with the fear and loathing of Jean Raspail's disturbing novel 'The Camp of the Saints'" or with the cheerful equanimity of a *Wall Street Journal* editorial." Reed states, "… I'm afraid I saw it as another half-million votes for the thuggish Jean-Marie Le Pen and his nativist National Front."

Camp of the Saints is a notorious racist novel about a flotilla of Indians reaching the shores of Europe and destroying Western civilization. Typical of Reed's indirect writing, the question not asked is why would the sight of Africans, Asians and Arabs participating in French national life, and celebrating Bastille Day, not be seen as a fairly good sign of assimilation by newcomers? Why should the parade instead lead to "fear or loathing" or provoke a person to join a racist political movement. What does Reed propose for the streets of Paris to get rid of this "fear or loathing? He doesn't say.

Reed writes, "'We're all from the Ganges now,' some of the less admirable characters in Raspail's novel chirp, and Goude seems to share that view." This statement implies that Reed shares Raspail's views.

Reed explains that "it was something of a relief" when he watched a military parade, in which "there was something clean and purposeful." Seeing so many minorities participating in a parade is evidently something from which Reed needs relief.

He concludes by what seems to be hinting at an apocalyptic race war in the future. He says that he now understands what Davidson felt and quotes him, "reminder, … that the processes of government, laboratory science, liberalism, and expertise must be depended upon sometime, somewhere, to reach a breaking point, at which breaking point the army takes over and the ancient battle begin once more," and that, "… after Goude's jour de gloire one can almost see Davidson's point."[305]

Jean Raspail's *The Camp of the Saints* is a loathsome novel portraying Europe overrun by Indian immigrants. In 1994 Reed in his list of recommended books in *Reason* magazine.[306] The *Chronicles* essay was republished in *Whistling Dixie: Dispatches from the South*, originally published by the University of Missouri Press in 1990. That press has published a fair number of books by neo-Confederates.[307]

Reed isn't some marginal member of society. He is a leader in the field of Southern studies and it is hard to believe his views weren't known about in that field, many of his books were published by the University of Missouri Press and he has been a significant figure in Southern nationalism and the neo-Confederate movement.

The cover title of the June 1999 *Chronicles* magazine was, "The Decline of the West: From the Alamo to Kosovo." This is issue covered what they saw as a decline from a fighting spirit from an earlier America. The issue also features the usual articles complaining about U.S. policy in the Balkans. William Murchison has his column titled, "Print the Legend: Retaking the Alamo" complaining about Hispanic rejections of the Alamo myth. Articles repeatedly connect the conflict in Kosovo to Hispanic immigration into the United States.

What is notable is a short item in the "Cultural Revolutions," section by Ronald F. Maxwell, director of the movies, *Gettysburg*, *Gods and Generals*, and *Copperhead*.

Maxwell complains that the West is preoccupied with Kosovo to the exclusion of a more immediate problem in America:

> Sadly for America, the southwestern United States could become a Tex-Mex-style Balkan powder keg in the not-too-distant future.

Maxwell projects a future in which the Southwest will be, as he sees it swamped by Hispanics, leading to violent "disaster." The United States instead of intervening in Kosovo Maxwell writes.

> … should be looking to our own country and its immediate neighbors, and seeking solutions for the generation now being born --- solutions that will spare them the agony of ethnic and sectarian violence or the scourge of civil war.[308]

Ron Maxwell was also interviewed in 2002 in the *Southern Partisan* for an issue with the cover theme "Gods and Generals" devoted to his movie with the same title.[309]

Donald Livingston is the founder of the Abbeville Institute. He is the speaker with a library of books behind him in the video at their website explaining the purpose of the Abbeville Institute. He has been a contributor of articles over the years to *Chronicles* magazine. He wrote, "We Are All Immigrants Now," in the Sept. 2001 *Chronicles* issue with a hysterical cover titled, "Strangers in a Strange Land," written in a horror font with a 1950s dressed white family looking over a landscape of an alien America.

The article is composed of Livingston's criticism of what he thinks is the over centralization of government, and the excessive size of the United States. He argues that America is an empire and adds commentary about immigration.

Livingston rejects the idea of the universal nation based on abstract principles as opposed to a nation based on ethnic origins. He writes:

> In the inverted world of American liberalism, the immigrant is more authentically American than those whose ancestors cleared the forests over 200 years ago and built the institutions, regions, peoples, and traditions. For the immigrant, America is naturally an abstraction, and he is encouraged by liberalism to think of it as reducible to a set of abstract principles – like a college student who thinks he has a good understanding of Shakespeare from reading *Cliff's Notes*.

Cliff's Notes are a series of pamphlets giving an overview of a subject or book. The title of the article refers to Livingston's argument that since most of the public believes in a United States based on abstract principles the general public resembles immigrants who also believe this and so the public in general are like immigrants who he claims don't understand the meaning of what he thinks is real Americanism.

Livingston sees immigration as a tactic of elites to destroy communities to centralize power.

> Empires have often used immigration policy for the purpose of centralization. The Soviets sought to eradicate the independence of the Baltic peoples through massive immigration, Tito followed the same policy in Kosovo, as China is currently in Tibet.

The United States he calls an empire. Livingston feels that the situation is hopeless and compares the situation to the Late Roman Empire and advocates the formation of separatist communities through secession stating, "Secession from a republic seems unpatriotic, but an empire is a different matter." Livingston doesn't say it directly but he is advocating the breakup of the United States into republics based on ethnicity.[310]

Chilton Williamson, in a January 2015 edition of *Chronicles* magazine, called the "Nation of Aliens: The *Chronicles* Immigration Issue," has an article, "The Revenge of the Confederacy," on the topic of immigration.

Williamson doesn't get to the topic of immigration until towards the end. The article first gives the standard neo-Confederate view of history. Williamson argues that the Civil War wasn't about slavery, but was a clash of different civilizations, and that preserving the Union, "prevailed over history, the Constitution, and social and political common sense." He states that Lincoln had "a bat in his stovepipe hat." Williamson believes in all the fictions of the Southern Agrarians, a reactionary literary movement in the early 20th century. The antebellum South wasn't about slavery but was some kind of agrarian society "grounded in nature and tradition," in contrast to an industrial "North."

Williamson describes what he believes were the destructive consequences of the Union victory in the Civil War:

> The result a century later was a country so culturally and politically grotesque that the New Left that developed subsequently in the vacuum created by the defeated traditionalist party was able to attack the United States from the left and establish itself as the sole effective opposition to the American political and cultural establishment that the unconditional surrender of 1865 had ensured.

These New Left radicals Williamson writes:

> … have adopted as their allies the scores of millions of angry and resentful foreigners, and the descendants of foreigners, admitted to the United States under the irresponsible immigration policies institutionalized by Congress at the behest of Northern industrialists in the second half of the 19th century.

These immigration policies Williams said are supported by "soft-minded churches" and "more or less vicious ethnic lobbies."

Note that Williamson sees the immigration problem starting in the "second half of the 19th century." Thus what he perceives as undesirable immigration evidently would include Germans, Scandinavians, Eastern Europeans, Southern Europeans, as well as modern immigrants from the rest of the world. Williamson argues that they are here for economic reasons only "or because, as Mencken said in another context, there is a warrant out for them somewhere else." H.L. Mencken was a famously biting journalist and author in the first half of the 20th century.

The result William writes:

Thus, the "Melting Pot" the North boasted of a century ago has come to resemble the brew being busily stirred by the witches Macbeth encountered on the heath, a writhing stew of snakes, toads, and eels, many of them poisonous and most of them an ecological threat to the native American habitat into which they have been thoughtlessly— and sometimes malevolently—introduced.

This "witches brew" Williamson explains "is the creation of the Union states that won the Civil War" and that:

For people whose hearts pump Confederate blood, a certain smugness is understandable, and even pardonable. Though their ancestors failed 150 years ago, Goliath has succeeded in destroying himself.[311]

Williamson sees Northern states as a witches' brew because of the immigration since the Civil War and thus the Confederacy is revenged. Also, implied is that Williamson sees himself as having a heart that pumps "Confederate blood."

Williamson was the editor of *Chronicles* magazine as of 2016. This was one of his columns prior to that job promotion.

This antipathy to immigration spills over into a resentment against soccer. Dan E. Phillips, assistant professor of psychiatry at Mercer University, has an article at the Abbeville Institute, "American Soccer Fandom as Cosmopolitan Affectation," published in 2014, attacking soccer fans. He writes, "I suggested that If Atlanta has self-respect left as a Southern city, then soccer should fail here as the foreign sport it is." He concludes the article with, "All us red-blooded yokels must fight its pernicious influence lest we be swallowed up by the cosmopolitan Borg." The "Borg" is a collective in the science fiction series *Star Trek: The Next Generation* which absorbs species into an ominous hive existence.[312] I wonder what Dan E. Phillips thinks of the movie *Concussion*?

MEXICAN AMERICAN WAR

In both the *Confederate Veteran* of the Sons of Confederate Veterans (starting in 2012) and in *UDC Magazine* of the United Daughters of the Confederacy (starting in 2004) there has appeared advertisements by the Descendants of Mexican War Veterans which was founded in 1989 in Dallas, Texas and had its first annual meeting in 1989 at the University of Texas at Arlington.[313]

The ad's headline reads, "Before Manassas, there was Mexico." Manassas is the Confederate name for a Civil War battle. The text of the ad reads"

Before the War Between the States leaders and troops got their start in the war with Mexico. Leaders like Lee, Jackson, Beauregard, Hardee, Johnson, and many of the soldiers they commanded saw action in the Mexican War.

The mailing address was in Richardson, Texas. The ad uses the neo-Confederate term for the Civil War and wants the readers to connect Confederate military leaders and soldiers to the War on Mexico.[314] Their current mailing address is in Garland, Texas.[315] Their publication is the *Mexican War Journal* with editorial advisors Dr. Gerald Saxon of the University of Texas at Arlington and Fellow at the Center for Greater Southwestern Studies and Dr. Anthony Knopp, professor emeritus, University of Texas at Brownsville.[316]

Abraham Lincoln denounced the war on Mexico. In the House of Representatives on January 12, 1848 he said, "The blood of this War, like the blood of Abel, is crying to Heaven against the President of the United States!"[317] Ulysses S. Grant, Union General who defeated the Confederacy and later president of the United States, called the Mexican American war, "one of the most unjust ever waged by a stronger against a weaker nation. It was an instance of a republic following the bad example of European monarchies, in not considering justice in their desire to acquire additional territory."[318] This sentiment was shared by many Americans at the time of the Civil War and by sensible historians since.

Regardless of what nonsense might be taught in Texas schoolbooks, Mexico abolished slavery throughout the Republic of Mexico except the Isthmus of Tehuantepec in Sept. 15, 1829, which alarmed the slave holders in Texas.

Neo-Confederate support for the Mexican American War has deep historical roots.

American slave holders abhorred the multiracial republics of Latin America. John Randolph of Roanoke, a hero to neo-Confederates today, made a long condescending and mocking speech about the Latin American republics in the U.S. Senate in 1826 when the United States was invited to a Congress of American States for the hemisphere, made a point of these republics having some degree of multiracial equality.[319]

Jefferson Davis praised an audience in an 1858 speech in Portland, Maine for keeping themselves racially pure unlike, "Among our neighbors of Central and Southern America, we see the Caucasian mingled with the Indian and the African. They have the forms of free government, because they have copied them. To its benefits they have not attained, because that standard of civilization is above their race."[320]

The United Daughters of the Confederacy celebrates Jefferson Davis as the chief hero of the Confederacy and have done so for generations. They have a Jefferson Davis gold medal for historians and awards named after him. They claim he was a great American patriot and one reason they give is that he fought as an officer in the Mexican American War. One example is an article, "Jefferson Davis at Buena Vista and the War With Mexico," by UDC Historian General Mrs. E.F. McEntire, (Juanita B.), for the June Program history program for the United Daughters of the Confederacy.

McEntire remembers the Alamo but the topic of slavery is nowhere to be found in the article. The origin of the war with Mexico is alleged to have been confusion as to the extent of the Louisiana Purchase and whether it included Texas and the Mexicans refusing to negotiate over the purchase's borders.[321]

The neo-Confederate movement sees the Mexican American War as just and Confederate leaders were heroes of that war. This celebration of the aggression against Mexico can't but have an antagonizing effect. It is history, and it should be remembered, but it should be remembered like another terrible American injustice the Philippine-American War.

LGBT AND THE CONFEDERATE FLAG AS AN ANTI-GAY FLAG

Neo-Confederates take pains to claim they aren't racist. They claim the existence of Black Confederates and assemble lists of Hispanic Confederates to have a Hispanic Confederate heritage. However, they are openly anti-LGBT (Lesbian Gay Bisexual and Transsexual). The attacks on LGBT in neo-Confederate writings are extensive.

The hostility towards LGBT exists in a framework of neo-Confederate ideas that the Civil War was a theological war of a heretical "North" against a Christian orthodox South.[322] The Confederate armies were conceived as being religious Christian armies that held religious revivals. Neo-Confederates today see themselves as continuing this struggle against anti-Christian forces. The Confederate flag is held to be a Christian symbol. The following are four examples of how prominent individuals in the SCV sees itself as an army of God fighting cultural wars.

SCV Chaplain-in-Chief Alister C. Anderson writes in his "Chaplain's Comments" in the *Confederate Veteran* magazine in 1999 that among the SCV members "there is an expanding intellectual awareness that the War for Southern Independence was a war for religious and theological independence as well as political and economic freedom." The SCV members "hunger for a spiritual union with the faith of our ancestors." Supporting the Confederate flag, "[advancing] the colors of the Confederacy," is not just for their ancestors, but also to "be a healing to the moral sickness of so many people and institutions of our beloved Republic." That is, Anderson is asserting, the efforts to defend and promote the Confederate flag is part of a religious effort to fight immorality.

Evans urges that the SCV members "emphasize the religious aspect of our brotherhood." He asks that members fast one meal between meetings and contribute the funds saved to defending the Confederate flag.

In the conclusion Alister asks the SCV members "to remember that we are soldiers in the Army of God and are organized along the lines of our solider ancestors." Explaining the purpose of this Evans, said, "I ask you to remember that the spiritual discipline within our brotherhood is crucial for the survival of our Republic in these dreadfully immoral times."[323]

Frank Conner in a 2004 *Southern Mercury* article, "Reorganizing the Sons of Confederate Veterans," writes "Right now we have neither the structured organization nor the fighters needed to engage our enemies in the culture war and win it." Conner explains what the issues are in this "culture war." In a section, "Step 3: Basic Training for the Culture War," Conner explains, "Very few know why the enemy is attacking us, and what our Confederate heritage is that we are supposed to be defending."

Conner to remedy this he proposes::

> The first training program will teach each SCV member what his Confederate heritage is the Protestant-based conservative belief system, and the set of values and way of life resulting from it, which were the essence of the Old South …

Conner explains further, "It will teach each SCV member why a people possessed of that viewpoint would (and will) demand and get good (constitutional) government, and maintain a moral society …"

The second training program he proposes is to teach the membership that the South has been under attack by "Northern liberals" since 1830. Jews aren't mentioned.

Conner is defining what "Confederate heritage" is – a right wing reactionary agenda – and he asserts that fighting for this agenda should be the purpose of the SCV.[324]

Another example of some of these ideas are presented by SCV Chaplain-in-Chief Mark W. Evans in his column "Chaplain's Comments. " One of those columns, titled, "Battle for Truth," was featured in 2010 in the *Confederate Veteran* magazine. He explains that "Our Southern ancestors had reverence for the Bible," and "remained steadfast in orthodox Christianity." In contrast Evans states, "false teachings took deeper root in the North in the South," and "Erroneous theories flowing from the Northeast were especially troublesome. One wave of heretical teaching followed another…" Evans explains how the rejection of what he considers "orthodox Christianity" leads to Deism, Unitarianism, and then to Transcendentalism.

Evans states that abolitionists were believers in these heretical theories and to get public acceptance were advocated for things like world peace, prison and labor reforms, and women's rights "with self-righteous zeal." Evans writes, "Their godless enthusiasm reached a pinnacle when they demanded the immediate elimination of slavery." This implies that their reform efforts were "godless enthusiasm" but not the peak of them.

Both Benjamin Palmer and James Henley Thornwell are quoted as saying that the struggle against slavery and the Civil War was about atheists, socialists, etc. against the "friends of order" and "religion." The Confederate army "startled the world with valor and military prowess. Undergirding the heroes of the Confederacy was a clear conscious before god." Evans gives an account of one soldier's faith in Christianity.

Evans writes, "Now, almost 150 years later, ungodly thinking has taken our land to the brink of destruction. It is time to return to the truths of God's Word." He quotes the Bible, "If God be for us, who can be against us?" Evans is calling on the SCV membership to fight against "ungodly thinking" today as the Confederate soldier fought against enemies of religion in the Civil War.[325]

Evans in 2011 authored for the *Confederate Veteran* magazine an article "Christian Warriors" as part of the SCV Chaplain-in-Chief column, "Chaplain's Comments." The title refers to the leaders of the Confederate army, in particular Confederate generals Robert E. Lee and Thomas J. Jackson as being Christian Warriors. Evans sees the purpose of the SCV as being to advance the cause of the Confederate Army in present day politics.

> As Sons of Confederate Veterans we maintain and defend our heritage. The principles motivating our ancestors came from the Bible. We need the same teachings spread through our land today. Our country is in danger from Marxism, humanism, atheism, secularism and other anti-Christian movements.[326]

The SCV has a *Charge* given to them by Confederate general Stephen D. Lee in an address to them in 1906. The origin of the exact text of the *Charge* has been a subject of some inquiry but there is a fairly standard text that has been used by the SCV for generations as a statement of their purpose.

The *Charge* is as follows:

> To you, Sons of Confederate Veterans, we will commit the vindication of the cause for which we fought. To your strength will be given will be given the defense of the Confederate soldier's good name, the guardianship of his history, the emulation of his virtues, the perpetuation of those principles which he loved and which you love also, and those ideals which made him glorious and which you also cherish. [327]

Boyd D. Cathey in 2012 in the *Confederate Veteran* magazine in an article, "The Land We Love: Southern Tradition and Our Future," opens his article with the discussion and full quotation of the *Charge*. He asserts that the General Stephan D. Lee's Charge isn't just about defending the Confederacy and secession stating:

> … but also of defending – the "perpetuation" of – the "principles" and the "culture" of the Southland: a set of beliefs, customs, traditions, a way of life.

Cathey then states, "What were these 'principles' General Lee refers to?" The essay is about explaining what these "principles" are with expectation that the SCV membership will support these "principles." The essay is an in depth summary of neo-Confederate ideology developed in the 20th century referring to conservative Richard M. Weaver of the University of Chicago and M.E. Bradford of the University of Dallas and drawing on sources going back to the Civil War. It focuses defining a reactionary South of hierarchy in opposition to egalitarianism and the civil rights movement. However, I will examine what might more directly impact LGBT.

Cathey says that the essay will explain, "… just how we differentiate ourselves from folks in the rest of the Federal union." One differentiating feature of the South according to Cathey is its "Christian religious orthodoxy," he states the South is "Christ haunted" quoting Flannery O'Conner. Cathey states, "Our Southern society is an outpost of Christian civilization." He states that because of "surrender to modernism by most mainline churches … our Southern way of life has come under increased attack." He laments, "In today's America to be an orthodox Christian in the traditional family is bad enough …" and defending the Confederacy is even more difficult. In closing he describes a plan to defend the Confederacy and Southern conservatism which includes being more politically active and also get into cultural fields to produce pro-Southern films, literature, music, etc. This is to be inspired by hope from "our orthodox Christian faith."[328]

What these four examples show is that the SCV isn't just a historical society with a sentimental attachment to the Confederacy. It is a group in which leading members see as, or should be, mobilized to fight culture wars, to be an army of God, not just to defend the Confederacy but fight for a reactionary agenda hostile to democracy in the present.

A key symbol of this struggle is the Confederate battle flag. In the 2010 *Confederate Veteran*, in "The Official Page of the Youth Enhancement Committee," is an article "Something to Intrigue the Mind: The Message in the Confederate Battle Flag." The message is, "The RED field represents the Blood of Christ Jesus. The WHITE boarder represents the Protection of God. The BLUE "X" represents the Christian Cross of Saint Andrew…"[329]

The Confederate battle flag is often asserted in the neo-Confederate movement to be a Christian symbol with a Christian cross of St. Andrew. Historically this is not true. Confederate general P.G.T. Beauregard gave to the Southern Historical Society a copy of a letter from Confederate Congressional Rep. William Porcher Miles, who was the chairman of the Congressional committee over the design of the Confederate battle flag concerning its design. These two were involved in designing the Confederate battle flag, Beauregard submitted to the committee two flags one with an upright cross and one with an "X" cross like you see on the Confederate battle flag.

In the letter of August 27, 1861 Miles writes to P.G.T. Beauregard explains why he choose the "X" version, "It avoided the religious objection about the cross (from the Jews and many Protestant sects), because it did not stand out conspicuously as if the cross had been placed upright."

Further Miles writes, "Besides, in the form I propose, the cross was more heraldic than ecclesiastical, it being the saltire of heraldry, and significant of strength and progress (from the Latin *salto*, to leap)."[330] This decision to avoid a Christian meaning is also explained by Beauregard to in an 1872 letter to the office of the New Orleans and Carrolton Railroad Company in which he writes, "but Colonel Walton's had the *Latin* cross, and Colonel Miles's the *St. Andrew's* which removed the objection that many of our soldiers might have to fight under the former symbol." [Italics in original.]

However, the historical record is never much of a barrier, if at all, to neo-Confederates when they want to believe something.

What might this neo-Confederate army of God think about LGBT.

The 4th Quarter 1996 *Southern Partisan* magazine had an article on how the Confederate flags were Christian flags published during the controversy over the Confederate battle flag being flown over the South Carolina capitol. The issue included a proclamation, "The Moral Defense of the Confederate Flag: A Special Message for Southern Christians." This was written when "Fifteen ministers representing a half dozen denominations worked with the editors of Southern Partisan in preparation of this statement." It was released in a press conference on Dec. 11, 1996 and co-signers were solicited. It was written "In the spirit of *The Address to Christians* (1863)," which was a defense of the Confederacy sent out by Confederate clergy during the Civil War. [Italics in original.]

In a section, "The St. Andrew's Cross," the article states, "It is important to emphasize that the Confederate Flag itself is a Christian symbol. It is based on the St. Andrews Cross, familiar in the wake of the movie *Braveheart* as the flag of Scotland" and "The X-shaped cross in both flags is also the Greek letter *chi* which has long been a Christian abbreviation for 'Christ.'"[Italics in the original.]

The article then has a section titled, "Confederate Flags As Christian Symbols," in which it refers to some Confederate flags having a Latin cross and others with words referring to God were stitched to Confederate battle flags. There were a lot of flags for regiments or particular armies which were not the Confederate battle flag or were modifications.

The article then has a section, "The Theology of the Flag – Old and New," which states the idea of the Civil War as a theological conflict and other sections, "The Cause of the South," and "The Shared Scourge of Political Correctness," that explain that the cause of the South is a reactionary agenda against "Political Correctness." An example given is a "liberal media makes its fashionable case" for "the normal nature of same sex marriages."[331] The Confederate flag is thus defined as an anti-LGBT flag.

This idea of the Confederate flags as Christian symbols had prior advocates, but with this proclamation and its release in the *Southern Partisan* it was widely disseminated in the neo-Confederate movement.

The SCV advocates the idea that the Confederate flag is a Christian symbol. SCV Chaplain-in-Chief H. Rondel Rumburg in the 2005 *Confederate Veteran* in his column "Chaplain's Comments," explains:

> The Confederate Flag stood for more than States Rights. Although it stood for that, it stood in the ultimate for the Triune God of the Bible, and the fact that 'the truth shall set you free.'"

He also explains, "The flag with Andrew's Cross (X) on it had two major aspects: it was symbolic of the Christian faith, as well as being identified with the origin of the people." Rumburg is arguing that the flag design is because the South was predominately Scots-Irish.[332] Rumburg's idea that the Confederate battle flag represents the ethnic origins of the South is nonsensical, but is a part the newer neo-Confederates theories of the Celtic origins and behaviors of white Southerners. The documentation of the flags origins has no reference to ethnicity and it can been seen that the flag was designed to be as broadly acceptable as possible to Confederate soldiers and not oriented to any one group. Additionally, the ethnic mythology of the time of the Civil War was that the South were the cultural inheritors of "Cavaliers" and the North were the cultural inheritors of the "Roundheads," both English groups. Lost Cause advocates have bragged about being more Anglo-Saxon than the North for generations.

Rumburg is the author of *Confederate Flags Matter: The Christian Influence on the Flags*, 2015, SBSS Press, Appomattox, Virginia. It is a book dedicated to arguing that the Confederate flags are Christian symbols. As mentioned earlier he is the editor of the *Sons of Confederate Veterans Chaplain's Corps Chronicles*.

Recently, in the Nov./Dec. 2015 *Confederate Veteran* Boyd D. Cathey in defense of the Confederate flag states:

> The Battle Flag bears a traditional Christian "saltire," the St. Andrew Cross, which has deep historical roots in Scotland, Spain, Burgundy, and Russia and in Christian iconography.[333]

With members in the SCV imagining that that the SCV is or should be a Christian army of God, like the original Confederate Army, and it could be asked what is their attitude towards LGBT people?

J.D. Haines, a Brigade Commander in the Oklahoma Division of the Sons of Confederate Veterans, has an article in 2006 in the *Southern Mercury*, "The Problem With Teaching Tolerance." According to Haines is that it leads to the abandonment of morals. He writes, "Teaching tolerance lies at the root of many juvenile behavioral problems in America today." Gaines states, "America is on a course of moral decline similar to that seen in the Roman Empire." He explains:

> The goals of teaching tolerance include denouncing racism, sexism and homophobia. In the school system's zeal to stamp out intolerance, the old-fashioned virtues have been lost, particularly if they are Christian values. Not killing, stealing or lying and honoring parents, for example, have taken a back seat to promoting the rights of minorities, females, and homosexuals.

He asserts that parents are confused because school prayer is not allowed, but schools "teach that homosexuality is an acceptable lifestyle."[334]

SCV Chaplain-in-Chief, Cecil A. Fayard, Jr. in his "Chaplain's Comments: America Is in Trouble Part 1," in the 2009 *Confederate Veteran*, states "God is not mocked" and so there will be consequences, "for whatever a man soweth, that shall he reap." And he lists what is going wrong with America which includes "We have sown immorality." Fayard states:

> We live in a very loose society, a wicked nation morally. All types of unspeakable and deplorable acts are being committed by deviant men and women.

And:

> Public schools teach our children how to practice various forms of immorality. One school curriculum teaches acceptance of homosexuality in the first grade and mutual masturbation in junior high.[335]

James Ronald Kennedy and Walter Donald Kennedy in the 2014 *Confederate Veteran*, contributed a lengthy article, "Our Re-United Country?: The Sad Reality of Reconciliation," that asserted that the South is oppressed and the United States is an empire without states' rights. In a section, "Political Subjugation – the Price of Reconciliation," they complain, "Even when the South enjoys a small Congressional victory – such as the Defense of Marriage Act – the ruling elite of the Federal Empire merely elect to refuse to enforce laws which are contrary to its interests."[336] This refers to the U.S. Supreme Court overturning the Defense of Marriage Act as being unconstitutional.

SCV Lieutenant Commander-in-Chief Thomas V. Strain Jr., in his "Report of the Lt. Commander-in-Chief," in the Sept./Oct. 2015 *Confederate Veteran* expressed anger that Dylann Roof's massacre in Charleston resulted in the Confederate flag being removed from the Confederate monument on the South Carolina capitol grounds and that the Southern Baptist Convention (SBC) called for the flag to be removed. Denouncing the SBC he declared, "The simple truth of the matter is this – while the SBC was worrying about the removing the Confederate Battle Flag from the Confederate monument in Columbia, the United States Supreme Court, in a five to four decision, decided that every state had to observe same sex marriages without regard to their own laws, or their own constitution."[337] Strain was elected SCV Commander-in-Chief of the SCV in 2016.

However, it is in the *Chaplain's Corps Chronicles of the Sons of Confederate Veterans* where SCV members are the most open about their hostility towards LGBT. Each camp, the local unit of the SCV, has a Chaplain, and there are chaplains for state divisions of the SCV as well the Chaplain-in-Chief for the whole SCV. This publication is distributed as a PDF and its online. It provides direction to the SCV as to religious values.

H. Rondel Rumburg is the editor of the publication and in his editorials his scathing hostility to LGBT is very evident.

In 2007 issue of the *Chaplain's Corps Chronicles of the Sons of Confederate Veterans* Rumburg writes in an editorial, "Scapegoating the South: Apologizing: the Result of Scapegoating," feels that the South is unjustly treated. This which his rejection of apologies:

> One of the horrendous results of scapegoating is the rash of apologies for the past being given to the supposed offspring of slaves, Indians, Mexicans, etc., by the supposed representatives of people long dead. Presently the legislature for the State of Virginia is hammering out an apology to the Indians, Africans, etc. for supposed wrongs done in the past by white Protestant Christians.

Rumburg feels instead these politicians "need to confess their own offenses to God" one of which Rumburg explains is that they are, "… guilty of protecting sodomites, thus spreading AIDS …"[338]

Rumburg in the 2009 *Chaplain's Corps Chronicles of the Sons of Confederate Veterans* laments that "Deconstructionists" have taken over educational institutions in the South, and "The result has been disastrous. There has been an enthroning of sodomy as a preferred lifestyle …"[339]

However, it is in a 2013 issue of the *Chaplain's Corps Chronicles of the Sons of Confederate Veterans* that Rumburg really explodes over LGBT rights. He states, "Now we have become Gemorrah's cesspool."

Rumburg asks, "Was your soul vexed over the latest Supreme Court ruling or the Boy Scout vote to include homosexuals?" If it was vexed over these things Rumburg states that the person is like Lot in the bible in regards to "Sodom." Rumburg quotes Pat Buchanan that "The new Americans … have replace the good country we grew up in with a cultural wasteland and a moral sewer that are not worth living in …"

Rumburg recounts the Biblical story of the destruction of Sodom and Gomorrah, and makes references to the Bible and states that God punished "the angles that sinned" and drowned the "old world" with a flood in the account of Noah. He believes that God is going to punish America and that "the wicked shall be turned into hell." One reason given is:

> America, is abandoned because she has given herself up to homosexuals, deviants, and perverts. They now have a role in all branches of

government. They may yet be in the minority but they are given the priority!

The "three branches of government" are denounced because, "They have masterminded this evil!" Rumburg then discusses how God might punish America because "it could be some other method than fire and brimstone." He lists "bubonic plaque or Black Death," "terrible disease," "tidal wave," or "cataclysmic event."

The SCV may argued that it is "Heritage Not Hate," but some of their members certainly want their membership to know that heritage is homophobia.

The neo-Confederate movement's hostility towards LGBT goes back to the modern movements beginnings.

James Ronald Kennedy and Walter Donald Kennedy in *The South Was Right!* asks if the government is just, "Can we say that this government, which has given us forced busing and demanded equality for homosexuals and communists in our classrooms, is doing the will of the people of the South?"[340]

The *Southern Partisan* magazine from the very first issue in 1979 and into the 21st century had numerous attacks on LGBT from small snipes in short items to entire articles.

The 1979 *Southern Partisan* inaugural issue, included a sarcastic complaint that the National Endowment of the Arts through the Coordinating Council of Literary Magazines gave "your" money to *Gay Sunshine*, *Gaysweek*, and *Sinister Wisdom* (a Lesbian magazine), and further complains, "… not to mention magazines dedicated to one or another 'minority' – Blacks, Indians, Women …" In another article in the issue, "Mom," Thomas Fleming complains about what he sees as the horrible breakdown in traditional gender roles, and in regards to the women's movement he comments, "… the harridans and homosexuals who make up that leadership of 'the movement.'"

A typical snide remark is the *Southern Partisan* reply to a 1986 letter to the editor about the historical accuracy of a picture of a Confederate general whether the pine trees were Southern or Californian, and how beneficial it would have been for the Confederacy to have gotten hold of Californian gold. Part of the *Southern Partisan* editor's reply to the letter is, "Unfortunately, not many of our men made it that far west. If they had, those boys in San Francisco would be dating girls and eating grits instead of quiche."[341]

In a July 2005 *Southern Partisan* published an unsigned article about the shortage of children in the public schools in San Francisco. The article sees the problem due to the presence of LGBT in the city. The article asks, "As for heterosexual parents, how many of them want their children to wander down the streets of a city glutted with sexual deviants known for their attraction to the young?" The article says that if the mayor really wants to bring children to San Francisco "he'll have to rid the city of homosexuals." To do this the article suggests:

> Maybe he should get a piper to lead them out of town – not a Pied Piper, since "pied" means "patchy in color" – but a Pink Piper, wearing a tutu and just a touch of rouge and lipstick."[342]

The editor of this issue is Christopher Sullivan, later Commander-in-Chief of the SCV.

However, the attack on gays in the *Southern Partisan* could be without any attempt at so-called humor and with deadly serious intent against LGBT.

In the 2003 *Southern Partisan*, P.J. Byrnes has an article, "A New Strategy to Fight the Gay Rights Movement," in which he proposes to use health legislation to go after the LGBT community. Byrnes explains that due to the change in public attitudes moral arguments such as "'hate the sin, love the sinner' are strategically flawed." He recommends, "In combating the gay rights movement in the political arena, we should approach homosexual conduct as a public health issue, not a moral one." He argues, "As a public health issue it is easy to defend sodomy laws." Byrnes argues that Acquired Immune Deficiency Syndrome (AIDS) is a compelling health issue with its costs and deaths. He concludes:

> With such an approach, defenders of traditional prohibitions against buggery would never have to spend time reassuring public officials and the rest of the world that they weren't bigoted or homophobic or religious zealots.[343]

In the 2004 *Southern Partisan*, in an essay, "A New Christian Right," P.J. Byrnes, he calls for a new Christian Right movement that is uncompromising and hard edged. One of the reasons Byrnes gives is the success of the LGBT movement, he states:

> Its anti-family, anti-Christian, anti-American agenda has swept the country. Homosexual activists have gotten everything they've demanded, including a Supreme Court green light to sodomize each other, special legal protection, and same-sex "marriage."

Byrnes also repeats his proposal on how to go after LGBT:

Homosexuality is best attacked as a public health issue. Homosexual behavior has resulted in over a half a million dead from AIDS and has cost American taxpayers billions of dollars every year. We need a non-religious, high-profile, pro-family lobbying group to confront weak-kneed politicians Washington.

He suggests not to have it led by religious leaders and to not use moral or religious arguments, but instead, "The scientific and medical evidence, if used properly, is more than sufficient to stop the gay movement dead in its tracks."[344]

If the reader thinks that this strategy is fanciful and couldn't be successful, they should know that there is already an effort underway to ban sexually explicit materials under the guise of health laws. If they prove successful the Christian Right would be very likely to pursue this "health" strategy against LGBT.

There is a lot of this shrill hostile rhetoric towards LGBT in the neo-Confederate movement and it would be a very long review to go over it all. However, one southern nationalists' writing needs to reviewed as an example of how LGBT is attacked by academics involved in the neo-Confederate movement. John Shelton Reed has been called the dean of Southern Studies. The University of Missouri has published many of his books, he was a founding co-editor of *Southern Cultures* published by the Univ. of North Carolina Press, and he was published extensively in southern journals.

Reed was in California at various times from 1986 to 1991. During that period Reed wrote about California in *Chronicles* magazine. He trashed the state. In a January 1986 issue he ridiculed Marin County in Northern California and then Southern California, concluding, "Look. If we can't secede, can we kick them out?"[345] In a 1991 Chronicles column mostly about the fiftieth anniversary of *The Mind of the South* by W.J. Cash, Reed, living in California ridicules San Francisco because they have "something called the National Sexuality Symposium." He jokes that he thought of asking *Chronicles* magazine for the fee to go and report on it, but jokes, "... but then I figured Tom Fleming doesn't really want me discussing the techniques for extended orgasm or erotic film making in these pages, much less whatever was said at the workshop on S&M for beginners." He also snidely states, "I am sorry to have missed the 'erotic costume ball'" and that he "had this *great* ideas for a costume." [Italics in the original.][346]

In another 1991 *Chronicles* article, "Hotel California," he spends time on how he finds California "strange in strange ways." He concludes that he would be happy if California was a separate country, stating, "But I don't like the idea that one American congressman in eight comes from here. I don't like to be held responsible as an American for what Californians do ..."[347]

It becomes apparent in reading Reed's *Chronicles* columns that though he is hostile to a region that is not very restrained by reactionary ideology it is the freedoms that LGBT have found there that really bothers him.

In a 1986 column with short items, he is upset that anti-smoking laws have been pioneered by San Francisco "the home of Sister Boom Boom" where the Democratic National Convention is scheduled to meet in 1984. (Sister Boom Boom was a drag performer who wore nun regalia, and who engaged in protests, often at political events such as outside the 1984 DNC, with a group called the Sisters of Perpetual Indulgence.) He states, "Leave it to the modern Democratic Party to meet in a city that regards smoking – and little else – as a crime against nature. Mama always said that you don't have to drink and smoke to have a good time, but I don't think San Francisco is what she had in mind." What the author sees as Reed's bigotry is often expressed in the form of a joke.[348]

However, it is Reed's 1988 column, subtitled, "Reservations Required," in *Chronicles* that really shows his fear of California as a place where LGBT might achieve civil rights leading to civil rights for LGBT everywhere in the United States. It isn't towards the end of the article that the reader realizes that the sinister title isn't about restaurants but internment camps for LGBT.

The column describes his visit to California and he says snide things about Marin, Berkeley, and San Francisco, but he focuses on gay men in San Francisco as the topic. The column starts out that he ate California cuisine which is evidently okay since he was in California and because he was a regionalist, and that such a restaurant would be okay in North Carolina, "… if it were plainly just another kind of foreign restaurant." However, Reed complains, "The problem with California stuff is that it won't stay exotic."

After explaining how beautiful the Bay Area is, he gets into the topic of the column, "But man is vile in ways that are downright startling to a boy whose vices run to S&D (smoking and drinking.) Of course, even without its most notorious deviants the place would be strange." Reed notes that the there is a large number of gay men in San Francisco, and that they are organized as a community, making the city, "the Rome, the Moscow, the Salt Lake City Of Inversion." [Capitols as in the original. "Inversion" is a 19th century term for homosexuality.]

Reed points out that the public in general has recognized that San Francisco has a large gay community and sees it damaging to its image. He jokes, "Even Rice-a-Roni, "the San Francisco treat," is getting nervous—dropping that tag, I read, apparently because market research has found that many now associate the words San Francisco with buggery and death."

Whereas Reed sees male homosexuality everywhere in San Francisco he is puzzled that his friends don't, writing:

> The strange thing is that my San Francisco friends don't seem to notice, either. It's not so much that they're tolerant as that they've become desensitized; they seem just to tune out the ubiquitous evidence of the homosexual presence. I really don't want to gross readers out here: let's just say that the kind of thing that gives sodomy a bad name is hard to avoid.

Reed seems to find vindication in the AIDS epidemic writing that gay men are defined by their sexual activity and "have in common its consequences, so something else they share, now, is the shadow of death from AIDS." This epidemic, Reed argues is just "theoretical" in North Carolina. Reed comments that in San Francisco, "Obituaries presented a steady drumbeat of young lives cut short: the wages of sin, to be sure, but a dirty trick on those who believed in the promise of sexual 'freedom'". Reed jokes about the ads advocating that condoms be used, writing, "although of course the only safe sex is with a faithful partner, and they say a good man is hard to find."

Reed fears LGBT political action, "Homosexuals' continuing fear of persecutions, however well-founded, has led them into some strange and even deadly political behavior." This "deadly" behavior is that they are "like some ethnic minorities, bloc-voters …" Reed says that this makes San Francisco politicians "grovel" to gays and notes "… the extent to which its homosexual population is treated with at least the semblance of respect…"

Reed re-states his fear that "Californianisms do seem to be contagious." He suggests "setting one or two American cities aside as something like reservations has a lot to be said for it…" And concludes, "Reservations haven't worked very well for Indians, but some such settlement may be the best of the bad choices we've got in this troublesome case."

Despite having written this column Reed seems to try to position himself as a neutral observer on the question, and says that he might later write about having reservations for LGBT, and feels that he will be "abused" by "people who think homosexuality is an abomination" and "those who think it's just an alternative life-style."[349]

However, besides this article, other items in Reed's writing show him to be as hostile as in this article, however seemingly joking he might express himself.

An example is a 1986 *Chronicle* column he writes about the refusal of the Southern Methodist University student union to recognize a LGBT organization. He quotes the rejection of the group by the student government that the proposed group, "is inconsistent with the goals, purpose, and philosophy and religious heritage of a Methodist university." Reed comments, "Does that mean it's wrong?"[350]

In 1990 *Chronicles* articles Reed writes in reaction to U.S. Senator Jesse Helm's wanting to deny funding for arts of which he didn't approve, including the art of photographer Mapplethorpe. Reed writes that he, "snuck off (in the interests of science) into Mr. Mapplethorpe's notorious photographs – and wish I hadn't." Commenting that it would "bend an impressionable young mind out of shape," he states, "Even I picked up a few images that will be with me for a while." Reed thinks Helms "chickened out" because he just wanted to deny funds for the exhibit. Reed states that "I'd shut it down and put an armed guard on the door."[351]

Fear of African American male sexuality has been a central element in white racist American thinking including that of neo-Confederates going back early into the 19th century if not before. One can only imagine the horror to Reed a Mapplethorpe exhibit could be.

The neo-Confederate movement has a hostility against the LGBT community which would deny their ability to exist except as persecuted individuals. It would behoove many LGBT to give up their plantation lullabies that seem to occupy their imagination, stop being *Gone with the Wind*, stop making excuses for the Confederacy, and reject the Confederacy.

12 DIVISION BY PREJUDICE: AFRICAN AMERICANS

The Confederacy was an attempt to preserve slavery and white supremacy. Afterwards the whole point of glorifying the Confederacy and its leaders was to preserve white supremacy. It would take a very long book to review the entire history of the attempts of neo-Confederates since the Civil War to maintain white dominance and political control. Some historical background will be given to provide a context for the more contemporary neo-Confederate efforts.

The 40 volumes of the *Confederate Veteran* published from 1893 to 1932, official publication of the United Confederate Veterans, Sons of Confederate Veterans, United Daughters of the Confederacy, and the Confederated Southern Memorial Associations, seethes with racism.[352]

In the Dec. 1916 *Confederate Veteran*, there is reprinted an address by Judge C.C. Cummings, historian of the Texas Division of the United Confederate Veterans (UCV) made to the convention of the Texas Division of the UDV. In the address Cummings makes a proposal to ship all African Americans to Africa. Part of his speech is about the Bible and the division of the races and segregation. Asians are held to be the result of humans interbreeding with "lower forms of life." This is a long quote, but it needs to be read to fully know the crazed racism of those who glorified the Confederacy.

> History is philosophy of teaching by example; and when we turn to the tenth chapter of Genesis we see where Father Noah got tired of trying to have his three sons live in peace together, and he then divided the known world among the three. To Ham he assigned Africa; to Shem, Asia; and to

Japheth, the elder, he gave a double portion by the right of primogeniture, and Europe and the isles of the sea fell to his share.

This was the first attempt at race segregation. But race amalgamation followed between Shem and Ham on the plains of Mesopotamia. They built great Babylon and the Tower of Babel, and race friction followed and confusion of tongues, and they were dispersed. The second experiment of race segregation, being under divine guidance, yet obtains. We read that in the midst of this race mixture the divine voice called Abraham into a strange country and separated his seed from the rest as a witness for all time of the steady influence of the one God over all pagan gods. After undergoing bondage under Ham for a time about equal to the bondage of Ham with us, Shem came out into the Promised Land. Now in the great war going on in Europe we expect to see the world again divided as old Father Noah did at first, and each son must return to his own—Shem back to the Promised Land, Ham back to Africa—all under the supervision of Japheth, whom Father Noah decreed should be so enlarged.

Another attempt of amalgamation was made by Japheth; and confusion ensued, as it ever must in race mixture. Japheth when he crossed over to his portion in Europe divided, and a part of him trekked westward over the Himalayan Mountains of Western Asia, amalgamated with lower forms of life, stagnated into castes, and so remains to-day non-progressive. The other part traveled to the northwest of Europe and has ever refused race mixture, but now stands out as the great white race which dominates the civilization of the world.

The South took up Ham as a savage and through "slavery has lifted him to his feet as a man. If he is the man he is claimed to be, he will hearken to the cry of 150,000,000 of his kind and go over and help them.[353]

Below is a 1903 article by *Confederate Veteran* editor S.A. Cunningham. He is upset that President McKinley invited African American Booker T. Washington to the White House for dinner. Notice the comment about "the distinctive color odor." Also, from this essay you can see where the expression "Solid South" comes from. "Negro" was not capitalized in the original. The title is spelled exactly as it was in the *Confederate Veteran*. Yes it is a lengthy quote, but I want to demonstrate with just two of these two of these articles the shrill racism that was part of the neo-Confederate movement in the past. Neo-Confederates when called out for their racism like to say that they are being quoted out of context knowing that the entire article can't be quoted without copyright violation. None of these articles in the old *Confederate Veteran* are copyrighted.

M'KINLEY, ROOSEVELT, AND THE NEGRO

The Southern people will remain "solid" on the race question. The most clannish of them are not fearful of disturbance upon that point. They conceded that their Northern fellow citizens may not realize the necessity of white supremacy and that good men among them, in undertaking to disturb the natural relations, deserve prayer from knowing not what to do.

All the world remembers how the South grieved in the death of McKinley, and how her people respect his memory. They cherish his noble utterance in behalf of caring for the graves of the Confederate dead, and are comforted in the memory of his Christian resignation when shot down by an assassin. They prefer to remember these things to his early official acts. It may be well, however, in this connection to review his administration on the negro question. Elected by as partisan a class as any of his predecessors, and misguided as much by that question as any of them, began appointing negroes to office in spite of the protestation of white people directly concerned. This emboldened the negroes to think that the bottom rail would indeed be on top, and they became more insolent than ever. The sin of it was so demonstrated in Wilmington, N.C. to note a single illustration, that the white people of that noted, conservative city determined, in spite of the power of the United States or all the world, that they would not submit to the outrages being there perpetrated. It was so bad that the white ladies could not walk the streets in safety. The wife of a merchant, for instance, was accosted by a burly negro, who walked up close by her on a public street and said, putting his face close to hers: "Won't you kiss me darling?" Public meetings were held, defiant speeches were made, and an organization was publicly perfected to annual the acts of the President of the United States. The men bound themselves by their sacred oaths to submit no longer, and blood ran in the streets.

These things induced the good McKinley to pause and consider his course on that subject. Impatient negroes held mass meetings and condemned the President. One of the speakers at such a gathering in the national capital demonstrated the animus of his race by saying that he "would concentrate those issues into one McKinley neck" and he "would hold the razor to cut the jugular vein."

The Spanish war coming on just then, men of the South rallied as promptly as those of the North to fight the battles of the United States, and the negro problem ceased to be considered. It is well remembered that McKinley did not further meddle with that question.

In the succeeding national campaign, McKinley's election was not regarded as the usual calamity in the election of a sectional and a partisan President, and many Southern people were not displeased that the remarkable leader of the "Rough Riders" in the Spanish-American war was ticketed with him. For his many admirable qualities that they had much hope that should he occupy the Presidency, Roosevelt would be a non-partisan, and that the deplored sectionalism would be obliterated before the patriotic soldiers of the Union and Confederate armies had all answered their answered their last call. The last-named class is at least equally as anxious for it as the former. The most opportune conditions possible were anticipated. President Roosevelt had the best opportunity that has ever occurred to restore primitive relations to the country. His versatility, his integrity, and his independence might have made him the most popular President that ever occupied the White House in the memory of any now living; but the worst mistakes are being made, and the writer voices the sentiments of many millions, surely, in expressing sorrow and anguish in the Booker Washington incident and for other events that have followed on the race question. Aside from the principle issues, those who know President Roosevelt personally -- those who have been fascinated and charmed by his qualities of good fellowship -- are the more grieved.

Surely his best friends should importune him to pause and mediate upon human imperfections. He has not the power, and the armies can't be made large enough, to force into the kind of subjection he seems to desire the white people of the South who were compatriots of his noble ancestors and their children.

These expressions are not of sectional consideration, but from a principle as old and as deep as the creation of white and black --- and the distinctive color odor. Let every possible influence be brought to bear with the President for the good of all people, black as well as white. Let his friends in the South be diligent to communicate with him upon the disastrous and grievous results that will come of playing with unquenchable fire.

It is our due to the President to state that his Southern blood induces our people to be much more exacting, and these remarks are as a plea to him rather than a criticism to injure.[354]

The article refers to a race riot started in Wilmington, North Carolina, in 1898, when local whites violently overthrew the local government in a black-majority city. A former Confederate officer, Alfred Ward Waddell, led 500 white rioters who attacked the offices of the *Wilmington Daily Record,* an African American-owned newspaper. Waddell was provoked by an editorial in the *Record* that attacked the hypocrisy of whites who justified the lynching of black men because they supposedly had a propensity to rape white women, while whites remained silent when white men sexually sexually assaulted black women. The rioters burned *Record*'s offices, forced an unknown number of African Americans to leave town, and murdered fourteen. Waddell's mob then forced the Republican-controlled city council to resign and illegally replaced it, with Waddell installing himself as mayor. Cunningham also referred to when President Theodore Roosevelt, on October 16, 1901, hosted African American educator Booker T. Washington for dinner at the White House, which provoked a huge backlash among Southern whites who accused the president of promoting racial equality. Senator Benjamin Tillman of South Carolina proclaimed that white men in the South would "have to kill a thousand niggers to get them back in their places."

One shrieking quote after another could be taken from the old *Confederate Veteran*. Also, it was understood in the old *Confederate Veteran* that the Confederate soldier was fighting for white supremacy.

In the 1925 *Confederate Veteran* U.S. Congressional Rep. John E. Rankin spoke at the battle field of Brice's Cross Roads. The speech opens with, "We are gathered to-day upon sacred ground. This hallowed spot was consecrated by the blood and sacrifices of the noblest army that ever followed a flag."

Rankin later makes it clear what they sacrificed for and what made this "sacred ground."

> Slavery was not the cause that actuated the soldiers of the South in that dreadful conflict. We are all glad that human slavery has disappeared; but the dread of the horrible alternative which some of our opponents would have imposed—that of placing the negro upon terms of social and political equality with the white man—aroused the latent indignation of the Anglo-Saxon South and called forth from the deep wells of human nature the most powerful resentment that ever inspired a human soul to willing sacrifice or battered down the barriers of self-restraint.
>
> Not only would they have placed the negroes on equality with the whites, but some would have placed them in control. To-day, the sons of those men who sixty years ago preached the doctrine of a black South, tell us that the South, with its pure American stock, its high ideals, and its inflexible fidelity to the great principles upon which our civilization rests, will someday be called upon to save this republic.
>
> Our people had before them at that time the horrible examples of negro insurrections in Haiti and Santo Domingo, where the blacks had revolted and put to death, in the most cruel and unspeakable manner, the white

men, women, and children of those unfortunate provinces. Such wanton cruelty was applauded by the opposition and was cited as conclusive evidence of the negro's fitness for self-government. Some of them even proclaimed that he had proved himself superior to the white man. Sixty years have passed away, and the negroes of Haiti and Santo Domingo have lapsed into a barbarism that would shame the jungles of darkest Africa. With three hundred years of training behind them; with a modern civilization thrust upon them; with a government already organized; with the sympathy and encouragement of the civilized nations of the earth; in a land extremely rich in climate, soil, and resources; with every possible advantage that could be laid at their feet—the negroes of Haiti have gradually drifted back into savagery, voodooism, and cannibalism, until to-day it requires the constant guard of American Marines to save them from themselves and to protect them from one another.

Yet those misguided individuals who advocated a black South would have had the world believe that the Confederate soldiers, who were fighting against those and similar possibilities, were doing so merely to maintain the institution of slavery.

A lost cause! You have won the great cause of white supremacy, by which alone our civilization can hope to endure![355]

Another arguments of the neo-Confederates is that the Ku Klux Klan in the 20th century gave the Confederate battle flag a bad reputation. However, the neo-Confederate groups in the early 20th century repeatedly emphasized that the Ku Klux Klan of Reconstruction was the heroic effort of Confederate soldiers and that the Ku Klux Klan of Reconstruction was Confederate heritage.[356] Some examples are at www.confederatepastpresent.org, a web page of primary historical documentation to demolish neo-Confederate mythmaking.

In any Ku Klux Klan revival the members of such a revival would imagine themselves as being Confederate because neo-Confederate groups had taught them that the Ku Klux Klan to be Confederate and so they would fly Confederate flags, and did not see themselves as appropriating them.

Also, during the 1950s in the newspaper *The Citizens' Council*, published by the White Citizens Council, you can see that the Confederate battle flag is understood to be a symbol of white supremacy by mainstream white Southerners. You can read all six years of the newspaper at www.citizenscouncils.com.

It isn't until later that suddenly various historical myths are concocted to argue that the Confederate flag is "Heritage not Hate," when significant efforts get underway to get rid of Confederate symbols in the 1980s and racism was no longer respectable.

Charles Lunsford appears to have popularized the slogan "Heritage Not Hate." In 1994 in the *Southern Heritage Magazine* he wrote an article on why he resigned as the Chairman of the Sons of Confederate Veterans Heritage Defense Committee. To defend the Confederate battle flag in South Carolina he worked with the notoriously racist Council of Conservative Citizens (CCC) in 1993 and in 1994 he spoke at one of their rallies in South Carolina. He calls the group "respected." This apparently got him into trouble with the SCV Commander-in-Chief Norman Dassinger. What is really interesting in the article is this statement by Lunsford.

> In a conversation with the Commander in Chief, he stated that his only concern was that I not use my SCV title when speaking to outside groups.

According to the article Dassinger isn't concerned that the chief of their heritage defense is working with the Council of Conservative Citizens, thinks it is a great organization, "only" that, the SCV not be associated with the group. When Lunsford finds out that Dassinger has given an ultimatum to a Chaplain General of the Military Order of Stars & Bars (MOSB) to resign from the CCC, Lunsford writes, "This was the final straw, I submitted my resignation as Heritage Chairman."357 However, Lunsford claim of a purge of Council of Conservative Citizens doesn't accord with the historical record. There continued to be overlap between the two groups.

The slogan "Heritage Not Hate" was popularized by a person who thought the Council of Conservative Citizens was "respected" group and wanted to work with them.

The neo-Confederate movement started with the agenda of white supremacy and it is not some recent agenda item because of some change in the SCV as has been alleged. There have been periods in the SCV past where they have been explicit in their racism and there has been periods when it appears they have decided that it would be strategic to be discreet about it and it appears the racism is kept off-stage, but it appears to have always been there.

Just a few examples are necessary to prove this point. Readers are directed to other resources such as www.confederatepastpresent.org, www.citizenscouncils.com, and the books, *Neo-Confederacy: A Critical Introduction*, and the *Confederate and Neo-Confederate Reader*. For further examples of neo-Confederate hostility against African Americans. The author is one of the editors of both books. Articles written by the author can be found at www.templeofdemocracy.com.

DIVISION BY PREJUDICE: AFRICAN AMERICANS

No Citizenship for African Americans

The SCV offers for sale reprints of *The Legal and Historical Status of the Dred Scott Decision*, by Elbert William R. Ewing originally published in 1909 by the Cobden Publishing Co. available for sale online at the SCV website, in at least six SCV merchandise catalogs since 2004, and in their publication *Confederate Veteran*.[358] It was offered in the SCV Merchandise Catalog 2013-2014 which was an insert in the Sept/Oct. 2013 *Confederate Veteran* but without a caption.[359]

The book defends the infamous Supreme Court decision handed out by Chief Justice Roger B. Taney in the Dred Scott case in 1857 before the Civil War which declared that "the black man has no rights that a white man is bound to respect," and denied that African Americans could be citizens.

The book quotes attorney John F. Denny in support of Taney, "Can it be that the Constitution binds so loathsome an excrescence to the vitals of any State? If so, that charter has certainly failed to secure some of the chief benefits for which it was formed…"[360]

Taney in his court opinion repeatedly states that the framers of the Constitution did not intend that descendants of Africans to ever become citizens. Thus the prestige and respect of the American founders, and the origin story of the American nation, is applied to deny the descendants of Africans citizenship.

It was no surprise to the author that neo-Confederates would defend the Dred Scott decision, but it was curious of all the obscure racist books of the 19th and 20th century that the SCV could choose from, they would select this one for sale and sell it year after year. The racism of the neo-Confederate movement is like a cluttered room and in examining one thing the importance of another thing can be overlooked. It wasn't until the author was organizing his notes for this chapter the significance of this book and its ominous importance became apparent.

The sale of Ewing's book in itself, and in conjunction with the neo-Confederate's long campaign attacking the legitimacy of Fourteenth Amendment to the Constitution seems to be about denying African Americans citizenship in the United States. The Fourteenth Amendment negated the Dred Scott decision. By making everyone who was born in the United States a citizen, it thus granted African Americans citizenship regardless of state laws. It also prevents the formation of any hereditary class of individuals in the United States without citizenship.

If the Fourteenth Amendment was made void and the Dred Scott decision held to be valid African Americans would not be citizens of the United States and would have as Chief Justice Taney stated, "... no rights that a white man is bound to respect." It is generally understood that one of the purposes of the Fourteenth Amendment was to make the Dred Scot decision void.

A campaign asserting that the Fourteenth Amendment was illegitimate and it was done with wrongful intent lessens its prestige and credibility and makes it much more vulnerable to repeal or modification.

Anti-immigration activists have called for the Fourteenth Amendment to be amended so that being born in the United States doesn't confer citizenship. The question has to be asked if a birth certificate showing that a person was born in the United States doesn't make a person a citizen, then what would be the requirement for citizenship? If the requirement was that one of the parents was a citizen then the question is then was the parent a citizen and on what basis? Citizenship could be a genealogical project. What classes of people would likely have resources to do genealogical documentation? The Dred Scott decision could possibly apply. If the Fourteenth Amendment was up for modification the nation would have politically fallen into the hands of racists and lunatics. The recent attempted voter suppression schemes in the South and elsewhere, only some of which have been struck down by the courts, to reduce minority voting gives a clear indication that the citizenship of minorities would be at great risk with a modification of the Fourteenth Amendment.

FOURTEENTH AMENDMENT

Both of the founding books of the modern neo-Confederate movement denounce the Fourteenth Amendment. As noted earlier these books have been praised in the *Confederate Veteran*, are sold online by the Sons of Confederate Veterans, and have been sold in their merchandise catalogs.

Michael Andrew Grissom in *Southern by the Grace of God*, (1989) complained that the Radical Republicans had a plan "to give the negro the right to vote." Of these potential voters Grissom writes, "There were nearly 4,000,000 negroes in Dixie, most of whom could neither read nor write. Most of them had no comprehension of matters beyond the boundary of the plantation."

Grissom further complains that the Radical Republicans were going to require state constitutions of the former Confederate states to be redone:

> Every southern state was required to rewrite its constitution in a constitutional convention of delegates chosen in a state wide election of *all* adult males, *except those with disqualifications*. This mean that many ex-Confederates could not vote, and it meant that negroes, even though they were not citizens, could vote. [Italics in the original.]

Grissom explains that to insure African Americans (Grissom never uses the term) could vote, the Radical Republicans worked to pass the Fourteenth Amendment. These two efforts to insure citizenship for African Americans Grissom calls, the "Radical's harsh program," "their bizarre scheme to force negro suffrage on the South," and a "diabolical scheme."[361]

James Ronald Kennedy and Walter Donald Kennedy in, *The South Was Right!* (1991, 1994) have multiple appendices in their book rejecting and denouncing the Fourteenth Amendment.

The six-page "Appendix VII," is a resolution from the New Jersey state legislature in which they rescind their approval of the Fourteenth Amendment declaring "… that the said proposed amendment being designed to confer, or to compel the States to confer the sovereign right of the elective franchise upon a race which has never given the slightest evidence, at any time, or in any quarter of the globe, of its capacity for self-government, which will render the right valueless to any portion of the people, was intended to overthrow the system of self-government …"

The two-page "Appendix IX" is an abstracted editorial from *U.S. News and World Report*, a publication that was hostile to the civil rights movement in the 20th century civil rights era, published in 1957 and in 1970 arguing that the Fourteenth Amendment was never legally ratified. The author, David Lawrence, is quoted saying the amendment "… is a disgrace to free government…" and "It's never too late to correct an injustice."

The three-page "Appendix X" is an abstract of an article by neo-Confederate Forrest McDonald, published in *The Georgia Journal of Southern Legal History* in which he argues that the Fourteenth Amendment was never legally ratified.

Not surprisingly, the book denounces the passage of the Fourteenth Amendment. One section on the Fourteenth Amendment is titled "The Enactment of a Fraud." However, the Kennedy brothers are careful not to mention African Americans by name. For example, about the election of the Southern state constitutional convention they write:

> The right to vote was denied to a large portion of white citizens, and new elections were ordered with illiterates enfranchised regardless of their lack of education or qualifications. New legislatures composed illiterates and others who had little or no governmental experience were elected to carry out the demands of the Northern Congress.

The Kennedy brothers discuss the Fourteenth Amendment as some plan to undermine states' rights. In this book, published in 1991, and republished in

1994, they take care to make it an issue of states' rights and not refer directly to African Americans.³⁶²

The Kennedy brothers were the speakers at the Sons of Confederate Veterans heritage luncheon at their 2015 national convention in Richmond, Virginia.³⁶³

Frank Conner in the *South under Siege*, published in 2002, also argues that the Fourteenth Amendment is not legitimate and is a scheme to oppress the South.³⁶⁴

There is an additional argument in not just neo-Confederate writings on the Fourteenth and Fifteenth Amendment, but in a great many history books that implies that soliciting African American voters is not legitimate.

Political parties always want to make sure their supporters are registered, make it to the polls and vote. Of course they do it for political gain for if your supporters don't vote, you don't win elections. Somehow the Republican Party's desire to enable African American voters to be able to vote and get their support is seen or implied as ethically wrong. The whole point of a democratic system with political parties is that these parties respond to voter concerns and seek their votes. The Republican Party had defeated secession, and during the Civil War gradually came to the realization that slavery had to be abolished and did so. What is wrong with them wanting African American votes during Reconstruction? Political parties seek to build alliances of interests. When you read an article, textbook, or history in which the desire of the Republican Party to get the votes of African Americans is somehow wrong, whether this critique is directly stated or hinted at, you have a fairly good idea of what the author's attitude is on race and what you are reading is garbage.

Attacking the Fourteenth Amendment is still on the contemporary neo-Confederate agenda. Retta D. Tindal, UDC Historian General, in the January Program for the UDC membership, in a 2012 article, in the *UDC Magazine*, "Reconstruction, 1865-1877," defends the infamous Black Codes passed by the legislatures of the former Confederate states immediately after the Civil War. These codes essentially reduced African Americans to a situation near slavery. Tindal writes that "Newly liberated Negroes were not prepared for their freedom …" Tindal justifies the Black Codes arguing "The Code, in effect, was no worse than the Northern apprentice laws." Tindal sees the Fourteenth Amendment deriving from unjust criticism of the Black Codes. She writes:

> Northern reformers and radicals, who had been deprived of any contact with field hands, protested that the Code limited the Negroes' civil rights and used this as an excuse to oppose the President's reconstruction plans and further hinder the South. … The direct results of their protest was the

enactment in Congress in 1866 of the Civil Rights Act as the Fourteenth Amendment to the Constitution.

The Fourteenth Amendment is held to have made race relations worse. Tindal writes, "The problem of the Negro was compounded to a greater degree than before the war. While it is a fact that the Negroes gained freedom and citizenship because of the war and Reconstruction, almost all of them were ill-equipped to support themselves and make sound political decisions." Tindal argues that African Americans (she never uses the term) did not do well with freedom. It is somehow the fault of the African Americans and not in the situation African Americans found themselves in and not the marauding's of groups like the Ku Klux Klan and the intense discrimination they faced that blocked African Americans from greater success. It is a classic blame the victim argument. Radical Republicans Tindal states "displayed a viciousness" in their Reconstruction efforts.[365]

The mentality of this UDC leader is also revealed in the use of the phrase, "The problem of the Negro."

This article is not just the opinion of one UDC member, it is the January Program of Historical Education for the entire UDC membership by the UDC Historian General.

The SCV hasn't focused on targeting the Fourteenth Amendment directly but it really doesn't have to since it has been favorably reviewing in their publications and offering for sale books that do. The Violence chapter of this book details how the neo-Confederate movement has favorably reviewed, *Southern by the Grace of God*, by Michael Andrew Grissom starting in 1989 and later offered it for sale. Also, in the Violence chapter of this book it is detailed how the SCV started selling *The South under Siege* by Frank Conner in 2004 and recommended it in the *Southern Mercury*.

In the earlier "Against Equality and Democracy" chapter it is detailed how the book, *The South Was Right!* was recommended in the *Confederate Veteran* in books reviews in 1991 and 1994, and has been offered for sale by the SCV since 2001.

It appears that the SCV doesn't have to spend time condemning the Fourteenth Amendment when they have been favorably reviewing or offering for sale books that do so instead starting in 1989 and now going on for 27 years. This would have the added advantage of pushing the idea that African American citizenship was a mistake without having to specifically state it in their periodicals, when they might be criticized for doing so.

PERNICIOUS

African American Men as Dangerous Beings

Retta D. Tindal, UDC Historian General, in the January program for the UDC membership, printed in the *UDC Magazine*, in 2012 argues in an article, "Reconstruction, 1865-1877," that:

> Newly liberated Negroes were not prepared for their freedom and wandered from town to town, sometimes living in shacks and makeshift tents in great congregations on the edges of town. They, too, were hungry, sick and unsure of their fate. Negroes greatly outnumbered the whites, and the women were terrified to pass the shantytowns. ... at times they had to ... so they fought back the dread and held their heads high.[366]

What is Tindal implying when she states "women were terrified" as opposed to "men and women were terrified" or "people were terrified?"

The idea of African Americans being dangerous animals goes way back in the neo-Confederate movement. This is an extract from an article in the *Confederate Veteran* in 1906 defending the notorious Atlanta Race Riots in which white people attacked the African American community. The author refers to "brutal degenerate negroes" whose "... mind is too feeble and shallow ..." to be deterred by fear of punishment in the commission of rape. The author writes about African Americans that they are, "returning to a state of brutal savagery, every day degenerating, as a whole, morally and becoming an increasing menace to civilization." The author explains the greatest menace is that African American men are likely to rape white women. (I know it is a long quote, but please read it so you appreciate the extent of the appalling nature of Confederate heritage.)

> The Southern white man's exact knowledge of conditions was discredited, his advice scorned, his warnings unheeded. Although he had demonstrated repeatedly his fidelity to the restored Union and had shown his willingness to serve his country in the field when the emergency arose, he was deemed unworthy of confidence in questions affecting the negro. He was told to observe the law, when the law was unable to save him or, what was a thousand times more important, to save the dearest thing on earth to him—his women. He was told to contain himself, to be patient and wait the results of long distance Northern theorizing.
>
> Meantime he was surrounded by a dense mass of ignorant negroes fast forgetting what little of self--control had been inherited from a former generation which had been trained to respect the white man and honor the white woman and rapidly returning to a state of brutal savagery, every day degenerating, as a whole, morally and becoming an increasing menace to civilization. Upon this vicious, ignorant, debased horde the puny

schemes of race elevation were as snowflakes falling into the seething ocean. Still the Southern whites protested, warned, and implored; but Northern sentimentality was proof against the natural appeals of race, the ties of kinship, and the dictates of nature.

Now it has at length come to pass that the deluge has broken, and this problem, long in the brewing of its malign factors, must be effectually settled not alone by the South, but by the North as well. We have had enough of theorizing, temporizing, philosophizing; it is time to act. Northern people are not generally aware of the fact, but it is nevertheless true that the state of the mass of negroes in the South is so debased, so utterly, hopelessly, fearfully lacking in moral conceptions, that there exists in many Southern States a condition which this or any other respectable journal would not dare describe except in the most general terms, so loathsome and shocking would the details be if truly and plainly stated.

White women and children are not safe; they cannot walk unguarded in the streets of the cities even in daytime. At night doors must be locked and windows barred, the revolver must be ready at hand if the black assailant is to be kept out. In many portions of the Black Belt the family of the white man lives in a constant state of siege; a fate worse than death awaits its members if they dare relax their vigilance for an hour. Northern people do not know the truth, and their journals are not enlightening them. The South, for very shame, is loath to let the facts be known; but a residence of even a few weeks in any portion of the country where the ignorant negro population is congested will convince the most skeptical that this hideous danger is always imminent and very real.

The crime of stealing is the very least of the negro's offenses against Southern society. The whites of the South have long since ceased to expect that he will respect the rights of property. Larceny is looked upon as a joke. As well might one expect the leopard to change his spots as the Southern negro to refrain from stealing. It is possible to protect against this comparatively minor offense; it is the hideous crimes, the unspeakable horrors, that are the real menace. Against these the law is powerless, because it recognizes no punishment adequate to the offense; it can devise nothing that will prevent its recurrence, and the harm done is irreparable.

Ordinary punishment, adequate in the North to check crime, fails entirely in the South to restrain the negro even from the commission of minor misdemeanors. The disgrace of imprisonment does not touch him, as a rule. In many Southern towns, when cold weather approaches and the shiftless and improvident blacks feel its chill, numbers of them deliberately and openly commit theft in order to be arrested, convicted, and sentenced to the penitentiary during the winter months, there to be maintained in comparative comfort at the State's expense until spring returns. When, once again at liberty, they come back, they are met at the train by their neighbors, relatives, and friends and escorted in triumph to their lurking places, as if they were heroes returning from an honorable undertaking instead of idle, vicious, debased criminals let loose from jail.

The fear of immediate and dreadful death is powerless to control the brutal, degenerated negro when his passions are aroused. His mind is too feeble and shallow to consider the consequences of his crime; and the brute in him, once awakened, reckons nothing whatever of future punishment. The force of example, even in its most terrifying form, when frenzied mobs wreak vengeance in burnings and sickening torture, does not impress itself upon this class for more than a very brief time. Its intellect is so inferior and its imagination so utterly diseased that the effect of such horrid spectacles soon wears off.[367]

Stephen Dill Lee wrote a lengthy article "The South Since the War," of 300 pages, incorporated in Vol. 12 of the serial set of books, *Confederate Military History*. This is the same Lee for whom the SCV Stephen Dill Lee Institute is named and gave the SCV *The Charge*. It is full of white supremacist statements about the inferiority of African Americans and defense of segregation. However, what is of interest here is his section, "Lynchings." (Spelled that way.)

Lee starts out by saying that lynching, "to the extent it has existed in the South is indefensible." However, after making that statement, he turns around and defends Southern lynching. The cause of lynching is civil rights for African Americans and the end of slavery.

> The crime invoking it began and has been continued solely by the irrepressible and worst element of the negro race, inaugurating a new crime, which was unknown and impossible in the days of slavery, and which, from that fact and the existence of slavery, invested it with peculiar horror and atrocity. That the race instinct is strongly implanted in human society is undeniable; and when this crime is committed under the peculiarly harrowing surroundings of isolation in sparsely-settled communities, upon helpless and unprotected white women, combined with the murder in many cases of the outraged female, it arouses a fierceness and revengeful spirit uncontrollable at times. It should be borne in mind, too, that a most abnormal state of society had pre-ceded the advent of this crime of rape, for which the Southern people were not alone responsible and which they tried to prevent. What is now regarded as a great political mistake was committed in the sudden enfranchisement and investment of the negro race with all the privileges of citizenship, including suffrage, lawmaking, and governing at the point of the bayonet a

> superior race, who had always been aggressive in the assertion of every political right. This race was under a ban as a punishment for so-called rebellion and insurrection. Their hands were tied when this great political and social reversion of the races was put in operation and upheld by the military government of the United States from 1867 to 1880 (almost). When the military power of the government in this period stood aside, apparently to see what the new State governments would do alone, those governments inaugurated a similar system only worse, in that negro militia, armed to the teeth, took the place of the white United States troops, and most offensively flaunted their newly-invested rights in the faces of the white people of the South, a proud, sensitive race.

And:

> Instead of realizing the dangerous situation, the new lawmakers began discussing, with most inflammatory language and bearing, the matter of intermarriage of the races, the further disfranchisement of classes of whites who might throw obstacles to their proposed plans, and mixed schools in common for all children, white and black. When it is recalled now that in some of the States the negroes were largely in the majority, and in others nearly equally divided, this complete social upheaval was enough to turn the heads of the worst element of a more fortunate race than that of the negro.

And:

> This new and hideous crime remained to be inaugurated by a younger generation of negroes, raised amidst the upheaval of those troublous times, while their fathers were mainly engaged in listening to inflammatory appeals, many of a social coloring, by designing and robbing strangers who held political power; and while their fathers themselves had laid aside their industrious habits of life and were leading a careless, wandering existence in their new-born freedom, not one-third of their time being given to productive labor.

> Amid such surroundings the new generation of negro boys and men was raised. Parents, in a measure, gradually lost control of their boys in that loose period, and they grew up in idleness and with distorted and ugly ideas of their rights. They felt that they had to assert those rights personally by insolence and bravado toward the white males and females, among whom they had lived. The young negroes remembered that their fathers were held in place by the white troops of the government which had given them freedom. They saw soldiers of their own race parading almost every plantation and town to keep down the whites and hold the

negroes in power. Even an ignorant negro boy could see that the "black man's party" was in power, and the "bottom rail on top."

And:

> Under these conditions, when the brains of the carpet-baggers were lost to the negroes by a change of government into the hands of the Southern property-holders and educated class, the young negroes could scarcely appreciate the import of the change, and they found that dreams of social equality had vanished forever. This dream had never taken strong hold on the older blacks, but it had seized the younger ones. They recalled all the discussions and talks of the dark days as to the inter-marrying of the races, and the crime of raping a white woman came into existence as a sequence.

After condemning lynching Lee then justifies it:

> The crime was indefensible; but those who condemn it must not forget the abnormal conditions. Those who engaged in lynching put them-selves outside of the law, but at the same time those who committed rape put themselves also outside of the law. It would always be better to abide by the law, for human society and civilization are based on the principle that the individual gives up his right of protection of life and property to the State which must perform this duty. But in the isolated spots where the crime was generally committed, it was almost impossible in many cases to get this legal protection promptly, and when it was needed, the community was swayed by a terrible cyclone of excitement and horror.

And Lee gives the standard neo-Confederate defense of anything bad in the South, that whatever is criticized exists somewhere in the "North":

> It should not be forgotten, too, that lynchings occur sometimes at the North under similar atrocious surroundings. Outraged communities in all parts of the world take the law in their own hands and lynch those who endanger the sanctity of home and society.

Finally Lee states, "It is possible that some few lynchings may have been meted out to innocent parties, but barely possible."[368] This is a classic argument that anything in the South can be excused if you can find a non-Southern locality that also has the same problem. I think knowing this method of rebuttal is a requirement for get a Ph.D. in Southern Studies.

The Sons of Confederate Veterans have offered for sale the book, *The Negro: The Southerners Problem*, by Thomas Nelson Page, originally published in 1904 in at least six of their merchandise catalogs including the 2015-2016 catalog. They currently they offer it online, but have not in the *Confederate Veteran* magazine.[369] It was also offered in the SCV Merchandise Catalog 2013-2014 which was an insert in the Sept/Oct. 2013 *Confederate Veteran* but without a caption.[370]

Page had collected together his earlier published essays and articles for the book. Its dedication reads, "To all those who truly wish to help solve the race problem, these studies are respectfully dedicated."

The 2004 SCV Merchandise catalog states, "Despite its politically incorrect title, this reprint of the 1904 original by Thomas Nelson Page is a thoughtful examination of the history of the Negro in the South and his place in American (and Southern) society. States that the chief cause of post-war racial tension in the South grew out of the ignorance of the North of actual Southern social conditions, and ignorance in the South of the power and temper of the North."

There is disclaimer, "Presented here for research purposes." This was included probably to provide for plausible deniability for the SCV given this book's notoriously racist content.

The book argues that African Americans (Page uses "Negroes") are racially inferior, portrays African American slavery as pleasant, and supports disfranchisement of African Americans. However, this book will focus on the books discussion of lynching.

In the chapter, "Lynching of Negroes – Its Cause and Its Prevention," Page opens up the discussion wanting to assure the reader, "To say that Negroes furnish most of the ravishers is not to say that all Negroes are rapists." (Ravishing is an archaic term for rape.)

Page sees the cause of lynching being the end of slavery and the period of Reconstruction during which he believes African Americans acquired a belief in racial equality.

Page writes, "… yet during the later period of slavery, the crime of rape did not exist, nor did it exist to any considerable extent for some years after emancipation." During the Civil War he asserts, "… the Negroes were the loyal guardians of the women and children" and were very secure.

Problems soon arose, according to Page:

> Then came the period and process of Reconstruction, with its teachings. Among these was the teaching that the Negro was the equal of the white, that the white was his enemy, and that he must assert his equality. The growth of the idea was a gradual one in the Negro's mind. This was

> followed by a number of cases where members of the Negro militia ravished white women; in some instances in the presence of their families.

Page sees a new generation of African Americans prone to violence and rape because they don't have the habits of the loyal slaves and do have ideas of racial equality. African Americans in general are held to condone the rape of white women.

> As the old relation, which had survived even the strain of Reconstruction, dwindled with the passing of the old generation from the stage, and the "New Issue" with the new teaching took its place, the crime broke out again with renewed violence. The idea of equality began to percolate more extensively among the Negroes. In evidence of It Is the fact that since the assaults began again they have been chiefly directed against the plainer order of people, instances of attacks on women of the upper class, though not unknown, being of rare occurrence.

> Conditions in the South render the commission of this crime peculiarly easy. The white population is sparse, the forests are extensive, the officers of the law distant and difficult to reach; but, above all, the Negro population have appeared inclined to condone the fact of mere assault.

And:

> The Negro had the same animal instincts in slavery that he exhibits now; the punishment that follows the crime now is quite as certain, as terrible, and as swift as it could have been then. So, to what is due the alarming increase of this terrible brutality? To the writer it appears plain that it is due to two things: first, to racial antagonism and to the talk of social equality that inflames the ignorant Negro, who has grown up unregulated and undisciplined; and, secondly, to the absence of a strong restraining public opinion among the Negroes of any class, which alone can extirpate the crime. In the first place, the Negro does not generally believe in the virtue of women. It is beyond his experience. He does not generally believe in the existence of actual assault. It is beyond his comprehension. In the next place, his passion, always his controlling force, is now, since the new teaching, for the white women.

Page argues that the South lives in terror of white women being raped. Page then gives justification for lynching, such as delays in the law, that fact that rape was by an African American man is especially horrifically awful because of his race, describing it as "unspeakable." The following paragraph sounds like something written for a story in the Cosmic Horror genre.

> They simply could not be put in print. It is these unnamable horrors which have outraged the minds of those who live in regions where they have occurred, and where they may at any time occur again, and, upsetting reason, have swept from their bearings cool men and changed them into madmen, drunk with fury and the lust of revenge.

Page points out that burning African Americans shocks the public, but advises:

> Only, a deeper shock than even this is at the bottom of their ferocious rage—the shock which comes from the ravishing and butchery of their women and children.

> It is not necessary to be an apologist for barbarity because one states with bluntness the cause. The stern underlying principle of the people who commit these barbarities is one that has its root deep in the basic passions of humanity; the determination to put an end to the ravishing of their women by an Inferior race, or by any race, no matter what the consequence.

Page then recounts some more horrific rape cases to inflame the reader to accept his argument. Page then points out that there is lynching of African Americans in the "North" which he asserts is worse. Page then sees the problem worsening.

> For a time, the assaults by Negroes were confined to young women who were caught alone in solitary and secluded places. The company of a child was sufficient to protect them. Then the ravishers grew bolder, and attacks followed on women when they were in company. And then, not content with this, the ravishers began to attack women in their own homes.

Page also argues, "The charge that is often made, that the innocent are sometimes lynched, has little foundation."

The chapter is a horror itself and goes on and on and can be considered an incitement to lynch in itself.[371] The book itself is the product of a smug racist and is truly idiotic. Yet, this is the book that the SCV merchandise catalog recommends to the SCV membership as "a thoughtful examination" on race relations.

Robert Slimp reveals the racial hysteria of neo-Confederates in "Americans Face the Worst Presidential Candidates In History," in 2009 in the *Southern Mercury*. Slimp states that "Obama doesn't understand the United States Constitution" and that "… he is a genuine racist."

Slimp writes, "It is very clear to me that if Barack Obama should be elected President, he would be extremely anti-white ..."

If elected Slimp thinks Obama would be a one-term president, but that:

> However, I believe that his rhetoric and anti-white legislative proposals would stir up racial riots. If he were running for re-election, these riots would turn into an exceedingly violent nature that would seriously damage race relations in America, and leave entire sections of some of our cities in ruins.[372]

Frank Conner in 2003 in the *Southern Mercury* in "Where We Stand Now And How We Got There," states that "... white Southerners had disfranchised and segregated blacks, in perhaps the mildest reaction possible at that time to the blacks transgressions. The blacks were – then a childlike people ...." Conner argues that when African Americans moved into towns, "... they did not understand town life, and the white Southerners lacked the resources to teach them; consequently, the blacks' crime rate soared. Their homicide rate became seven times that of the whites. In sheer self-defense, the Southern whites, segregated the blacks."[373]

The age old neo-Confederate idea that the African Americans are less than human and dangerous beasts continues to be advocated.

Against Civil Rights

The Sons of Confederate Veterans didn't have a journal of their own in the 1950s and 60s. Local SCV camps sometimes had their own journals and the UDC for a while gave the SCV a section in their publication.

The *Dallas Morning News* reported in 1953 that the SCV John B. Hood Camp, "... Tuesday resolved to resist attempts to enforce racial integration and said those attempts were efforts to 'destroy our civilization.'"

This John B. Hood camp later in 1965 published the *John B. Hood Journal*.

In one issue they sold a Whites Only sticker:

> The Journal has available for immediate shipment a small supply of signs to display Early American-Southern tradition. They read "White Only" and are professionally done, They measure 3 x 5 inches with black letters on a white background. They are self-adhesive with waterproof ink. Think of the possibilities. On your personal bathrooms, etc., anywhere they are still legal. The nominal cost is 15¢ apiece or 2 for 25¢. Send your quarter

to: Whites Only (simply WO, if you prefer) XXXX XXXX Drive, Dallas, Texas. [Address redacted.]

In another issue they reprinted *The Negro 23rd Psalm*.

> Lyndon is my shepherd, I shall not work,
> He maketh me to lie down in from of theatres;
> He leadeth me to White Universities.
> He restoreth my welfare check.
> He leadeth me in the paths of sit-ins for Communism's sake.
> Yea, though I walk through the Heart of Dixie,
> I shall fear no policeman, for Lyndon is with me,
> His Federal troops and "Marshalls", they comfort me.
> He prepareth a table for me in the presence of White people,
> He amointeth my hair with anti-kink hair straightener.
> My Cadillac tank runneth over.
> Surely the Supreme Court shall follow me all the days of my life, and I shall dwell in the Federal Housing Projects forever,

Another article announced that the segregationist ex-governor Mississippi Ross R. Barnett was given an honorary life membership by Col. John A. May, SCV Commander-in-Chief at their 70th Annual Reunion. Barnett spoke to the convention about preserving the constitution in reference to upholding segregation.

Confederate "heritage" was understood by the editors of the journal as being against racial equality. From the *John B. Hood Journal*.

> There is no place in the Sons of Confederate Veterans for persons who do not subscribe to the principals of the men from which they are descended. We, of the organization, sully the memory of our illustrious ancestors, if we accept or retain persons in our organization who by their daily actions desecrate the memory of the soldier of the South ... [The article gives the history of the term Scalawag and denounces Lyndon Johnson and Ralph Yarborough as such.] ...All of these persons are working in direct contradiction of what their ancestors stood for. Lyndon Johnson has sponsored more legislation to destroy the South than any man who ever occupied the White house, Among the many pieces of despicable legislation sponsored by this turncoat, is the misnamed Civil Rights Act and the Voting Rights Act which though patently unconstitutional will be upheld by a Supreme Court with no regard to the constitution. Ralph Yarborough worked for and voted for the Civil Rights Act and the Voting Rights Act, and he is and has been the fair haired boy of the NAACP, CORE, and other negro agitating groups, .., it is right and proper that we keep alive the historical aspects of the War Between the

States, but I believe it is more important that we stand for the ideals and principles of the men who served in that great conflict. If we do not, our recalling of their great service is hollow indeed.[374] [Comments in brackets that of the author of this book.]

At the Sons of Confederate Veterans national convention in Dallas, Texas in 1977 the "entertainment" for one evening is given as, "'Birth of a Nation,' a classic D.W. Griffith silent film about the Reconstruction era, will be shown after the choral presentation."[375]

Later defenders of the Confederate battle flag would say that the Ku Klux Klan gave it a bad reputation. However in the 1977, the SCV offered at their convention a pro-Klan movie.

SCV Commander-in-Chief William M. Beard in 1957 in the *United Daughters of the Confederacy Magazine*, denounces the May 17, 1954 *Brown vs. Board of Education* Supreme Court decision integrating the schools and the NAACP. These are some quotes:

> The problems of desegregation must be solved by the people of the South. People who live in the North should keep hands off in this crisis in the Southern way of life.

> The tactics of Representative Adam Clayton Powell and of the N.A.A.C.P. have caused intense racial tensions in the Southern States.

> Where before May 17, 1954 there was harmony between the white people and the Colored people in the South, we now have uneasy racial tensions.[376]

Later it seems that the SCV realized that in their battles to defend the Confederacy being open about their views on the Ku Klux Klan, African Americans and civil rights legislation would harm their cause. The *Confederate Veteran* when it was revived in the 1980s avoided direct comments about Civil Rights. It wasn't until the 21st century that articles in SCV publications again became open about their opposition to civil rights.

The United Daughters of the Confederacy also attacked civil rights in the 1950s. From about 1957 until mid-1959, they mostly attacked the Supreme Court decision of *Brown vs. Board of Education* and defended segregation. Some of these anti-civil rights articles were serialized over three issues and some issues had no less than three anti-civil rights serialized articles.

A typical example is a June 1958 *United Daughters of the Confederacy Magazine* with the article "Jefferson Davis – The Man America Needs Today," by Bruce

Dunstan. Dunstan feels that the ideas of Davis were needed to defeat the mid-20th century civil rights movement. Dunstan writes:

> Millions of millions of Americans' hard-earned tax dollars are annually squandered in foreign lands in far too many foolish ways to list here. This constant waste of America's wealth, together with forced shameful race-mixing, that causes lowered educational standards, immorality, and finally a mongrelized people, will bring the downfall of America, as integration of races doomed the once cultured, and prosperous cities and nations of Carthage, Athens, Rome, and Sparta; and made of Egypt the weak world power that she is today.
>
> Also as this invisible government gained control of both our once great and patriotic political parties, and has carefully plotted this long range, devilish plan, to weaken America, economically and racially to the end that we shall be forced to make our Constitution subject to the will of the United Nation, or in other words, be compelled to adopt One World Government ..."[377]

There is an abrupt end of the tirades against civil rights which coincides with the start of the Civil War Centennial mid-1959. It would hardly do to try to represent the Confederacy in a sentimental light, talking about "heritage," when your publication is raging about "mogrelization."

Since then the UDC and their magazine hasn't had articles like this, which the author considers explicitly racist. Clara Erath wrote the "Confederate Notes" column for *UDC Magazine*. Starting in 1989 until 1999 her columns discreetly pushed the neo-Confederate movement. Columns recommended *Southern Partisan* magazine to readers. Univ. of Dallas professor M.E. Bradford, who spent his life campaigning against civil rights is praised and his writing recommended. However, if you were to read the columns and if you didn't already know anything about *Southern Partisan* magazine, the books recommended or the individuals praised, the author doesn't think it likely that you would know that these magazines and books are hostile to civil rights and these individuals were hostile to civil rights.

Erath in 1990 enthusiastically reviewed and strongly recommended Richard M. Weaver's *The Southern Tradition At Bay*, a racist book originally published in 1968 by Arlington House and republished by Regnery Gateway in 1989.[378] This book was critical in the origins of the modern Neo-Confederate movement containing many of its core ideas. Since this book was recommended in the *United Daughters of the Confederacy Magazine* repeatedly it would be instructive to examine this book to understand what type of book they were recommending.

The book was originally Weaver's dissertation, *The Confederate South, 1865-1910: A Study in the Survival of a Mind and a Culture*, at Louisiana State University for his doctorate in English in 1943. Weaver died in 1963, and in 1968 it was posthumously published with two editors, George Core and M.E. Bradford, the latter a campaigner for George Wallace. The Forward was written by segregationist and Southern Agrarian Donald Davidson. The books basic thesis that there is a southern tradition and philosophy but that it hadn't properly been developed as Weaver explains in his Epilogue:

> The South possesses an inheritance which it has imperfectly understood and little used. It is in the curious position of having been right without realizing the grounds of its rightness.

He further explains:

> The South committed two great errors in its struggle against the modern world, errors characteristic for it, but of disastrous consequence. The first was a failure to study its position until it arrived at metaphysical foundations. No Southern spokesman was ever able to show why the South was right *finally*. In other words, the South never perfected its world view. [Italics in the original].[379]

Weaver decides to take on this task and sees southern culture as being anti-modern, anti-democratic, hierarchal, religiously pre-modern, and feudal in origins. Weaver advocates the restoration of this culture as a solution for what he sees as the problems of modern society.

In his book he paints slavery and large plantations as idyllic. He portrays slavery as somehow worse than working for wages.

> In the midst of traffic in human beings there was, paradoxically, less evidence of the cash nexus than in the marts of free labor, and even the humble could have the deep human satisfaction that comes of being cherished for what one is. Between the expression "our people," euphemistic though it may have been, and the modern abstraction "manpower" lies a measure of our decline in humanity.[380]

"Our people" was a euphemism for slaves used by slave owners. Weaver sees free labor as a decline from slavery.

Another apologetic for slavery follows:

> The Northern public has generally displayed a strange credulity with respects to stories of abuses emanating from the South, and when these are multiplied tenfold, as they were in Reconstruction days, it is little

wonder that many Northerners of good will, whom a visit to the South would have undeceived, went on believing that slave holders had subjected their Negroes to deliberate and systematic brutalizing. Somewhere between two opinions distorted by passion lay a truth: on the one hand, Southerners had done less than they might have toward civilizing the blacks, and on the other hand, Northerners, accepting the dogma that the Negro had the white man's nature and capacities, had conceived an imperfect notion of the problem.[381]

Emancipation is seen as a problem for African Americans, Weaver writing:

> That the presence of the African had been the chief source of Southern misfortunes was a common admission; yet his very childlikeness, his extraordinary exhibitions of loyalty, and his pathetic attempts to find his place in the complicated white man's civilization ...[382]

Also, Weaver writes that African Americans can't comprehend their civil rights quoting Virginia Clay accounts during Reconstruction.

> The Negro's first disillusionment came when he tried to grasp tangible form the benefits which the new dispensation was expected to confer. Stories are told of his coming to town with a sack to carry back the franchise which was to be given him, and of his confusion of the "Freedmen's Bureau" with the well-known article of furniture. "Whar's dat bureau? Was sure to be the first question," Virginia Clay wrote.

Virginia Clay is claiming that African Americans actually thought they were going to get a piece of furniture, a bureau.

This type of racist disparagement of African Americans goes on and on in Weaver's book.

Curious for a book advocated by a women's organization, in Weaver's epilogue he advocates the revocation of suffrage for women arguing:

> Distinctions of many kinds will have to be restored, and I would mention especially one whose loss has added immeasurably to the malaise of our civilization – fruitful distinction between the sexes, with the recognition of respective spheres of influence. ... Southerners were adamant, and even today, with our power of discrimination at its lowest point in history, there arises a feeling that the roles of the sexes must again be made explicit. ... and I think that women would have more influence actually if they did not vote, but, according to the advice of Augusta Evans Wilson, made their firesides seats of Delphic wisdom.[383]

However, in reading Erath's commentary on the book in the *UDC Magazine* you would have no hint of Weaver's views on race or opposition to woman's suffrage. Instead Erath speaks about non-materialism versus science, and in other general terms and concluding the article with a quote from Weaver's book:

> The Old South may indeed be a hall hung with splendid tapestries in which no one would care to live; but from them we can learn something of how to live.

Thus a nasty racist book is recommended to the readers of *UDC Magazine* in romantic terms entirely omitting race.

As mentioned earlier in the chapter on violence, the UDC has brought to the attention of the readers of UDC Magazine Michael Andrew Grissom's book, *Southern by the Grace of God*.

In the 21st century there are similar efforts. In 2005 Clara Erath has an article in *UDC Magazine* complaining that Southern universities have become "politically correct" and promoted membership in the Abbeville Institute and their meeting at the Young-Sanders Center.[384] Again in 2005 we find that Abbeville Institute co-founder Donald Livingston was honored by the UDC which presented him with a Jefferson Davis gold medal.[385]

In the 21st century the Sons of Confederate Veterans periodicals first start having articles denouncing the civil rights movement in the *Southern Mercury* with Frank Conner's article, "Where We Stand Now And How We Got There," in 2003.

Conner sees the entire civil rights movement as an attack on the South. Conner writes "… liberal Democrat Harry Truman pressured the Congress to enact the radical civil rights bill aimed squarely at the white South …" The Supreme Court decision *Brown vs. Board of Education* integrating the schools is also denounced.

Conner sees the white South the victim of a propaganda campaign and states:

> As a result, the US Congress enacted the patently-unconstitutional Civil Rights Act of 1964 and the Voting Rights Act of 1965 … The Old South was destroyed, and its belief system and way of life were discredited outside the South.

Conner then has a section, "The Liberals Begin Final Stage of their Culture War Against the White South." This stage is the promotion of "multiculturalism," and liberals and "black activists" attacking "big corporations as racist." Conner also states, "That coalition," referring to liberals and African Americans, "is presently promoting hate-crime legislation as the final weapon to intimidate the whites (particularly the white southerners) into total impotence via thought-crime laws." All this Conner writes, "… is steadily shredding white society …"

Conner in the article argues that liberalism has failed and, "So liberalism is now vulnerable; it can be taken."[386] In 2016 in the year of Donald Trump's presidential campaign this is certainly not an impossibility.

In "The Land We Love: Southern Tradition and Our Future, in 2012 in the *Confederate Veteran* Boyd D. Cathey makes a direct statement against civil rights legislation.[387] Cathey argues that after Reconstruction "there had developed an unwritten 'understanding' between North and South… after 1877, more or less left the South alone to manage its own internal affairs."

Cathey sees the coming of the civil rights movement and civil rights legislation as an attack on the South. Cathey states:

> But this understanding began to break down in the 1950s and 1960s. The decisions of the Supreme Court, the triumph of the *civil rights* movement which in some ways was a frontal attack on constitutional republicanism and the rights of property, and the triumph of political correctness and cultural Marxism, all signaled the beginning of a "Second War of Northern Aggression" aimed at totally reshaping and restructuring our culture and at rejecting the principles and beliefs of our ancestors. [Italics in the original.]

Cathey uses italics for "civil rights" to indicate that he doesn't see them as civil rights.

The article starts out with Cathey discussing the Charge of the Sons of Confederate Veterans by Gen. Stephen D. Lee, which as discussed earlier in the book calls on the members of the SCV to honor the Confederate veteran through "the perpetuation of those principles which he loved and which you love also, and those ideals which made him glorious and which you also cherish." Cathey argues, "What were those 'principles' General Lee refer to?"

In the article Cathey states that civil rights legislation is in opposition to the principles of the Confederate soldier and so the Charge of the Sons of Confederate Veterans, which is held to be the very purpose of the SCV, is opposition to civil rights legislation.

There are two other items in this essay of Cathey which don't mention civil rights at all, but direct the reader to anti-civil rights readings. Cathey recommends and discusses the book, *The Southern Tradition at Bay*, by Richard M. Weaver, which has been mentioned in this chapter previously.

Cathey also recommends the book, *Remembering Who We Are: Observations of a Southern Conservative*, by M.E. Bradford. Bradford dedicated most of his life against civil rights. The author is working on a short book length manuscript about him. In reading Cathey you might get the impression of him as some vaguely romantic traditional agrarian. The author has read this book through and studied it and can testify that the book's dust jacket very ably summarizes this book in a few sentences.

> The United States was not founded, Bradford argues, with the idea of creating a society dedicated to either justice or equality, and all attempts to turn America in that direction have resulted in a perversion of the nation's true origins in the struggle for liberty from oppression of a remote and sometimes hostile government. Discussing some of those attempts, several of the pieces in the collection examine recent efforts by the federal government to impose a single vision on the diversity of America, to transform the nation from a land of liberty to one that promotes equality.[388]

The opposition to civil rights in this article is consistent with its general argument that Southern society is inherently anti-egalitarian and thus would be inherently in opposition to any type of civil rights legislation.

There is so much about how the neo-Confederate movement has campaigned against African Americans that isn't covered in this chapter. There are the attacks on Maya Angelou and Martin Luther King. There are the books written by neo-Confederates and sold by the Sons of Confederate Veterans defending or excusing African American slavery. However, the themes explored here in depth give a fairly good idea of how neo-Confederates deny the humanity of African Americans and seek to deny them human rights and the subtle means they employ in pursuit of this agenda.

13 ENABLERS: BANAL WHITE NATIONALISM

The neo-Confederates are assisted and enabled, in achieving their goals by groups and individuals.

This assistance can come in different forms. Neo-Confederates are enabled when a church, school or other organization provides space for the Sons of Confederate Veterans or the United Daughters of the Confederacy to meet, have an event, or function. These spaces provided are often prestigious, which gives credibility to neo-Confederate groups. Assistance can be rendered when a person or groups defends a Confederate named park, a Confederate monument or criticizes those who criticize these parks or monuments. Assistance can be subtle or explicit.

Surprisingly, individuals and groups the public would think would never associate with neo-Confederate ideas often provide such assistance.

Some of these enablers would not enable the neo-Confederate movement if this link became generally known to the public. Exposing the neo-Confederate enablers provides a key opportunity to oppose the neo-Confederate movement.

The author has observed that people tend to have stereotypes of who racists are and also have preconceived ideas what type of organizations that might be involved in enabling neo-Confederates. They can have very limited definitions of what racism is and who these racists might be, and have preconceptions of racist groups as always consisting of extremists individuals engaged in violent or outrageous behavior. They blurt racist slurs, they have angry shouts.

Indeed the concept of "hate" groups serves to provide cover for racists who don't fit this stereotype. The calm and deliberative racist is not recognized because we don't perceive emotional hysteria, the deliberative racist doesn't blurt out racist slurs.

When a person discovered that they are part of an enabling organization, or that someone they admire is an enabler, rather than reacting that this enabling is unacceptable, this person will often rationalize this relationship with a racist movement.

These preconceptions about who a racist might be can lead people to not recognize neo-Confederates or understand the negative consequences of a neo-Confederate agenda. More importantly these preconceptions can allow neo-Confederates and their enablers essentially to advance their agenda with lessened opposition. Thus before discussing enablers there needs to be a discussion of banal white nationalism and the stereotypes of who racists are.

BANAL WHITE NATIONALISM

The fact that in 2016 Confederate monuments have not been long since swept away is due to the prevalence of banal white nationalism and is why I am discussing this concept in depth here.

The public's concept of a racist generally is a stereotype. Much of the public invariably imagines the racist to be a belligerent person, perhaps wearing strange clothing, screaming racial slurs and with open hostility against some minority group. Additionally the racist is uneducated, perhaps mentally unstable or deficient, and has a marginal economic position in society.

These stereotypes of who a racist is, has multiple significant negative effects. Based on these assumptions people can avoid confronting their own attitudes on race because they see the racist as their "other," an alien type with whom they share no characteristics. They can believe that they themselves aren't racists since they don't shout and they are educated and they have good middle class decorum, they don't fit the stereotype. Denouncing neo-Nazis, the Ku Klux Klan and similar groups can make individuals feel good about themselves. They can contrast themselves with these extremists and congratulate themselves on how superior they are to flamboyant racists who wear swastikas or white sheets.

The second negative effect of these preconceptions is that individuals often don't recognize, let alone challenge, racism in people they know since their friends, spouse, relative, co-worker, boss, subordinate, or neighbor doesn't fit the stereotype. I have repeatedly gotten an outraged reply, when I find an individual involved with neo-Confederacy. I am asked how I could possibly think this or that person is racist since that individual in question is well mannered or is "nice" and "charming." If you don't foam at the mouth, it is believed, you couldn't possibly be racist.

As Tony Horowitz makes clear in an April 28, 1995, *Wall Street Journal* article, "The Faces of Extremism Wears Many Guises – Most of them Ordinary," other racist groups are overlooked as the media chases the Ku Klux Klan. Horwitz describes attention a meeting of Confederate flag supporters:

> The breakfast crowd at the Capitol Restaurant looked about as rabid as the Rotary Club.

One of attendees is friendly and introduces himself to Horowitz:

> "I'm Walt," he said, ... "I'm here to defend my race against the government and Jewish-controlled media."

> Ostensibly, he and 40 others were there to march in support of the Confederate flag that flew atop the nearby statehouse. But as Walt and his cohorts ... quickly made clear, the rebel flag was simply a symbol of resistance against a tyrannical government and its co-conspirators: blacks, the liberal media, feminists, gays, immigrants, Jews ...

> In the four months since, traveling across eight Southern states, I've repeatedly encountered similar groups ... Its typical camouflage is the ordinary appearance and occupations of most far-right adherents.

Horowitz discusses how groups like this are ignored by the media but groups which fit the stereotype get a lot of media attention.

> On the other hand, no one ever misses groups like the Ku Klux Klan. Soon after the flag march in South Carolina, I watched a rally by the Knights of the KKK. The "grand dragon" for the "realm of Kentucky" led 10 others down the street, with twice that number of police and TV cameras looking on. ...

However, on another date at a nearby location an event gets no coverage as Horowitz explains:

> This time the Klan didn't come, but the scene was far more menacing, with ... speakers who spewed venom at the state and its presumed agents among liberal and minority groups.

> ... Yet this speech and others even more inflammatory didn't make the nightly news.

> One reason: Mr. [Michael] Hill wore a tie instead of a hood and took the podium as head of the blandly-named Southern League. [389]

Another negative impact is that if someone is anti-KKK they are assumed to be anti-racist. They merely may have a different strategy for racism and they feel that the KKK undermines it. You are told that so and so was anti-KKK as if that proves that person isn't or wasn't racist. The 1950s White Citizens Councils in their publications very emphatically told their members not to support any Klan activity since it undermined the effort to support segregation. Neo-Confederates often denounce what they call "hate groups" realizing that the Klan has a poisonous public image but the public might not recognize a more conventionally dressed, more verbally evasive group with a similar agenda.

Middle class, consciously racist groups are quite well aware of this stereotype and the public's reluctance to label anyone as racist who doesn't fit this stereotype. These middle class racist groups exploit these stereotypes to give themselves protective coloration. These are excerpts from a 2004 column, "Neo-Confederates of the GOP rise again," by Stanley Crouch, a columnist for the *New York Daily News*, published in the *San Francisco Chronicle*, when U.S. Senator Trent Lott's and U.S. Rep. Bob Barr's ties to the Council of Conservative Citizens (www.cofcc.org) became news.

> Somewhere in the material of the Council of Conservative Citizens the statement is made that one should be a Nazi – but never use the word.
>
> That seems to be the approach the council is taking now that more and more light is being cast on its white supremacist doctrine, its vision of Negroes as "monkeys," its belief there was no such thing as the holocaust.
>
> … What appears before us now is clear: Neo-Confederates with a disguised racial policy have risen to the top of the GOP.
>
> But this rise is something that has to remain under wraps, because in the era of Michael Jordan, one cannot just come out and be hardcore racist. That would be impolitic.
>
> … The racist of old would come right out and call an insulting name at those who raised his paranoia. But these guys are cagier. Or more cowardly.
>
> …. There is a very sophisticated kind of bigot among us who doesn't want to be stopped along the way by his opinions. This one wants power. He is far more dangerous.[390]

Crouch sees that these groups make sure they don't fit the popular stereotype of racists. On the other hand Crouch is wrong about this marking a difference between old racism and new racism. He also overrates the sophistication of the supposedly "new" racists. These "new" racists are just not idiots and can figure out that publically venting their racism in crude terms before the public will not advance their agenda. This strategy probably goes back some time. Richard M. Weaver, an English professor at the University of Chicago in the mid-20th century is even today still considered a legitimate thinker by the conservative movement, even though he was a racist and a smug one at that.[391]

The idea that some racists are really clever likely derives from the discovery of racist groups that aren't just raging maniacs. In a sense it still incorporates the stereotype.

The old/new racist idea is flawed in another way. In reading the history of the South you come across endless racists who proclaim their concern for the "negro." William D. McCain, a leading figure of the Sons of Confederate Veterans for decades in the middle 20th century, and president of the University of Southern Mississippi made speeches outside the state on behalf of the Sovereignty Commission, an agency of the State of Mississippi to suppress civil rights activists in the state, outside the state. In the speech he expresses his concerns for the welfare of the "negro" though he fought to make sure African Americans couldn't be admitted to his university.

This is not to say I don't appreciate the reporting by Stanley Crouch about Trent Lott and the Council of Conservative Citizens. Had he not made it an issue it might very well have not been generally reported and I think his help was essential. He was the first major media figure to start talking about racists who didn't fit stereotypes and even though it is now nearing 20 years ago I have not forgot how well he explained it.

The media focuses on obvious racists – Klansman burning crosses, for instance, because it is comforting to have reaffirmation that you aren't racist, and neither the people you know, because you are not like the racists on the screen. There is a sort of fascination with these racists, the photogenic strange clothing and the burning crosses. Everyone can wallow in their moral superiority. These groups also won't argue that they aren't racist. The reporter doesn't have to critically review claims of racism because Nazis and Klansmen shout out that they are. On the other hand, a reporter might get outraged denial from a group that doesn't fit the stereotype and public criticism that he labeled a group as racist.

Again, the use of the expression "Hate Group" is one that reinforces the stereotypes of what a racist group is and provides cover for those groups that don't fit the stereotype. It is simplistic and an obstacle to understanding racist processes in society.

Who is a white nationalist? What is white nationalism? The first thought comes to mind is of persons living in a compound in Idaho or perhaps some other remote rural location. The white nationalist is explicitly a racist who is violent and hostile towards African Americans and has an explicitly white supremacist agenda.

Another white nationalism that comes to mind is the paternalistic racist. This type of racist is to some extent recognized. The White Citizens Councils of the 1950s are described as the "uptown Klan." "Uptown" in this case means upscale and middle class persons with community respectability. However, this term "uptown Klan" is somewhat a problem. It implies that the KKK is the reference standard for defining racism, and suggests that the White Citizens Councils were nothing more than a Klan keeping their agenda undercover. However, reporters operating in such a stereotypical framework can be excused for using this short hand.

However, paternalistic racism is a racism of its own type not derivative of another type of racism. This type of racism is openly racist but argues that they have a concern for African Americans. This concern turns out to be that African Americans be given a subordinate place in society, a position the paternalistic racist feels they are best suited as inferior beings.

Again, the problems with these overt white nationalist groups like the neo-Nazis and Ku Klux Klan members is that they become the idea of what a racist group is, and so other racist groups are not recognized as such.

Additionally, I think there are other forms of white nationalism in which those who are these types of white nationalists don't recognize themselves as white nationalists. These are the most powerful forms of white nationalism, since they are exercised without opposition, without understanding that these forms exist, thus there is not recognition of persons and groups as having these forms of white nationalism. There is often no self-recognition that they are these types of white nationalists.

It is undeniable that those who label themselves as white nationalists are racists, as are those who are currently generally recognized as white nationalists, but there are additional white nationalists who don't fit within these recognized types.

Michael Billig in his landmark book, *Banal Nationalism* discusses the fact that the discussion of nationalism usually resolves around extremists to the exclusion of seeing the banal nationalism in everyday life. Billig contrasts the focus of the usual analyst of nationalism to the analyst of banal nationalism as follows:

> The analyst of banal nationalism does not have the theoretical luxury of exposing the nationalism of others. The analyst cannot place exotic nationalist under the microscope as specimens, in order to stain the tissues of repressed sexuality, or turn the magnifying lens on to the unreasonable stereotypes, which ooze from the mouth of the specimen. In presenting the psychology of a Le Pen or Zhirinovsky, 'we' might experience a shiver of fear as 'we' contemplate 'them', the nationalists, with their violent emotions and 'their' crude stereotyping of the Other. And 'we' will recognize 'ourselves' among the objects of this stereotyping. Alongside the 'foreigners' and the 'racial inferiors', there 'we" will be – the 'liberal degenerates', with 'our' international broadmindedness. 'We' will be reassured to have confirmed 'ourselves' as the Other of 'our' Other.
>
> By extending the concept of nationalism, the analyst is not safely removed from the scope of investigation. We might imagine that we possess a cosmopolitan broadness of spirit. But, if nationalism is a wider ideology, whose familiar commonplaces catch us unawares, then this is too reassuring. We will not remain unaffected. If the thesis is correct, then nationalism has seeped into the corners of our consciousness; it is present in the very words which we might try to use for analysis. It is naïve to think that a text of exposure can escape from the times and place of its formulation. It can attempt, instead, to do something more modest: it can draw attention to the powers of an ideology which is so familiar that it hardly seems noticeable. [392]

(Jean-Marie Le Pen was the founder and leader of the xenophobic National Front Party in France from 1972 to 2011, a party his daughter Marine now leads. Vladimir Zhirinovsky led the similar Liberal-Democratic Party in Russia shortly after the fall of the Soviet Union in 1991.)

If there can be a banal nationalism, could there also be a banal white nationalism? Would we be able to see it? Are we so sure that we ourselves aren't banal white nationalists and in the use of the term "we" here, I include African Americans? I don't think that anyone is automatically immune to banal white nationalism.

Unconscious white nationalists would be furious if they heard the label applied to them.

I believe this form of white nationalism is likely fairly extensive, though I don't think banal white nationalism will be fully excavated and revealed until there is a politics challenging it. I think it might well be that a fairly significant fraction of the public might be banal white nationalists.

In discussing white nationalism and racism, we have a difficulty with the assumption that they are identical concepts. Certainly, a white nationalistic concept has racist implications and is racist. However, white nationalism is a concept, and ideology that often results in racist actions and behaviors. It is not a distinction without a difference. In understanding the distinctions between white nationalism and racism a person can conceptualize a process of one leading to the other, of A causing B. You can see banal white nationalism working through multiple channels to have racist impacts. This is a particularly useful understanding in where the banal white nationalism doesn't incorporate in itself an explicitly racist ideology.

The unacknowledged and unlabeled white nationalism has the potential to have a greater impact because it is more widespread and is more subtle and most importantly unrecognized as such and thus unopposed.

These white nationalists, of which I suggest exist, can think that Martin Luther King is a hero, support February Black History month, and are supportive of the civil rights revolution. Does this seem like an outrageous thing to say? If so, does it seem to be outrageous because you are thinking of some white nationalists holed up in Idaho? Could not a person have a concept of a white nation but want to see that a space is created for non-whites in the white nation? Couldn't a person, not consciously a white nationalist, but internally embracing the idea of the white nation, but not consciously doing so, want to accommodate non-whites? Wouldn't that keep peace and stability for the white nation and legitimatize the white nation? For some, doesn't a February Black history month allow January, March, April, May, June, July, August, September, October, November, and December to be essentially the white history months? A strategy for civil rights could merely assure stability for a nation that is conceptualized as white and pacify non-whites. Could it not be just an affirmation for these type of white nationalists on just how good as white people they are to the non-whites?

A white nationalism which creates a historical narrative which constructs a heroic white nation and which obscures the troubled history of race in America is the most powerful form of white nationalism. It constructs a white nation with perhaps non-whites accommodated in the guest house, maybe a nice guest house, but still a guest house.

Another form of white nationalism doesn't feature hostility against African Americans. These white nationalists see African Americans as having no consequence, as being of no concern, as a nullity in society. In this form of white nationalism, African Americans are never part of "us" or "we."

When the author first conceptualized the idea of white banal nationalism he wasn't sure to what extent it is existed. He discussed the idea with a co-worker. He detailed his investigations and developing thoughts. The co-worker thought banal white nationalism was an interesting idea and asked to what extent I thought that this worldview existed in the white population. I replied that I didn't know and that it could be anything from 5% to 80+% percent. The co-worker then blurted out, "There are black nationalists too!" I suddenly realized then that the co-worker was leaping to the defense of the white race. Yet the discussion was not about judging one race versus another. I began from that time forward to realize that banal white nationalism might pervade a large percentage of the white population. Of course there are nationalists of all races, I wasn't comparing races at all, but analyzing historical memory as it works in a dominate group. The co-worker I think was expecting a small percentage that the co-worker might feel superior to, not something that might include the co-worker.

CONSTRUCTING THE WHITE NATION

What ways could you construct a white nation? It could be historical narratives which value whites and directly or indirectly negates the value of non-whites as human beings. It could be historical narratives which obscure the racism in the American national story to give whites a more heroic role, or deny the historical narrative which could provide the basis of claims for social justice for non-whites. It could be historical narratives which obscure elements from which a challenge to the white nation could be made or narratives that might discredit the white nation. It could be toleration for historical narratives that are supportive of white nationalism and racism. White nationalism could be opposing historical narratives which undermine or oppose white nationalism. In this case historical narratives are the focus, but similarly white nationalism could operate in other spheres.

These historical narratives supporting white nationalism can happen in multiple ways from the high school history textbooks, book reviews, news reporting, magazines, and wherever a historical narrative is written. One of the more atrocious examples is Ken Burn's *Civil War* and the Public Broadcasting System stations giving out copies of Shelby Foote's Civil War book trilogy.

White nationalism can be activities to mark the nation as a white nation and mark the landscape as a white landscape, to make the nation's territory a white geographical space and do activities on the landscape to support historical narratives of white nationalism.

The dominating historical narrative, what is in textbooks and the stories told by monuments are like a braid of multiple historical narratives woven together. It incorporates the neo-Confederate historical narrative as one strand. The neo-Confederate historical narrative is grossly racist. It is the glorification of the attempted creation of a nation to support slavery and maintain white supremacy. It has been used for generations, over a century, to support white supremacy. Yet the neo-Confederate narratives are pandered to by the government and by institutions regarded as respectable. Until recently it was not frequently challenged by others. It is still woven into the braid of American history. This is done even though many in the public and many scholars have pointed out that the Confederacy was about slavery and white supremacy in the press.

The Neo-Confederate narrative is indefensible but it will be defended and not just by neo-Confederates. Challenging this narrative has the potential of revealing the banal white nationalism of those who support the Confederacy, not just those in the neo-Confederate movement, but also the enablers of the neo-Confederacy, of those who are willing to go along with it, or make excuses for it, and those who are indifferent to a historical narrative that lessens the humanity of African Americans. Exposure of banal white nationalism would reveals those to whom Black lives don't matter much or not at all.

A campaign against neo-Confederacy will reveal white solidarity when neo-Confederates are challenged over Confederate symbols, monuments, holidays, etc. which are supported by this racist historical narrative and when people outside the neo-Confederate movement will come to the defense of the Confederate symbols, monuments, holidays, etc. It is revealed when I hear the angry wail of protest by someone that their neighbor or co-worker or fellow committee member or friend or associate is so nice, and has so many laudable traits, that he or she couldn't possibly be racist, and that I am so wicked to raise any question about that person's support of the Confederacy.

Understanding banal white nationalism is necessary to understand how neo-Confederacy is accommodated and enabled in society, and also how deep and extensive white banal nationalism is in America.

UNITED STATES MILITARY ACADEMIES

"We honor others to honor ourselves" is an old saying. By giving an award to someone we necessarily define ourselves as being worthy enough that getting an award from us is an honor to the recipient of the award.

The United Daughters of the Confederacy appropriates itself the prestige of the U.S. military by giving awards to cadets at all the United States Military Academies with these awards, except one, named after Confederates. These are the awards which the UDC gives out annually at military academies as listed in the May 2009 UDC Magazine.[393]

- The Robert E. Lee Sabre at the U.S. Military Academy at West Point, New York.

- The Commodore Matthew Fontaine Maury Award at the U.S. Naval Academy, Annapolis, Maryland

- The Lieutenant General Claire L. Chenault Award at the U.S. Air Force Academy, Colorado Springs, Colorado

- The Admiral Raphael Semmes Award at the U.S. Coast Guard Academy, New London, Connecticut

- The Matthew Fontaine Maury Award at the U.S. Merchant Marine Academy, Kings Point, New York

- The Stonewall Jackson Award at the Virginia Military Institute, Lexington, Virginia

- The William Porcher DuBose Award at The Citadel, Charleston, South Carolina

In the November 2015 UDC Magazine in a page of photos of military cadets receiving these awards. Additionally there is this award.

- The Sir Moses Ezekiel Award given at the Virginia Military Academy.

Robert E. Lee was a racist who worked against African Americans civil rights after the Civil War. His attitudes are best described by his son Robert E. Lee Jr.

This is from the *"Recollections and Letters of General Lee,"* by R.E. Lee, Jr. which was published by Doubleday, Page & Company in 1904. The following is a section about R.E. Lee Sr. visiting "Corbin Braxton's widow" for dinner with some friends. His son gives an account on page 168 in the 1988 reprint by Broadfoot Publishing Co., of Lee Sr.'s conversation with Colonel Carter.

> In talking with Colonel Carter about the situation of farmers at that time in the South, and of their prospects for the future, he urged him to get rid of the negroes left on the farm — some ninety odd in number, principally women and children, with a few old men — saying the government would provide for them, and advised him to secure white labour. The Colonel told him he had to use, for immediate needs, such force as he had, being unable at that time to get the whites. Were upon General Lee remarked:

> "I have always observed that wherever you find the negro, everything is going down around him, and wherever you find the white man, you see everything around him improving."

Robert E. Lee signed the notorious *White Sulphur Manifesto* to undermine and oppose the Republican Party civil rights policies in the presidential election of 1868. This letter stated:

> It is true that the people of the South, in common with a large majority of the people of the North and West, are, for obvious reasons, inflexibly opposed to any system of laws that would place the political power of the country in the hands of the negro race. But this opposition springs from no feeling of enmity, but from a deep-seated conviction that, at present, the negroes have neither the intelligence nor the other qualifications which are necessary to make them safe depositories of political power. They would inevitably become the victims of demagogues, who, for selfish purposes, would mislead them to the serious injury of the public.

The historical record shows Lee in support of slavery and believing that Virginia would be better off without African Americans.[394] A good book exploding the Lost Cause myths about Robert E. lee is *Lee Considered: General Robert E. Lee and Civil War History*, by Alan T. Nolan.

The earliest record of the Robert E. Lee award being given at West Point so far discovered by the author is in the 1948 *United Daughters of the Confederacy Magazine*. However, the article states:

> In former years the award in honor of General Lee, for the highest rating in Mathematics, was a saber. At the request of the Superintendent of the Academy to our President-General this year the award was a wrist watch, suitably inscribed.[395]

This practice obviously had gone on for some time prior to 1948. In the 1954 *United Daughters of the Confederacy Magazine*, an article on the award, states that the first presentation of the Robert E. Lee sword was given in 1931 at West Point at the graduation ceremonies.[396] The *UDC Magazine* page where they have photos of cadets getting awards from the UDC at different academies has not had a photo or mention of an award given at West Point in 2014 and 2015. However, in an Oct. 2015 article in *The Chronicle of Higher Education* by Peter Schmidt states that "all five of the nation's service academies continue to offer annual awards financed by the United Daughters of the Confederacy."

The article also states that in response to his inquiries about the award:

... [t]he White House and the Pentagon directed inquiries to the service academies, whose spokesmen described the awards as noncontroversial and among hundreds annually given out.[397]

The article references an earlier letter by Edward H. Sebesta sent to the White House asking that the awards be stopped and documenting the racism of several of the Confederate leaders for whom the awards are named.

It is curious that this award hasn't recently been included in the awards page the UDC usually publishes in their magazine even though it seems to be still given out. Though the author can't offer any proof, it might be that the UDC is not reporting the award so that they can continue to give it but allow West Point to avoid controversy. As the author continues to write and get journalists interested in the enablers of the Confederacy some activities become harder to track.

Though an award given by a group with a long documented record of racism named after a Confederate general who was a traitor, who fought for the Confederacy and who was against African American civil rights during Reconstruction isn't controversial at West Point, Black power salutes evidently are. In a 2016 *New York Times* article, "Raised-Fist Photo by Black Women at West Point Spurs Inquiry," a group of African American women cadets did a group "Old Corps" photo which resulted in a storm of outrage in right wing media. The article reports:

> West Point opened an investigation on April 28 into whether the women violated Army rules that prohibit political activities while in uniform. Now, as the women wait to hear if they will be punished, they are gaining supporters who say they were simply making a gesture of solidarity and strength.[398]

In an article in *The Atlantic*, the West Point officer investigating called the photo "inappropriate," and this officer stated:

> Based on the fact that the photo has caused a perception of impropriety on the part of the sixteen female Cadets, I recommend all photographed individuals receive a block of instruction designed and implemented by the Simon Center for Professional Military Excellence, intended to educate the Cadets on the impact of their actions. I recommend this instruction be completed prior to the May graduation of the USMA Class of 2016. I do not feel the graduation of any of the sixteen Cadets in the photograph should be delayed, so long as they display an understanding of how their actions as Cadets and future Officers were inappropriate, at the conclusion of the instruction.[399]

The article says the cadets "won't be punished," but it seems that they are, in fact, being punished and a message is being sent to future African American cadets. A supposed "Black power" salute is, according to West Point "political" and in violation of the academy's code, however, having cadets photographed posed with a representative of the United Daughters of the Confederacy getting an award named after a Confederate general year after year is somehow politically neutral.

The Commodore Matthew Fontaine Maury award has been given to a cadet of the U.S. Naval academy starting in 1931.[400] Another Maury award was also first given at U.S. Merchant Marine academy starting in 1962.[401]

Maury after the defeat of the Confederacy could not face the end of the Old South and attempted to recreate it in Mexico. Quoting Gaines M. Foster in his book, *Ghosts of the Confederacy*, (which has a section about ex-Confederates hoping to revive a version of the antebellum South):

> The dream received its boldest and clearest expression in the plan of Matthew Fontaine Maury. This former Confederate naval leader sought to recruit two or three hundred thousand from the best families of Virginia – which in actuality would have entailed recruiting all the families of Virginia – for emigration to Mexico. They would bring with them a proportional number of "negro skilled laborers in agriculture" who would enter the country as "peons" – a concession that caused Maury to consider himself an abolitionist. Together, the best families and faithful peons would build a "New Virginia" in a part of Mexico that reminded Maury of the Valley of the Shenandoah.[402]

To accomplish this, Maury worked with and was supported by French puppet Emperor Maximilian, and so thus worked against the struggles for freedom of the Mexican people lead by Benito Juarez for the restoration of the Mexican republic.

Maury also worked at length for a scheme to colonize the Amazon River basin of Brazil with African American slaves, and sent an agent, William Herndon, to the Amazon to scout it out. Maury's contempt for Brazilians and his plans for this slave expansion are shown in these excerpts in a letter of instruction to Herndon:

> … [W]ho shall people the Great Valley of this Mighty Amazon? Shall it be peopled with an imbecile and an indolent people or by a go ahead race that has energy and enterprise equal to subdue the forest and to develop and bring forth the vast resources that lie hidden here?

> [I]t [Brazil] cannot no more prevent American citizens from the free, as well as from the slave states, from going there with their goods and chattels to settle and to revolutionize and republicanize and Anglo Saxonize that valley, than it can prevent the magazine from exploding after the firebrand that has been thrown into it. That valley is to [be] the safety valve for our Southern States, when they become over-populated with slaves, the African Slave Trade will be stopped, and they will send their slaves to the Amazon. Just as the Mississippi Valley has been the escape valve for the slaves of the Northern, now free, States, so will the Amazon be to that of the Mississippi.

Herndon's report of his findings of this mission sold 30,000 copies in the first two printings in 3 months.[403] To further promote this expansion of slavery Maury resorted to the fear mongering of race war. In *De Bow's Review* in an article advocating the transfer of African American slaves to the Amazon, Maury writes:

> The fact must be obvious to the far-reaching minds of our statesmen, that unless some means of relief be devised, some channel afforded, by which the South can, when the time comes, get rid of the excess of her slave population, that she will be ultimately found, with regard to this institution, in the predicament of the man with the wolf by the ears—too dangerous to hold on any longer, and equally dangerous to let go.

> To our mind, the event is as certain to happen as any event is [sic] which depends on the contingencies of the future, viz.: that unless means be devised for gradually relieving the slave states from the undue pressure of this class upon them—unless some way be opened by which they may be rid of their surplus black population,—the time will come—it may not be in the next nor in the succeeding generation—but, sooner or later, come it will, and come it must—when the two races will join in the death struggle for the mastery.[404]

A columnist in 1958 in the *UDC Magazine* in an article praising Maury, lists the attempt to make the Amazon River basin a slave empire as an example of his intellect along with his other accomplishments and awards. Further the columnist quotes Maury writing to his cousin that transferring African American slaves to the Amazon "…would be relieving our own country of the slaves, it would be hastening the time of our deliverance, and if it would be putting off indefinitely, the horrows [sic] of that war of races, which without an escape is surely to come.[405]

The earliest record the author has of the Raphael Semmes award given at graduation ceremonies at the U.S. Coast Guard ceremonies is in the August 1959 *United Daughters of the Confederacy Magazine*.[406]

Professor Gerald Horne, in his book, *The Deepest South: The United States, Brazil, and the African Slave Trade*, discusses the obsessive racism of Raphael Semmes. In Mexico Semmes erected a tombstone that said, "… in memoriam of Abraham Lincoln, President of the late United States, who died of nigger on the brain, 1ˢᵗ January 1863." Brazilian society displeased Semmes because of racial antipathies. Horne quotes Semmes in his rejection of post-war colonization of Brazil as follows:

> "The effete Portuguese race," he sputtered, "has been ingrafted [sic]upon a stupid, stolid Indian stock in that country … this might be a suitable field enough for the New England schoolma'am and carpet-bagger, but no Southern gentleman should think of mixing his blood or casting his lot with such a race of people."

Horne explains that while Semmes, as a Confederate naval officer during the Civil War, was hosted and feted by Brazilian society he was obsessed with their racial composition. Horne writes:

> He was disgusted with "amalgamation" in Brazil, thinking it provided a poor example for North America, as it was leading to "mongrel set of curs" that would "cover the whole land." He was more pleased with South Africa where "the African has met the usual fate of the savage, when he comes in contact with civilized man. He had been thrust aside, and was only to be seen as a straggler and stranger in his native land." As he saw it, "the inhabitants of the Cape Colony seemed to resemble our own people" in their penchant for white supremacy.

Horne also questions Semmes being considered a hero and writes:

> The "damage done by Raphael Semmes to the commerce of the United States" amounted to "ten millions of dollars." Yet despite this mayhem he inflicted on the U.S. during the course of his treasonous revolt, after the war his "statue" was placed prominently on "Mobile's busiest thoroughfare, standing near the sea he so long loved and dominated."[407]

Certainly a racist and treasonous destroyer of American shipping is an inappropriate name for an award to be given to a cadet of the U.S. Coast Guard academy.

As reported in the *UDC Magazine* in 2008 the South Carolina Division of the UDC has given a Wade Hampton Sabre annually to a cadet at the Citadel for 36 years.[408]

Wade Hampton was the leader of the Red Shirts who conducted a violent and successful campaign to restore white supremacy in South Carolina ending the multiracial democracy of Reconstruction. Wade Hampton is a hero to the UDC South Carolina Division precisely because he restored white supremacy to South Carolina and overthrew Reconstruction.

The UDC South Carolina Division issued a publication, *United Daughters of the Confederacy, South Carolina Division: Golden Anniversary 1896-1946*. In it on page 13 is an article titled, "Oakley Park, Edgefield's Red Shirt Shrine." Oakley Park is an old Plantation house which the South Carolina UDC division had decided in October 1944 to restore. The importance of this house for restoration is stated in the article, "Oakley Park was the home of General Martin Witherspoon Gary, who with his Red Shirts, in 1876, did so much to restore white supremacy in South Carolina."

The article explains further:

> The "Red Shirts" were largely ex-Confederate soldiers under the leadership of their one-time military commanders. Forbidden to organize into military companies and regarding the gray uniform of the Confederacy as inappropriate, the men arrayed themselves in red shirts and formed mounted bands which patrolled the State in the interest of the Democratic nominee for Governor, which was Hampton, against the Republican nominee, Chamberlain. "A white man's government", they said. Then followed a long struggle for control. The Republicans held the State House, and were sustained by United States troops. Conditions were desperate! The Democrats were determined to get the government back into the hands of the white people.

> The Red Shirts, who gathered at Oakley Park and rode out from there were a great factor in achieving this, and in the election of Hampton in 1876, and thus was accomplished the overthrow of that "blackest abomination" – The Radical Government of South Carolina."[409]

The author hasn't completed biographical studies of all the persons for whom the awards are named. Excepting Chennault, they are all named after individuals who fought for the Confederacy.

It is bad policy to give awards at American military academies named after leaders who waged war on the American government and were traitors. The history of republics has numerous cases where the military, which is supposed to defend the republic, has instead overthrown or attempted to overthrow the republic. This goes back to the fall of the Roman Republic to the fall of the Italian Republics and unto this this year (2016) with an attempted coup d'état against the Republic of Turkey.

It is dangerous to have an officer swear to uphold the Constitution but allow the officer to receive an award named after an individual who betrayed his oath of allegiance. At that moment not all treason is odious.

In the many years of the UDC awards program there is no record of a single cadet refusing the award. If you decide to enlist in the American military you might be serving under an officer that was glad to get a neo-Confederate award.

JUNIOR RESERVE OFFICER TRAINING CORPS

In American high schools the U.S. military has a Junior Reserve Officer Training Corps (JROTC). The H.L. Hunley was a Confederate submarine named after its inventor Horace Lawson Hunley.

The SCV announces the, "Junior ROTC H.L. Hunley Awards Program," in 2009 in the *Confederate Veteran*. The article explains that formerly it was a local award of the South Carolina Division of the SCV and the General Executive Council of the SCV had decided to make it a national SCV awards program in 2009. This article also mentions "more than 200 awards" had been presented in South Carolina already.[410]

The purpose of this award is explained by A.C. Wilson III, National Chairman of the H.L. Hunley Award, in 2014 in the *Confederate Veteran*.

Wilson opens with:

> Every year I have two or three camp commanders asking just exactly what this program does that contributes to our fulfilling General Stephen Dill Lee's Charge to the Sons.

Wilson explains why the SCV has this program. The SCV gets to sit in at the awards programs and as he explains further:

> Tomorrow's leaders are sitting in these auditoriums … As these young Americans are recognized … they remember who recognized their hard work and sacrifices. We … sit among the … leaders who are there representing the Sons of the American Revolution, Daughters of the American Revolution, Scottish Rite, American Legion, Veterans of Foreign Wars, Military Order of Purple Hearts and many others… We are meeting high school administrators, teachers and parents and will be asked to make presentations to classes on the War Between the States and share with these students the true history of the South, students who represent our future generations.

The article announces that, "In 2010/2011 we sent out more than 250 awards, and that this year, "we gave out more than 400 awards," and that, "We have only touched the tip of the iceberg because there are more than 6,000 JROTC units in the country." The article also points out that "a year and a half ago" that they got "official approval from the US Navy and Army JROTC Headquarters," and that the Air Force sent out their guide which included the H.L. Hunley award.

The SCV apparently sees this award as an opportunity to use African American students to legitimize themselves. In the article Wilson tells how an African American store employee was happy because he had gotten a H.L. Hunley award from the SCV when he was in JROTC at Eau Claire High School which Wilson points out "is about 98 percent black."[411]

In 2013 another issue of the *Confederate Veteran*, included the article "Junior ROTC – Implementing the Charge." The publication made a point of having a photograph of a smiling African American cadet receiving an award.[412] The title of the article makes it clear that the purpose of this award is to advance the *Charge* of Stephen D. Lee. In other articles in the *Confederate Veteran* it becomes clear to the author of this book that the *Charge* includes opposition to civil rights. In addition, The Charge was written by a person who excused the lynching of African Americans.

The author in 2015 wrote all four military services letters asking that they not permit the H.L. Hunley award and provided information both about the SCV and the SCV's agenda behind this award. Two of the services replied with very brief letters that evaded the issues raised and two didn't reply.

The United Daughters of the Confederacy has decided to give out a JROTC medal, the UDC President General announcing that the UDC was going to copyright the medal in the 2014 *UDC magazine*.[413] In 2016 the UDC President General stated that, "The JROTC Medals have been being [sic] awarded in rapid fashion" and "… we have awarded 125 medals to date."[414] Less is known about this program.

The young people who join the JROTC trust that the persons running the program have their interests in mind. To allow these students to be exploited for a neo-Confederate agenda is a disgrace.

The U.S. Military has a tremendous amount of prestige in the United States. Allowing the neo-Confederates to glom onto that prestige allows them to legitimize themselves, and to advance their agenda.

Religious Denominations

The Sons of Confederate Veterans and the United Daughters of the Confederacy get the use of church facilities for monthly meetings, Confederate Memorial Day events, other neo-Confederate events, and for their national conventions. For national conventions they typically choose a historic church that is a prominent and prestigious architectural landmark. The denominations which lend the UDC and SCV these the facilities are not fringe denominations but major mainstream denominations. (I am excluding cemeteries in this discussion of facilities.)

The prestigious building lends its prestige to the neo-Confederate organization. There is prestige in that the neo-Confederate organization has the influence to obtain the use of such a building. Further the denomination also confers legitimacy on the neo-Confederate groups. It is not likely that any mainstream denomination would lend their facilities to an organization that was generally understood to be racist or on the fringe.

There is a preconception that churches that might host the Sons of Confederate Veterans and the United Daughters of the Confederacy must be some very conservative denomination. However, that is the exception, as the following bar graphs will show. The bar graphs are also online at http://www.templeofdemocracy.com/churches-of-the-confederacy.html. The website includes the extensive correspondence which the author has mailed to churches and denominational leaders along with a description of their response can be read. This has been an interesting project since, in addition to opposing the neo-Confederate movement, I realized that I am mapping out the reality of American Christianity and its true views of race beneath all the surface rhetoric. I have file boxes filling up with correspondence, certified letter receipts and post cards, and proof of mailing receipts, and documentation.

This is a bar graph of denominations which have hosted the United Daughters of the Confederacy at their national conventions from 1990 to 2015.

PERNICIOUS

United Daughters of the Confederacy National Convention Hosting Churches by Denomination 1990 to 2015.

Denomination	Count
Episcopal	13
United Methodist	4
Presbyterian USA	2
Roman Catholic	2
Southern Baptist Convention	1
American Baptist Church	1
Historic Richmond Foundation	1
No Church	1

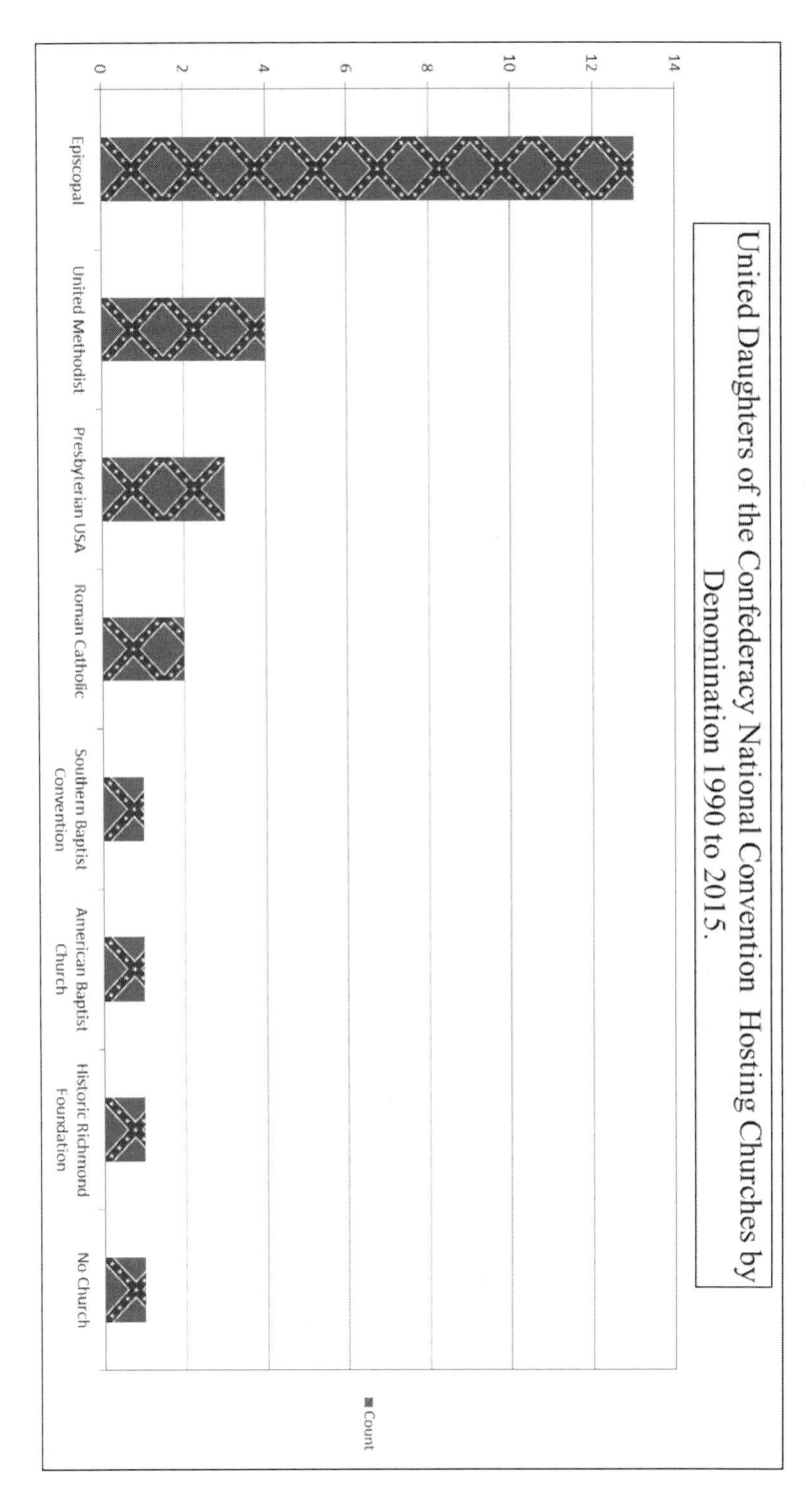

This is the bar graphs of denominations which have hosted the Sons of Confederate Veterans at their national conventions.

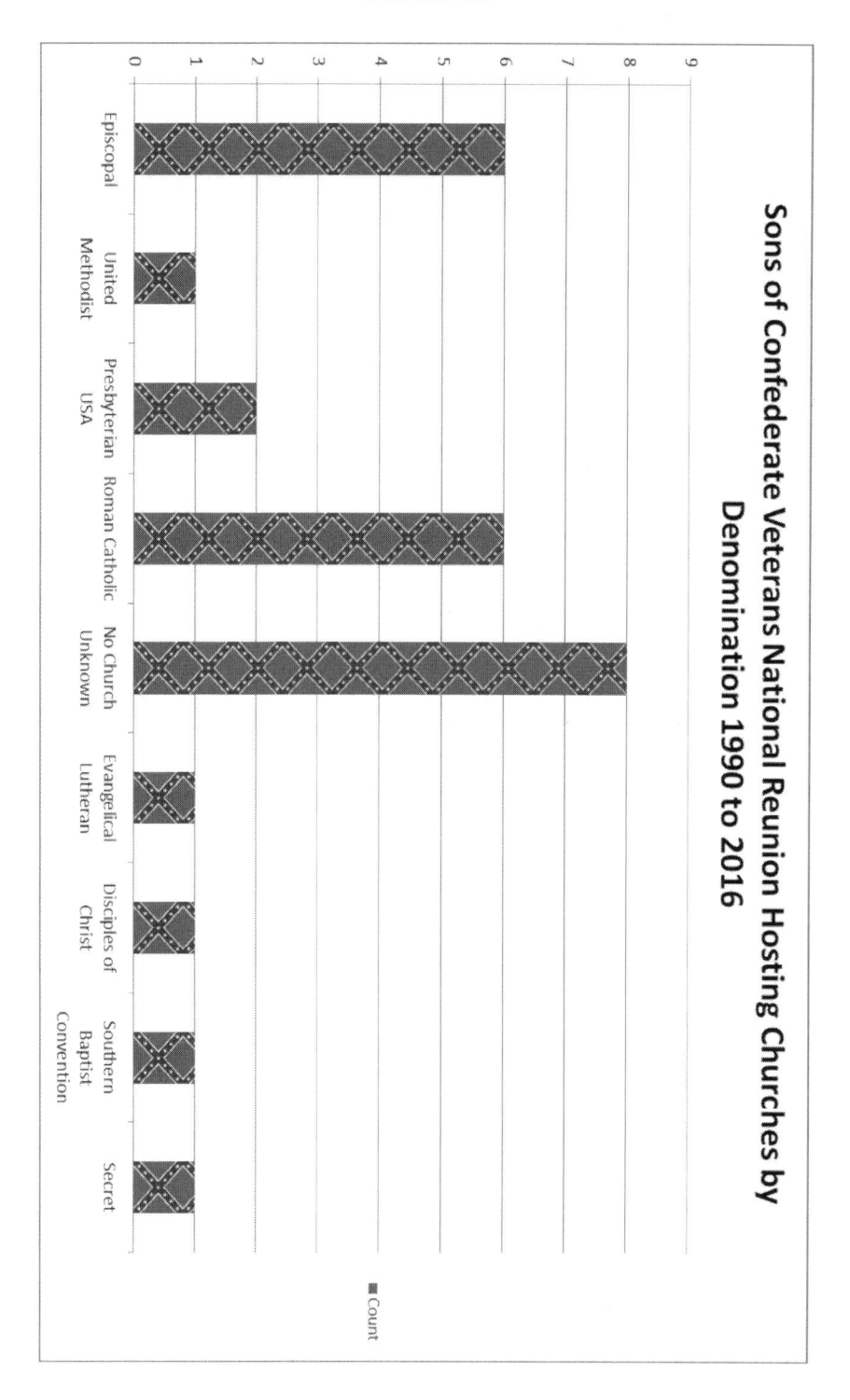

Sons of Confederate Veterans National Reunion Hosting Churches by Denomination 1990 to 2016

Denomination	Count
Episcopal	6
United Methodist	1
Presbyterian USA	2
Roman Catholic	6
No Church Unknown	8
Evangelical Lutheran	1
Disciples of Christ	1
Southern Baptist Convention	1
Secret	1

ENABLERS: BANAL WHITE NATIONALISM

This is the bar graph of denominations which have hosted the Children of the Confederacy. (An organization run with the oversight of the United Daughters of the Confederacy.

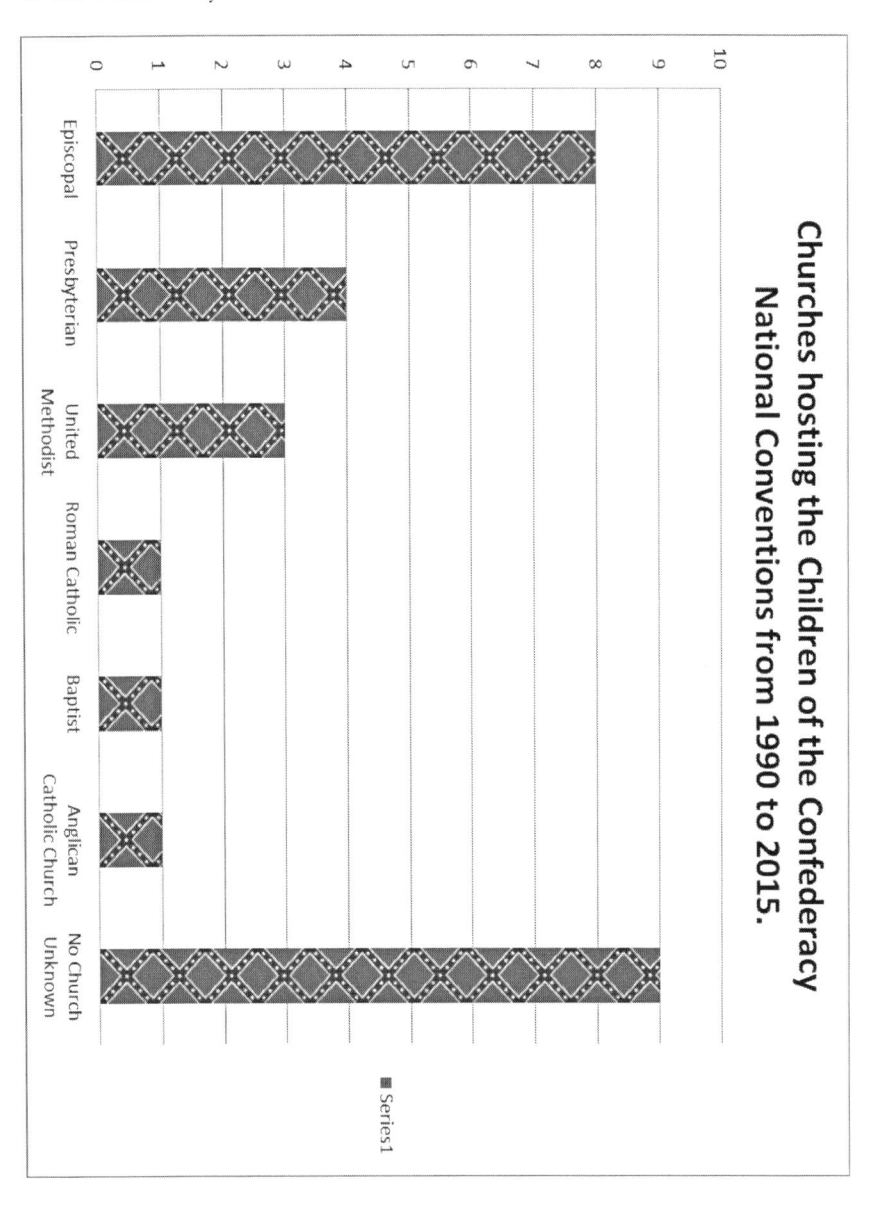

Churches hosting the Children of the Confederacy National Conventions from 1990 to 2015.

Denomination	Count
Episcopal	8
Presbyterian	4
United Methodist	3
Roman Catholic	1
Baptist	1
Anglican Catholic Church	1
No Church Unknown	9

The author has received three types of responses from denominations evading the question when there is a response at all.

1. The recipient doesn't know of any churches hosting a neo-Confederate group. However, whether the recipient checked to see if any church is hosting a neo-Confederate group or that an assumption is being made is not specified. The recipient did not say whether or not they advised the churches not to host neo-Confederate groups is not mentioned. Nor, finally, will there be any action to discuss the matter with church leadership, to pass a resolution, or have a public statement or discussion on the topic.

2. Another response confines the question to the narrow topic that they can't compel a church not to host. In such responses, the recipient ignores that they could make a statement on their own, and fail to commit to raising the question within their denomination. Such respondents could work to persuade churches to not host neo-Confederate groups. However, in the end, either their denomination is hosting neo-Confederate groups or it is not and excuses are irrelevant.

3. The third type of response is to write back and mention how many minority members they have in their denomination and avoid the question entirely. One variant of this response is to mention that they are having a joint function with an African American church. Another variant is to reference some statement or resolution their denomination has issued against racism.

Episcopal Church

Though the Episcopal Church has hosted the United Daughters of the Confederacy the most, the great majority of these events were at St. Paul's Episcopal Church in Richmond, Virginia where they have met every other year in the past. In 2014 the author emailed and wrote letters to the clergy, vestry, and others at St. Paul's Episcopal Church asking them not to host. At the same time the author wrote the entire executive council of the Episcopal Church, and other groups within the Episcopal Church with enclosed bar graphs.

St. Paul's Episcopal Church decided not to host the United Daughters of the Confederacy and also decided to review how their church has identified with the Confederacy.

The National Cathedral in Washington D.C. has decided to remove their Confederate stain glass.

However, Episcopal churches are still hosting United Daughters of the Confederacy events at the local level. The Episcopal Church hasn't passed any resolution against the Confederate flag. Also, they haven't, as a denomination discussed the issue. I didn't get any response from the national leadership either. So though there have been some positive developments, members of the Episcopal Church should ask some questions about whether their church is hosting neo-Confederate events.

The Dallas Episcopal Diocese was written in 2014 concerning the 2016 SCV convention in the Dallas area and the first response was that the bishop didn't know of any and there was no follow up response to another letter sent in 2016. This is unfortunate since it was a real possibility that one Episcopal Church might have hosted the SCV.

Roman Catholic Church

Generally the response has been no response. There was a response from the Archdiocese of San Antonio that parish matters were the responsibility of the Dallas Diocese, but the Dallas Diocese didn't respond at all. Included in the letter was a quote from a resolution against discrimination. The Richmond Diocese's response to the first letter was that they didn't know of any such event planned and they thus avoided the issue. In response to a follow up letter there was no response.

In looking at the websites of the Dioceses of the Roman Catholic Church you will see they are outspoken on a great many things. Dealing with the issue of the Confederacy is not one of them.

Presbyterian Church USA

I haven't started a letter writing campaign with them. I was hoping that one of the other denominations would set a precedent I could refer to as an example. They haven't lent their facilities that often, but as other denominations refuse neo-Confederates their denomination might become the alternative choice.

I wrote the Presbytery that includes Richmond, Virginia twice and got very legalistic responses. The author will need to re-read the Gospels and see if previously he had overlooked a passage in which Christ passes the bar exam. I didn't get any response for the letter sent to the Presbytery that includes Dallas in regards to the SCV's 2016 convention in Richardson, Texas, a suburb of Dallas.

Southern Baptist Convention

To prevent a church from lending their facilities to the SCV in 2014 in Charleston, South Carolina area, I wrote the leaders there of the United Methodists Church, both factions of the Episcopal Church, the Roman Catholic Church, and the Presbyterian USA Church asking them not to host the SCV in 2014. The SCV got the Ashley River Baptist Church to host their national convention service in 2014. I hadn't written the Southern Baptist Convention (SBC) leaders since I thought their apology over slavery meant something such they wouldn't host a neo-Confederate group. I was wrong. The neo-Confederates have denounced the SBC with vitriol for their apology over slavery which I also thought would be another reason the SBC would not host.

I have since written the entire leadership and executive board of the SBC asking that they not host neo-Confederate groups and providing documentation on the racism of the SCV and UDC. I received no response. In response to the SCV's planned 2016 convention in Dallas, Texas I wrote the leadership and board of the Texas SBC, and the leader of the Dallas Baptist Association. I did get replies. The Texas SBC responded that they have minority members and the leader of the Dallas Baptist Association stated he didn't know of any churches that were hosting.

Recently the SBC has passed a resolution against the Confederate battle flag but the resolution needs to be examined very carefully. The resolution is based on the idea that the Confederate battle flag is offensive, not that the Confederacy was wrong. The resolution says nothing about neo-Confederate groups or allowing them the use of facilities. So it is very likely that SBC churches will continue to host neo-Confederate groups.

Though in the past the SBC has hosted a few events, in the future they may host more since some other denominations, whether they respond to my correspondence or not, have seemed to have stopped lending their facilities to the more visible neo-Confederates events such as national conventions. After two years of letters to the Richmond area the SCV could not find a church to host their national convention service in 2015. So in Memphis in 2017 and Franklin, Tennessee outside Nashville in 2018 the SCV may choose a Southern Baptist Church since other denominations might turn them down.

In terms of the church organizational arguments that they can't compel an individual church to do anything, the SBC does kick out churches that aren't anti-gay as the New Heart Community Church in La Mirada, California discovered.[415] The old adage, "Where there is a will, there is a way," comes to mind.

United Methodist Church

The African Episcopal Church, the African Episcopal Zion Church and the Christian Methodists, which is a historically African American Methodist denomination have never hosted a neo-Confederate group for anything.

The United Methodist Church (UMC) however, has the worst track record of hosting neo-Confederate groups despite being asked not to. The UMC has been evasive over the issue if they respond at all.

In 2013 the Boston Avenue United Methodist Church in Tulsa, Oklahoma hosted the United Daughters of the Confederacy. *UDC Magazine* latter featured multiple pictures of their members and leadership in and in front of the church appropriating to the UDC the prestige of this architectural landmark. This was despite letters to the UMC national leadership and the leadership of the Boston Avenue congregation.

The response in 2014 to a request that the UMC in Richmond not host the UDC was that individual churches couldn't be compelled to not host a neo-Confederate group, and in 2015 the response to a request that they not host the SCV in Richmond there was no response at all.

The North Carolina Division of the United Daughters of the Confederacy had on their website for the 2015 UDC national convention in Raleigh, North Carolina that it was to be held at the Edenton Street United Methodist Church, which was then replaced with a new web page for the 2015 UDC national convention without a specific church mentioned. The minister of the church replied to a letter that there had never been an arrangement to do so. However, prior to that letter I got emails from someone purporting to be a member of the church using a personal email account inquiring about the convention and I referred the person to a Google cache and later a www.archive.org copy of the website showing that the Edenton Street church was scheduled to be the location of the UDC service. However, when writing an inquiry to the person by letter and also sending emails to the person's official account I got no reply. Not sure exactly what happened.

The deletion of the web page was prior to this person's inquiry. It may demonstrate that there is a growing campaign of secrecy in arranging these church events.

I wrote The Court Street United Methodist Church in Lynchburg, Virginia in 2015 asking them not to host the group Children of the Confederacy. I got no reply.

When I sent a request in 2014 to not host the SCV to the Dallas UMC in 2014 not to host the SCV I got no response. In 2016 I got an email in reply from Bishop Michael McKee that he was unaware of any church hosting neo-Confederate groups and that was all.

It appears that the United Methodist Church is very likely to continue to hosting neo-Confederate groups.

At this time the campaign to get churches to not host neo-Confederate groups is making limited progress. None of the major denominations will take a stand on it or even discuss it. The SCV staring in 2014 has not stated where they are having their services and not listing it in their published schedules. I only found out that they met at the Ashley River Baptist church in a news article. In 2015 no church would accept them, according to published reports. In 2016 the SCV had in their schedule they had a church "TBA" (to be announced), the author doesn't know what church it was. The UDC may also follow this strategy. It has to be asked if churches that assist this secrecy in hosting Confederate functions are acting in collusion.

The United Methodist Churches seem to be shifting to a legalistic argument that they can't compel churches, but in doing research the author found out that they acted very quickly and decisively to go after ministers that performed gay marriages, and talked about connectivity in doing so. It seems connectivity is acceptable to enforce homophobia, but not to reject neo-Confederacy. The policy of the UMC seems to be, homophobia, connectivity, racism, dis-connectivity.

IN GENERAL

While writing to church leaders in various cities I would also write or contact by email various alliances of churches that purported to be concerned with social justice. They were uniformly not helpful and from the Tulsa Metropolitan Ministry I got an angry tirade from Director Ray Hickman who, after the fact, denied me permission to publish his comments and in writing their Board of Directors about the letter there was no reply.

Collectively the major American denominations are enabling the neo-Confederate groups by refusing to respond to or raise the issue. If some of the denominations would reject hosting neo-Confederate groups, focus could be on those that do. If the issue was raised before the public, many church attendees would ask questions of their leadership.

Members of these denominations are likely to point out that they do this or that to fight racism, and in some cases this effort is sincere like that of the St. Paul's Episcopal Church, the National Cathedral and some other Episcopal churches. However, for many of the others I would like to repeat a summary statement an African American friend said upon learning of my efforts, "It's a lot of white people fooling around to feel good about themselves." I am afraid it is.

The author is having to send out a tremendous amount of correspondence to keep pressure on the churches, and even then the focus is only on five major denominations.

These are the things that the reader could do that would make a difference.

1. Ensure that your church is not hosting a neo-Confederate event or group. Do not think that your church is so good on the issues of race that they would not host a neo-Confederate group.

2. Don't make excuses for your denomination hosting neo-Confederate groups.

3. Raise the issue in your denomination. A simple discussion panel would make the membership of the denomination realize that it is an issue and that their denomination is hosting neo-Confederates or keep their denomination from hosting neo-Confederates..

4. Tell others about the issue at other churches in your denomination and in interfaith groups.

5. Let others know about this issue.

These five steps would stop many churches from enabling the neo-Confederate movement. When the word gets around, a lot of churches, even if they really don't care about the issue, will not host neo-Confederate groups to avoid the controversy. Possibly even some organization or church leader will make a public statement on the issue and it could start a national debate. Finally, keep up with the web page on Churches of the Confederacy at www.templeofdemocracy.com.

For those who are members of historically African American denominations when some church organization wants to have an interracial event, ask what their policy is regarding neo-Confederate groups. One of the replies I got from a minster in the United Methodist Church was that they had a joint activity with an African American church which somehow made it okay that they were hosting meetings of the SCV. Make sure that you and your church isn't being used.

"Patriotic" Societies

The American Legion and Veterans of Foreign Wars (VFW) should consider whether it is patriotic to lend their facilities to neo-Confederate groups who honor those who would have destroyed our nation if they had succeeded. I am still occasionally finding that local chapters of these organizations are doing so.

What is disturbing is that in a 2014 in *Confederate Veteran*, Gene Hogan, SCV Chief of Heritage Operations, presented the following as a viable strategy:

> Finally, another means of effective communication is cooperation... However, because we live in a society that often has trouble remembering, and consequently, valuing, any sacrifice from the past, we must, when possible, make common cause with the SAR, DAR, VFW, American Legion and any other similarly chartered organizations. [SAR is the Sons of the American Revolution, and the DAR is the Daughters of the American Revolution.][416]

It is not surprising that they have this expectation. In 2009, in the *Confederate Veteran* there is a notice that a SCV member has been elected President General and Chairman of the Board of the Sons of the American Revolution. The notice states that SAR President Butler extended an invitation to the SCV Commander-in-Chief to attend a meeting of the SAR Leadership.[417] Evidently the SAR is aware of the American Revolution, but apparently not the civil rights revolution.

In another 2014 issue of the *Confederate Veteran* we find that the Sons of the American Revolution (SAR) has rejected an ad by the SCV. This shouldn't necessarily be taken as proof that these organizations have moved apart. SCV Lt. Commander-in-Chief Charles Kelly Barrow writes that the SAR had run their ad in an issue of their publication, but the SAR membership had reacted to it negatively. However the negative reaction seems to be towards the radical language that the SCV was using, and the SAR would have been willing to run an ad for the SCV without such radical language. [418]

These societies which claim to be patriotic should be told in no uncertain terms that they are not patriotic at all when they enable neo-Confederate groups. When they do work with neo-Confederate they should be publically condemned as unpatriotic.

The idea of hereditary castes of individuals who are somehow more American than others is fundamentally against the American democratic idea. These hereditary groups will often say that their purpose is to advance the history of some part of the American past. However, if that was true then the groups should not be hereditary and they should be historical societies, not "Sons of" and "Daughters of." They should be open to everyone who was interested in the groups historical focus. These societies are about exclusion and it is not surprising they have a long record of working with neo-Confederate groups.

The next time a member of one of these groups speaks to your class or group ask them questions if they are a member of a neo-Confederate group and if so why. Ask them about their working with neo-Confederate groups. They need to get the message. Also, ask this of any representative of a local historical society of any type and preservationist societies.

Yale University and Others

The previously mentioned enablers were selected because they significantly enable neo-Confederates. The churches, U.S. Military academies mentioned above and JROTC show that institutions which seem to have nothing to do with neo-Confederates are in fact enablers.

There are many other enablers. That there were historical societies that campaigned for the retention of the Confederate monuments in New Orleans, which was mentioned earlier in this book, was not at all surprising to the author. The academic fields of Civil War history and the field of Southern Studies have some serious issues. Discussing these other enablers would be a book in itself. The author is contemplating a book on the neo-Confederate intelligentsia in America which would be largely a study of Southern Studies.

However, enabling is not confined to just these venues just mentioned. Enabling neo-Confederacy can happen where ever banal white nationalism permeates America and this permeation seems to be very wide spread in American intellectual life. One example is an article in a recent issue (June 8, 2016) of the *New York Review of Books*, David Cole, professor in Law and Public Policy at Georgetown University Law Center, in an interview with Yale University President Peter Salovey discusses his decision not to change the name of Calhoun College at Yale University named after John C. Calhoun a leading defending of slavery in America before the Civil War. Salovey gives basically the argument which is used to defend Confederate monuments everywhere. Cole questions are not too demanding, but serve as platforms for Salovay to justify his actions.

In response to a question by Cole on how does Yale confront the legacy of John C. Calhoun since Yale "has celebrated Calhoun in a public way?" Salovay denies that Yale has been celebrating Calhoun with this response:

> I would not call naming a residential college for Calhoun necessarily celebrating him, although it does memorialize him.

This response is nonsensical. Names for buildings are chosen, and not drawn out of a hat. This naming was meant to celebrate Calhoun. Memorialization is a means of celebrating the accomplishments of the dead.

Salovay describes a "principle" which justifies keeping the name.

> To me, the principle that is most compelling is that we should attempt to confront our history in order both to learn from it and to change the future. We shouldn't obscure our history, or run from it. ... But to me the appropriate response is to ask what we can learn about the history of racism in this country, and thereby motivate ourselves to work towards a better future.

Salovay here is attempting to portray his decision to continue to have John C. Calhoun glorified on Yale University and the maintaining the campus' racial landscape as equivalent to confronting America's racist past and defending history. He has transformed himself as some type of combatant against racism.[419]

This is similar to other banal white nationalists' arguments in defense of Confederate monuments that the removal is erasing history, thus positioning the defender of the monument as a defender of history.

Salovay then discusses a variety of ways that his school is going to do to fight racism. These are obviously mentioned to justify the retention of the John C. Calhoun name. Then the conversation wanders far away from Calhoun College to discuss other issues of race.

Confronting racism would be changing the name of John C. Calhoun so Yale would not continue to glorify Calhoun and give Yale a white racialized landscape. Keeping the name continues to send a message that obscures history since it is the practice to name buildings after people who we feel should be honored. It is one reason that few libraries are knowingly named after serial killers.

Keeping the name sends a very powerful message that one of Yale University's core values involve keeping the Calhoun name.

I think that the real reason the name Calhoun was kept is that a lot of alumni were upset.

The Calhoun College had, until recently, a stain glass window of African slaves picking cotton. Not long after this interview was published in *The New York Review of Books*, Corey Menafee, an African American dishwasher who had worked in Calhoun College since 2007, on impulse, knocked it out of the window, stating, "It's 2016, I shouldn't have to come to work and see things like that." Menafee called the window "racist, very demeaning." Menafee was arrested, and Yale made a statement that the falling glass had endangered students.[420] Yale did later rehire him under the condition that he not speak about the matter, effectively gagging him.[421]

Menafee also smashed the rationalizations of Salovay, Cole, and the staff of *The New York Review of Books*. Evidently there was one employee who didn't exactly understand the "principle" on how Yale was going to "confront" racism.

The importance of this example is where this enabling occurred and in which publication the retention of the Calhoun name for the college was justified.

This wasn't some building in some college in the South. In fact in the South these things are really getting confronted, it was at Yale, one of the most prestigious universities in the nation.

This article and interview didn't appear in some benighted journal which still rhapsodizes about the Southern Agrarians or admires racist M.E. Bradford, or some stridently conservative publication, but in *The New York Review of Books* which supposedly has editors who engage in critical thinking. For the record they are: Editor, Robert B. Silvers; Senior Editors, Michael Shae, Hugh Eakin, Eve Bowen, and Jana Prikryl.

The New York Review of Books article and interview shows that banal white nationalism is extensive in our nation as is the solidarity of these banal white nationalists. This worldview appears at places, at institutions, where we would likely least expect it. This is the great power which supports neo-Confederates.

I think we need to start calling people like Salovay, Cole, and others banal white nationalists and bring to the surface this banal white nationalism. Until we acknowledge the existence of something we can't fight it.

Nor is this type of thing unique to Yale University. The University of Texas at Austin had four Confederate statutes on their main mall: Confederate General Albert Sidney Johnston, Jefferson Davis, Robert E. Lee, and Confederate Postmaster John H. Reagan. Someone had spray painted "Davis Must Fall" and "Emancipate UT" on the Jefferson Davis statue, and "Black Lives Matter" on the Lee and Johnston statues.[422] In June 2015 the University of Texas at Austin announced a task force to review the Jefferson Davis statue on campus. The twelve members of this task force were:

Gregory J. Vincent, Vice President for Diversity and Community Engagement (chair)

Laura Beckworth, Law School alumna; Chair of UT Austin Development Board

Daina Berry, Associate Professor, Departments of History and African and African Diaspora Studies

Hector de Leon, Law School Alumnus; past president of both the UT Law Alumni Association and the Texas Exes; 2010 Distinguished Alumnus

Edmund "Ted" Gordon, Chair, Department of African and African Diaspora Studies

Rohit Mandalapu, Vice President, Student Government; Senior, College of Liberal Arts

Carlos Martinez, Associate Vice President for Governmental Relations

Lorraine Pangle, Co-director, Thomas Jefferson Center for the Study of Core Texts and Ideas; Professor, Department of Government

Xavier Rotnofsky, President, Student Government; Senior, College of Liberal Arts

Frederick "Fritz" Steiner, Dean, School of Architecture

Marisa Swanson, President, Social Work Council; Member, Senate of College Councils; Senior, School of Social Work and College of Liberal Arts

Brian Wilkey, President, Graduate Student Assembly; Graduate Student, College of Natural Sciences

Though the task force was asked to have particular focus on Jefferson Davis, all the Main Mall statues were to be reviewed.[423] One of the options the task force considered was removing all four statues.[424]

The decision was to remove just the Jefferson Davis statue, and not the other three. The decision University of Texas President Fenves told the press was that other three had "deep ties" to Texas and Jefferson Davis didn't. Fenves, also says, "While every historical figure leaves a mixed legacy, I believe Jefferson Davis is in a separate category, and that it is not in the university's best interest to continue commemorating him on our Main Mall." The decision was based on the idea that Jefferson Davis didn't have "deep ties" to Texas. The few years that Robert E. Lee spent in Texas as an army officer before the Civil War was evidently enough to be considered "deep ties."[425]

Jefferson Davis wasn't moved because he was the Confederate president and the Confederacy fought for slavery, but because he didn't have "deep ties" to Texas. Similarly three historical figures who were part of the Confederacy, an attempted nation created to preserve white supremacy were okay. This is a decision made by a task force headed by the University of Texas at Austin Vice President of Diversity and Community Engagement. In reviewing the task force decision the reader can see there that this group had no concept at all of the idea of a racialized landscape or recognition that the Confederacy was formed to preserve white supremacy. In the report they were concerned with being seen as "politically correct."

In 2015 Baltimore, Maryland had a Special Commission to review whether to retain or remove its four Confederate monuments: the Confederate Soldiers and Sailors Monument located on Mount Royal Avenue near Mosher Street; the Confederate Women's of Maryland, located at Bishop Square Park; the Roger B. Taney Monument, located on Mt. Vernon Place in North Park; and the Lee & Jackson Monument, located in Wyman Park Dell.

The mayor included our members from the Baltimore City Commission for Historical and Architectural Preservation (CHAP), and three members from the Baltimore City Public Arts Commission. The members of this commission were:

1. Dr. Aaron Bryant: Commission Chair, Andrew Mellon Foundation Curator of Photographer at National Museum of African American History and Culture, and member of CHAP.

2. Dr. Elizabeth Nix, assistant professor of public history at University of Baltimore and author and co-editor of Baltimore '68 Riots and Rebirth in an American City, and member of CHAP.

3. Donna Cypress, director of library services at Lincoln College and member of Maryland Commission on African American History and Culture, and member of CHAP.

4. Larry Gibson, professor of law at the University of Maryland at Baltimore and author of Young Thurgood: The Making of a Supreme Court Justice, and member of CHAP.

5. Elissa Blount-Moorhead, partner TNEG films, independent curator, cultural advisor to contemporary, and member of Baltimore City Public Arts Commission

6. Elford Jackson, prominent civil engineer, and member of Baltimore City Public Arts Commission.

7. Mary Demory, representative of the City Council President's office, and member of Baltimore City Public Arts Commission.[426]

Six of the seven commissioners were African American.

It might be thought that a city with an African American mayor and where seven of fourteen city council members were African American, a city not in the South, would remove all four monuments. However, the Special Commission, as the *Baltimore Sun* reported, "voted narrowly to remove two of them." By a 4 to 3 margin, the commission voted to remove the Lee & Jackson Monument and the Roger B. Taney Monument. By a 6-1 margin the commission decided to keep the Confederate Soldiers and Sailors Monument and the Confederate Women's Monument.

African American Elford Jackson, according to the *Baltimore Sun* argued "he wanted to see more art in Baltimore, not less," and commented "They are pieces of art." The *Baltimore Sun* reports that Alexander E. Hooke, "... described the statute of Lee and Jackson as a 'stunning statue,' and compared it to artwork 'one might find in Paris or Vienna." He also argued that the statue could be a "teachable moment" and called the vote "very sad."[427] The *Baltimore Sun* ran articles by Hooke that opposed efforts to remove Confederate monuments. One article was, "My run in with liberal fascists" where he claimed that he unexpectedly ran into a protest at the Robert E. Lee and Thomas J. "Stonewall" Jackson statue in Wayman Park. Another article compared those who wanted to remove the statues with the Taliban in Afghanistan.[428]

What is even more appalling about the decision of this group is that they are not asking for the monuments to be but into a history museum or some other place where they can be contextualized. They wanted to have the statues moved to other locations where they would still serve a function of glorifying the Confederacy and antebellum slave owners.

As reported by *Reuters,* the Commission's report suggested that the Lee and Jackson monument be given to the National Park Service and placed at the Chancellorsville Battlefield in Virginia.

As of 9/15/2016 the City of Baltimore can't find anyone to take the statues. A spokesperson stated:

> We're going to be reaching out across the state to see if anyone would be interested in partnering with the city of Baltimore in obtaining these monuments.

This requirement might be the pretext to keep the statues where they are.[429] Indeed reported in the *Baltimore Sun* on is an editorial, "No more foot-dragging on Confederate monuments." It complains, "we don't understand why Mayor Staphanie Rawlings-Blake is dragging her feet." It demolishes the excuses made for the statues. It points out that the idea of giving the statue to the National Park Service "is a non-starter" since rules to place new statues there involve legislation to do so and much meet a requirement for the parks purpose. They point out somewhat humorously, "It's a buyer's market now with regard to Confederate-related monuments, with many cities and towns seeking to get rid of them and not many looking to add them." The article suggests placing the status in a warehouse.[430]

There are members of white elites who have Confederate ancestors and their donations might be vital to a future political campaign. Among the white population the Confederacy has significant support and their votes might be important for a state-wide election.

Is it really surprising that what happened to Freddie Gray, a man who died of being roughly handled by the police, happened in Baltimore and that in the Baltimore legal system there was no consequences to those whose actions resulted in Gray's death?

Support for the Confederacy is widespread. When there are attempts to remove monuments of Confederates or pro-slavery leaders who are considered heroes by the neo-Confederate movement all sorts of rationalizations are employed to justify these monuments. By opposing these monuments we will see who will do neo-Confederate bidding and who will go along with them. But much more importantly we will surfaced the banal white nationalism of America and will see the nation as it really is.

14 AMERICAN HISTORY TEXTBOOKS

I wrote at the beginning of this book that it would not be primarily about history, but neo-Confederate ideas are communicated to new generations and are given legitimacy when they are transmitted through history textbooks. Consciously or not, white nationalism often becomes the curriculum of public schools. In a review of a history textbook there will be some discussion of history.

It should not be surprising that a great portion of the public are banal white nationalists, that is persons for whom black lives don't matter or don't matter much. The public school systems in their American history classes have taught children banal white nationalism and not so banal white nationalism for generations with banal to not so banal white nationalistic American history textbooks.

The author has purchased American history textbooks both for the public schools and the private Christian schools at various times over the last 20 years to review them. The school books written for the private Christian schools have been abysmal and won't be reviewed here.

Though there has been some progress in American history textbooks in recent years, the improvement has been relative from a low level. When the author reviewed the new notorious Texas teaching standards regarding the Civil War and Reconstruction for *Politics and the History Curriculum: The Struggle Over Standards in Texas and the Nation*, (Palgrave Macmillan, 2012), he told the editor that though the new standards were really bad, the prior standards weren't very good either. (The author purchased all the new Texas teaching standards American history textbooks and hopes to review them some day.)

In reading these new textbooks, it is clear that even with their substantial improvements over their predecessors, the newer texts still incorporate a banal white nationalist message, in particular, of those banal white nationalists who want to have a nice guest house for minorities.

So for this section two of the better American history textbooks were selected and read for review. One book is the Teacher' Edition, for the AP Edition for the 16th edition of *The American Pageant: History of the American People*, by David M. Kennedy of Stanford University and Lizabeth Cohen of Harvard University and Thomas A. Bailey, now deceased, who wrote the original editions which Kennedy and Cohen have updated. It is published by Cengage Learning headquartered in Boston, Massachusetts in 2015.

The other is *The American Journey: A History of the United States*, Vol. 1 which is to 1877, and Vol. 2 which is since 1865, 8th edition by David Goldfield of the Univ. of North Carolina, Charlotte, Carl Abbott of Portland State University, Virginia DeJohn Anderson of Univ. of Colorado, Boulder, Jo Ann E. Argersinger of Southern Illinois University, Peter H. Argersinger of Southern Illinois University, and William L. Barney of Univ. of North Carolina, Chapel Hill. It is published by Pearson Education Inc., of Hoboken, New Jersey, copyright 2017. The Library of Congress listing has David R. Goldfield as the author. Unfortunately, given that the review of *American Pageant* has made this section over 9,000 words, *American Journey* will need to be reviewed elsewhere and at a later time no matter how richly it deserves criticism.

Before *American Pageant* can be reviewed, three concepts need to be understood.

1. What slavery really was in the antebellum South.

2. White nationalism, banal and not, and African slavery.

3. The historical lateness of emancipation of slavery in America.

Slavery

The appalling nature of slavery is often not deeply and fully understood. This is revealed when people compare slavery to a low wage industrial jobs in the same historical period. Indeed these comparisons when made reveal the mentality of the person doing the comparisons regarding race. Being a slave is more than about no pay. Too many history textbooks discuss this or that particular aspect of slavery without giving a total picture.

As Harvard professor Orlando Patterson, explains in his book, *Slavery and Social Death*, to be a slave is to not exist as a person. As a slave you exist as if you are cattle, a horse, a thing.[431]

You will work in the fields from sunup to sundown and you will work grueling hard days to the limits of your endurance. You won't be able to slack off. That is why slave owners have the lash. You will toil six days a week and you might get Sunday off only because otherwise you might collapse. Sunday will be the time to clean your hovel and mend your clothes and recuperate from six days of grinding work. (12 x 6 = 84 hours a week.) You will have no retirement, no pay, no expectations of being able to change your life or to advance yourself. All your tomorrows will be grinding labor and recuperation from exhaustion. You have no future, and you can expect that neither will your children, grandchildren and the generations that come after for all time to come them will have a future. All their tomorrows will be the same grinding labor.

You will die having spent your entire life doing grinding labor under the fear of the lash.

It is likely you will die early.

An example would be the mortality of the slaves on Jefferson Davis's Brierfield plantation in Mississippi; many were worked to an early death. As William J. Cooper explains in *Jefferson Davis, American*, "The Continuing imbalance towards younger slaves on Brierfield strongly indicates that only a small percentage of Davis's bondspeople lived past forty," and "This rarity of the elderly also helps explain why the master of Brierfield evinced such affection for the ancient slave known as Uncle Bob. He had practically no peers." Cooper explains that Davis was a steady purchaser of young slaves. His plantation was a slow death camp.[432] Jefferson Davis was the one and only president of the Confederate States of America.

As a slave you will have no choice in food. It will be what the owner thinks is the most economical choice between cost and providing enough food calories so the owner can work you as hard as possible. Your clothes will be economical, the minimum needed to keep you alive and avoid complaints regarding community standards of modesty. (Yes there were occasions of such complaints.)

Each of your child's births will mark the beginning of another appalling life of slavery, where they will have no life of their own either, where they will be worked to the limits of their endurance for the rest of the days of their life, where they won't get an education, might be forbidden to learn to read and write, where you won't be able to protect them from cruelty, physical abuse, and rape. There will be the constant risk of you children being sold away from you, or you being sold away from them. In the 19th century having a relative sold away often meant you would never hear from them again. Slave owners didn't care.

If you are a woman you will run the risk of rape since you don't have any real rights. Teenage sons of slave owners as well as the slave owners themselves may want to use you for their sexual purposes. A child you give birth to might well be a child whose father was a rapist and the child will know as well as anyone else that they were conceived as a result of a rape.

As for some shallow talk that is heard in the media about African Americans being descendants from famous white people who owned slaves, it needs to be asked whether a slave can truly give consent to a person who might whip them or whip a brother or sister, a parent or child. The slave owner could whip to death or permanent injury a relative or sell away a relative or reassign a relative who is a house slave into the harsher labor in the fields. Can consent be freely given to a person who also controls all the possible rewards in your life, perhaps a little more for your children, perhaps a reassignment of a relative to a job out of the fields, perhaps leniency from the lash for a brother, a child, a parent? Can you freely give consent to the man who demands sex from you when he controls your entire universe and is the master of a system of terror?[433] Slavery in the antebellum South was often sex slavery.

Slavery is a system of terror using violence and other means of terror. How else do you get people to work at the limits of their endurance for their entire lives for nothing and not have any life and to endure the endless suffering and to dissuade these slaves from running away?

The system of terror doesn't necessarily have to involve physical punishment, though it frequently was. There can be the threat to sell a child or a spouse away, or you away from them. Imagine having your 4 year old child being sold away with the likelihood that you would never seeing that child again.

Much blather is said about the frequency of whipping or how many masters where "cruel" or "kind." Slavery is cruelty and some masters were crueler than others. I think though a detailed description of a whipping removes whipping from the realm of abstraction into a felt reality. The following is an eye witness account of a slave whipping using salt quoted from the book *An Empire for Slavery: The Peculiar Institution in Texas, 1821-1865*, by Randolph B. Campbell.

> This white man was whipping him and the blood was all over this nigger and he was saying "o, master, o, master, I pray you not to hit me anymore. Oh, Lordy, oh, Lordy, has mercy on me. Master, please has mercy on me, please has mercy." But this man wouldn't stop a minute and spits tobacco juice and cuss him and then starts in whipping him again. This nigger was

jumping around on the ground all tied up, just like a chicken when you chops his head off when this man was whipping him and when the white folks would stop awhile this nigger would lay there and roll from side to side and beg for mercy.

... Then he tells some of the slaves to wash him off and put salt in the cut places and he stood there to watch them to see that they did. He was chewing his tobacco, spitting and cussing that nigger and when they gets him washed off and puts salt in the raw places he sure did scream and groan.

But when he groaned they just keeping putting the salt in to the wounds on his poor old beat up body.[434]

Sometimes it wasn't salt but brine. This is an account of the whippings Confederate General Robert E. Lee gave to his runaway slaves Wesley Norris who, in an interview, in 1866 described the event:

I was born a slave on the plantation of George Parke Custis; after the death of Mr. Custis, Gen. Lee, had been made the executor of the estate, assumed control of the slaves of Mr. Custis, in number about seventy; it was the general impression among the slaves of Mr. Custis that on his death they should be forever free; in fact this statement had been made to them by Mr. C years before; at his death we were informed by Gen. Lee that by the conditions of the will we must remain slaves for five years; I remained with Gen. Lee for about seventeen months, when my sister Mary, a cousin of ours, and I determined to run away, which we did in the year 1859; we had already reached Westminster, in Maryland, on our way to the North, when we were apprehended and thrown into prison, and Gen. Lee notified of our arrest; we remained in prison fifteen days, when we were sent back to Arlington, we were immediately taken before Gen. Lee, who demanded the reason why we ran away; we frankly told him that we considered ourselves free; he then told us he would teach us a lesson we never would forget; he then ordered us to the barn, where, in his presence, we were tied firmly to posts by a Mr. Gwin, our overseer, who was ordered by Gen. Lee to strip us to the waist and give us fifty lashes each, excepting my sister, who received but twenty; we were accordingly stripped to the skin by the overseer, who, however had sufficient humanity to decline whipping us; accordingly Dick Williams, a county constable, was called in, who gave us the number of lashes ordered; Gen. Lee, in the meantime, stood by, and frequently enjoined Williams to 'lay it on well,' an injunction which he did not fail to heed; not satisfied with simply lacerating our naked flesh, Gen. Lee then ordered the overseer to thoroughly wash our backs with brine which was done.

At the end of this interview, Norris states that there were at least a dozen witnesses to substantiate his statements.[435] Anyone who has ever had even a small cut come into contact with vinegar, salt or lemon juice knows how much it burns for just a tiny cut. Imagine your body cut up all over and getting brine washed over the cuts. It must have been like suffering in a burning hell.

Robert E. Lee was a man who had people tortured by having them tied up, whipped, and left in agony with brine poured on their wounds. On page 424 Kennedy and Cohen write, "Most conspicuous among a dozen or so first-rate commanders was grey-haired General Robert E. Lee, whose knightly bearing and chivalric sense of honor embodied the Southern ideal."

You can bet that the slaves on Robert E. Lee's plantation and those on the plantation in Texas where salt was packed into the wounds of a whipped slave made really sure that they didn't get their owners angry or give them reason or rage to whip them. A lot of blather is said about whipping wasn't that frequent to minimize the horror of slavery, it doesn't need to be to have a system of terror. What risk would you be willing to take of a whipping such as these two here described?

Above all this, you are exploited, brutalized, abuse and raped by those who have contempt for your human worth and frequently and publically make racist statements that you are inferior and degraded and not fully a human being or having human capacities even though they are the monsters.

BANAL AND NOT SO BANAL WHITE NATIONALISM

There are those in history who found African slavery intolerable and those today who find African slavery in history appalling. These people had and are sicken about African slavery as if it could or could have happen to them or their families or friends or neighbors. They imagine the African slave as a fellow human being.

Then there are those who don't really care that much. There are those who think slavery was bad and are glad it is gone, but it is just another progressive agenda item in American history like building the highway system or establishing public schools. They might celebrate Black History Month. However, deep down, they don't see the abolition of slavery as an imperative, that every year it persisted as a horror. They certainly don't consider any means necessary to liberate the slaves. To these banal white nationalists freeing the slaves is good as long as it doesn't cause too much trouble.

It comes down to who is really part of your "us" or who is part of your "them" or "others."

Late

As it was, slavery was only abolished in the United States of America in 1865 with the passage of the Thirteenth Amendment to the Constitution. In 1860 there was no official plan to abolish slavery in the United States. At the time the question was how much slavery was **not** going to expand into the spoils of the Mexican American War or by conquest of Latin America.

Without the Civil War, perhaps, and only perhaps, sometime, eventually slavery would have been abolished, perhaps in the 21st century or later. What trends there might be at that time leading to the eventual abolition of slavery were not moving quickly or at much speed at all and facing the opposition of slave owners every step of the way.

As the world changed with the increase of education and the improvement of communication such the development and spread of newspapers, radio, and later television and travel, what would have happen if slavery had lasted into the modern world? It would have to be a very dark world in which America would still have slavery in a world of phones, television, and jet travel. It would have to be a dark world in which world public opinion would not see a modern slave America as deserving the enmity of all humanity. In such a world, talk of the president of the United States as being the leader of the free world would be laughable.

In such a world to be a patriotic American would have meant that you were a vicious person, and to have a moral sense a person would have to be unpatriotic.

Slavery is a system of terror by violence and as the anti-slavery movement moved forward the slave owners were ready to be violent at all hazards and consequences to defend slavery and were violent from the very beginning towards abolitionists and violently suppressed slave revolts. The future was coming and abolition was faced with this violent enemy.

The American Pageant

The *American Pageant*, textbook communicates the old "blundering generation" idea of the Civil War which sees the Civil War as resulting from the lack of compromise and political leadership. This is the idea that abolitionists and fire-eaters (radical slave owners) drove the nation to the Civil War and that there were supposedly no great compromisers in the late 1850s and in 1860 to make compromises to prevent civil war, such as those who made the Compromise of 1850 which is supposedly was a great compromise. It is essentially dismissive of the humanity of African Americans since it is their humanity which is compromised, nullified, and ignored by these so-called great white negotiators and their supposedly great compromises. Basically it is an idea that abolitionists needlessly were troublemakers by making a big fuss about slavery.

This book, like so many American history text books, ahistorically uses the term "North" and "South" as if they were homogenous blocks, particularly in reference to the Federal government and the Confederacy. By treating the term "South" as identical with "Confederacy" this textbook instructs students in the "South," however that might be defined, that the South and the Confederacy are the same thing and instruct white students in Southern nationalism. Instead of the Confederacy being a regime that happened in the history of the former slave states, it is embedded into Southern identity. The consequences of the repetitious use of South instead of Confederacy might not be apparent to the everyday public but surely it should be understood by anyone with any understanding of the educational process.

It can be immediately seen how some might think the Confederate flag is a symbol of the South with a textbook that confuses the Confederacy with the South.

The textbook minimizes slavery.

It is not difficult to see who David M. Kennedy and Lizabeth Cohen identify with. In their chapter "The South and the Slavery Controversy" the authors say the following about the slave owners, "… and this select group provided the cream of the political and social leadership of the section and the nation." The percent of butterfat isn't given by the authors, but a more historically competent description would be "this small group formed the dominating political and social elite of the section and the nation."

On page 342 there is a Currier & Ives print of slaves harvesting cotton giving the past an idealized glow. The authors state:

> Unhappily, the moonlight-and-magnolia tradition concealed much that was worrisome, distasteful, and sordid.

A better term than "unhappily" is "dishonestly" "Unhappily" might be a term I would use for a dinner party that ended badly with perhaps a loud argument or a collapsed soufflé. Similarly "worrisome," and "distasteful" are rather minimizing terms. If by some chance of fate Kennedy and Cohen were kidnapped, perhaps by the "cream" of some criminal group, and one was whipped and the other was next in line to be whipped, perhaps the authors would find the experience "distasteful" and "worrisome" while the whipped one was shrieking. A note to Kennedy and Cohen: next edition try words like "brutal," "horrible," and "dehumanizing."

"Distasteful" is also mentioned on page 392 in which there is reference to the "distasteful Fugitive Slave Law." This is the law which drove African Americans to flee to Canada, resulted in free African Americans kidnapped into slavery, and drove African American communities to form groups in their own defense. The Fugitive Slave Law of 1850 was "distasteful" indeed, probably much worse than a burnt pop tart though.

Rather obliquely the authors state, "The natural reproduction of enslaved African Americans also distinguished North American slavery from slavery in more southerly New World societies and implied much about the tenor of the slave regime and the condition of family life under slavery in the United States."

It is true that in many slave societies to the south of the United States the life spans of slaves was very short. However, what is "implied" isn't clearly stated by Kennedy and Cohen, but this could be interpreted to mean that slave life in the United States was not so bad.

From what follows in their textbook does tend to indicate that this is was their intention. Their statements resemble those in a neo-Confederate text in defense of slavery. For example, on page 347 they state, "Slaves where the primary form of wealth in the South, and as such they were cared for as any asset is cared for by a prudent capitalist."

Kennedy and Cohen on pages 348 and 349 state some of the horrors of slavery and mention that, "Floggings were common, for the whip was the substitute for the wage-incentive system and the most visible symbol of the planter's mastery." How symbolic this is when you are the person being flogged I leave to the reader to decide.

Kennedy and Cohen also pose the question, "How did the slaves actually live?" They answer this as follows:

> There is no simple answer to this question. Conditions varied from region to region, from large plantation to small plantation, and from master to master.

No doubt there was variation from plantation to plantation, from region to region, and from master to master. I am sure that this is a very useful sentence to have when someone on the textbook selection committee has an ancestor that owned slaves or in a region where there was slavery. There a problem with the historical memory of slavery of people being told that these or those slave owners were better than average. It is discussed among professional historians. As persons with some claim to be historically educated Kennedy and Cohen should know better.

What these statements are leading to is the statement minimizing slavery:

> But savage beatings made sullen laborers, and lash marks hurt resale value. There are, to be sure, sadistic monsters in any population, and the planter class contained its share. But the typical planter had too much of his own prosperity riding on the backs of his slaves to beat them bloody on a regular basis.

I am not sure what an "unsavage" beating is, but I suspect every beating is "savage" or otherwise don't make happy individuals. More interesting question is whether Kennedy and Cohen think there were "unsullen" slaves, for what is the antonym of "sullen?" It is cheerful. Were the owners of slaves really concerned with their slaves' happiness? If they were why didn't they set them free?

In any case, anyone who beats even one person with a whip, even briefly, for personal enrichment is a monster. Furthermore, a typical slave owner had all or nearly all of his prosperity extracted through the exploitation of the slaves, and using the term "exploitation" would be better than the phrase "riding on the backs." This is slavery and not horse racing though Kennedy and Cohen may be revealing something of themselves here in this comparison of slaves to horses.

However, the most outrageous thing about this paragraph is the clever wording, "beat them bloody on a regular basis." It is a misdirection of sorts and somewhat confusing. Did Kennedy and Cohen think that people might believe some owners would actually schedule beatings on a "regular basis?" Was that a real possibility? Were they trying to avoid the term frequently? Either way what frequency of beatings do Kennedy and Cohen think would acceptable? As discussed earlier slave owners needed to terrorize their slaves, and whippings were very effective to do this, but there would be no need to whip just for whipping itself and it is not likely too many whippings would be necessary to terrorize the slaves.

This reference to the frequency of whippings by Kennedy and Cohen leads the reader to consider the question of the frequency of whippings rather than the horror of having to live a life in fear of whippings and the horror that a person could just whip you when they wanted to.

There are likely students who think slave whippings were done all the time. A better explanation is that slavery as a system of terror, not that some slave owners were "prudent capitalists."

Finally this argument that the self-interest of slave owners somehow protects the slaves is a classic element of the neo-Confederate/Lost Cause defenses of antebellum slavery.

Are Kennedy and Cohen thinking about the message they are sending with their use of some of these 19th century prints? Are they even aware that there can be a sub-text in such a picture?

The authors state on page 350 that, "Slavery was intolerably degrading to the victims. They were deprived of their dignity and sense of responsibility that comes from independence and the right to make choices," and then moves to discuss briefly the laws against instructing slaves.

Of course slavery does deny a person dignity and under it you don't get a chance to make choices and this is degrading. However, this really avoids discussing the horrors of slavery. Later the authors mention "the inhumanity of slavery." I think some concrete descriptive graphic examples of what "creamy" slave owners did to the slaves would be useful in an American textbook if the goal is to actually instruct students and not sell bound wads of paper.

It also seems that a few statements are thrown in that the authors can point to if someone questions their textbook. Slavery is bad, but not too bad, but bad, but not too bad, goes the book.

One rather bizarre statement that the authors make is, "But most Blacks had no wish to be transplanted into a strange civilization after having become partially Americanized." By what measure or reference standard were Blacks partially Americanized as opposed to other Americans? I ask the reader to pause and reflect on what is being asserted by Kennedy and Cohen.

However, what is most noteworthy is how Kennedy and Cohen refer to abolitionists who found slavery intolerable.

Kennedy and Cohen constantly snipe at the anti-slavery figures in American history and also blame the abolitionists for the Civil War. They suggest that abolitionists caused a lot of trouble over the issue of African Americans freedom because they were fanatics.

On page 352 we learn that abolitionist Theodore Dwight Weld is, "Humorless and deadly earnest," rather than serious and dedicated. Weld's pamphlet, "Slavery as It Is," is referred to as a "potent propaganda pamphlet." "Propaganda" has a stigmatized meaning. Though technically correct, a better statement might be that, "with this pamphlet he communicated effectively to the American public the horrors of slavery."

On page 353 we learn that Garrison is, "The emotionally high strung son of a drunken father and a spiritual child of the Second Great Awakening." On the same page, readers are told regarding Garrison with his publication, *The Liberator*," was:

> Stern and uncompromising, Garrison nailed his colors to the masthead of his weekly. He proclaimed in strident tones that under no circumstances would he tolerate the poisonous weed of slavery but would stamp it out at once, root and branch.

They quote his masthead, "I will be as harsh as truth and as uncompromising as Justice," and that Garrison won't "equivocate – I will not excuse."

Here. Kennedy and Cohen are painting Garrison as a fanatic. Was Garrison "stern" and "uncompromising" or just serious and not willing to accept rationalizations for slavery? Were his tones "strident" or forthright and just stating things as they are? What his masthead a statement of his philosophy of not accepting rationalizations or are we to believe that Garrison was "harsh" and "uncompromising" personally, that maybe he shouted "no butter on my toast you moron" at breakfast sometimes.

The textbook authors tell us that Garrison with *The Liberator*, "… triggered a thirty-year war of words and in a sense fired one of the opening barrages of the Civil War."

On page 353 there are more criticisms of Garrison being, "… more interested in his own self-righteousness than in the substance of the slavery evil itself." An example of Garrison's "self-righteousness" is given, that he burned a copy of the Constitution on the 4th of July in 1854 saying it was a pact with hell. Given that the Constitution supported slavery wasn't it?

At the Constitutional Convention in in 1787 the issue of slavery was discussed. Delegates rationalized Constitutional provisions for slavery, but one voice was raised against bondage.

> Col. George Mason [VA]. This infernal traffic originated in the avarice of British merchants. The British government constantly checked the attempts of Virginia to put a stop to it. The present question concerns not the importing states alone, but the whole Union. The evil of having slaves was experienced during the late war. Had slaves been treated as they might have been by the enemy, they would have proved dangerous instruments in their hands. But their folly dealt by the slaves as it did by the Tories. He mentioned the dangerous insurrections of the slaves in Greece and Sicily; and the instructions given by Cromwell, to the commissioners sent to Virginia, to arm the servants and slaves, in case

other means of obtaining its submission should fail. Maryland and Virginia, he said, had already prohibited the importation of slaves expressly. North Carolina had done the same in substance. All this would be in vain, if South Carolina and Georgia be at liberty to import. The western people are already calling out for slaves for their new lands, and will fill that country with slaves, if they can be got through South Carolina and Georgia. Slavery discourages arts and manufactures. The poor despise labor when performed by slaves. They prevent the emigration of whites, who really enrich and strengthen a county. They produce the most pernicious effect on manners. Every master of slaves is born a petty tyrant. They bring the judgment of Heaven on a country. **As nations cannot be rewarded or punished in the next world, they must be in this. By an inevitable chain of causes and effects, Providence punishes national sins by national calamities.** He lamented that some of our eastern brethren had, from a lust of gain, embarked in this nefarious traffic. As to the state being in possession of the right to import, this was the case with many other rights, now to be properly given up. He held it essential, in every point of view, that the general government should have power to prevent the increase of slavery.[436] [Boldface added by author.]

Yes, one of the American founders thought the Constitutional provisions for slavery were a national sin for which America would be punished by God. How radical is Garrison's statement that the Constitution was a "pact with hell?"

There is reference to "extreme Garrisonians" on page 359 and "extreme anti-slavery" on page 373. There is reference to abolitionists as "zealots" or "zealous" on pages 359, 375, and 381.

The abolitionists are held to be responsible to their own beatings by anti-abolitionists mobs. On page 359 Kennedy and Cohen write:

> Repeated tongue-lashings by the extreme abolitionists provoked many mob outbursts in the North, some lead by respectable gentlemen.

The textbook has an underlying message that the Civil War being started by fanatical abolitionists, not by rapacious, ruthless slave owners. This is the historical narrative of the neo-Confederates.

Astoundingly on page 360 the authors recommend the writings of two neo-Confederates, Eugene Genovese, a contributor to *Southern Partisan* magazine and a defender of pro-slavery theologians and Elizabeth Fox-Genovese for the issue of gender and slavery, and whose interview in *Southern Partisan* about gender is reviewed earlier in this book. On page 419 Eugene Genovese is again cited as a credible source.

On page 400 Harriet Beecher Stowe's book, *Uncle Tom's Cabin*, is called a "trouble brewing book," and public enthusiasm for the book is dismissively referred to as "Tommania," and on page 399 the book is called a "literary incendiary."

On page 402 John Brown is called a "fanatical figure" and the book informs us that he had "glittering gray eyes," but evidently was not a vampire in the *Twilight* movie and his attack in Kansas called "terroristic." On pages 410 & 411, in a passage about John Brown's raid on Harper's Ferry, Virginia, which was intended to ignite a slave rebellion he is further denounced. We are told that "… thirteen of his near relations were regarded as insane, including his mother and grandmother" and "Though perhaps of unsound mind, he was clever enough to see that he was worth much more to the abolitionist cause dangling from a rope than in any other way." "Dangling from a rope" instead of "hanged" is another way for the authors to dismissively mock Brown.

The reader of this book might consider the book, *Allies for Freedom & Blacks on John Brown*, by the distinguished 20th century African American historian Benjamin Quarles published in 1974 by Oxford University Press and republished since. African Americans have regarded Brown as a hero for generations. In this book you can read Harlem Renaissance writer Langston Hughes praise for John Brown on the centennial of Harper's Ferry and Malcolm X's exhortation to liberals that they need to be like John Brown.[437]

Distinguished professors Ira Berlin of the University of Maryland, Barbara J. Fields of Columbia University, Joseph P. Reidy of Howard University, and Leslie S. Rowland of the University of Maryland dedicated their book, *Slaves No More: Three Essays on Emancipation and the Civil War*, published by Cambridge University press every member of John Brown's party, listing their names and making the statement, "Who Risked All at Harper's Ferry." To some academics African lives matter.

When we imagine white people being enslaved violence is considered very acceptable. In the movie *The Ten Commandments* we see the Red Sea drowning Pharaoh's army as right. We cheer on Errol Flynn in *Captain Blood* and applaud his fellow pirates who have escaped slavery. We are glad to see the Philistines get theirs when Victor Mature as the title hero pulls down pillars in *Samson and Delilah*. And who would admit to being against the slaves in *Spartacus* when Kirk Douglas leads them in a rebellion against the Roman army?

If someone came into your neighborhood and kidnapped members of your family the loved ones of friends and neighbors, which you knew they were being beaten and raped, would you use a machine gun to free them if one became available to you?

Imagine this. You and your mother got up early in the morning before sunrise and are making a run for it. You are running through the woods and miles away from the plantation. However, one of the house slaves has betrayed you. You are running as fast as you can but your mother, worn down by years of bondage, is moving as fast as she can. But she just isn't fast enough and you can hear the dogs in the distance. "Mother," you cry, "You need to go faster!" And then, oh my God, oh my God, you can hear that they are getting very close and that they will soon be upon you. Your mother is crying in fear and urging you to run and leave her behind. But you were lucky and foresighted enough to have stolen a gun. You are not going to be a slave anymore at all cost and hazards. Suddenly around the bend, right there with snarling dogs is Thomas Jefferson, he is shouting, "I see them, I see them!" What would you do? I propose to every student of American history everywhere and every reader of this book an assignment to write what you would do next and why. You have permission to quote this narrative as part of this assignment and change the name from Thomas Jefferson to another slave owner if you wish.

Kennedy and Cohen strongly imply that abolitionist U.S. Senator Charles Sumner's infamous canning by South Carolina U.S. Rep. Preston Brooks, an 1856 near-fatal sneak attack Brooks made while Sumner was sitting in the U.S. Senate chambers, and beat him unconscious and nearly killed him as somehow Sumner's own fault for his famous speech "The Crime Against Kansas," given on May 19, 1856 in the U.S. Senate.

Like other anti-slavery figures in *American Pageant*, Sumner is labeled as being personally aberrant. Kennedy and Cohen calls him "cold, humorless, intolerant, and egotistical," and "the most disliked men in the Senate." In contrast, we are informed that Brooks is "Ordinarily gracious and gallant ..." Readers are given an explanation, or perhaps rationalization is a better term, of why Preston canned Sumner. We are informed one of the reasons is that Sumner had insulted South Carolina U.S. Senator Andrew Butler, "... one of the best liked members of the Senate." Other popularity rankings of U.S. Senators at the time are not provided by Kennedy and Cohen.

Sumner's "The Crime Against Kansas," speech is denounced by Kennedy and Cohen, and on page 403 they refer to its "coarse language." On page 404 they call it an "abusive speech" and "intemperate speech." It isn't referred to as direct and forthright.

What reveals Kennedy's and Cohen's attitudes, and is simply outrageous, is their use of the terms "merciless nagging of abolitionists" on page 358, and "abolitionist nagging" on page 418. According to Kennedy and Cohen "sensitive" (page 359) slave holders had to bear "nagging," and not just "nagging" but "nagging" that was "merciless" by abolitionists who we are to assume are merciless because they engaged in "merciless nagging." It is telling that this adjective, "merciless," is applied to denunciations of slavery, but not to slavery itself. The use of "nagging" entirely trivializes the value of the lives of the African American slaves as well as trivializing the enormity of the crime of slavery. It mocks the abolitionists and reinforces the idea that abolitionists, and not the slaveholders were extremists.

In discussing the Underground Railroad on page 386 Kennedy and Cohen write:

> Unlike cattle thieves, the abolitionists who ran the Underground Railroad did not gain personally from their lawlessness.

African American slaves are compared to cattle and the abolitionists to thieves by Kennedy and Cohen. The abolitionists aren't rescuers in this textbook.

Then there is this statement on page 386 regarding the anger of the slave owners about the Underground Railroad and the assistance rendered escaping slaves by abolitionists:

> But to the slaveowners, the loss was infuriating, whatever the motives. The moral judgements of the abolitionists seemed, in some ways, more galling than outright theft. They reflected not only a holier-than-thou attitude but a refusal to obey the laws solemnly passed by Congress.

The authors could claim that the last sentence in this quote from their textbook simply represents the attitudes of the slave owners, but, in fact, the sentence is a comment on the abolitionists by the authors themselves. It is the "moral judgements of the abolitionists" which "reflected" a "holier-than-thou attitude." The "they" in the sentence is the "moral judgements of the abolitionists."

Reading "American Pageant" you might get the impression that the slave owners were shoved out of the Union by the harassment of abolitionists.

On page 354, in the discussions about the beginnings of abolitionism Kennedy and Cohen construct false opposites as follows:

> High-minded and courageous, the abolitionists were men and women of good will and various colors who faced the cruel choice that people of good conscious in many ages have had thrust upon them: when is evil so enormous that it must be denounced even at the risk of precipitating bloodshed and butchery?

The abolitionists here are made responsible for the choices made by the slave owners to defend slavery at all costs including "bloodshed and butchery."

On page 357, a neo-Confederate interpretation again appears, "Elsewhere in the Americas, enslaved peoples secured their freedoms gradually and in stark contrast to the United States, peacefully." This is an assertion is contrary to the historical record as will be discussed.

We are told on page 419 that "looming over" the debate as to the causes of the Civil War is the "… stark fact that the United States was the only state to fight a war to rid itself of slavery."

This latter is a very clever statement which implies that the United States' Civil War was a unique political failing in which violence being needed to abolish bondage. This statement would exclude the revolt of the slaves in Haiti since they weren't technically a state until after the slave revolution succeeded. The successful Haitian revolt inspired other slave revolts. As Manisha Sinha explains in her book, *The Slaves' Cause: A History of Abolition*, published by Yale University Press:

> The Haitian Revolution stimulated black assertiveness throughout the Western hemisphere. In the 1790s black Jacobinism spread to Rio de la Plata in Uruguay and to Maracaibo, Cartagena, Demerara, and Caro in Venezuela, and the Second Maroon War broke out in Jamaica. In 1812 the Aponte uprising of slaves and free people of color in Cuba came on the heels of the institution of a liberal constitution and the debate over abolition in the Spanish Cortes at Cádiz.
>
> … Christophe of the northern kingdom of Haiti helped rebels in neighboring Santo Domingo against Spanish rule. In 1821 Haiti conquered Santo Domingo and enacted abolition there.[438]

Maroons are Africans who escaped slavery in the Americas and formed independent settlements. They didn't wait for "gradual freedom." Of course a Second Maroon War indicates that there was a First Maroon War.

The Texan revolt over Mexican prohibition against slavery would be excluded since in that case state violence prevented the abolition of slavery. In fact their account of the Mexican American War is somewhat astounding but won't be dealt with in this review.

It was violence that precipitated the British abolition of slavery. As Manisha Sinha explains in her book, *The Slaves' Cause*:

> While slave resistance prompted debates over emancipation in America, it precipitated British abolition. In December 1831 the charismatic Samuel "Daddy" Sharpe led the so-called Baptist War or Christmas Rebellion in Jamaica, which involved nearly sixty thousand slaves. It was preceded by a wave of slave resistance and free black activism in the West Indies. ... One week after Sharpe's execution in 1832, Parliament appointed a select committee to explore the expediency of "effecting" the Extinction of Slavery throughout the British Dominions." The Reform Act, which democratized parliamentary elections, and abolitionist petitions ensured the passage of emancipation in 1833.[439]

Sharpe's sixty thousand didn't constitute a state so this violence wouldn't fall under the author's careful wording. Kennedy's and Cohen's phrasing cleverly excludes the revolts of Africans outside the United States and erases them. Of course the Baptist War was not peaceful nor was the British Emancipation gradual.

The abolition of slavery in Latin America is part of the revolutions of independence from Spain. To quote Hugh Thomas in his book, *The Slave Trade*:

> Bolívar thought that the abolition of slavery was the key to Spanish American independence, and liberated his own slaves. The Supreme Junta of Caracas, the first government of an independent Venezuela, abolished the trade in slaves in 1811; and in New Granada (Columbia) in 1812 ..."[440]

As Sinha explains in *The Slaves Cause*:

> Latin American revolutionaries like José San Martin and Simón Bolívar turned to Haiti for assistance in their anticolonial struggle against Spain. Petion sent aid to them on the condition that abolition and black rights be part of their revolutionary agenda. ... The Haitian Revolution was an important precedent for slave runaways and free black soldiers who demanded emancipation during the Latin American Wars of Independence. ... By the 1820s nearly all the former Spanish colonies in Latin America where abolition was expedited by warfare had decreed a gradual end to slavery.[441]

In Brazil there were revolts and brutality. Thomas states:

> There had been a Hausa rising in Brazil in 1807, a more general Islamic one in 1809, and less easily identifiable rebellions in 1814, 1816, 1822, and 1826; and thereafter an upheaval almost every year. Many whites were killed before the rebellions were at last crushed.[442]

Thomas in talking about the anxiousness of slave owners there in the 1830s explains:

> For another serious rebellion of slaves, the "revolt of Male," with strong Islamic undercurrent, broke out in 1835. It was repressed with brutality: whippings with five hundred or more strokes were common punishments for mullahs accused merely of teaching friends to read the Koran in Arabic.[443]

It seems that abolition in the Americas wasn't so peaceful and war had something to do with it. Kennedy and Cohen in their textbooks erase the heroic struggles of Africans in the Americas, which is atrocious.

Perhaps in the Spanish Americas there was "persistencia implacable" and in Brazil "irritante impiedosa" by "abolicionistas" which accounts for all this violence over slavery that occurred there.[444]

I recommend reading Hugh Thomas *The Slave Trade*, in particular for persons who were taught world or "Western" history it shows that the whole idea that European exploration was for spices is a myth, but instead Europe's voracious appetite for slaves drove the exploration. Yes, if the explorers could make a profit bring back spices or other goods they were willing to do so, but it is clear that the demand for slaves was, if not the primary, one of the leading driving forces behind exploration. Prince Henry the Navigator should be renamed Prince Henry the Kidnapper.

The fact that in some places abolition comes more easily without war and others it takes war is likely due to particular circumstances. The slave owners in the British Caribbean could hardly mount a secession movement when they were entirely dependent on the British government to sustain them against slave revolts on islands where they were vastly outnumbered. They would have miniscule resources to mount a revolt against the British Empire. Additionally, these slave owners were to be compensated.

The populations of slaves in other countries like Mexico, Chile and Argentina were very small and the slave owners were hardly in a position to stage any revolt against the leaders of the revolution for independence from Spain.

And what did peace bring to localities that did have politically powerful slave owners? Delayed freedom, Cuba didn't abolish slavery until 1886 and in Brazil in 1888. In the accomplishment of abolition in these two countries it has to be considered that one of the factors was that there were no major slave powers remaining. Slavery had been abolished in America and American ships were no longer illegally engaged in the Atlantic slave trade under the American flag thus through legal technicalities evading and undermining the African Squadron.

There was a proposal in the U.S. Congress to use the sale of federal lands to pay slave holders for their slaves and relocate them back to Africa. It was introduced into the U.S. Senate on Feb. 18, 1825. It enraged slaveholders. This is an extract from the, "Message of Governor Troup of Georgia on May 25, 1825," regarding the proposal:

> Since your last meeting, our feelings have been again outraged by officious and impertinent intermeddlings with our domestic concerns. Beside the resolution presented for the consideration of the Senate by Mr. King, of New York, it is understood that the Attorney General of the United States, who may be presumed to represent his Government faithfully, and to speak as its mouth piece, has recently maintained, before the Supreme Court, doctrines on this subject, which, if sanctioned by that tribunal, will make it quite easy for the Congress, by a short decree, to divest this entire interest, without cost to themselves of one dollar, or of one acre of public land. This is the uniform practice of the Government of the United States; if it wishes a principle established which it dare not establish for itself, a case is made before the Supreme Court, and the principle once settled, the act of Congress follows of course. Soon, very soon, therefore, the United States' Government, discarding the mask, will openly lend itself to a combination of fanatics for the destruction of everything valuable in the Southern country ; one movement of the Congress unresisted by you, and all is lost. Temporize no longer—make known your resolution that this subject shall not be touched by them, but at their peril; but for its sacred guaranty by the constitution, we never would have become parties to that instrument; at this moment you would not make yourselves parties to any constitution without it; of course you will not be a party to it, from the moment the General Government shall make that movement.
>
> If this matter be an evil, it is our own—if it be a sin, we can implore the forgiveness of it—to remove it we ask not even their sympathy or assistance: it may be our physical weakness—it is our moral strength. ... I entreat you, therefore, most earnestly, now that it is not too late, to step forth, and, having exhausted the argument, to stand by your arms.[445]

This document is from one of the document collections edited by Herman Ames that the Univ. of Pennsylvania published in the early 20th century. They can be downloaded free from the Internet Archive and are quite illuminating as to the motives of the slave owners.

Even then in 1825, thirty-five years before secession, when the accumulative "merciless nagging" of abolitionists must have been much less, an offer to pay for the slaves and relocate them enrages slave owners and brings threats of violent secession.

In 1785 Methodist Bishop Thomas Coke took a tour from New York to North Carolina to defend the Methodist rules against slaveholding and in Virginia encountered threats of violence against his anti-slavery message. Quoting from H. Shelton Smith's, "In His Image, But ...: Racism in Southern Religion, 1780-1910:"

> But two days later he ran into a hornet's nest, when he preached against slavery at Martin's barn. "A high-headed lady ... told the rioters (as I was afterwards informed) that she would give fifty pounds, if they would give that little doctor one hundred lashes." The angry mob might well have flogged the preacher if a friendly justice of the peace had not intervened. Yet on April 11 another mob showed up for his sermon at "brother Baker's," armed "with staves and clubs." Their attack was frustrated only because the "little doctor" did not touch on the offensive subject.

Indeed for the rest of his visit Bishop Coke did not bring up the topic of slavery. [446] This is somewhat puzzling though, how much accumulated "merciless nagging" by abolitionists could there have been in 1785 to make slave holders violent? Slave owners are violent when their exploitation is threatened.

On pages 415-416 Kennedy and Cohen in a section titled "Collapse of Compromise" they discuss the Crittenden Amendments, which were six constitutional amendments and four resolutions for the U.S. Congress to prevent secession. Kennedy and Cohen state:

> President-elect Lincoln flatly rejected the Crittenden scheme which offered some slight prospect of success, and all hopes of compromise evaporated. For this refusal Lincoln must bear a heavy responsibility.

The Crittenden amendments were monstrous and if Lincoln accepted them it would have been an outrage against humanity.

The authors minimize and obscure what the Crittenden amendments were.

The textbook explains that below a latitude of 36° 30″ slavery would be permitted in the territories but a state formed from there could be slave or free and further states, "Federal protection in a territory south of 36° 30″ might conceivably, though improbably, turn the entire area permanently towards slavery." The use of "improbably" is to indicate to the reader that this provision wasn't likely to result in a new slave states.

The authors argue that Lincoln rejected them based on the principle of his platform "even though gains for slavery in the territories might be only temporary." They then state:

> Larger gains might come later in Cuba and Mexico. Crittenden's proposal, said Lincoln, "would amount to a perpetual covenant of war against every people, tribe, and state owning a foot of land between here and Tierra del Fuego."

Lincoln was quite right since all territories south of the United States would be slave territories per the Crittenden Amendments and irresistible temptation to slave holders. Even before the Civil War slave owners were organizing military expeditions, "filibusters," they called them to seize territories in Latin America for slavery. Vice President of the Confederacy Alexander H. Stephens in his speeches talked about the need to acquire territories in Latin America for slavery.

However, the Crittenden amendments were about much more than a latitude for slavery. If adopted it would have fasten slavery upon the U.S. Constitution for all time and would have made total violent revolution the only solution for the abolition of slavery in the United States. Indeed what were these compromises in American history which Kennedy and Cohen find great, but just a kicking the can down the road, leaving emancipation for a future generation to accomplish.

As stated, the Crittenden Amendments were six articles and four resolutions for the U.S. Congress.

Article II states that Congress will have no power to abolish slavery in areas of which it is in control of and which is within a slave state. That is Congress couldn't forbid slavery in a fort or national park if it was within a slave state.

Article III states that Congress will have no power to abolish slavery in the District of Columbia as long as it is between Maryland and Virginia.

Article IV states that Congress will have no power to prohibit or hinder the interstate transportation of slaves between slave states.

Article V is more ominous. If a slave was aided in his escape by intimidation or violence or rescued by force, the owner of the escaping slave could sue the county in federal court for damages equal to the value of the slave, losses they might suffer in the attempted recapture, with interest. The county in which the slave evaded capture could then sue the persons aiding the slave's escape for what the county had to pay the slave owner. This would have made every abolitionist aiding a slave's escape by force by necessity a revolutionary against the national government. It would set every county against the abolitionist. It also shows that states' rights counted for nothing when it was in the way of the defense of slavery.

Article VI establishes that there can be no amendment to these five articles proposed by Crittenden and no amendment would be permitted to give Congress the power to abolish slavery or interfere with it in any slave state.

Further this article VI establishes that the sections of the Constitution that were already protecting slavery could not be amended: the third paragraph of the second section of the first article of the Constitution in which slaves were to be counted as $3/5^{th}$ of a person, which insured the overrepresentation of slave states in the Congress; and the third paragraph of the second section of the fourth article, which required that slaves that escaped into another state had to be returned.

In the four resolutions there is a call upon the U.S. House and Senate that federal laws be passed to punish those who help slaves escape and nullify state liberty laws protecting African Americans in the non-slave holding states.

The Crittenden amendments are only a possibility if you think that complete capitulation to the interest of slavery is acceptable. These proposed amendments would have bolted down slavery on to the Constitution for all time.

As for the impossibility of slavery in the Southwest territories, Jefferson Davis didn't see it that way. In the U.S. Senate, on Feb. 14, 1850 he stated:

> One of the positions laid down by the honorable Senator from Kentucky, and which he denominated as one of his two truths, was, that slavery was excluded from the Territories of California and New Mexico by a decree of Nature. From that opinion I dissent. I hold that the pursuit of gold-washing and milling is better adapted to slave labor than to any other species of labor recognized among us, and is likely to be found in that new country for many years to come. I also maintain that it is particularly adapted to an agriculture which depends upon irrigation. Till the canals are cut, ditches and dams made, no person can reclaim the soil from Nature; an individual pioneer cannot settle upon it with his family, and support them by the product of his own exertion, as in the old possessions of the United States, where rain and dew unite with a prolific soil to reward freely and readily the toil of man. It is only by associated labor that such a country can be reduced to cultivation. They have this associated labor in Mexico under a system of peonage. That kind of involuntary servitude, for debt I suppose, cannot long continue to exist under American institutions; therefore the only species of labor that can

readily supply its place under our Government would, I think, be the domestic servitude of African slavery; and therefore I believe it is essential, on account of the climate, productions, soil, and the peculiar character of cultivation, that we should during its first settlement have that slavery in at least a portion of California and New Mexico. It is also true, that in certain climates only the African race are adapted to work in the sun. It is from this cause perhaps more than all others that the products of Mexico, once so important and extensive, have dwindled into comparative insignificance since the abolition of slavery. And it is also on that account that the prosperity of Central and Southern America generally has declined, and that it has been sustained in Brazil, where slavery has continued; that Jamaica and St. Domingo have now, from being among the most productive and profitable colonies, sunk into decay, and are relapsing to desert and barbarism; and yet Cuba and Porto Rico continue to maintain; I might say to increase, their prosperity. I therefore deny what is affirmed by the Senator from Kentucky to be his second truth, and in support of that denial call attention to the wealth and productiveness of Mexico when slavery existed there, and invite a comparison between that and its condition at present.[447]

Historically mining has used slave labor and there is no reason that irrigated land could not be worked by slave labor and irrigation projects prior to modern technology did require large amounts of manual labor.

On page 418 Kennedy and Cohen write:

Worldwide impulses of nationalism – then stirring in Italy, Germany, Poland, and elsewhere – where fermenting in the South. This huge area, with its distinctive culture, was not so much a section as a subnation.

This is a key neo-Confederate nationalist concept and makes the Confederacy integral to Southern identity.

I would like to contrast what Kennedy's and Cohen's world historical view of the Civil War with what Ira Berlin, Barbara J. Fields, Steven F. Miller, Joseph P. Reidy and Leslie S. Rowland say in *Slaves No More*:

With emancipation in the South, the United States enacted its part in a world-wide drama. Throughout the western world and beyond, the forces released by the American and French revolutions and by the industrial revolution worked to undermine the political regimes based upon hereditary privilege and economic systems based upon bound labor. … Almost simultaneously with the great struggle in the United States, the vestiges of serfdom in central and eastern Europe yielded to the pressure of the age. Only small pockets in Africa and Asia remained immune, and their immunity was temporary. The fateful lightning announced by the victorious Union army was soon to strike, if had not already struck, wherever men and women remained in bonds of personal servitude.[448]

Berlin et all see a great world struggle for freedom, Kennedy and Cohen see Confederate-Americans.

On pages 444 & 445 the authors of bring up another neo-Confederate talking point in a section titled, "A Proclamation without Emancipation," in which the authors explain, "The presidential pen did not formally strike the shackles from a single slave." Further they state, "In short where he *could* he would not, and where he *would* he could not." [Italics in the original.]

The Emancipation Proclamation converted the American armies into armies of liberation and with every future advance slaves would be liberated and in the end the system of slavery in the seceded states was destroyed. The authors' logic is like saying roads don't transport things, which is true. Whether gravel or concrete or asphalt a package put on a road will not be moved by the road.

The authors do state that the Emancipation Proclamation did inspire some slaves to run away to the American armies, but this misses the entire point of the importance of the Emancipation Proclamation. Perhaps it is some concession to which they can point.

On page 458 Kennedy and Cohen state:

> Lincoln expired in the arms of victory, at the very pinnacle of his fame. From the standpoint of his reputation, his death could not have been better timed if he had hired the assassin. A large number of his countrymen had not suspected his greatness, and many others had even doubted his ability. His dramatic death helped erase the memory of his short comings and caused his nobler qualities to stand out in sharper relief.

A standard neo-Confederate talking point is that Lincoln wasn't great and was a villain and that his assassination caused him to be seen as a hero. This is the assertion of persons who hate Abraham Lincoln from the notorious racist M.E. Bradford to the writings of Thomas D. Lorenzo at Loyola University in Baltimore.

It is profoundly disrespectful and really creepy.

The book's treatment of Reconstruction has the well-worn ideas that Reconstruction was oppressive to the seceded states. On page 459 the authors argue that Lincoln would have been moderate and kindly shielding the South from "vindictive" treatment implying the old idea that Radical Republicans were vindictive. Thaddeus Steven's a leader of the Radical Republicans who campaigned for the rights of African Americans and on page 475 is called "crusty and vindictive." On page 471 we are told Radical Republicans "believed that the South should atone more painfully for its sins." On page 483 Reconstruction is characterized as harsh with the authors writing, "the wonder is that Reconstruction was not far harsher than it was."

The reason the Radical Republicans were called radical and after the fall of Reconstruction have been subject to so much abuse is because they worked very hard for the human rights of African Americans.

President Andrew Johnson during Reconstruction acted to undermine the rights of African Americans. He was a slave holder. He was racist. He became president upon the assassination of Lincoln. Johnson opposed the Fourteenth Amendment giving citizenship to African Americans. He vetoed a civil rights bill in 1865. He was selected to be on the vice-presidential candidate running with Lincoln during the 1864 presidential election to get the votes of some Democrats, a party that was at that time controlled by white supremacists.

The Radical Republicans attempting to advance the rights of African Americans and prevent Johnson from undermining their efforts passed the Tenure of Office Act. Johnson violated it and Congress acted to impeach him.

On page 482 Kennedy and Cohen comment on the failure to impeach Johnson, "The nation thus narrowly avoided a dangerous precedent that would have gravely weakened one of the three branches of government." If Johnson had been impeached there was a fighting chance that Reconstruction could have succeeded and Civil Rights would have come to African Americans much earlier. However, Kennedy and Cohen write, "From the standpoint of the radicals, the greatest crime had been to stand inflexibly in their path," obscuring the fact that the path of the Radical Republicans had fought for civil rights for African Americans.

Finally on page 483 Kennedy and Cohen state:

> The Republicans acted from a mixture of idealism and political expediency. They wanted both to protect the freed slaves and to promote the fortunes of the Republican party [sic]. In the end their efforts backfired badly.

The term "backfired" implies that the Reconstruction policies of the Radical Republicans were a mistake and had consequences that were opposite then were intended, which would be that the Radical Republican policies contributed to racism in the South. The Radical Republicans did fail, but they were defeated by the disaster of Andrew Johnson becoming president and the violent campaign of terror in the former slave states. However, their efforts weren't a mistake and our nation would be so much better today if they had succeeded. Perhaps the author's read seriously Hodding Carter's book, *The Angry Scar: The Story of Reconstructions*, where racism in the South is blamed on the attempts of Radical Republicans to secure civil rights for African Americans.

As for the reference of "political expediency" doesn't every political party work to insure its fortunes by working for the interests of its supporters and insuring that they can vote? Isn't that how democracy works? I am sure efforts in 2015 and 2016 to defeat voter suppression of minorities is based on idealism and expediency. It seems that the spirit of William Archibald Dunning one of major racist historians in American history whose writings portrayed Reconstruction as a mistake haunts the pages of *American Pageant*.

Finally on page 482 we learn that Thaddeus Stevens was crippled. In discussing the anger of "Diehard Radicals," those who were really committed to the rights of African Americans and not willing to give it up, Kennedy and Cohen write "'The Country is going to the Devil!' cried the crippled Stevens as he was carried from the hall," when the effort to impeach Johnson failed. Upon reading this the author decided to Google and see if Stevens also had a hunchback. He didn't.

In contrast to the comments regarding Stevens, Sumner, and the abolitionists this is what Kennedy and Cohen write in their section about the creamy slave owners on page 341 in describing their aristocratic lives:

> Their money provided the leisure for study, reflection, and statecraft, as notably true of men like John C. Calhoun (a Yale graduate) and Jefferson Davis (a West Point graduate.) They felt a keen sense of obligation to serve the public.

The money of the slave owners gave them the power and time to dominate society and work for the preservation of slavery. The "statecraft" of both of these men was to fight for slavery and to serve their own interests.

This review is already too long, and not every aspect of this textbook is reviewed. It should be enough however to demonstrate the nature of this specific textbook and make the reader aware of the problems with public school American history textbooks in 2016.

W.E.B. DuBois wrote in "The Lie of History as It Is Taught Today," in 1960:

Thus we train generations of men who do not know the past, or believe a false picture of the past, to have no trustworthy guide for living and to stumble doggedly on, through mistake after mistake, to fatal ends. Our history becomes "lies agreed upon" and stark ignorance guides our future.[449]

Yet it is 56 years later and we are still teaching a banal white nationalistic history. When will this stop?

15 CONCLUSION

With the triumph of democracy in the Western world in the 19th and 20th century, and with its adoption elsewhere, at a time in which even dictators and totalitarian systems attempt to imitate the forms of democracy and use the vocabulary of democracy to legitimize themselves, many don't realize that there are some who still reject modern democracy.

There are groups in the West that reject democracy and its egalitarian ideals in favor of older, pre-modern systems of privilege, who idealize older societies run by patriarchal elites who command subordinates and where slavery and serfdom were be acceptable. These groups would have societies they claim are traditional with values that would limit individual freedoms in actions and beliefs.

Some are monarchists, others would have aristocratic societies, and yet others would have some form of republic in which an elite would rule. Neo-Confederates talk about ordered liberty which would be largely the liberty of elites to order you around.

This reactionary resistance to modern democratic society has persisted into the present. In America this reactionary resistance is to a large extent the neo-Confederate movement and its goal is nothing less than to undermine and subvert our modern American democratic society.

This book has not dwelt on the intelligentsia of the neo-Confederate movement. It has not provided an intellectual history of the neo-Confederate movement. I instead have focused on describing the movement's real effects and the specific practical agenda items, its goals and its toolbox of tactics and strategies. However, there is a reactionary current of thought drawing on the antebellum slave past and the Confederacy which continues into the present.

The author is working on a manuscript to describe this reactionary intellectual history.

Given the great popularity of our democratic society this movement has had to carefully select the methods that it has used and has avoided being overt. Thus the public has been largely unaware of this hidden agenda. The author hopes that this book helps remedy this situation and educate the public about this movement, its methods, its goals.

Nations, philosophies, religions, ideas, and knowledge ultimately exist in the minds of humanity and persist only as humanity may persist in believing in them. As such nothing in history is ever truly fixed and absolutely impervious to change. All these socially constructed realities are in continual flux.

Our democratic society in America is an ongoing project and needs ongoing support. The neo-Confederate movement seeks instead to bring it down and defeat our democratic society. To defend democracy we need to defeat the neo-Confederate movement.

However, our efforts should not be seen as entirely defensive. In defeating neo-Confederacy and their historical misrepresentations we have a revolutionary opportunity, an opportunity for a Third American Revolution. The first is the American Revolution for independence, the second being the Civil War, which historians have called the Second American Revolution. Without a major geographic region of the nation being defined by the Confederacy that has served as a reactionary fortress with all its consequences to American national life, without Americans being taught white banal nationalism in the schools, without neo-Confederacy in our nation's culture, we will have a new idea of what America is and a new idea of who we are as Americans.

This is the opportunity for a third American Revolution.

EPILOG

In the preface, it was stated that book was written to mobilize people to oppose the neo-Confederate movement.

As stated in the conclusion of this book, failure to defeat the neo-Confederate movement could lead to a dark future for our nation, but that defeating the neo-Confederate movement would greatly advance the United States of America in the direction of social justice. It would lead to a third American Revolution.

The reason that the neo-Confederates haven't been defeated is that they have been organized and have worked for their goals over generations, whereas there is no group organized to oppose neo-Confederacy and what efforts that there have been are intermittent.

Enablers know that after a few months opposition to neo-Confederacy will fade away, but the neo-Confederates will still be there.

Yet the neo-Confederate movement is vulnerable and could be defeated with not that many people and not that much effort. What is needed is that there be an informed organized effort to defeat neo-Confederacy.

One reason this hasn't happened is that it hasn't been understood that the national future is at stake in fighting neo-Confederacy and instead it is thought it is about haggling over 19th century history. This book should dispel that misunderstanding.

Another reason is that the research materials and information to make an informed opposition to neo-Confederacy hasn't been available. Now with this book, other books, online informational websites and more information forthcoming there are the resources to start and enable an informed effort against the neo-Confederate movement.

I call upon the readers of this book to join in an effort to defeat neo-Confederacy and to contact the author though www.templeofdemocracy.com. The author plans on working to mobilize an effort against neo-Confederacy using the Internet including social media and hopes that the reader will join us in our efforts.

FIVE RECOMMENDED HISTORY BOOKS

Though I had said that neo-Confederacy isn't about arguing over the past but fighting over America's future one of the neo-Confederate's tactics is the misrepresentation of history. Knowledge of history could prove useful in defeating this tactic. Also, the reader might have acquired an interest in this history but not know where to start in their reading.

So this basic five book bibliography is provided for the reader **if** they wish to read some history. However, the author wants to emphasis that opposing neo-Confederates doesn't require that the reader read any of these five books and if the reader doesn't want to read these books that is fine also.

1. *The Half Has Never Been Told: Slavery and the Making of American Capitalism*, Edward E. Baptist, Basic Books, 2014.

2. *The Slave's Cause: A History of Abolition*, by Manisha Sinha, Yale University Press, 2016.

3. *The Fall of the House of Dixie: The Civil War and the Social Revolution That Transformed the South*, Bruce C. Levine, Random House, 2013.

4. *Reconstruction: America's Unfinished Revolution, 1863-1877*, Eric Foner, Revised 2nd edition, Harper Perennial Modern Classics, 2014.

5. *Trouble in Mind: Black Southerners in the Age of Jim Crow*, Leon F. Litwack, Vintage Books an imprint of Random House, 1999. Also, published in 1998 by Alfred A. Knopf Inc. In the early years when fighting neo-Confederacy was a very uphill battle reading this book made me promise to myself to never give up.

Saving money on purchasing books.

You can often purchase used books on www.ebay.com as well as Amazon.com and save a considerable amount of money on both the hard cover and soft cover copies. Often for less than $5 a used paper back copy is available.
I generally do not work with a used book seller with a rating below 90% unless I have to. I prefer scores of 95% or higher. Of course there are e-book versions of some of these books which also is a savings.

AN ANTI-CONFEDERATE FLAG

Introduction

The anti-Confederate flag shown in black & white on the title page of this book was designed with several considerations in mind to make sure it would convey a strong message concerning the neo-Confederate agenda. The full color version can be seen at www.templeofdemocracy.com.

Considerations

First, the anti-Confederate flag shouldn't contain a Confederate flag. For example there have been attempts to design an anti-Confederate symbol by putting the international prohibition sign over the Confederate battle flag. As a design that approach doesn't work out well since the Confederate battle flag has a cross on it and the slash in the prohibition sign goes over a cross bar in the Confederate flag. Additionally, if you wear this design on a t-shirt, from a distance it looks like you are wearing the Confederate flag. We don't want to wear Confederate flags, not even with prohibition signs. We want our flag to express positive values and not just in opposition to the Confederate flag.

Second, we want to have this flag be accessible to everyone, a flag that everyone who is for democratic values can call his or her own. We want an anti-Confederate and pro-American democratic flag that doesn't exclude anyone and draws together different people to be united in their opposition to neo-Confederacy. The flag can't specifically oriented to any one group in society since that would make it one group's flag and hence not anyone else's.

Third, we want a flag that is distinctive from other flags and not likely to be confused with any other flag.

Fourth, we want a flag that is readily recognizable and stands out and draws attention.

Fifth, it needs to be a flag with a design compatible with flag design.

Sixth, it should draw on anti-Confederate flags in history.

Seventh, the flag should have an appealing design so that people want to wear it because it has an appealing design.

ANTI-CONFEDERATE FLAGS IN HISTORY

During the Civil War there were many anti-Confederate flags. These were modified American flags. Some Americans rearranged the stars in the phalanxes or square pattern symbolizing readiness to face attacks on America from any direction.‡ The popularity of flying an American flag started with the Civil War. Prior to the Civil War American flags were flown at Federal buildings such as the Post Office. With the Civil War, the manufacturers were suddenly faced with a tremendous demand for American flags which people flew as anti-Confederate flags. The American flag with or without modifications was seen as the anti-Confederate flag.§

The nickname "Old Glory" for the American flag comes from one Civil War episode. Capt. Driver, a retired sea captain who moved to Tennessee in the Nashville area before the Civil War, had taken with him in his retirement the American flag that he had flown on his ship. He was very proud of this flag and exhibited it frequently and called it "Old Glory." When the Civil War broke out his flag was threatened and he hid it inside a quilt. When the American armies liberated Nashville, he was brought before the liberating troops and Capt. Driver exhibited his flag. This episode was picked up by the press at the time and though Capt. Driver and his flag are largely forgotten, the nickname "Old Glory" for the American flag is still remembered.**

The Confederates saw the American flag as an Anti-Confederate flag. Mobs in New Orleans tore down an American flag and dragged it through the mud of the streets and then "tore it to shreds, and distributed the pieces among the crowd." In Memphis the burial of the American flag was publicly celebrated.††

Unfortunately, with the overthrow of the multi-racial democracy of Reconstruction and the nation rejecting an Abolitionist vision of America, by the 1920s the Ku Klux Klan felt comfortable flying the American flag and even

---

‡ The Phalanx pattern is shown on page 131 in "The Stars and the Stripes: The American Flag as Art and as History from the Birth of the Republic to the Present," published by Alfred A. Knopf, New York, 1973.
§ Guenter, Scot M., "The American Flag, 1777-1924: Cultural Shifts from Creation to Codification," Fairleigh Dickinson University Press, 1990. For history of the American flag during the Civil War is Chapter 4, "Symbol of the Union: Flag Use During the Civil War," pages 66-87. For changes in flag manufacturing to supply demand during the Civil War page 89-90.
** Harrison, Peleg D., "The Stars and Strips and Other American Flags," pub. Little, Brown & Co., Boston, 1917, pages 304-307.
†† Preble, George Henry, "Origin and History of the American Flag," 2nd Edition, Vol. II, pub. Nicholas Brown, Philadelphia, 1917, pages 468-493.

claimed that they represented 100% Americanism. So the American flag by itself has lost an anti-Confederate meaning.

The Phalanx flag and Capt. Drivers flags can't be used since they are so similar to an American flag they aren't distinctive and can't be readily recognized as being something other than an American flag.

The Anti-Confederate Pro-American Flag Design

This anti-Confederate flag meets all seven of the considerations listed above. One, it doesn't contain a Confederate flag. Two, it is for every one of all backgrounds and isn't specific to one group. Three, it is certainly distinctive from any other flag. Four, it is readily recognizable, even from a distance. Five, it is compatible with flag design. Six, it draw on the Civil War history of anti-Confederate flags by being a flag based on the American flag. Seven, it is a design that is appealing to people.

It isn't just a flag against something, is a flag for the modern multi-racial democratic America and in opposition to the anti-democratic and racist values of the Confederacy.

It has fifty stars in a blue region like the American flag and has red and white strips like the American flag. However, both the blue canton of the American flag and the stripes has been transformed. The stars aren't aligned which is a design feature that has been used in the past to give them "sparkle." This gives the flag a novel and distinctive appearance so it won't be confused with an American flag, but will suggest the American flag. It is also an energetic pattern suggestive of an active struggle against neo-Confederacy. The swallowtail ends of the flag on the right side give the flag charm and further novelty.

ANTI-CONFEDERATE FLAG

Copyright Edward H. Sebesta 2009 Anti-Confederate flag.

ABOUT THE AUTHOR

In 2015 he was awarded the Spirit of Freedom Medal by the African American Civil War Museum in Washington, DC for his lifetime work.

He has been investigating and fighting the neo-Confederate movement for over 20 years. An autobiographical account of his research and efforts, "Has Neo-Confederacy Fallen?" was published at *Black Commentator* in 2015 and can be accessed for free at: (http://blackcommentator.com/613/613_cover_confederacy_fallen_sebesta_guest.html).

An alternative way to find the *Black Commentator* article is to go to www.templeofdemocracy.com and view the curriculum vitae.

INDEX

A

A Theological Interpretation of American History, 127, 128
Abbeville Institute, 1-5, 8, 46-48, 53, 54, 71, 88, 102, 109, 118, 120, 122, 134, 135, 144, 147, 190, 279
Affordable Health Care Act, 1, 2, 5
African Americans, vii, xv, 8, 18, 21, 31, 32, 35, 36, 38, 42-44, 53, 61, 70, 77, 78, 90, 91, 97-99, 105, 109, 111, 113, 114, 125, 164, 168, 170, 171, 173-176, 178, 181, 183, 184, 186, 189, 190, 192, 198-201, 203-205, 212, 237, 240, 242, 244, 247, 256, 259, 260
AIDS, 157, 159, 161
Alamo, v, 143, 148
amalgamation, 79, 80, 165, 209
American Legion, 211, 224, 225
American Pageant, 235, 240, 248, 249, 260
American Renaissance, 55, 114, 137
Amin, Idi, 137
An Empire for Slavery, 237
anti-Christian, 149, 151, 159
anti-democratic, 23, 24, 57, 73, 74, 188, 268
anti-egalitarian, 37, 73, 192
anti-Semitism, 110, 112, 114, 122, 124-127, 132
Anti-Suffrage, 22
apologies, 156
Aristocracies, 67
Arminians, 128
atheists, 82, 127, 128, 150

B

Baltimore, Maryland, 230
Banal Nationalism, 199
banal white nationalism, 195, 200, 201-203, 226, 228, 232, 234
bar graphs of denominations, 216
Barnett, Ross R., Governor MS, 185
Barrow, Cassie S., 89
Bassani, Marco, 65
Bay Area, 161
bias crimes, 107
Bible, 128, 129, 133, 138, 150, 151, 154, 157, 164
Billig, Michael, 199
Birth of a Nation, 98, 101, 102, 186
Black Lives Matter, 3, 43-45, 119, 120, 228
Black power salutes, 206
Black Studies, 121
Boas, Franz, 123
Bob Jones University, 129
Bradford, M.E., v, 27, 41, 55, 72, 152, 187, 192, 228, 258
Bradshaw, David, 46
Brown vs. Board of Education, 47, 51, 70, 186, 190
Buchanan, Pat, 48, 65, 66, 68, 157

C

Calhoun College, 226, 227
Calhoun, John C., 41, 226, 227, 260
California, 38, 69, 120, 123, 132, 139, 160, 161, 221, 256
Camp of the Saints, 142
Campbell, Ellen, 23
Cathey, Boyd C., 141

Cathey, Boyd D., 71, 73, 130, 132, 151, 155, 191
Chafets, Zev, 125
Charge of the Sons of Confederate Veterans, 71, 141, 151, 178, 191, 211, 212
Chodes, John, 88, 90, 103
Chronicles, 45, 46, 54, 55, 61, 66, 71, 85, 86, 125, 132-134, 141, 143-145, 147, 154, 156, 157, 160-162
Cinco de Mayo, 38, 119, 120
Citadel, 46, 108, 109, 121, 204, 209
Citizen Informer, 54, 99, 137
civil religion, 17, 24
Civil Rights, 31, 42, 47, 61, 91, 111, 129, 136, 175, 184-186, 190, 259
Confederate Americans, 42
Confederate Gift, 112
Conner, Frank, 110-115-125, 127, 149, 150, 152, 174, 175, 184, 190, 191
Crocker, H.W. III, 48
cultural Marxists, 136
culture war, 2, 150
culture wars, 2, 3, 113, 152
Cunningham, S.A., 165
Curry, Jabez L.M., 88-91

D

Dabney, Robert Lewis, 53, 76-78, 80-88, 118, 132
Dark Enlightenment, 45
Davidson, Donald, 141, 187
Davis, Jefferson, 2, 5, 28, 33, 48, 54, 100, 148, 186, 190, 228, 229, 236, 256, 260, 279
Defense of Marriage Act, 156
Democracy, The God That Failed, 62, 73

Department of Agriculture, 91
DeRosa, Marshall, 46
Descendants of Mexican War Veterans, 147
Di Lorenzo, Thomas, 46
Dickey, Chris, 140
Dred Scott, 171, 172
Dwyer, John J., 129, 130

E

Eanes, Greg, 5
Educational PAC, SCV, 111, 112
Ellison, Keith Congressman, 133
Emancipation Proclamation, 8, 258
empire, 81, 144, 145, 156, 208
Episcopal Church, 94, 219, 220-223
Equal Rights Amendment, xiii, xv, 9, 14, 16, 92, 118
ERA, 9, 16, 25, 28
Erath, Clara, 82, 187, 190
Ewing, Elbert William R., 171
existentialists, 128

F

Federal Election Bill, 22
feminism, 3, 118, 120, 122
Feminists, 120, 121
Fifteenth Amendment, 8
Finney, Charles, 129, 130
Fleming, Thomas, 54, 66, 125, 134, 158
Fourteenth Amendment, 8, 171-175, 259
French Revolution, 82, 125
Fukuyama, Francis, 66

G

Garland, Merrick, 126, 147
Genovese, Elizabeth Fox, 120
Georgia state flag, 18
Gibson, Mel, x, 125, 230
Gods and Generals, 143, 144
Gottfried, Paul, 46, 109, 122
Gramsci, Antonio, 88
Gretna, Louisiana, 57, 96
Griffith, D.W., 98, 101, 102, 186
Grissom, Michael Andrew, 96-101, 109, 172, 173, 175, 190
Gumbel, Bryant, 54
Gutzman, Kevin R., 47

H

Haiti, 168, 250, 251
Ham, 164, 165
Hampton, Jack Judge, 107
Hate crime, 106
hate crimes, 108, 109, 110, 114, 115
Hayes-Bautista, David, 38, 120
Hill, Michael, x, 53, 61, 126
Hines, Richard T., 27
Hispanic, v, 120, 135, 136, 140, 143, 149
homosexuals, 64, 107, 108, 155, 157, 158
Hoppe, Hans-Hermann, 62, 63, 66, 84

I

immigration, 3, 55, 64, 66, 69, 81, 119, 123, 134-147, 172
Institute for Historical Review, 132
Intercollegiate Studies Institute, 62
International Jewry, 127
IQ, 123
Irish, 69, 119, 135, 154

Islam, 132-134

J

Jewish intellectuals, 114, 115, 124, 125
Jewish-controlled, 115, 196
Jews, 3, 64, 81, 114, 115, 123-127, 131, 150, 153, 196
Jones, Rickey L., 32
JROTC, 211, 212, 226

K

Kennedy, James Ronald, 57, 90, 156, 158, 173
Kennedy, Walter Donald, 57, 90, 156, 158, 173
Kennedys, James and Walter, 57-59, 61
Kirk, Russell, 48
Knights of the White Camellia, 98
Kosovo, v, 143-145
Ku Klux Klan, x, 9, 21, 38, 42, 51, 90, 94, 95, 98, 100-103, 106, 169, 175, 186, 195, 196, 199, 267
KuKoranKlan, 134

L

Lamar, Dolly Blount, 22
landscape, 17, 18, 31, 32, 51, 137, 144, 202, 227, 230
League of the South, ix, x, 46, 53, 54, 61, 66, 71, 83, 86, 90, 125, 126, 140
Lee, Robert E., 2, 48, 151, 204, 205, 228, 229, 231, 238, 239
Lee, Stephen Dill, 3, 71, 141, 151, 178, 191, 211, 212
LGBT, 3, 107, 149, 152-163
Liberty Caucus, 2, 4

Lincoln, Abraham, 25, 29, 39, 52, 54, 55, 57, 94, 96, 101, 102, 145, 147, 209, 230, 254, 255, 258, 259
Livingston, Dpnald, 46, 53, 71, 144, 190
Lost Cause, iv, 18, 21-23, 28, 38, 154, 205, 244
Ludwig von Mises Institute, 46, 54, 62, 63, 73, 84
lynching, 99, 101, 109, 168, 178, 180-183, 212

M

MacDonald, Kevin, 123
Mankiller, Wilma Pearl, 119
map, 12-14
Mapplethorpe, 162, 163
maps, 11, 12, 15, 20, 24
Maxwell, Ronald F., 143, 144
McClanahan, Brion, 47
McKinley, William President, 165-167
Mexican War Journal, 147
Mexico, 20, 69, 120, 137, 139, 147-149, 207, 209, 252, 255, 256
micro-aggression, 110
Mississippi state flag, 18
Montgomery, Marion, 120
Moore, E. Ray, 89
Morill Act, 91
Moscow, Idaho, 86, 87
multiculturalism, x, 64, 68, 86, 113, 114, 137, 190
Murchison, William, 71, 143
Muslims, 3, 69, 132-134
Myths of American Slavery, 57

N

National Cathedral in Washington D.C, 219
National Council of La Raza, 139
Native American Studies, 121
neo-Reactionary, 45
Nesmith, Kevin, 109
New Orleans, 36, 116, 153, 226, 267
Nineteenth Amendment, xiii, 8, 13, 21, 22, 23
Norris, Wesley, 238
nullification, 1, 2, 3, 4, 8

O

Oakley Park, 42, 103, 104, 210
Obama, Barack President, 19, 52, 70, 119, 126, 134, 140, 183
Obamacare, 1, 2
odor, 165, 167
Orange Lives Matter, 119
orthodox (Christianity), 46, 129, 130, 131, 149, 150, 152
Owens, Collie, 82

P

paleoconservatives, 45, 55, 66
paleolibertarians, 45
Paul, Ron U.S. Representative, 139
Pelican Publishing Company, 96, 125
Pew Research Center, 18, 279
police shootings, 43
Polin, Claude, 67
Politically Incorrect Guide, 46, 47, 48
Politically Incorrect Guide to American History, 46, 47
Poll, 18, 36, 279

poll tax, 13, 16, 23, 59
polling results, 18
polls, 19, 20, 33, 174
Presbyterian and Reformed Publishing Co., 129
PRESBYTERIAN CHURCH USA, 220
Public Policy Polling, 19, 279
Puerto Rican, 135
Puerto Ricans, 135

Q

Quinn, Richard M., 27

R

Randolph, John (of Roanoke), 78, 148, 237
Rankin, John E., 168
rape, 110, 122, 136, 168, 176, 178, 180-183, 236, 237
Raspail Jean, 69, 142, 143
reactionary fortress, 24, 263
Reconquista, 69
Reconstruction, 18, 21-23, 35, 41-43, 52, 60-62, 70, 87, 88, 90, 91, 97, 98, 101-103, 105, 106, 111, 116, 169, 174-176, 181, 182, 186, 188, 189, 191, 206, 210, 234, 258-260, 265, 267
Red Shirts, 9, 21, 42, 51, 95, 99, 103, 104-106, 210
Reed, John Shelton, v, 141-143, 160-163
Regenstein, Lewis, 122
Regnery Press, 46-49, 187
Rembert, James, 46
Republican Party, 19, 20, 22, 25-27, 53, 54, 60, 97, 98, 104, 168, 174, 205, 210, 259

Rethinking the American Union for the 21st Century, 5
Riley, Leslie, 83
Roman Catholic Church, 70, 220, 221
Roof, Dylann, 36, 53, 55, 94, 133, 156
Rumburg, H. Rondel, 45, 131, 154, 156
Rutherford, Mildred, 22

S

Sale, Kirkpatrick, 68
Sandal, Matthew, 109
Schlafly, Phyllis, 16, 118, 279
Scott, Wiillard, 54
SCV, 2-5, 28, 42, 43, 45, 52, 57, 62, 71, 100-103, 106, 110-114, 116, 122, 124, 127, 128, 131-133, 135, 136, 140, 141, 149-152, 154-158, 170, 171, 175, 178, 180-186, 191, 211, 212, 214, 220-225
Second Vatican Council, 70
sexual deviants, 158
Simpson, Barry D., 84
Singers, C. Gregg, 127, 129
slavery, x, xiv, 8, 20, 21, 31-33, 35, 41, 53, 57, 65, 70, 73, 76, 82, 85, 86, 91, 96, 97, 100, 129, 132, 145, 148, 150, 164, 165, 168, 169, 174, 178, 181, 182, 188, 192, 203, 205, 208, 221, 226, 229, 232, 235-237, 239, 240-256, 258, 260, 262
Sobran, Joe, 48, 65
soccer, 147
Sons of Confederate Veterans, v, 2, 4, 28, 35, 42-45, 52, 57, 62, 71, 83, 84, 96, 101, 106, 109-113, 122, 125, 132, 133, 136, 139, 140, 141, 147, 149, 151, 154-157, 164, 170, 172, 174, 180, 184-186, 190-192, 194, 198, 214, 216

Sons of the American Revolution, 211, 225
Southern Baptist Convention, 156, 220, 221
Southern Cultures, 141, 160
Southern Partisan, v, ix, 16, 23, 25-28, 46-48, 54-65, 66, 71, 73, 82, 88, 89, 94, 99, 100, 107-109, 118, 120, 121, 135, 141, 144, 153, 154, 158, 159, 187, 246, 279
Sprinkle Publications, 82
Sprinkle, Lloyd, 82
Sproul, R.C. Jr., 85
states' rights, 4, 5, 18, 21-23, 28, 61, 63, 70, 112, 156, 173
Stephen D. Lee Institute, 3
Stephen Dill Lee Institute, 141, 178
student, 2, 62, 108, 109, 145, 162, 248
suffrage, 22, 60, 67, 73, 78, 91, 129, 173, 178, 189
Supreme Court, 7-9, 51, 69, 91, 107, 111, 126, 156, 157, 159, 171, 185, 186, 190, 191, 230, 253

T

Taney, Roger B. Chief Justice, 171, 172, 230, 231
Taylor, Jared, 114
Texas Nationalist Movement, 19, 279
The Camp of the Saints, 69, 142, 143
The Culture of Critique, 123
The Journal of Historical Review, 132
The Legal and Historical Status of the Dred Scott Decision, 171
The Negro 23rd Psalm, 184
The New York Review of Books, 227, 228
The South Under Siege, 111, 123

The South Was Right!, ix, 56, 57, 61, 73, 90, 96, 158, 173
The Southern Tradition at Bay, 72, 191
Third-World, 136
Thornwell, James Henley, 127, 128, 130-132, 150
TNM (Texas Nationalist Movement), 19, 20, 279
Tocqueville, Alexis de, 62, 66, 68, 70, 73
Tolerance, 136, 155
Transaction Press, 62
transcendentalists, 128
Trifkovic, Srdja, 134
Truth in History, 131
Tubman, Harriet, 119
Twenty-Fourth Amendment, 13, 23, 59

U

U.S. Air Force Academy, 204
U.S. Merchant Marine Academy, 204
U.S. Military Academy at West Point, 204-207, 260
U.S. Naval Academy, 204
Unitarianism, 128-131, 150
Unitarians, 3, 81, 127-129, 132
United Methodist Church, 138, 221-224
United States History for Christian Schools, 129
United States Military Academies, 203
University of Idaho, 87
University of Louisville, 32
University of Texas at Arlington, 147
University of Texas at Austin, 228, 230

V

Vanderbilt Lambda Association, 108
Veterans of Foreign Wars, 211, 224
Virginia Dare, 55
Virginia Military Academy, 204
Virginia Military Institute, 121, 204
Vogler, James N. Jr., 61, 100
voter suppression, 116, 172, 260
voting, 3, 7, 16, 19, 22-24, 58-60, 78, 98, 138, 140, 172, 279
Voting Rights Act, 7, 60, 61, 111, 185, 190

W

Was Jefferson Davis Right?, 57
Watkins, Watkins Jr., 54
Weaver, Richard M., v, 41, 72, 152, 187, 191, 198
White Citizens Council, 53, 88, 169
White League, 98

Williams, Scott Whitten, 83
Williamson, Chilton Jr., 55, 62, 66, 145
Wilson, Clyde, x, 70, 88, 90, 102, 103
Wilson, Clyde N., 54, 55
Wilson, Douglas, 86, 129
Wilson, William, 46
women, xiii, xv, 8, 9, 16, 17, 21, 22, 52, 110, 120-122, 124, 136, 150, 155, 158, 168, 169, 176-178, 181-183, 189, 204, 206, 249, 258
Women's Studies, 121
women's suffrage, 16, 21
Woods, Thomas E., 46

Y

Yale University, 226-228, 250, 265
Younge, Gary, 31

Z

Zappa, Ann Rives, 111

FOOTNOTES

[1] No author, "Compatriots! Learn About the Abbeville Institute," full page ad, *Confederate Veteran*, inside back cover, Vol. 73 No. 6, Nov./Dec. 2015, pp. 73 (inside back cover). Ad was also run: Vol. 71 No. 6, Nov./Dec. 2013, pp. 66; Vol. 72 No. 1, Jan./Feb. 2014, pp. 73; Vol. 72 No.4, July/Aug. 2014, pp. 74; Vol. 72 No. 6, Nov./Dec. 2014, pp. 73; Vol. 73 No. 1, Jan./Feb. 2015, pp. 69; Vol. 73 No. 2, March/April 2015, pp. 67; Vol. 73 No. 4, July/Aug. 2015, pp. 65; Vol. 73 No. 5, Sept./Oct. 2015, pp. 65.

[2] Eanes, Greg, "Enduring Principles: Remarks Delivered at the 50th Anniversary of the United Daughters of the Confederacy Massing of the Flags in Honor of Confederate President Jefferson Davis," The Eanes Group, city not given but listed as a Virginia business, 2015, pp. 17-21.

[3] "Phyllis Schlafly," *Southern Partisan*, Vol. 2 No. 3, Summer 1982. (Note cover wrongly lists issue as Vol. 3 No. 3, but inside the magazine is the correct volume and number.), pp. 36-39. Note the *Southern Partisan* was frequently late and sometimes very late.

[4] CNN Opinion Research Poll, for release April 12, 2011, i2.cdn.turner.com/cnn/2011/images/04/11/rel6b.pdf, printed out 2/16/13.

[5] The Pew Research Center for the People & the Press, "Civil War at 150: Still Relevant, Still Divisive," www.people-press.org/2011/04/08/civil-war-at-150-still-relevant-still-divisive/1/, printed out 2/10/2013.

[6] No author, "Georgia Miscellany," Public Policy Polling, http://www.publicpolicypolling.com/main/2012/12/georgia-miscellany.html, printed out 4/23/2016.

[7] "Poll: 29 percent of Mississippians would back a new Confederacy," http://www.sunherald.com/news/politics-government/politics-columns-blogs/crawdaddy/article36566313.html#storylink=cpy, printed out 4/23/2016.

[8] Phillips, Amber "The Texas secession debate is getting kind of real," *Washington Post*, April 19, 2016, https://www.washingtonpost.com/news/the-fix/wp/2016/04/19/the-texas-secession-movement-is-getting-kind-of-serious/, printed out 4/23/2016.

[9] Baddour, Dylan, "Texas GOP official wants secession on the primary ballot," Nov. 15, 2015, http://www.chron.com/news/houston-texas/texas/article/texas-independence-secession-republic-TNM-texian-6654896.php, printed out 4/23/2016.

[10] Tilove, Jonathan, "Texas GOP votes not to put secession on primary ballot," Austin American-Statesman, Jan. 5, 2015, http://www.statesman.com/news/news/state-regional-govt-politics/texas-gop-votes-not-to-put-secession-question-on-p/npczK/, printed out 4/23/2016. For the Texas Nationalist Movement account of them photographing the vote, http://www.thetnm.org/breakdown_of_srec_voting, printed out 4/23/2016

[11] Miller, Daniel, "Special message from TNM President: Convention Update," http://www.thetnm.org/2016_convention_update, printed out 4/23/2016; Baddour, Dylan, "In Texas, some local GOPs call for statewide vote on secession," http://www.chron.com/news/politics/texas/article/texas-secession-

independence-nationalist-movement-7248746.php, printed out 4/23/2016; for the 270 count of conventions, Phillips, Amber "The Texas secession debate is getting kind of real," Washington Post, April 19, 2016, https://www.washingtonpost.com/news/the-fix/wp/2016/04/19/the-texas-secession-movement-is-getting-kind-of-serious/, printed out 4/23/2016.

[12] Baddour, Dylan, "GOP committee ends talk of secession at party convention," Houston Chronicle, Friday, May 13, 2016, http://www.chron.com/news/houston-texas/texas/article/GOP-committee-ends-anticipation-of-secession-7466700.php, printed out 8/4/2016.

[13] Johnson, Kenneth R., "White Racial Attitudes as a Factor in the Arguments Against the Nineteenth Amendment," *Phylon*, Vol. 31 No. 1, 1st Qtr. 1970, pp. 31-37. The articles reference is to the *Woman Patriot*, Vol. 3, June 28, 1919, pp. 6-7.

[14] McRae, Elizabeth Gillespie, "Caretakers of Southern Civilization: Georgia Women and the Anti-Suffrage Campaign, 1914-1920," *The Georgia Historical Quarterly*, Vol. 82 No. 4, Winter 1998, pp. 801-828.

[15] Campbell, Ellen, "Trampled Ground," *Southern Partisan*, Vol. 3 No. 1, Winter 1983, pp. 23-24.

[16]

[17] No author, "A Southern Partisan Conversation: The Reverend Jerry Falwell," *Southern Partisan*, Vol. 2 No. Spring 1982, pp. 22-29.

[18] Gragg, Rod, "Partisan Conversation," *Southern Partisan*, Vol. 6 No. 1, Winter 1986, pp. 39

[19] No author, "A Southern Partisan Conversation: Interview With The Rev. Donald Wildmon, President and Founder of the American Family Association," *Southern Partisan*, Vol. 9 2nd Qtr., 1989, pp. 36-39. Note: The issues of the Southern Partisan changed their system of issues over time. Sometimes the cover would not match the contents. There were other irregularities. The issue identification given for this paper are based on inspection of the magazines themselves.

[20] Baldwin, Donald, "Byrd of Virginia: A Closer Look," *Southern Partisan*, Vol. 2 No. 4, Fall 1982, pp. 12-14.

[21] Baldwin, Donald, "A Partisan Conversation: Phil Gramm," *Southern Partisan*, Vol. 3 No. 3 Summer 1983, pp. 30-33.

[22] Baldwin, Donald, "A Partisan Conversation: Jesse Helms," *Southern Partisan*, Vol. 4 No. 2, Spring 1984, pp. 34-38.

[23] Hines, Richard T., "A Partisan Conversation With Trent Lott," *Southern Partisan*, Vol. 4 No.4, Fall 1984, pp. 44-48.

[24] Goolsby, Charles, "Partisan Conversation: Congressman Dick Armey," *Southern Partisan*, Vol. 10 3rd Qtr. 1990, pp. 26-29.

[25] Goolsby, Charles, "Partisan Conversation: Thad Cochran," *Southern Partisan*, Vol. 15 3rd Qtr., 1995, pp. 32-36.

[26] No author, "Partisan Conversation: Senator John Ashcroft, Missouri's Champion of States' Rights and Traditional Southern Values," Southern Partisan, Vol. 18 2nd Qtr., 1998.

[27] No author, "Partisan Conversation: Congressman Lindsey Graham," *Southern Partisan*, Vol. 19 1st Qtr. 1999, pp. 42-45.

[28] Bradford, M.E., Address given on June 3, 1986 at Arlington Cemetery on the occasion of President Jefferson Davis's birthday and then was published in *Southern Partisan* Vol. 8 No. 4, Winter 1988, pp.19-23 from "Against the Barbarians: and Other Reflections on Familiar Themes," Univ. of Missouri Press, Columbia, MO, 1992, pp. 215-21. Readers might recall George Orwell's novel "1984" about a future totalitarian state published in 1949. In the novel the slogan of the totalitarian state was "Who controls the past, controls the future: who controls the present controls the past." However, the author is not restating this idea. Being dominate in the present will greatly assist in dominating the past, but it might be that working to undermine this domination of the past can work to change the present and future which is the author's idea.

[29] Gary Younge, *No Place Like Home: A Black Briton's Journey Through the American South* (Jackson: University Press of Mississippi, 2002), 67. From, "The Jefferson Davis Highway: Contesting the Confederacy in the Pacific Northwest," Euan Hague, Edward H. Sebesta, 2011, *Journal of American Studies*, Cambridge Journals, Vol. 45 No. 2, May 2011, pp. 281-301. Abstract online at http://journals.cambridge.org/action/displayAbstract?fromPage=online&aid=8267705.

[30] O'Brian, Brendan, "Confederate monuments to be removed from University of Louisville campus," Reuters, 4/29/16, http://www.reuters.com/article/us-kentucky-monument-idUSKCN0XR02P, printed out 5/1/2016.

[31] Bailey, Phillip M., "Confederate memorial at U of L to be removed," *Courier-Journal*, 4/29/2016, http://www.courier-journal.com/story/news/local/2016/04/29/ramsey-fischer-discuss-confederate-statue/83695160/, printed out 5/1/2016.

[32] The author can't remember if this comparison was something adapted or inspired by someone's earlier writings or entirely from earlier writings and hasn't been able to find an attribution, but it isn't an entirely original comparison by the author. Perhaps the author's idea is derived from a statement b Rev. Floyd Rose of Georgia. http://www.wctv.tv/home/headlines/Organizations-Asking-Georgia-To-Stop-Endorsing-The-Confederacy-268165812.html, printed out 5/1/2016.

[33] Brammer, Jack, "Panel votes to keep statue of Confederate President Jefferson Davis in Kentucky Capitol," Lexington Herald Leader, Aug. 5, 2015, http://www.kentucky.com/news/politics-government/article44613948.html, printed out 5/1/2016.

[34] Williams, Jessica, "'Death threats,' 'threatening calls' prompt firm tasked with removing Confederate monuments to quit," *The Advocate*, Jan. 14, 2016, Baton Rouge, LA, http://theadvocate.com/news/neworleans/neworleansnews/14572522-93/firm-tasked-with-confederate-monument-removal-pulls-out-after-company-receives-

death-threats-threate printed out 4/30/2016, printed out 4/30/2016; Adelson, Jeff, "Potential Problems? City of New Orleans again pushes back deadline for bids on Confederate monument removal," *The Advocate*, Baton Rouge, LA, April 24, 2016.

[35] Dutten, Sarah, De Pinto Jennifer, Salvanto, Anthony, "Poll: Views on Charleston shooting, Confederate flag," *CBS News*, July 23, 2015, http://www.cbsnews.com/news/cbs-news-poll-charleston-shooting-and-the-confederate-flag/, printed out 4/30/2016; No author, "Majority of Louisianans oppose removing Confederate statues," *CBS News*, 4/19/2016, http://www.cbsnews.com/news/majority-of-louisianans-oppose-removing-confederate-statues/, printed out 4/30/2016.

[36] Adelson, Jeff, "Those hoping to keep Confederate monuments in place face uphill battle in court, federal judge says," *The Advocate*, Baton Rouge, LA, Jan. 14, 2016. Local historical societies Monumental Task Committee and the Louisiana Landmark Society joined a lawsuit with the local Sons of Confederate Veterans chapter to keep the monuments. http://theadvocate.com/csp/mediapool/sites/Advocate/assets/templates/FullStoryPrint.csp?cid=14571610#&preview=y, printed out 4/30/2016.

[37] Blinder, Alan, "Momentum to Remove Confederate Symbols Slows or Stops," *New York Times*, March 13, 2016, http://www.nytimes.com/2016/03/14/us/momentum-to-remove-confederate-symbols-slows-or-stops.html?_r=0, printed out 5/1/2016.

[38] Harris, Donna, "Oakley Park: Only Shrine of Its Kind," *United Daughters of the Confederacy Magazine*, June/July 2001, pp. 23-24.

[39] Parker, Ray L., "Is There Not a Cause?," *Confederate Veterans*, Vol. 74 No. 3, May/June 2016, pp. 12-13.

[40] Strain, Thomas V. Jr., "Courage," *Confederate Veteran*, March/April 2015, pp. 8-9; "Continue the Fight," *Confederate Veteran*, July/August 201, pp. 8-9.

[41] Strain, Thomas V. Jr, "General Order 2016-01," http://www.scv.org/pdf/2016GeneralOrder01.pdf, printed out 9/9/2016.

[42] Strain, Thomas, V., "Looking to the future," *Confederate Veteran*, Vol. 74 No. 5, Sept./Oct. 2016, pp. 4-5.

[43] Rumburg, H. Rondel, "Confederate Flags Matter: The Christian Influence on the Flags," SBSS, Appomattox, Virginia, 2015. For his role in the periodical and past office in the SCV, see Chaplain's Corp Chronicles of the Sons of Confederate Veterans, May 2016, No. 125, http://chaplain-in-chief.com/custom3_1.html. For further information, http://www.biblicalandsouthernstudies.com/. Printed out 5/29/2016.

[44] No author, "Confederate Gifts from GHQ," *Confederate Veteran*, Vol. 74 No. 4, July/August 2016, pp. 70-71.

[45] Abbeville Institute had a list at their website www.abbevilleinstitute.org up until 2013, but the list disappeared in 2014. You can however go to www.archive.org and view earlier versions of their website and see who is listed. The scholars listed here are from an archive.org capture of https://web.archive.org/web/20130814222550/http://www.abbevilleinstitute.org/

printed out 4/27/2016. The author has printed out hard copies of neo-Confederate web pages since 1996 and archived them. The Internet Archive does a fairly good job, but not all gets captured, some of which is very critical.

[46] http://www.regnery.com/imprint/politically-incorrect-guides/, printed out 4/27/2016.

[47] https://mises.org/profile/thomas-e-woods-jr, printed out 4/28/16.

[48] Articles in *Southern Patriot* are: Woods, Thomas E. Jr., "Copperheads," Vol. 2 No. 1, Jan.-Feb. 1995, pp. 3-5; "The Abolitionists," Vol. 2 No. 5, Sept.-Oct. 1995, pp. 36-37.

[49] https://web.archive.org/web/20130814222550/http://www.abbevilleinstitute.org/ printed out 4/27/2016.

[50] http://www.abbevilleinstitute.org/support/selected-books-and-dvd-videos-by-abbeville-scholars/, printed out 4/27/2016. If you visit the page you won't find directly the page, you have to use their search engine and put in the term "dvd" to have it show up as a search result.

[51] *Chronicles* magazine articles are: Vol. 20 No. 5 May 1996 "Battling Cyberhate" where he attacks campaigns against cyberhate; Vol. 20 No. 7, July 1996, "Ron Pau and the Two GOPs," defending Ron Paul as a true conservative; Vol. 24 No. 1, Jan. 2000, pp. 32-33, book review of the 50th anniversary republishing of "The Roosevelt Myth," by John T. Flynn; Vol. 26 No. 9, Sept. 2002, pp. 26-28, book review of "Perpetual War for Perpetual Peace: How We Got to Be So Hated," by Gore Vidal; Vol. 27 No. 5, May 2003, pp. 28-30, book review of "God and the World," by Cardinal Joseph Ratzinger.

[52] Woods, Thomas E. Jr., "Christendom's Last Stand," *Southern Partisan*, Vol. 17 2nd Qtr., 1997; "Sitting Amidst the Ruins: The South vs. The Enlightenment," *Southern Partisan*, Vol. 21 2nd Qtr. 2001, pp. 16-22. The other articles in *Southern Partisan* are: "Derailing the Constitution," Vol. 16 1st Qtr. 1996, pp. 48-49; "A New Strategy Against Terrorism," 4th Qtr. 2001, pp. 12; Sept.-Oct. 2002, pp. 31-34, book review of "Revolt from the Heartland" by Joseph Scotchie; Vol. 24 Qtr. 1, pp. 27-29, book review of "Speaking of Liberty" by Lew Rockwell; Vol. 24 No. 5, pp. 30-31 book review of "Reclaiming Liberty," by James Ronald Kennedy; Vol. 20 No. 2 pp. 20-21, book review of "Lincoln Unmasked: What You Are Not Supposed to Know About Dishonest Abe," by Thomas J. DiLorenzo.

[53] http://tomwoods.com/about/. Printed out 4/28/16; Thomas E. Woods, doesn't provide any information about his neo-Confederate writings. To correct this lack, the author of this book keeps a web page listing all the writings. http://www.templeofdemocracy.com/thomas-e-woods.html. The Abbeville Institute web page listing books and DVD videos by member scholars is http://www.abbevilleinstitute.org/support/selected-books-and-dvd-videos-by-abbeville-scholars/, printed out 4/27/2016.

[54] https://www.cv.edu/?page_id=6873, printed out 5/1/2016. From Chattahoochee Valley website.

[55] Brion McClanahan was listed as recently as Aug. 3, 2015 as the editor of Abbeville Review at the Abbeville Institute website, https://web.archive.org/web/20150809122556/http://www.abbevilleinstitute.org/blog/july-top-ten/, fortunately the Internet Archive has archived their website. Printed out 4/28/2016.
[56] Directory listing at www.lewrockwell.com, https://www.lewrockwell.com/author/brion-mcclanahan/, printed out 4/29/2016.
[57] http://www.brionmcclanahan.com/, printed out 5/1/2016.
[58] McClanahan, Brion, Vol. 12 No. 3, May-June 2002, *Southern Partisan*, "Fire Martial," review of "A Fire Eater Remembers: The Confederate Memoirs of Robert Barnwell Rhett," by William C. Davis.
[59] http://www.kevingutzman.com/bio/bio.html, printed out 5/1/2016.
[60] Gutzman, Kevin R. *Southern Partisan* articles are: Vol. 15 4th Qtr. 1995, pp. five reviews, no titles, "John C. Calhoun: A Biography," by Irving H. Barlett, "Taming the Storm: The Life and Times of Judge Frank M. Johnson Jr. and the South's Fight Over Civil Rights" by Jack Bass, "The Reintegration of American History: Slavery and the Civil War," by William W. Freehling, "Juries and Judges Versus the Law: Virginia's Provincial Legal Perspectives, 1783-1828," by Thornton F. Miller, "The Confederate Republic: A Revolution Against Politics," by George C. Rable, pp. 48-52; Vol. 16 No. 1 1996, three reviews, "Andersonville: The Horrors of a Georgia Movie," review of "Andersonville," Turner Network Television, 1996, pp. 39-41, "Ode to Father Abraham," review of "Lincoln" by David Herbert Donald, pp. 44-45, 53, no title, "All Over the Map: Rethinking American Regions," by Edward L. Ayers, Patricia N. Limerick, Stephen Nissenbaum, Peter S. Onuf, pp. 49; Vol. 16 2nd Qtr. 1996, six reviews, "First in Our Hearts," review of "Founding Father: Rediscovering George Washington," by Richard Brookhiser, pp. 40-42, no title, "The South and the New Deal," by Roger Biles, pp. 50-51, and "Republics Ancient & Modern: Classical Republicanism and the American Revolution," by Paul A. Rahe, pp. 51-52, "Richard Hurdis: A Tale of Alabama," by William Gilmore Simms and edited by John Caldwell Guilds, pp. 52-53, "The Age of Federalism: The Early American Republic, 1788-1800," pp. 53, "The Intellectual Construction of America: Exceptionalism and Identity From 1492 to 1800, pp. 53-54; Vol. 17 1st Qtr. 1997, "Madison's Third Way," review of "The Sacred Fire of Liberty: James Madison & the Founding of the Federal Republic," by Lance Banning, pp. 48-49; Vol. 17 2nd Qtr. 1997, two reviews, "Original Meanings: Politics and Ideas in the Making of the Constitution," by Jack N. Rakove, pp. 44, "Sectional Crisis and Southern Constitutionalism," by Don E. Fehrenbacher, pp. 44-45; Vol. 18, 1st Qtr. 1998, three reviews, "In Search of the Real Jefferson," review of "Thomas Jefferson: A Ken Burns Film," and "American Sphinx: The Character of Thomas Jefferson," by Joseph Ellis, pp. 34-35, "The Inner Jefferson: Portrait of a Grieving Optimist," by Andrew Burstein, pp. 46-47 , "The Long Affair: Thomas Jefferson and the French Revolution, 1785-1800," by Conor Cruise O'Brien, pp. 47; Vol. 18 4th Qr. 1998, "The Randolph-Clay Duel," pp. 16-20.

[61] The scholars listed here are from an archive.org capture of https://web.archive.org/web/20130814222550/http://www.abbevilleinstitute.org/ printed out 4/27/2016.
[62] https://www.lewrockwell.com/author/kevin-r-c-gutzman/, printed out 5/1/2016. Article critical of the Supreme Court decision, http://archive.lewrockwell.com/orig8/gutzman5.html, printed out 5/1/2016.
[63] Franck, Matthew J., "Whistling Dixie," *Claremont Review of Books*, Vol. 8, No. 1, Winter 2007/08, accessed online at http://www.claremont.org/crb/article/whistling-dixie/, printed out 4/28/2016.
[64] http://www.kevingutzman.com/, printed out 5/1/2016.
[65] H.W. Crocker, III, *Southern Partisan* articles are: Vol. 17 2nd Qtr. 1997, three reviews, "Shades of Blue and Gray: An Introductory Military History of the Civil War," by Herman Hattaway, pp. 50, "The Blue & The Gray on the Silver Screen: More than 80 Years of Civil War Movies," by Ray Kinnard, pp. 50, "John Randolph of Roanoke: A Study in American Politics," 4th edition, by Russell Kirk, pp. 50; Vol. 17 4th Qtr. 1997, review of "Conceived in Liberty: Joshua Chamberlain, William Oates, and the American Civil War," by Mark Perry, pp. 44; Vol. 18 1st Qtr. 1998, book review of "Stonewall Jackson: The Man, the Soldier, the Legend," by James I. Robertson, pp. 50; Vol. 18 2nd Qtr. 1998, book review of "Confederate Tide Rising: Robert E. Lee and the Making of Southern Strategy, 1861-1862," by Joseph L. Harsh, pp. 47; Vol. 18 4th Qtr. 1998, three book reviews, "General George E. Pickett in Life and Legend," by Lesley J. Gordon, pp. 46-47, "Private Soldiers and Public Heroes: An American Album of the Common Man's Civil War," by Milton Bagby, pp. 47, "Mrs. Robert E. Lee," by Rose Mortimer Elizey MacDonald, introduction by Douglas Southall Freeman, pp. 47; Vol. 19 2nd Qtr. 1999, "Smoke Never Clears," book review of "Memoirs of Confederate War for Independence: A Prussian Officer with J.E.B. Stuart in Virginia," by Heros von Borcke, pp. 42. (Cover wrongly indicates volume 23), in the same issue on page 26 he gives his list of recommended books for an article, "Recommended Readings for All Southern Partisans,"; Vol. 19 3rd Qtr. 1999, "Smoke Never Clears," book review of "Grey Ghost: The Life of Colonel John Singleton Mosby," by James A. Ramage, pp. 36; Vol. 19, 4th Qtr. 1999, "Smoke Never Clears," review of two books, "Confederate Wizards of the Saddle," by Bennett Young, and "The Campaign that Won America: The Story of Yorktown," by Burke Davis, pp. 33-34.
[66] http://www.nationalreview.com/author/h-w-crocker-iii, printed out 5/1/2016. His defense of the British Empire in *National Review* is online http://www.nationalreview.com/article/285212/paleo-conservative-guide-british-empire-h-w-crocker-iii?target=author&tid=902910, printed out 5/1/2016.
[67] http://www.crisismagazine.com/author/crocker, printed out 5/1/2016.
[68] http://spectator.org/bios/h-w-crocker-iii, printed out 5/1/2016.
[69] Crocker, H.W. III, *American Spectator*, 10/20/2008, http://spectator.org/articles/42815/how-would-jefferson-davis-vote, printed out 5/1/2016.
[70] http://www.regnery.com/about/leadership/, printed out 5/1/2016.

[71] http://www.penguinrandomhouse.com/books/33664/robert-e-lee-on-leadership-by-hw-crocker-iii/, printed out 5/1/2016.
[72] Statement of Circulation, *UDC Magazine*, Vol. 78 No. 9, Oct. 2015, pp. 26.
[73] There are numerous examples of the UDC praising the Ku Klux Klan. UDC Historian General recommends S.E.F. Roses book on the Ku Klux Klan in a 1913 address to the UDC convention, the book is endorsed by the UDC, and S.E.F. Rose succeeds Rutherford as UDC Historian General, see www.confederatepastpresent.org for all the historical references; in 1956 and 1957 the UDC Magazine ran many articles attacking the Supreme Court on school integration, one article which is really hysterical is Bruce, Dunstan, "Jefferson Davis – The Man America Needs Today," United Daughters of the Confederacy Magazine, June 1958, pp. 19, 23, 26, 27. This article and others like it are online at www.confederatepastpresent.org and in the book, "The Confederate and Neo-Confederate Reader," Univ. Press of Mississippi, 2010. The magazine often ran articles divided over two or more issues and some issues had no less than three such articles in them at one time; The *UDC Magazine* helped launch Michael Andrew Grissom's pro-KKK "Southern by the Grace of God," with an excerpt in their Sept. 1988 issue, and called the book a "treasure" in a column by Retta D. Tindal, "Confederate Classics: For Research, Reference, or Refresher," *UDC Magazine*, Vol. 70 No. 10, Nov. 2007, pp. 15.
[74] Baird, Randy, "Hog and Hominey Licks Carpetbaggers," Vol. 23 No. 3, March 1960, pp. 20.
[75] Foster, Gaines M., "Ghosts of the Confederacy: Defeat, the Lost Cause, and the Emergence of the New South," Oxford Univ. Press USA, 1987, pp. 107-108.
[76] No author, *Confederate Veteran*, Vol. 74 No. 5, Sept./Oct. 2016, pp. 1.
[77] Barrow, Charles Kelly, "Numbers – Do They Really Matter?" *Confederate Veteran*, Vol. 70 No. 6, Nov.-Dec. 2012, pp. 8-9. Note: The Volume number system of the Confederate Veteran has widely varied since its publication started in the 1980s. What is given in these citations are what was printed in the magazine.
[78] No author, *Southern Mercury*, Vol. 6 No. 5, Sept./Oct. 2008, pp. 4.
[79] Slimp, Robert, "Americans Face the Worst Presidential Candidates in History," Southern Mercury, Vol. 6 No.3, May-June 2008, pp. 28-33; Stang, Alan, "Republican Party: Red From the State," *Southern Mercury*, Vol. 6 No. 2, March/April 2008, pp. 26-29.
[80] http://samdavis.scv.org/, printed out 5/8/2015. The references to "Beavis & Butthead" are in the 1st application form in the *Confederate Veteran*, Vol. One 2003, Jan.-Feb. pp. 43, which though now very out-of-date hasn't been updated in recent ads. (The *Confederate Veterans* for some years adopted a system of six volumes per year starting with volume One, Two, Three, and then starting over the next year. The volume and numbering system has varied widely.) For article describing assignment on secession, Taylor, Fred D., "Educating Our Youth – The Successes of the First Sam Davis Youth Camp," March/April 2004, *Confederate Veteran*, pp. 26-28, Oratory contest mentioned on page 27 3rd column.

[81] Wilson, R.G., "Report from the Commander-in-Chief," *Confederate Veteran*, Volume Two 2003 (March-April), pp. 2-3; Pastor John Weaver, Taylor, Fred D., "Educating Our Youth – The Successes of the First Sam Davis Youth Camp," March/April 2004, *Confederate Veteran*, pp. 26-28, Weaver as instructor on page 27, 2nd column.

[82] "Southern League News," *Southern Patriot*, Vol. 1 No. 1, Sept.-Oct. 1994, pp. 7.

[83] "Purpose," http://www.abbevilleinstitute.org/principles/, printed out 5/7/2016.

[84] Hill, Michael, "Re: The Bitter Fruits of Empire: 11 September 2001," League of the South News Service, press release Sept. 12, 2001, archived by archive.org at https://web.archive.org/web/20011201103034/http://216.157.8.33/ls-press-releases/11sept-terrorism.htm, printed out 5/2/2016; Carlson, Wayne, "Why Should God Bless America?," archived by archive.org at https://web.archive.org/web/20020105123804/http://www.dixienet.org/dn-gazette/god-bless.htm, printed out 5/7/2016.

[85] The League of the South is often adopting new websites and abandoning others so it an internet search engine might be the best method of locating their websites.

[86] League of the South Institute page, archived at archive.org https://web.archive.org/web/20011021163848/http://www.dixienet.org/ls-institute/los-institute.htm#staff, printed out 5/7/2016.

[87] Wilson, Clyde, "New From Southern Pens, Part 4," April 20, 2016, http://www.abbevilleinstitute.org/blog/new-from-southern-pens-part-4/, printed out 5/8/2016.

[88] Edsel, Tom, "Lott Renounces White 'racialist' Group He Praised in 1992," Washington Post, Dec. 16, 1998, page A2. My last name is misspelled as "Sebasta."

[89] "About Mises," https://mises.org/about-mises, printed out 5/7/2016, "Faculty and Staff," https://mises.org/faculty-staff, printed 5/7/2016, "About," https://www.lewrockwell.com/about/, printed out 5/7/2016.

[90] Neal, Terry, "Racial Issues Dog GOP Foes; McCain Won't Fire Aide, Bush Pressed on Bob Jones, Flag," *Washington Post*, Feb. 18, 2000, page A6; Jim Schutze, "Rebel Hunter: Oak Cliff's Ed Sebesta helped topple Trent Lott," *Dallas Observer*, Jan. 9, 2003.

[91] Gragg, Ron, "A Partisan Conversation With Willard Scott," interview of Willard Scott, "Southern Partisan," Vol. 4 No. 3 Summer 1984, pp. 31-35. I have always thought that more was going on then was reported.

[92] Fleming, Thomas, "A League of Our Own," *Chronicles*, Vol. 17 No. 2, Feb. 1993, pp. 12-15.

[93] No author, "Southern league news," *Southern Patriot*, Vol. 1 No. 1, Sept.-Oct. 1994, pp. 7, lists board of directors and founding members on committees.

[94] No author, no pagination, outside mailing covers on *Southern Patriot* issues: Vol. 4 No. 5, Sept.-Oct. 1997; Vol. 4 No. 6, Nov.-Dec. 1997; Vol. 6 No. 1, Jan.-Feb. 1998; Vol. 6 No. 2, March-April 1998.

[95] Wilson, Clyde, "A Real Place," book review of "A Gallery of Ashevilleans: A History of a the People of a Mountain Town," by Joseph Scotchie, Vol. 40 No. 4, April 2016, pp. 15; in the same issue, Watkins, William J. Jr., "Antonin Scalia's Flexible Constitution," pp. 11-3. Fleming, Thomas (1993) "A League of our own," Chronicles: A magazine of American culture, 17.2 12-15.

[96] *Chronicles*, Vol. 39 No. 8, August 2015, series of short articles upset with the rejection of the Confederate battle flag: Denis Petrov, "Abolishing America," pp. 5-6; Richert, Scott P., "The Color of Money," pp. 7-8; Williamson, Chilton Jr., "Two Flags," pp. 8; Trotter, Jack, "Enter the Vandals," 8-9, Wolf, Aaron D., "Life on the Frontier."

[97] Williamson, Chilton, Jr., "The Revenge of the Confederacy," Chronicles, Vol. 39 No. 1, Jan. 2015, pp. 36-37. Williamson has the article online at http://www.chiltonwilliamson.com/articles/the_revenge_of_confederacy.html, printed out 5/29/2016.

[98] Landess, Thomas Jr., "Life, Literature, & Lincoln," Chronicles Press, Rockford Institute, Rockford, Illinois, 2015. Online ad for book is http://www.chroniclesmagazine.org/life-literat-and-lincoln-hardcover-/, printed out 5/29/2016.

[99] Wilson, Clyde N., "Chronicles of the South: Garden of the Beaux Arts," (Vol. 1), and "Chronicles of the South: Justice to so Fine a Country," (Vol. 2), Chronicles Press, Rockford Institute, Rockford, Illinois, 2010.

[100] Gordon, David, "Southern Cross," *American Conservative*, April 1, 2010, pp. 34-36.

[101] Online story, www.scv.secure-site.bix, printed out 8/11/2016. Sons of Confederate Veterans Merchandise Catalog 2004-2005, page 29; Sons of Confederate Veteran Merchandise Catalog 2005-2006, page 29; Sons of Confederate Veteran Merchandise Catalog 2008-2009, page 28; Sons of Confederate Veteran Merchandise Catalog 2009-2010, page 28; Sons of Confederate Veteran Merchandise Catalog 2011-2012, page 28; Sons of Confederate Veteran Merchandise Catalog 2015-2016, page 28 . Note, the author only possesses six of these catalogs, there may be others which might also have had this book listed. For the online store. First sold in *Confederate Veteran*, "Classic Southern Reprints," Vol. 3 2001, pp. 42. For several years the issues of Confederate Veteran were six volumes a year.

[102] 2013-2014 SCV Merchandise Catalog, pp. 15, insert after page 20 in *Confederate Veteran*, Vol. 71 No1. 5, Sept./Oct. 2014.

[103] Givens, R. Michael, "Report of the Lt. Commander-in-Chief," *Confederate Veteran*, Vol. 66 No. 5, Sept./Oct. 2008, pp. 8-9.

[104] Hill, Michael, "The Good Kennedys," *Chronicles*, Vol. 20 No. 10, December 1996, pages 44-45.

[105] Vogler, James N. Jr, "Books in Print," Confederate Veteran, Nov. – Dec. 1991, page 10.

[106] Vogler, James N. Jr, "Books in Print," *Confederate Veteran*, Nov. – Dec. 1994, page 4.

[107] Sons of Confederate Veterans Merchandise Catalog 2004-2005, page 29; Sons of Confederate Veteran Merchandise Catalog 2005-2006, page 29; Sons of Confederate Veteran Merchandise Catalog 2008-2009, page 28; Sons of Confederate Veteran Merchandise Catalog 2009-2010, page 28; Sons of Confederate Veteran Merchandise Catalog 2011-2012, page 28; Sons of Confederate Veteran Merchandise Catalog 2015-2016, page 28 . Note, the author only possesses six of these catalogs, there may be others which might also have had this book listed. For the online store. SCV Online store, http://scv.secure-sites.us, printed out 7/23/2016. The first add in Confederate Veteran magazine where the SCV itself is selling the book is in an advertising section, "Christmas Ideas from SCV International Headquarters," Vol. 5 2001, pp. 22-23. The *Confederate Veteran* at one time had a system of volume number of Volumes 1, 2, 3, 4, 5, 6 each year.

[108] Williamson, Chilton, Jr., "After Tocqueville: The Promise and Failure of Democracy," ISI Books, Intercollegiate Studies Institute, Wilmington, Delaware, 2012, www.isibooks.org. Intercollegiate Studies Institute, www.isi.org.

[109] No author, "Profiles: Hans-Hermann Hoppe," https://mises.org/profile/hans-hermann-hoppe, printed out 5/18/2016.

[110] Hoppe, Hans-Herman, "Democracy: The God that Failed," Transaction Press, New Brunswick, NJ, 2007, pp. 40.

[111] Hoppe, Hans-Herman, "Democracy: The God that Failed," Transaction Press, New Brunswick, NJ, 2007, pp. 38.

[112] Hoppe, Hans-Herman, "Democracy: The God that Failed," Transaction Press, New Brunswick, NJ, 2007, pp. 41. Other examples I found are on pages 80, 101n, 113n, 208n, 277n, 288, and 291.

[113] Hoppe, Hans-Herman, "Democracy: The God that Failed," Transaction Press, New Brunswick, NJ, 2007, pp. 43.

[114] Hoppe, Hans-Herman, "Democracy: The God that Failed," Transaction Press, New Brunswick, NJ, 2007, pp. 139-41.

[115] Hoppe, Hans-Herman, "Democracy: The God that Failed," Transaction Press, New Brunswick, NJ, 2007, pp. 145-47.

[116] Hoppe, Hans-Herman, "Democracy: The God that Failed," Transaction Press, New Brunswick, NJ, 2007, pp. 166.

[117] Hoppe, Hans-Herman, "Democracy: The God that Failed," Transaction Press, New Brunswick, NJ, 2007, pp. 174-75.

[118] Hoppe, Hans-Herman, "Democracy: The God that Failed," Transaction Press, New Brunswick, NJ, 2007, pp. 180.

[119] Hoppe, Hans-Herman, "Democracy: The God that Failed," Transaction Press, New Brunswick, NJ, 2007, pp. 262.

[120] Hoppe, Hans-Herman, "Democracy: The God that Failed," Transaction Press, New Brunswick, NJ, 2007, pp. 291-92.

[121] Sobran, Joseph, "The Sobran View," *Southern Partisan*, Jan.-Feb. 2002, pp. 37. This issue did not have an assigned volume or number.

[122] Bassani, Luigi Marco, "Democracy: An Indictment That Will Not Wash Away," *Southern Partisan*, Vol. 23 No. 4, the date printed in the magazine is July/August 2003, pp. 31-34.
[123] https://mises.org/profile/luigi-marco-bassani, printed out 5/22/2016.
[124] Fleming, Thomas, "Back to Althusius," *Chronicles*, Vol. 26 No. 3, March 2002, pp. 27-28.
[125] See "About" at http://www.chiltonwilliamson.com/about.html, printed out 5/29/2016. Also, http://www.chroniclesmagazine.org/about/editorial-staff/, printed out 5/29/2016. When Williamson became Senior Editor wasn't found.
[126] Williamson, Chilton, Jr., "After Tocqueville: The Promise and Failure of Democracy," ISI Books, Intercollegiate Studies Institute, 2012, pp. 74.
[127] Williamson, Chilton, Jr., "After Tocqueville: The Promise and Failure of Democracy," ISI Books, Intercollegiate Studies Institute, 2012, pp. 94.
[128] Williamson, Chilton, Jr., "After Tocqueville: The Promise and Failure of Democracy," ISI Books, Intercollegiate Studies Institute, 2012, pp. 97.
[129] Williamson, Chilton, Jr., "After Tocqueville: The Promise and Failure of Democracy," ISI Books, Intercollegiate Studies Institute, 2012, pp. 87-88.
[130] Williamson, Chilton, Jr., "After Tocqueville: The Promise and Failure of Democracy," ISI Books, Intercollegiate Studies Institute, 2012, pp. 87-88.
[131] Williamson, Chilton, Jr., "After Tocqueville: The Promise and Failure of Democracy," ISI Books, Intercollegiate Studies Institute, 2012, pp. 111.
[132] Williamson, Chilton, Jr., "After Tocqueville: The Promise and Failure of Democracy," ISI Books, Intercollegiate Studies Institute, 2012, pp. 90.
[133] Williamson, Chilton, Jr., "After Tocqueville: The Promise and Failure of Democracy," ISI Books, Intercollegiate Studies Institute, 2012, pp. 99-112.
[134] Williamson, Chilton, Jr., "After Tocqueville: The Promise and Failure of Democracy," ISI Books, Intercollegiate Studies Institute, 2012, pp. 115.
[135] Williamson, Chilton, Jr., "After Tocqueville: The Promise and Failure of Democracy," ISI Books, Intercollegiate Studies Institute, 2012, pp. 116.
[136] Williamson, Chilton, Jr., "After Tocqueville: The Promise and Failure of Democracy," ISI Books, Intercollegiate Studies Institute, 2012, pp. 9-10. Pat Buchanan was a contributor and editor for *Southern Partisan* and a member of the Sons of Confederate Veterans. Kirkpatrick Sales is currently active in the Abbeville Institute and is a speaker at the SCV's Stephen Dill Lee Institute. He is the author of "Emancipation Hell: The Tragedy Wrought By the Emancipation Proclamation 150 Years Ago," self-published, 2012, which condemns the proclamation.
[137] Williamson, Chilton, Jr., "After Tocqueville: The Promise and Failure of Democracy," ISI Books, Intercollegiate Studies Institute, 2012, pp. 114-115.
[138] Williamson, Chilton, Jr., "After Tocqueville: The Promise and Failure of Democracy," ISI Books, Intercollegiate Studies Institute, 2012, pp. 116-117.
[139] Williamson, Chilton, Jr., "After Tocqueville: The Promise and Failure of Democracy," ISI Books, Intercollegiate Studies Institute, 2012, pp. 142.
[140] Williamson, Chilton, Jr., "After Tocqueville: The Promise and Failure of Democracy," ISI Books, Intercollegiate Studies Institute, 2012, pp. 203.

[141] Williamson, Chilton, Jr., "After Tocqueville: The Promise and Failure of Democracy," ISI Books, Intercollegiate Studies Institute, 2012, pp. 142-143.
[142] Williamson, Chilton, Jr., "After Tocqueville: The Promise and Failure of Democracy," ISI Books, Intercollegiate Studies Institute, 2012, pp. 143.
[143] Williamson, Chilton, Jr., "After Tocqueville: The Promise and Failure of Democracy," ISI Books, Intercollegiate Studies Institute, 2012, pp. 144.
[144] Williamson, Chilton, Jr., "After Tocqueville: The Promise and Failure of Democracy," ISI Books, Intercollegiate Studies Institute, 2012, pp. 144-149.
[145] Williamson, Chilton, Jr., "After Tocqueville: The Promise and Failure of Democracy," ISI Books, Intercollegiate Studies Institute, 2012, pp. 173.
[146] Williamson, Chilton, Jr., "After Tocqueville: The Promise and Failure of Democracy," ISI Books, Intercollegiate Studies Institute, 2012, pp. 169.
[147] Williamson, Chilton, Jr., "After Tocqueville: The Promise and Failure of Democracy," ISI Books, Intercollegiate Studies Institute, 2012, pp. 213.
[148] Williamson, Chilton, Jr., "After Tocqueville: The Promise and Failure of Democracy," ISI Books, Intercollegiate Studies Institute, 2012, pp. 124.
[149] Williamson, Chilton, Jr., "After Tocqueville: The Promise and Failure of Democracy," ISI Books, Intercollegiate Studies Institute, 2012, pages, 9, 41, 51, 59.
[150] Williamson, Chilton, Jr., "After Tocqueville: The Promise and Failure of Democracy," ISI Books, Intercollegiate Studies Institute, 2012, page55-57, Clyde Wilson, pp. 55, Reconstruction amendments and quote on page 57.
[151] Murchison, William, "How We Got Here," Chronicles, Vol. 36 No. 11, Nov. 2012, pp. 26-27.
[152] Weaver, Richard M., "The Southern Tradition at Bay: A History of Postbellum Thought," Arlington House, New Rochelle, New York, 1968. "Paradise" quote pp. 51.
[153] Bradford, M.E., "Remembering Who We Are: Observations of a Southern Conservative," Univ. of Georgia Press, Athens, Georgia, 1985, dust jacket.
[154] Boyd, Cathey, D., "The Land We Love: Southern Tradition and Our Future," *Confederate Veteran*, Vol. No. , March/April 2012, pp. 16-23, 56-60. Quotes on pages 20 & 21.
[155] For an in-depth article on Confederate Christian nationalism and their defenses of slavery and concept that the Civil War was a theological conflict see, Hague, Euan, Sebesta, Edward H., "The US Civil War as a Theological War: Confederate Christian Nationalism and the League of the South," *Canadian Review of American Studies*, Vol. 32, No. 2, 2000, pp. 253-284.
[156] As just one example, the reader might visit http://www.scv.org/about/chaplainsChronicle.php, and review the issues of the Chaplains' Corps Chronicles of the Sons of Confederate Veterans, and see the constant reference to Dabney as an authoritative theological source and as a great Confederate.
[157] Dabney, Robert Lewis, "Defense of Virginia and through her the South," E.J. Hale & Son, New York, NY, 1867, pp. 103, 107,118. This book has been

reprinted over the years, and is also available at www.archive.org in both pdf and text formats, as well as other formats.

[158] Dabney, Robert Lewis, "Discussions," Vol. 4, Presbyterian Committee of Publications, Richmond, Virginia, 1897, "The Negro and the Common School," pp.176-190, "blood boil" comment on page 177, "pretended education," pp. 178-179, third reason given starting page 180, "brain fever," pp. 181-182, amalgamation pp. 185-186. These volumes have been reprinted many times and are easily available today both in in print and online. The article is also online at www.confederatepastpresent.org, and elsewhere.

[159] Dabney, Robert Lewis, "Discussions," Vol. 4, Presbyterian Committee of Publications, Richmond, Virginia, 1897, "Fee Schools," pp. 261-262, quote from page 260-261. Originally published in the *Southern Planter and Farmer*, Jan. 1879.

[160] Cathey, Boyd, "Robert Lewis Dabney And the New South Creed," *Southern Partisan*, Vol. 4 No. 3, Summer 1984, pp. 47-50.

[161] Snapp, Byron, "Partisan Conversation: Lloyd Sprinkle," *Southern Partisan*, Vol. 14 2nd Qtr., 1994, pp. 28-31. Their webpage is http://www.sprinklepublications.net/.

[162] Earth, Clara, "Confederate Notes," UDC Magazine, Vol. 58 No. 5, May 1995, pp. 11.

[163] Owens, Collie, "R.L. Dabney, Confederate Prophet," *Southern Partisan*, Vol. 15 2nd Qtr. 1995, pp. 28-31.

[164] Williamson, Scott Whitten, "Seven Reasons to Homeschool," *Southern Patriot*, Vol. 5 No. 4, July-August 1998, pp. 11.

[165] Riley, Leslie, "Save the Children (and the South): Don't Send Them to Marx's Schools," Southern Patriot, Vol. 8 No. 1, Jan.-Feb. 2001, pp. 14.

[166] Simpson, Barry D., "The Cultural Degradation of Universal Education: The Educational Views of Robert Lewis Dabney," *Journal of Libertarian Studies*, Vol. 20, No. 3, summer 2006, pages 47-60. Also online at https://mises.org/library/cultural-degradation-universal-education-educational-views-robert-lewis-dabney.

[167] Sproul, R.C. Jr., "The Heart's Own Instinct," *Chronicles*, Vol. 27 No 9, Sept. 2003, pp. 43-45.

[168] For online information on the Association of Classical Christian Schools see www.accsedu.org, printed out 6/4/2016.

[169] "The War Between the States: America's Uncivil War," is by John J. Dwyer, as author, with contributing editors George Grant, J. Steven Wilkins, Douglas Wilson, and Tom Spencer, copyright 2005, previously published by American Vision, and now published and by the Western Conservatory of Arts and Sciences, http://westernconservatory.com/store. See also www.bluebonnetpress.com. "Southern Slavery As It Was," by Douglas Wilson and Steve Wilkins of the Auburn Avenue Church in Monroe, Louisiana, was published as monograph in 1996 by Canon Press. Used copies are quite expensive. It is online however, at http://reformed-

theology.org/html/books/slavery/southern_slavery_as_it_was.htm. Printed out 6/5/2016.

[170] Wilson, Douglas, "Bad Moon Rising: The Coming Break-Up of These United States," *Credenda Agenda*, Vol. 8 No. 1, no date, but I printed out a copy as early as April 29, 2001.

[171] "Saints and Scoundrels," Sixth Annual Credenda/Agenda American History Conference. Cannon Press, 2001. Conference was held at the University of Idaho, Student Union Ballroom, in Moscow, Idaho.

[172] Moore, E. Ray Jr., "Lost Southern History Recovered," *Southern Partisan*, Vol. 26 No. 1, March/April 2007, pp. 30-31; Barrow, Cassie A., "Destroying the Republic: Jabez Curry and the Re-Education of the Old South," *Confederate Veteran*, Vol. 67 No.3, May/June 2009, pp. 25,45. Abbeville Institute article, Wilson, Clyde, "Origins of the Educational Nightmare," publication date, Jan. 29, 2015, http://www.abbevilleinstitute.org/clyde-wilson-library/origins-of-the-educational-nightmare/, printed out 5/6/2016.

[173] Alderman, Edwin Anderson, Gordon, Armistead Churchill, "J.L.M. Curry: A Biography," MacMillan Co., New York City, 1911.

[174] Wilson, Clyde, "Origins of the Educational Nightmare," publication date, Jan. 29, 2015, http://www.abbevilleinstitute.org/clyde-wilson-library/origins-of-the-educational-nightmare/, printed out 5/6/2016.

[175] Barrow, Cassie A., "Destroying the Republic: Jabez Curry and the Re-Education of the Old South," Confederate Veteran, Vol. 67 No. 3, May-June 2009, pp. 25, 46.

[176] Moore, E. Ray, Jr., "Lost History Recovered," *Southern Partisan*, Vol. 26 No. 1, March/April 2007, pp. 30-32. Towards the end the dates in the Southern Partisan often had official dates and printing dates, and this issue just has this date and it is not clear if it is a printing date or "official" date. The last issue of *Southern Partisan* was dated Jan.-Feb. 2009 and arrived after a long cessation in publishing with the cover "We Are Back!" and it was the last issue.

[177] Announcement for League of the South 2007 Conference in Oct., *Free Magnolia*, Vol. 1 No. 3, July-Sept. 2007, page 9.

[178] Chodes, John Jr., "The Union League: Uncle Sam's Klan," *Southern Partisan*, Vol. 22, March/April 2002, pp. 23-26. An issue number was not found in the magazine. Also, League of the South Position Paper No. 4, published in 1999.

[179] Chodes, John, "The Union League During Southern Reconstruction," Shotwell Publishing, Columbia, South Carolina, 2016. Shotwell Publishing is online at www.shotwellpublishing.com. Printed out 6/12/2016.

[180] Chodes, John, "Destroying the Republic: Jabez Curry and the Re-Education of the Old South," Algora Publishers, www.algora.com, 2005, New York, Chapters 1 to 5; pp. 90 quotation of James and Walter Kennedy.

[181] Chodes, John, "Destroying the Republic: Jabez Curry and the Re-Education of the Old South," Algora Publishers, www.algora.com, 2005, New York, see bibliography on page 311.

[182] Chodes, John, "Destroying the Republic: Jabez Curry and the Re-Education of the Old South," Algora Publishers, www.algora.com, 2005, New York, pp. 106-108, 14th Amendment, pp. 108-111.

[183] Chodes, John, "Destroying the Republic: Jabez Curry and the Re-Education of the Old South," Algora Publishers, www.algora.com, 2005, New York, pp. 232. Chodes gives as a reference for this speech, Edwin Burritt Smith, "Education in the South – National Aid," an address before the Chicago Congregationalist Club, Feb. 20, 1888, pp. 10, 11, 14.

[184] I recommend three books for the reader for the periods of Reconstruction and the period afterwards. Eric Foner's "Reconstruction: America's Unfinished Revolution"; John Litwack's "Trouble In Mind," is excellent about African Americans living in the South before the mid-20th century Civil Rights Era; and Rayford W. Logan's "Betrayal of the Negro: From Rutherford B. Hayes To Woodrow Wilson." They are available in paperback.

[185] Chodes, John, "Destroying the Republic: Jabez Curry and the Re-Education of the Old South," Algora Publishers, www.algora.com, 2005, New York, pp. 149.

[186] Chodes, John, "Destroying the Republic: Jabez Curry and the Re-Education of the Old South," Algora Publishers, www.algora.com, 2005, New York, pp. 247.

[187] Chodes, John, "Destroying the Republic: Jabez Curry and the Re-Education of the Old South," Algora Publishers, www.algora.com, 2005, New York, pp. 247 -250, Morrill Act and Agricultural Experiment Stations; pp. 254 conspiracy theory about the Dept. of Agriculture going to Europe; pp. 255-256, nature training in New York State.

[188] Chodes, John, "Destroying the Republic: Jabez Curry and the Re-Education of the Old South," Algora Publishers, www.algora.com, 2005, New York, pp. 256-257.

[189] Smith, Glenn, Boughton, Melissa, Behre, Robert, "Nine dead after 'hate crime' shooting at Emanuel AME," *The Post and Courier*, Charleston, SC, http://www.postandcourier.com/article/20150617/PC16/150619408, printed out 6/15/2016.

[190] OKC Bombing Trial Transcript – 05/29/1997 16:25 CDT/CST, published 5/29/1997, *The Oklahoman*, Oklahoma City, OK, http://newsok.com/article/1074807, printed out 6/15/2016. Author has this t-shirt in his artifact collection. It was sold by the *Southern Partisan* magazine in their Christmas catalog which the author received November 1995. He ordered the t-shirt and received a letter dated Dec. 3, 1995 from *Southern Partisan* explaining that due to the demand for the t-shirt they were out of the size ordered and substituted a different size. Catalog in author's research collection.

[191] For primary historical documentation as for the reasons for secession in the secessionists own declarations and statements, see "The Confederate and Neo-Confederate Reader," editors James Loewen and Edward H. Sebesta, published by the University Press of Mississippi, 2008.

[192] Grissom, Michael Andrew, "Southern by the Grace of God," Pelican Publishing Company, Inc., Gretna, Louisiana, 1988; Also, Rebel Yell, Nashville, Tennessee, 1988. Michael Andrew Grissom had a website http://www.michaelandrewgrisssom.com which no longer exists but is archived at www.archive.org. Look at captures in the years 2007 and prior.

[193] Grissom, Michael Andrew, "Southern by the Grace of God," pp. 127, Pelican Publishing Company, Gretna, 1992.

[194] Grissom, Michael Andrew, "Southern by the Grace of God," pp. 128, Pelican Publishing Company, Gretna, 1992.

[195] Grissom, Michael Andrew, "Southern by the Grace of God," pp. 151, Pelican Publishing Company, Gretna, 1992.

[196] Grissom, Michael Andrew, "Southern by the Grace of God," pp. 166, Pelican Publishing Company, Gretna, 1992.

[197] Grissom, Michael Andrew, "Southern by the Grace of God," pp. 162-164, Pelican Publishing Company, Gretna, 1992.

[198] Grissom, Michael Andrew, "Southern by the Grace of God," pp. 165-171, Pelican Publishing Company, Gretna, 1992.

[199] Grissom, Michael Andrew, "Southern by the Grace of God," pp. 167, Pelican Publishing Company, Gretna, 1992.

[200] Grissom, Michael Andrew, "Southern by the Grace of God," pp. 173-178, Pelican Publishing Company, Gretna, 1992.

[201] Grissom, Michael Andrew, "Southern by the Grace of God," pp. 173-4, Pelican Publishing Company, Gretna, 1992.

[202] Grissom, Michael Andrew, "Southern by the Grace of God," pp. 180-181, Pelican Publishing Company, Gretna, 1992.

[203] Grissom, Michael Andrew, "Southern by the Grace of God," pp. 181-182, Pelican Publishing Company, Gretna, 1992.

[204] Grissom, Michael Andrew, "Southern by the Grace of God," pp. 446-448, Pelican Publishing Company, Gretna, 1992.

[205] Grissom, Michael Andrew, "Southern by the Grace of God," pp. 411-418, Pelican Publishing Company, Gretna, 1992.

[206] Grissom, Michael Andrew, "Southern by the Grace of God," "Southern Horizons" recommended on page 532, "The Clansman" recommended on page 533, "The Leopard Spots" recommended on page 535, *Southern Partisan* and *Citizen Informer* recommended on pages 538-9, Pelican Publishing Company, Gretna, 1992.

[207] Grissom, Michael Andrew, name given as "Mike," "The Mystery of John Hunt Cole," The United Daughters of the Confederacy Magazine, Vol. 51 No. 9, Sept. 1988, pp. 27-29.

[208] Tindal, Retta D., "Confederate Classics: For Research, Reference, or Refresher," *United Daughters of the Confederacy Magazine*, Vol.70 No. 10, Nov. 2007, pp. 15.

[209] No Author, "General Historical Programs September 2011 – August 2013," *United Daughters of the Confederacy Magazine*, Vol. 74 No. 5, May 2011, pp. 10-11.

[210] Back outside cover of "American Terrorists," by Michael Andrew Grissom and published through Create Space in 2016. Purpose of the medal is stated by the United Daughters of the Confederacy on their web site. http://www.hqudc.org/objectives/, printed out 9/11/2016.
[211] Vogler, James N. Jr., "Books In Print," *Confederate Veteran*, Sept. – Oct. 1989, page 37.
[212] Hilderman, Walter, C., "Book Notes," *Southern Partisan*, Vol. 8 No. 3, Fall 1988, page 45.
[213] No author, "Classic Southern Reprints," *Confederate Veteran*, Vol. 3 2001, pages 42-43, book notice on page 42.
[214] https://scv.secure-sites.us/store.php, printed out 5/26/2013.
[215] Sons of Confederate Veterans Merchandise Catalog 2004-2005, page 29; Sons of Confederate Veteran Merchandise Catalog 2005-2006, page 29; Sons of Confederate Veteran Merchandise Catalog 2008-2009, page 28; Sons of Confederate Veteran Merchandise Catalog 2009-2010, page 28; Sons of Confederate Veteran Merchandise Catalog 2011-2012, page 28; Sons of Confederate Veteran Merchandise Catalog 2015-2016, page 28. Note, the author only possesses six of these catalogs, there may be others which might also have this book listed.
[216] 2013-2014 SCV Merchandise Catalog, pp. 15, insert after page 20 in *Confederate Veteran*, Vol. 71 Nol. 5, Sept./Oct. 2014.
[217] Grissom, Michael Andrew, "When the South Was Southern," Pelican Publishing Company, Gretna, Louisiana 1994, pp. 322-325, quote on page 323.
[218] Online at www.scv.secure-sites.biz, printed out 8/9/2016, Sons of Confederate Veteran Merchandise Catalog 2005-2006, page 29; Sons of Confederate Veteran Merchandise Catalog 2008-2009, page 28; Sons of Confederate Veteran Merchandise Catalog 2009-2010, page 28; Sons of Confederate Veteran Merchandise Catalog 2011-2012, page 28; Sons of Confederate Veteran Merchandise Catalog 2015-2016, page 28. Note, the author only possesses six of these catalogs, there may be others which might also have this book listed.
[219] 2013-2014 SCV Merchandise Catalog, pp. 15, insert after page 20 in *Confederate Veteran*, Vol. 71 Nol. 5, Sept./Oct. 2014.
[220] Rose, S.E.F., "The Ku Klux Klan or Invisible Empire," published L. Graham Co. Ltd., New Orleans, 1914. Quote in unpaginated front pages. To read excerpts of the book go to www.confederatepastpresent.org and use search term "Klan" to find other books praising the Klan published by neo-Confederates.
[221] No author, "Classic Southern Reprints," Confederate Veteran, 2001 Vol. 1, pages 28-29, quote from page 28.
[222] No author, "Classic Southern Reprints," Confederate Veteran, 2001 Vol. 3, pages 42-43, quote from page 43.
[223] No author, "Classic Southern Reprints," Confederate Veteran, 2002 Vol. 1, pages 44-45, quote from page 45.
[224] https://scv.secure-sites.us/store.php, printed out 5/25/2013.

[225] Sons of Confederate Veterans Merchandise Catalog 2004-2005, page 37; Sons of Confederate Veteran Merchandise Catalog 2005-2006, page 37; Sons of Confederate Veteran Merchandise Catalog 2008-2009, page 36; Sons of Confederate Veteran Merchandise Catalog 2009-2010, page 36; Sons of Confederate Veteran Merchandise Catalog 2011-2012, page 36; Sons of Confederate Veteran Merchandise Catalog 2015-2016, page 36. Note, the author only possesses six of these catalogs, there may be others which might also have this video listed.

[226] 2013-2014 SCV Merchandise Catalog, pp. 17, insert after page 20 in *Confederate Veteran*, Vol. 71 Nol. 5, Sept./Oct. 2014.

[227] Wilson, Clyde, "Reconstruction: Violence and Dislocation," Abbeville Institute web site, posted Oct. 39, 2914, http://www.abbevilleinstitute.org/clyde-wilson-library/reconstruction-violence-and-dislocation/, printed out 6/13/2016, originally the final part of a lecture delivered at the Abbeville Institute 2009 Summer School titled, "Reconstruction in the Experience of the Southern People."

[228] Chodes, John, "Washington's KKK: The Union League During Reconstruction," Shotwell Publishers, Columbia, South Carolina, 2016, pp. x.

[229] Sons of Confederate Veterans Merchandise Catalog 2004-2005, page 30; Sons of Confederate Veteran Merchandise Catalog 2005-2006, page 30; Sons of Confederate Veteran Merchandise Catalog 2008-2009, page 29; Sons of Confederate Veteran Merchandise Catalog 2009-2010, page 29; Sons of Confederate Veteran Merchandise Catalog 2011-2012, page 29. Note, the author only possesses six of these catalogs, there may be others which might also have had this book listed.

[230] 2013-2014 SCV Merchandise Catalog, pp. 14, insert after page 20 in *Confederate Veteran*, Vol. 71 Nol. 5, Sept./Oct. 2014.

[231] Harris, Donna, "Oakley Park: Only Shrine of its kind," *UDC Magazine*, Vol. 64 No. 6, June/July2001, pp. 23-24.

[232] "United Daughters of the Confederacy, South Carolina Division: Golden Anniversary 1896-1946," no author, "Oakley Park, Edgefield's Red Shirt Shrine," pages 13.

[233] Walker, Cornelia, "Report of Oakley Park, The 'Red Shirt Shrine,'" pp. 189-91, "The Minutes of the Fifty-Fifth Annual Convention of the United Daughters of the Confederacy," 1948; Walker, Cornelia, "Oakley Park Report ("The Red Shirt Shrine", located at Edgefield, SC)," pp. 188-191, ""The Minutes of the Fifty-Sixth Annual Convention of the United Daughters of the Confederacy," 1949; Walker, Cornelia, "Oakley Park: The Red Shirt Shrine (Final Report)," pp. 189-192, ""The Minutes of the Fifty-Seventh Annual Convention of the United Daughters of the Confederacy," 1950. Most issues of *UDC Magazine* for 1948 & 1949.

[234] Until the latter part of the 20th century members of the UDC often used only their husband's name and what the author's name often isn't known. The names used are the names that the authors used for themselves.

[235] Tindal, Retta D., "General Wade Hampton III," *UDC Magazine*, Vol. 76 No. 5, May 2013, pp. 15-16.
[236] No author, "Confederate Gifts from IHQ," *Confederate Veteran*, Vol 62. No.3, May/June 2004, pp. 62.
[237] No author, "Confederate Gifts from IHQ," *Confederate Veteran*, Vol 67. No.1, Jan./Feb. 2009, pp. 62.
[238] Sons of Confederate Veterans Merchandise Catalog 2004-2005, page 30; Sons of Confederate Veteran Merchandise Catalog 2005-2006, page 30; Sons of Confederate Veteran Merchandise Catalog 2008-2009, page 29; Sons of Confederate Veteran Merchandise Catalog 2009-2010, page 29; Sons of Confederate Veteran Merchandise Catalog 2011-2012, page 29; Sons of Confederate Veteran Merchandise Catalog 2015-2016, page 29 . Note, the author only possesses six of these catalogs, there may be others which might also have had this book listed. For the online store. SCV Online store, http://scv.secure-sites.us, printed out 5/15/2016.
[239] 2013-2014 SCV Merchandise Catalog, pp. 14, insert after page 20 in *Confederate Veteran*, Vol. 71 Nol. 5, Sept./Oct. 2014.
[240] No author, "Texas," *Southern Partisan*, Vol. 9 4th Qtr., 1989. Note there are two issues of Southern Partisan which are 4th Qtr., 1989, one is Vol. 8 4th Qtr. 1989, and one is Vol. 9 4th Quarter 1989. As always with *the Southern Partisan* determining which issue is which requires detailed attention.
[241] No author, "Maryland: Gay Ole Time," *Southern Partisan*, Vol. 13 3rd Qtr., 1993, pp. 17.
[242] No author, "Tennessee," Southern Partisan, Vol. 20 3rd Qtr., 2000, pp. 16.
[243] No author, "Texas," *Southern Partisan*, Vol. 23 No. 6, "Issue date Nov./Dec. 2003, published August 2004," pp. 15. The *Southern Partisan* towards the end had these dual dates on each issue.
[244] "Around the Nation; Citadel Board to Review Hazing Incident," Associated Press, run in *New York Times*, Oct. 28, 1986, http://www.nytimes.com/1986/10/28/us/around-the-nation-citadel-board-to-review-hazing-incident.html, printed out 6/20/2016;"Around the Nation; Black Cadet at the Citadel Leaves Over Harassment," United Press International, run in *New York Times*, 11/15/1986, http://www.nytimes.com/1986/11/15/us/around-the-nation-black-cadet-at-the-citadel-leaves-over-harassment.html, printed out 6/20/2016; Bill McAllister, "Citadel Incident Divides Charleston," *Washington Post*, Nov. 21, 1986, https://www.washingtonpost.com/archive/politics/1986/11/21/citadel-incident-divides-charleston/7e95dbaa-7835-4686-ad82-66151dff3f3a/, printed out 6/20/2016.
[245] Sandal, Matthew, "Criticus Essay: What Really Happened at the Citadel?" Southern Partisan, Vol. 6 No. 4, Fall 1986, Vol. 7 No. 1, Winter 1987, pp. 47-48. This was a double issue.
[246] Gottfried, Paul, "Our American Cultural Revolution," May 27, 2016, http://www.abbevilleinstitute.org/review/our-american-cultural-revolution/, printed out 6/21/2016.

247 No author, full page advertisement, "At Last!: The Real History That the Southern Historians Weren't Allowed to Write," *Confederate Veteran*, Vol. 51 No. 4, July/August 2003, pp. 2; Vol. 51. No. 6, Dec. 2003, pp. 2.

248 No author, full page ad, *Confederate Veteran*, Vol. 51 No. 5, Sept./Oct. 2003, pp. 51.

249 No author, full page ad, *Confederate Veteran*, Vol. 62 No. 2, March/April. 2004, pp. 17. **(From 2003, to 2004 the volume of the *Confederate Veteran* jumps from Vol. 51 to Vol. 62. The author uses the volume and number as printed in the magazines themselves.)**

250 No author, full page ad, *Confederate Veteran*, Vol. 62 No. 3, May/June 2004, pp. 65.

251 No author, "Confederate Gifts from IHQ," *Confederate Veteran*, Vol. 62 No.4, July/August 2004, pp. 62.

252 No author, http://scv.secure-sites.biz/store.php, printed out 6/24/2016.

253 Sons of Confederate Veterans Merchandise Catalog 2004-2005, page 29; Sons of Confederate Veteran Merchandise Catalog 2005-2006, page 29; Sons of Confederate Veteran Merchandise Catalog 2008-2009, page 28; Sons of Confederate Veteran Merchandise Catalog 2009-2010, page 28; Sons of Confederate Veteran Merchandise Catalog 2011-2012, Sons of Confederate Veteran Merchandise Catalog 2015-2016 page 28. Note, the author only possesses six of these catalogs, there may be others which might also have this book listed.

254 2013-2014 SCV Merchandise Catalog, pp. 15, inserted in the Confederate Veteran, Vol. 71 No. 5, Sept.-Oct. 2013, insert was glued in between pages 20-21.

255 *Confederate Veteran* issues: July/August 2011, pp. 62; Sept./Oct. 2012, pp. 75; Sept./Oct. 2013, pp. 70; Jan./Feb. 2014, pp. 71, July/August 2014, pp. 70; May/June 2015 pp. 70. (These pages are the first page of the "Confederate Gifts from IHQ" ad.)

256 Conner, Frank, "Death of a Nation?: The Almost Forgotten Body and Soul of the Sons of Confederate Veterans," *Southern Mercury*, Vol. 1 No. 1, July/August 2003, pp. 8-13.

257 Conner, Frank, "Where We Stand Now: And How We Got Here," *Southern Mercury*, Vol. 1 No. 2, Sept./Oct. 2003, pp. 10-14.

258 Conner, Frank, "The Enemy's Strategy," *Southern Mercury*, Vol. 2 No. 1, Jan./Feb. 2004, pp. 5-7, 32-33.

259 Conner, Frank, "Reorganizing the Sons of Confederate Veterans," *Southern Mercury*, Vol. 2 No. 3, Jan./Feb. 2004, pp. 8-11, 27.

260 For vote to remove statues, Woodward, Alex, "New Orleans City Council votes to remove four Confederate statues," *Gambit*, Dec. 17, 2014, http://www.bestofneworleans.com/blogofneworleans/archives/2015/12/17/new-orleans-city-council-votes-to-remove-four-confederate-statues, printed out 6/25/2016; Williams, Jessica, "Confederate monument removal bid process stalled amid threats, unresolved court case, city of New Orleans says," *New Orleans Advocate*, May 23, 2016,

http://www.theneworleansadvocate.com/news/15879336-63/confederate-monument-removal-bid-process-stalled-amid-threats-unresolved-court-case-city-says, printed out 6/25/2016; for the burning of a contractor's Lamborghini sports car see, Danielle Kinchen, "$200,000 Lamborghini found burned in Baton Rouge raises questions about possible link to New Orleans monuments debate," *The Advocate*, Jan. 10, 2016, http://theadvocate.com/news/14619162-75/lamborghini-found-burned-to-the-ground-in-front-of-baton-rouge-business-that-backed-out-of-removing-, printed out 6/25/2016; for contractors wanting to remain anonymous and do the work overnight, Williams, Jessica, "Confederate monument removal bid process stalled amid threats, unresolved court case, city of New Orleans says," New Orleans Advocate, May 23, 2016, http://www.theneworleansadvocate.com/news/15879336-63/confederate-monument-removal-bid-process-stalled-amid-threats-unresolved-court-case-city-says, printed out 6/25/2016.

[261] This article is available from multiple sources online including www.confederatepastpresent.org.

[262] Rosesch, James Rutledge, "The Cause of Jackson is the Cause of Us All," online at the Abbeville Institute, publication date April 26, 2016, http://www.abbevilleinstitute.org/review/the-cause-of-jackson-is-the-cause-of-us-all/, printed out 6/26/2016.

[263] Cathey, Boyd, "The Eternal 'Rebel Yell'," online at the Abbeville Institute, publication date March 26, 2015, http://www.abbevilleinstitute.org/blog/the-eternal-rebel-yell/, printed out 6/26/2016.

[264] Interviewer not given, "Partisan Conversation: Elizabeth Fox Genovese," *Southern Partisan*, Vol. 17 1st Qtr., 1997, pp. 42-47.

[265] Regenstein, Lewis, "An Honorable Cause: Why the Confederate Battle Flag Today?" *Southern Mercury*, Vol. 1 No. 1, July/Aug. 2003, pp. 3-4.

[266] Online store, https://scv.secure-sites.biz/store.php, printed out 6/27/2016, books. For catalog sale; [266] Sons of Confederate Veterans Merchandise Catalog 2004-2005, page 16; Sons of Confederate Veteran Merchandise Catalog 2005-2006, page 16; Sons of Confederate Veteran Merchandise Catalog 2008-2009, page 16; Sons of Confederate Veteran Merchandise Catalog 2009-2010, page 16; Sons of Confederate Veteran Merchandise Catalog 2011-2012, page 16; Sons of Confederate Veteran Merchandise Catalog 2015-2016, page 14.

[267] Conner, Frank, "Where We Stand Now: And How We Got Here," *Southern Mercury*, Vol. 1 No. 2, Sept./Oct. 2003, pp. 10-14, quote on page 12, 2nd column.

[268] See, "Evolutionary Psychology's Anti-Semite," *Slate*, January 24, 2000, http://www.slate.com/articles/news_and_politics/culturebox/2000/01/evolutionary_psychologys_antisemite.html, printed out 9/13/2016; Greenberg, Brad A. ,"The Professor the Anti-Semites Love: Kevin MacDonald, Cal State Long Beach, and the downside of academic freedom," *Jewish Journal*, May 8, 2008, http://www.jewishjournal.com/los_angeles/article/the_professor_the_antisemites_love_20080509/, printed out 9/13/2016.

[269] Conner, Frank, "The South Under Siege: 1830-2000," Collards Publishing Company, Newnan, Georgia, 2002; quote regarding IQ on page 393, quote differentiating "Northern liberals" from "Northern Jews" page 397; strategy statement, pp. 396-97, no possibility of a civil rights move/26/2016ment without Jews, pp. 400; deadliest enemy statement, 406; three chapters, pp. 406. The first edition has a binding error and the name on the binding is "The South Under Seige."

[270] Fleming, Thomas, "Mel, Poor Mel," in his online blog "Hard Rights," at www.chroniclesmagazine.org. Though since deleted from the *Chronicles* website it is online at https://web.archive.org/web/20060927170427/http://www.chroniclesmagazine.org/cgi-bin/hardright.cgi/Mel,_Poor_Mel.html?seemore=y, printed out 6/26/2016, author also has an original copy somewhere in his files about the time it was published; Zev Chafets, "Slurring More than His Words," *Los Angeles Times*, Aug. 1, 2006, available online https://web.archive.org/web/20060929080515/http://www.latimes.com/news/opinion/commentary/la-oe-chafets1aug01,0,7422072.story?coll=la-opinion-center, printed out 6/26/2016.

[271] "The Alan Colme Show," August 19, 1999, NewsTalk 1050 WEVD, New York, with Alan Colmes, Michael Hill, Edward H. Sebesta, transcript of show in author's possession. It is available online at http://www.templeofdemocracy.com/curriculum-vitae.html.

[272] Hill, Michael, "Another Jew nominated for the US Supreme Court," http://leagueofthesouth.com/another-jew-nominated-for-the-us-supreme-court1389/, printed out 6/29/2016.

[273] Hill, Michael, "What was World War Two really about?" http://leagueofthesouth.com/what-was-world-war-two-really-about/, printed out 6/29/2016.

[274] Singer, Greg C., "A Theological Interpretation of American History," A Press, 1994. It is still in printed by other publishers. Originally it was published in 1964 by the Presbyterian and Reformed Pub. Col. in Philadelphia.

[275] Thornwell, James Henley, "The Rights and the Duties of the Masters: A Sermon Preached at the Dedication of a Church Erected in Charleston, S.C., For the Benefit and Instruction of the Coloured Population," Charleston: Steam Powered Press of Walker & James, 1850, pp. 14, also available in "The Collected Writings of James Henley Thornwell,' volume 4, under the title, "Relation of the Church to Slavery." The four volumes have been republished at least twice in the latter half of the 20th century.

[276] Anderson, Alister C., "Chaplain's Comments," page 52-53, *Confederate Veteran*, Vol. 5 1998.

[277] Weaver, John, "Chaplain's Comments," *Confederate Veteran*, 2000 Vol. 5, pp. 60-61. (For several years each year was six volumes. The volume and numbering system of the Confederate Veteran magazine varies widely.);

Thornwell, James Henley, "The Rights and the Duties of the Masters: A Sermon Preached at the Dedication of a Church Erected in Charleston, S.C., For the Benefit and Instruction of the Coloured Population," Charleston: Steam Powered Press of Walker & James, 1850, pp. 14, also available in "The Collected Writings of James Henley Thornwell,' volume 4, under the title, "Relation of the Church to Slavery." The four volumes have been republished at least twice in the latter half of the 20th century.

[278] Weaver, John, "Chaplain's Comments," Confederate Veteran, Volume One, 2003, pp. 60-61.

[279] Chambers, Glen and Fisher, Gene, "United States History for Christian Schools," page 284, Bob Jones University Press, 1982, Greenville, South Carolina.

[280] Dwyer, John, Grant, George, Wilkins, J. Steven, Wilson, Douglas, Spencer, Tom, "The War Between the States: America's Uncivil War," Western Conservatory of the Arts and Sciences, 3rd edition, 2013, quotes and section condemning Finney pages 152-155. See also http://www.bluebonnetpress.com/wbts_index.html, printed out 7/2/2016.

[281] Boyd, Cathey D., "The Land We Love: Southern Tradition and Our Future," *Confederate Veteran*, March/April 2012, pp. 16-23, 56-60. Quotes on page 22.

[282] Truth in History website, http://truthinhistory.org/, article "Jewish Hatred Against Jesus Christ," http://truthinhistory.org/jewish-hatred-against-jesus-christ.html, printed out 7/2/2016; article about Jews not being Israelites, "The House of Israel and The House of Judah," http://truthinhistory.org/the-house-of-israel-and-the-house-of-judah.html, printed out 7/2/2016; "The Seventy Weeks of Daniel," http://truthinhistory.org/the-seventy-weeks-of-daniel-2.html, printed out 7/2/2016.

[283] http://truthinhistory.org/contact-us/index.php, printed out 7/3/2016.

[284] https://web.archive.org/web/20070201233218/http://truthinhistory.org/, printed out 7/3/16.

[285] Baker, Charles Estell, "Chaplain's Comments," Confederate Veteran, Jan.-Feb. 1993, pp. 44. This issue doesn't have a volume or number.

[286] The website www.biblicalandsouthernstudies.com seems to be primarily devoted to publishing H. Rondel Rumburg's writings, but doesn't give much information who is in charge. The page http://www.biblicalandsouthernstudies.com/?page=shop/privacy, does list H. Rondel Rumburg as the contact individual for the group. However, Gary Lee Roper does mention that Rondel Rumburg is the founder of the Society for Biblical and Southern Studies in "Antebellum Slavery: An Orthodox Christian View," Gary Lee Roper publisher, 2008, pp. 179. The first issue of the *Chaplain's Corps Chronicles of the Sons of Confederate Veterans*, Jan. & Feb. 2006, has him as Chaplain-in-Chief writing an editorial, http://www.scv.org/pdf/chaplains/2006_Jan.pdf, printed out 7/3/2016, and he is listed as the editor in the June 2016 issue, http://www.scv.org/pdf/chaplains/2016_Jun.pdf, printed out 7/3/16. For the

listing of the 3rd edition of the "Enlarged Sesquicentennial Edition" of the "Chaplain's Handbook," http://chaplain-in-chief.com/catalog.html, printed out 7/3/2016.

[287] https://web.archive.org/web/20010203165300/http://ihr.org/jhr/jhrindex.html, printed out 7/3/2016. Later archived pages don't list the Editorial Advisory Committee.

[288] Miller, Scott, "Denial of the Holocaust," http://www.socialstudies.org/system/files/publications/se/5906/590607.html, printed out 7/3/2016. This is the website of the National Council for the Social Studies, an organization for social studies education and was founded in 1921.

[289] Sampley, Ted, "What Thomas Jefferson Learned From The Q'uran," pages 12-13, *Southern Mercury*, Vol. 5 No. 2, April 2007. The article can be found online.

[290] Parker, Ray, "Editorial," *Chaplain's Corps Chronicles of the Sons of Confederate Veterans*, Feb. 2016, http://www.scv.org/pdf/chaplains/2016_Feb.pdf, printed out 7/3/2016.

[291] Parker, Ray, "Editorial," *Chaplain's Corps Chronicles of the Sons of Confederate Veterans*, June. 2016, http://www.scv.org/pdf/chaplains/2016_Jun.pdf, printed out 7/3/2016.

[292] Fleming, Thomas, "From Under the Rubble: The Wearin' of the Cross," Abbeville Institute, http://www.abbevilleinstitute.org/blog/from-under-the-rubble-the-wearin-of-the-cross/, printed out 7/3/2016.

[293] Sullivan, Christopher M., "Partisan View," *Southern Partisan*, Vol. 20 1st Qtr. 2000, pp. 7. The mailing cover for the magazine says "Fourth Quarter 1999." However, the volume and quarter and year come from the cover of the magazine.

[294] Web page listing papers, http://www.scv.org/research/edPapers.php, printed out 7/4/2016; "Hispanic Heritage Month: Hispanics in Gray and Blue," http://www.scv.org/documents/edpapers/hispanichistory.pdf, printed out 7/4/2016.

[295] No author, "Classic Southern Reprints," Confederate Veteran, Vol. 2 2002, p. 36.

[296] Masters, Michael W., "The Tolerance Scam," *Southern Mercury*, Vol. 4 Nol. 4, July/Aug. 2006, pp. 8-9,30-34.

[297] Masters, Michael W., "The Morality of Survival, Part I," American Renaissance, Vol. 6 No. 7, July 1995, online http://www.amren.com/archives/back-issues/july-1995/, printed out 7/4/2016, and "The Morality of Survival, Part II," American Renaissance, Vol. 6 No. 8, August 1995, http://www.amren.com/archives/back-issues/august-1995/, printed out 7/4/2016.

[298] Sentell, Lynda, "Immigration Around the World," *Southern Mercury*, Vol. No. April 2007, pp. 16-20; No Author, "American Congressmen Speak Out On Immigration," pp. 20.

[299] The article is available at www.thesocialcontract.com, http://www.thesocialcontract.com/artman2/publish/tsc1103/article_978.shtml, printed out 7/5/2016.
[300] Childress, Rev. Edwin, "The 'Sojourner' Argument: Scripture Texts Are Often Misused by Religious Communities To Advocate High Immigration," *Southern Mercury*, Vol. 5 No. 2, April 2007, pp. 24-27.
[301] Slimp, Robert, "The North American Union May End Our Constitutional Republic," *Southern Mercury*, Vol. 5 No. 3, Aug. 2007, pp. 12-15.
[302] Vega, Cecilia M., "San Francisco Promotes Services for Illegal Immigrants," *Southern Mercury*, Vol. 6 No. 5, Sept./Oct. 2008, pp. 32-33. Note states that it was originally on Page B-1 of the *San Francisco Chronicle*, Thursday, April 3, 2008.
[303] Givens, R. Michael, "Report of the Lt. Commander-in-Chief," Confederate Veteran, Vol. 66 No. 5, Sept./Oct. 2008, pp. 8-9.
[304] Cathey, Boyd D., "Land We Love: Southern Tradition and Our Future," Confederate Veteran, Vol. 70 No. 2, March/April 2012, pp. 16-23, 56-60.
[305] Reed, John Shelton, "Letter From the Lower Right: Allons, Enfants de la Patrie," *Chronicles*, Vol. 13 No. 11, November 1989, pp. 46-48. This essay was republished in "Whistling Dixie: Dispatches from the South," Harcourt, Brace, Jovanovich, 1992.
[306] Reed, John Shelton, his selection in, "Extracurricular Reading," *Reason*, Dec. 1994, http://reason.com/archives/1994/12/01/extracurricular-reading/5, printed 8/7/2016.
[307] See my short piece at http://www.blackcommentator.com/633/633_cover_missouri_library_of_evil.html.
[308] Maxwell, Ronald F., no title, in "Cultural Revolutions" section, *Chronicles*, Vol. 23 No. 6, June 1993, pp. 6-7.
[309] Issue was Vol. 22 No. 6, which places it as Nov.-Dec. 2002, the Vol. 22 No. 5 issue was Sept./Oct. 2002, and the next Vol. 23 No.1 was Jan./Feb. 2003.
[310] Livingston, Donald, W., "We Are All Immigrants Now," *Chronicles*, Vol. 25 No. 11, Nov. 2001, pp. 20-21.
[311] Williamson, Chilton, Jr., "Revenge of the Confederacy," *Chronicles*, Vol. 39 No. 1, Jan. 2015, pp. 36-37.
[312] Phillips, Dan E., "American Soccer Fandom as Cosmopolitan Affectation," http://www.abbevilleinstitute.org/blog/american-soccer-fandom-as-cosmopolitan-affectation/, printed out 7/4/2016.
[313] Listing of their annual meetings, http://www.dmwv.org/dmwv/org-meeting.htm, printed out 7/9/2016; founding, http://www.dmwv.org/mwvets/mexvets.htm, printed out 7/9/2016.
[314] Advertisement, *UDC Magazine*, Vol. 67 No. 9, Oct. 2004, pp. 17.
[315] "About the DMWV," http://www.dmwv.org/dmwv/org-app.htm, printed out 7/9/2016.
[316] Page about Mexican War Journal, http://www.dmwv.org/dmwv/mwj.htm, printed out 7/10/2016; listing of staff of The Center for Greater Southwestern

Studies at UT Arlington, http://www.uta.edu/southwesternstudies/aboutus.html, printed out 7/10/2016.

[317] Borit, G.S., "Journal of the Illinois State Historical Society," Vol. 67 No. 1, Feb. 1974, pp. 79-100, quote on page 70. From "Collected Works of Abraham Lincoln," Rutgers Univ. Press, Vol. 1, p. 439.

[318] Grant, Ulysses S., "Personal Memoirs of U.S. Grant," Dover Publications, New York, New York, reprint 1995, pp. 16. Originally published by Charles L. Webster & Co. New York City, 1885.

[319] Randolph, John, senate speech, Gales and Seaton's Register of Debates in Congress, 19th Congress, 1st Session, Commencing Dec. 5, 1825 and ending May 22, 1826, speech pp. 112-132. It is available online at www.confederatepastpresent.org.

[320] Davis, Jefferson, "Speech of Jefferson Davis at the Portland Democratic Convention, August 23, 1858," from "Jefferson Davis Constitutionalist: His Letters, Papers, and Speeches," collected and edited by Dunbar Rowland, Vol. 3 Pages 284-288, printed by the Mississippi Department of Archives and History, Jackson Mississippi, 1923.

[321] McEntire, Juanita B. (Mrs. E.F.), "Jefferson Davis at Buena Vista and the War With Mexico," *United Daughters of the Confederacy Magazine*, Vol. 47 No. 5, May 1984, pp. 8-10. Not until much later did UDC members use their own names instead of their husband's names for articles. The author was only able to track this name down since it was a June Program article hence the Historian General of the UDC and it just happened that the in the Historian General article in the issue she included her name. Generally, it is difficult or impossible to know what the author's name is except by the name the author used for the article and in that case that is the name used. The name of the magazine of the UDC has changed over time.

[322] Hague, Euan, Sebesta, Edward H., ""The US Civil War As A Theological War: Confederate Christian Nationalism and the League of the South," in *Canadian Review of American Studies*, Vol. 32 No. 3, 2002, pp. 253-284, has a good overview of Confederate Christian nationalism and the idea of the Civil War being a theological conflict. Also, in "Neo-Confederacy: A Critical Introduction," Editors, Euan Hague, Heidi Beirich, and Edward H. Sebesta, Univ. of Texas Press, Austin, 2008, has a chapter of neo-Confederates idea of the Civil War being a theological conflict.

[323] Anderson, Alister C., "Chaplain's Comments," *Confederate Veteran*, Vol. 6 1999, pp. 60-61.

[324] Conner, Frank, "Reorganizing the Sons of Confederate Veterans," *Southern Mercury*, Vol. 2 No. 3, May/June 2004, pp. 8-11, 27.

[325] Evans, Mark W., "Chaplain's Comments: Battle for Truth," *Confederate Veteran*, Vol. 68 No. 6, Nov./Dec. 2010, pp. 12-13.

[326] Evans, Mark W., "Christian Warriors," *Confederate Veteran*, Vol. 69 No. 2, March/April 2011, pp. 12-13.

[327] This is the standard text that is stated as "The Charge," but the origins of the "The Charge" is not known except it was reputedly stated by Stephen D. Lee to the SCV. There has been some inquiry into the matter by neo-Confederates.
[328] Boyd, Cathey, D. "The Land We Love: Southern Tradition and Our Future," Confederate Veteran, Vol. No., March/April 2012, pp. 16-23, 56-60.
[329] No author listed, but the Chairman of the Committee was Kirk Carter, "Something to Intrigue the Mind: The Message in the Confederate Battle Flag," Confederate Veteran, Vol. 68 No. 2, March/April 2010, pp. 19.
[330] Preble, George Henry, "Origin and History of the American Flag," Vol. 2, Nicholas Brown, Philadelphia, 1917, pp. 512-513.
[331] 15 Southern Ministers, "The Moral Case for the Confederate Flag: A Special Message for Southern Christians," Southern Partisan, Vol. 16 4th Qtr. 1996, pp. 16-21.
[332] Rumburg, H. Rondel, "Chaplain's Comments," Confederate Veteran, Vol. 63 No. 5, Nov./Dec. 2005, pp. 12-13, 49.
[333] Cathey, Body D., "A New Reconstruction: The Renewed Assault on Southern Heritage," Confederate Veteran, Vol. 73 No. 6, Nov./Dec. 2015. Pp. 16-19, 56-59.
[334] Haines, J.D., "The Problem with Teaching Tolerance," Southern Mercury, Vol. 4 No. 2, March/April 2006.
[335] Fayard, Cecil A. Jr., "Chaplain's Comments," Confederate Veteran, Vol. No. , Sept./Oct. 2009, pp. 12-13, 45.
[336] Kennedy, James Ronald, Kennedy Walter Donald, "Our Re-United Country?: The Sad Reality of Reconciliation," Confederate Veteran, Sept./Oct. 2014, pp. 16-22, 24,56, 62, 64-65. Quote on page 22.
[337] Strain, Thomas V. Jr., "Report of the Lt. Commander-in-Chief," Confederate Veteran, Vol. 73 No. 5, Sept./Oct. 2015, pp. 8-9.
[338] Rumburg, H. Rondel, "Scapegoating the South: Apologizing: the Result of Scapegoating," Chaplains' Corps Chronicles of the Sons of Confederate Veterans, March 2007, http://www.scv.org/new/wp-content/uploads/2015/10/2007_Mar.pdf, article printed out 7/10/2016.
[339] http://www.scv.org/new/wp-content/uploads/2015/10/2009_Sep.pdf, printed out 7/10/2016.
[340] Kennedy, James Ronald, Kennedy, Walter Kennedy, "The South Was Right!", 2nd Edition, Pelican Publishing Company, 1994, Gretna, Louisiana, pp. 264.
[341] Editorial reply to "Pining For the South," Southern Partisan, Vol. 6 No. 1, Winter 1986, pp. 3-4.
[342] No author, "Obiter Dicta: The Pink Piper," Southern Partisan, Vol. 24 No. 4, issue date, July/August 2004, published July 2005, pp. 9. The Southern Partisan had a confusing date system and the actual arrival of the printed magazine could be even months later.
[343] Byrnes, P.J., "A New Strategy to Fight the Gay Rights Movement," Southern Partisan, Vol. 23 No. 2, March/April 2003, pp. 40.

[344] Byrnes, P.J., "A New Christian Right," *Southern Partisan*, Vol. 24, No. 1, Issue Date, Jan./Feb. 2004, Published Nov. 2004, pp. 36. The *Southern Partisan* had a confusing date system and the actual arrival of the printed magazine could be even months later.

[345] Reed, John Shelton, "Letter From the Lower Right," *Chronicles*, Vol. 10 No. 1, Jan. 1986, pp. 45.

[346] Reed, John Shelton, "Letter From the Lower Right," Chronicles, Vol. 15 No. 4, April 1991, pp. 41-42.

[347] Reed, John Shelton, "Letter From the Lower Right," subtitle, "Hotel California," Chronicles, Vol. 15 No. 5, May 1991, pp. 45-46.

[348] Reed, John Shelton, "Letter From the Lower Right," Chronicles, Vol. 10 No. 1, Jan. 1986, pp. 45.

[349] Reed, John Shelton, "Letter From the Lower Right," subtitle, "Reservations Required," *Chronicles*, Vol. 12 No. 11, Nov. 1988, pp. 46-48. For some reason in this issue it is given as No. 10 printed in it, but there is a Vol. 12 No. 10 Oct. issue. It seems to be a misprint in the Nov. issue.

[350] Reed, John Shelton, "Letter from the Lower Right," *Chronicles*, Vol. 10 No. 2, Feb. 1986, pp. 45.

[351] Reed, John Shelton, "Letter from the Lower Right," *Chronicles*, Vol. 14 No. 4, April 1990, pp. 41-42.

[352] The Sons of Confederate Veterans revived in the 1980s the use of the name "Confederate Veteran" and also at times listed its volumes and numbers as if it was a continuation of the *Confederate Veteran* of the early 20th century, but it is a publication started in the 1980s.

[353] Cummings, C.C., "Annual Address by the Historian of Texas Division U.C.V.," Confederate Veteran, Vol. 24 No. 12, Dec. 1916, pp. 569. The address can be read in full at www.confederatepastpresent.org where examples of the white supremacist writings of the neo-Confederate groups in the 19th and 20th century are made available.

[354] Cunningham, S.A., "M'Kinley, Roosevelt, and the Negro," *Confederate Veteran* Vol. 11 No.1, Jan. 1903, pp. 4.

[355] Rankin, John E., "Forrest at Brice's Crossroads," *Confederate Veteran*, Vol. 33 No. 8, August 1925, pp. 290-2.

[356] Examples are at www.confederatepastpresent.org, and also in Loewen, James, Sebesta, Edward H., "The Confederate and Neo-Confederate Reader: The 'Great Truth' about the 'Lost Cause,'" Univ. Press of Mississippi, Jackson, Mississippi, 2010.

[357] Lunsford, Charles P., "Heritage Defense in the SCV," *Southern Heritage Magazine*, Vol. 2 No. 4, July/Aug. 1994, given a date in the article of May 1994, pp. 14-17.

[358] For online, https://scv.secure-sites.biz/store.php, printed out 7/18/2016. *Sons of Confederate Veterans Merchandise Catalog 2004-2005*, page 27; *Sons of Confederate Veteran Merchandise Catalog 2005-2006*, page 27; *Sons of Confederate Veteran Merchandise Catalog 2008-2009*, page 26; *Sons of Confederate Veteran Merchandise Catalog* 2009-2010, page 26; *Sons of*

Confederate Veteran Merchandise Catalog 2011-2012, pp.25 Sons of *Confederate Veteran Merchandise Catalog 2015-2016* page 26. Note, the author only possesses six of these catalogs, there may be others which might also have this book listed.

[359] 2013-2014 SCV Merchandise Catalog, pp. 13, insert after page 20 in *Confederate Veteran*, Vol. 71 Nol. 5, Sept./Oct. 2014.

[360] Ewing, Elbert William R., "Legal and Historical Status of the Dred Scott Decision", Cobden Publishing Co., Washington D.C., 1909, pp. 72. Quote from pamphlet, "An Enquiry into the Political Grade of the free Colored population under the Constitution of the United States," John F. Denny, of the Chambersburg, Pennsylvania bar, 1834.

[361] Grissom, Michael Andrew, "Southern by the Grace of God," Pelican Publishing Co., Gretna, Louisiana, 1989, pp. 165-169.

[362] Kennedy, James Ronald, Kennedy, Walter Donald, "The South Was Right!," Pelican Publishing Co., Gretna, Louisiana, 1994, for writing on Reconstruction, pp. 169-176, and Appendices as mentioned.

[363] www.jebstuartcamp.org/jebstuartcamp.org/2015reunion/docs/Speakers%20and%20Performances.pdf, printed out 6/5/2015.

[364] Conner, Frank, "The South Under Siege: 1830-2000," Collards Publishing Company, Newman, Georgia, 2002, pp. 180-187.

[365] Tindal, Retta, D., "Reconstruction, 1865-1877," *UDC Magazine*, Vol. 75 No. 11, Dec. 2012, pp. 11-14.

[366] Tindal, Retta, D., "Reconstruction, 1865-1877," UDC Magazine, Vol. 75 No. 11, Dec. 2012, pp. 11-14.

[367] Editorial reprinted from the Bellman of Minneapolis, Minnesota, "Northern View of Race Troubles," *Confederate Veteran,* Vol. 14 No. 12, Dec. 1906, pp. 546-47. This article in its entirety is available online at www.confederatepastpresent.org.

[368] Lee, Stephen Dill, "The South Since the War," Vol. 9, of the serial set, Confederate Military History, Confederate Publishing Company, 1899, Atlanta, Georgia. Article is pp. 267-568. The section, "The Negro Problem," starts on page 346. The section, "Lynchings," pp. 352-360. NOTE: This serial set has been reprinted several times since the original serial set was published and it has been expanded with additional volumes.

[369] Online store, https://scv.secure-sites.biz, printed out 8/7/2016. *Sons of Confederate Veterans Merchandise Catalog 2004-2005*, page 30; *Sons of Confederate Veteran Merchandise Catalog 2005-2006*, page 30; *Sons of Confederate Veteran Merchandise Catalog 2008-2009*, page 29; *Sons of Confederate Veteran Merchandise Catalog* 2009-2010, page 29; *Sons of Confederate Veteran Merchandise Catalog 2011-2012*, pp.29 Sons of *Confederate Veteran Merchandise Catalog 2015-2016* page 29. Note, the author only possesses six of these catalogs, there may be others which might also have this book listed.

[370] 2013-2014 SCV Merchandise Catalog, pp. 13, insert after page 20 in *Confederate Veteran*, Vol. 71 No1. 5, Sept./Oct. 2014.
[371] Page, Thomas Nelson, "The Negro: The Southerner's Problem," Charles Scribner's Sons, New York, New York, 1904, Chapter, "The Lynching of Negroes – Its Cause and Its Prevention," pp. 86-118.
[372] Slimp, Robert, "Americans Face The Worst Presidential Candidates In History," Southern Mercury, Vol. No. , May/June 2008, pp. 28-33, quote on page 32.
[373] Conner, Frank, "Where We Stand Now And How We Got There," *Southern Mercury*, Vol. 1 No. 2, Sept./Oct. 2003, pp. 10-14.
[374] John B. Hood Journal, holdings at the Dallas Public Library, bound volume, 973.742 J65, four volumes published in 1965, published by the John B. Hood Camp of the Texas Division of the Sons of Confederate Veterans. Whites only sticker in Vol. 1 No. 2, "Negro 23rd Psalm" in Vol. 1 No. 3, and the denunciation of supporters of Civil Rights as scalawags in Vol. 1 No. 4.
[375] Sons of Confederate Veterans Official Program national convention 1977 in Dallas, Texas. Copy at the Dallas Public Library. "Birth of a Nation" showing and M.E. Bradford's agenda "Call to Order," pp. 3.
[376] Beard, William M., "Our Common Heritage," *United Daughters of the Confederacy Magazine*, Vol. 20 No. 6, June 1957, pp. 17, 20-21, 24-25, 38-39.
[377] Dunstan, Bruce, "Jefferson Davis – The Man America Needs Today," *United Daughters of the Confederacy Magazine*, Vol. No. , June 1958, pp. 19, 23, 26-27.
[378] Erath, Clara, "Confederate Notes," page 9, *United Daughters of the Confederacy Magazine*, Vol. 53 No. 10, October 1990.
[379] Weaver, Richard, "The Southern Tradition At Bay," pages 388-389, published by Arlington House, New Rochelle, New York, 1968.
[380] Weaver, Richard, "The Southern Tradition At Bay," page 52, published by Arlington House, New Rochelle, New York, 1968.
[381] Weaver, Richard, "The Southern Tradition At Bay," page 168, published by Arlington House, New Rochelle, New York, 1968.
[382] Weaver, Richard, "The Southern Tradition At Bay," page 169, published by Arlington House, New Rochelle, New York, 1968.
[383] Weaver, Richard, "The Southern Tradition At Bay," page 394, published by Arlington House, New Rochelle, New York, 1968.
[384] Erath, Clara, "The Value of Southern Tradition: Abbeville Institute Promotes Critical Study of the War," *UDC Magazine*, Vol. 68 No. 7, Aug. 2005, pp. 17.
[385] No author, boxed article, "Abbeville Institute Co-Founder & President Honored," *UDC Magazine*, Vol. 69 No. 10, Nov. 2005, pp. 18.
[386] Conner, Frank, "Where We Stand Now And How We Got There," *Southern Mercury*, Vol. 1 No. 2, Sept./Oct. 2003, pp. 10-14.
[387] Cathey, Boyd D., "The Land We Love: Southern Tradition and Our Future," Confederate Veteran, Vol. 70 No. 2, March/April 2012, pp. 16-23, 56-60.
[388] Bradford, M.E., "Remembering Who We Are: Observations of a Southern Conservative," Univ. of Georgia Press, Athens, Georgia, 1985, dust jacket.

[389] Horwitz, Tony, "The Faces of Extremism Wear Many Guises – Most of them Ordinary," page 1, *Wall Street Journal*, Vol. 95 No. 83, April 28, 1995. Southern League was the old name of the League of the South.
[390] Crouch, Stanley, "Neo-Confederates of the GOP rise again," *San Francisco Chronicle*, January 5, 2004, page A-15.
[391] The reader could read "Life Without Prejudice" in which he rejects the civil rights movement. It is available online at multiple websites. The Intercollegiate Studies Institute, the group which supports the conservative student newspapers at the universities has it online at https://home.isi.org/life-without-prejudice, 9/16/2016.
[392] Billig, Michael, Banal Nationalism, from the Introduction, page 12, Sage Publications, Thousand Oaks, 1995. A challenging book which I strongly recommend reading.
[393] Jane G. Durden, "From the Desk of the President General," *UDC Magazine*, Vol. 72 No. 5, May 2009, page 5.
[394] Robert E. Lee, "Memoranda on the Civil War," *Century Illustrated Monthly Magazine*, Vol. 36 No. 4, August. 1888, 600-01 for his views on slavery; ---, *Report of the Joint Committee on Reconstruction at the First Session Thirty-Ninth Congress*, (Washington: GPO, 1866), 135-36 for his views of ridding Virginia of African Americans.
[395] No author, "General Robert E. Lee West Point Award," *United Daughters of the Confederacy Magazine*, Vol. 11 No.7, July 1948, pp. 20. The name of the magazine was shorten later.
[396] Duval, Ruby R., "The Robert E. Lee Sword," *United Daughters of the Confederacy Magazine*, Vol. 17 No. 10, Oct. 1954, pp. 4.
[397] Schmidt, Peter, "Bowdoin Ends Confederate-Heritage Award Like Many Still Offered by U.S. Service Academies," *The Chronicle of Higher Education*, Oct. 26, 2015, http://chronicle.com/blogs/ticker/bowdoin-ends-confederate-heritage-award-like-many-still-offered-by-u-s-service-academies/106066, printed out 7/30/2016.
[398] Phillips, Dave, "Raised-Fist Photo by Black Women at West Point Spurs Inquiry," New York Times, May 7, 2016, page A1. Also, online, http://www.nytimes.com/2016/05/07/us/raised-fist-photo-by-black-women-at-west-point-spurs-inquiry.html, printed out 7/30/2016.
[399] Calamur, Krishnadev, "The Controversy Over a Photograph At West Point," *The Atlantic*, May 11, 2016, http://www.theatlantic.com/national/archive/2016/05/west-point-cadets-photograph/482250/, printed out 7/30/2016.
[400] Duval, Ruby R., "The Robert E. Lee Sword," *United Daughters of the Confederacy Magazine*, Vol. 17 No. 10, Oct. 1954, pp. 4.
[401] No author, "New UDC Award Presented," captioned photo, *United Daughters of the Confederacy Magazine*, Vol. 25 No. 9, Sept. 1962, pp. 4.
[402] Foster, Gaines M., "Ghosts of the Confederacy," page 16, Oxford University Press, Oxford, 1987.

[403] Gerald Horne, "The Deepest South: The United States, Brazil, and the African Slave Trade," pp. 113-16, New York University Press, New York, 2007. Maury's plan is discussed from page 112 to 127.
[404] Matthew Fontaine Maury, "Direct Foreign Trade of the South," *De Bow's Review*, Vol. 12 No. 2 Feb. 1852, pp. 147.
[405] Col. John C. Lawton, "Matthew Fontaine Maury," *UDC Magazine*, Vol. 21 No. 3, March 1958, pp. 6-7, 10, 17.
[406] No author, "Cadet Garret T. Bush III Receives Admiral Semmes Award at Academy," *United Daughters of the Confederacy Magazine*, Vol. 22 No.8, August 1959, pp. 34.
[407] Gerald Horne, "The Deepest South: The United States, Brazil, and the African Slave Trade," pp. 190-91, New York University Press, New York, 2007.
[408] No author, photo with caption of Wade Hampton Sabre being given to a Citadel cadet, *UDC Magazine*, Vol. 71 No. 6, June/July 2008, pp. 28. Also, no author, photo with caption of same, *UDC Magazine*, Vol. 49 No. 12, Dec. 1986, pp. 7.
[409] "*United Daughters of the Confederacy, South Carolina Division: Golden Anniversary 1896-1946,*" no author.
[410] No author, "Junior ROTC H.L. Hunley Awards Program," *Confederate Veteran*, Vol. 67 No. 6, Nov./Dec. 2009 pp. 52-53.
[411] Wilson, A.C. III, ""SCV JROTC H.L. Hunley Award," *Confederate Veteran*, Vol. 72 No. 1, Jan./Feb. 2014, pp. 62-64.
[412] Hardy, William N., "Junior ROTC – Implementing the Charge," *Confederate Veteran*, Vol. 71 No. 6, Nov./Dec. 2013, pp. 56-57.
[413] Likins, Jamie, "From the Office of the President General," *United Daughters of the Confederacy Magazine*, Vol. 77 No. 11, Dec. 2014, pp. 5.
[414] Trammell, Mrs. Harold Jay (Pam), "From the Desk of the President General," United Daughters of the Confederacy Magazine, Vol. 79 No. 9, Oct. 2016, pp. 5.
[415] Roach, David, " Third way church disfellowshiped from SBC," Sept. 23, 2014, *Baptist Press*, http://bpnews.net/43416/third-way-church-disfellowshipped-from-sbc, printed out 9/16/2016.
[416] Hogan, Gene, "Forward the Colors," *Confederate Veteran*, Vol. 72 No.10, May/June 2014, pp. 10-11.
[417] No author, in section, "Notices From Around the Confederation," title, "SCV Member Elected to lead National Society Sons of American Revolution," Vol. 67 No. 6, Nov./Dec. 2009, pp. 48.
[418] Barrow, Charles Kelly, "Report of the Lt. Commander-in-Chief," *Confederate Veteran*, Vol. 72 No. 2, March/April 2014, pp. 8-9.
[419] Cole, David, "Race & Renaming: A Talk with Peter Salovey, President of Yale," *New York Review of Books*, Vol. 63 No. 10, pp. 42-44. The author because of this article and similar articles reflecting a banal white nationalism is not renewing his subscription. This is another print media trapped in the past. The article is available online http://www.nybooks.com/articles/2016/06/09/race-renaming-peter-salovey-yale/, and a copy was printed out 8/14/2016.

[420] Brighenti, Daniela, Xu, Qi, and Yaffe-Bellany, David, "Worker Smashes 'Racist' Panel, Loses Job," New Haven Independent, July 11, 2016, http://www.newhavenindependent.org/index.php/archives/entry/corey_menafee/, printed out 7/31/2016.
[421] Megan, Kathleen, "Charges Dropped Against Yale Dining Hall Worker," *Hartford Courant*, July 26, 2016, http://www.courant.com/education/hc-yale-menafee-court-0727-20160726-story.html, printed out 7/31/2016. Also, Brighenti, Daniela, Xu, Qi, and Yaffe-Bellany, David, "Yale Gags Rehired Cafeteria Worker," *New Haven Independent*, July 26, 2016, http://www.newhavenindependent.org/index.php/archives/entry/menafee/, printed out 7/31/2016.
[422] Gay, Eric, "University is moving Jefferson Davis statue, but Robert E. Lee's stays," *Association Press*, as carried by the *Los Angeles Times*, August, 15, 2015, http://www.latimes.com/nation/nationnow/la-na-nn-texas-jefferson-davis-statue-20150814-story.html, printed out 8/21/2016.
[423] No author, "Task Force to Review Jefferson Davis Statue on Campus,"Press Release, The University of Texas at Austin, June 24, 2015, http://news.utexas.edu/2015/06/24/task-force-to-review-jefferson-davis-statue-on-campus, printed out 8/21/2016.
[424] "Task Force on Historical Representation of Statuary at UT Austin: Report to President Gregory L. Fenves," August 10, 2015, page 7, http://diversity.utexas.edu/statues/2015/08/10/task-force-report-available-for-download/, downloaded 9/13/2016. http://mtsu.edu/forresthall/docs/UT-Austin-Report-2015.pdf,
[425] Gay, Eric, "University is moving Jefferson Davis statue, but Robert E. Lee's stays," *Association Press*, as carried by the *Los Angeles Times*, August, 15, 2015, http://www.latimes.com/nation/nationnow/la-na-nn-texas-jefferson-davis-statue-20150814-story.html, printed out 8/21/2016.
[426] http://mayor.baltimorecity.gov/news/press-releases/2015-09-04-mayor-rawlings-blake-announces-appointment-members-special-commission, printed out 9/13/2016.
[427] Broadwater, Luke, "Baltimore City commission recommends removal of two Confederate monuments," Baltimore Sun, Jan. 14, 2016, online at http://www.baltimoresun.com/news/maryland/baltimore-city/bs-md-ci-confederate-monuments-20160114-story.html, printed out 8/21/2016.
[428] Hooke, Alexander E., both *Baltimore Sun* articles, "My run in with liberal fascists," Feb. 2, 2016, http://www.baltimoresun.com/news/opinion/oped/bs-ed-liberal-fascism-20160202-story.html, printed out 9/13/2016; "Politically incorrect statues provide teachable moments," Oct. 27, 2015, http://www.baltimoresun.com/news/opinion/oped/bs-ed-confederate-lessons-20151027-story.html, printed out 9/13/2016.
[429] Reporting by Ian Simpson, editing by Alden Bentley, "Baltimore panel calls for removal of Confederate monuments," Reuters, 9/14/2016, http://www.reuters.com/article/us-maryland-monuments-idUSKCN11K2NX, printed out 9/15/2016.

[430] Editorial, "No more foot-dragging on Confederate monuments," Baltimore Sun, Sept. 15, 2016, http://www.baltimoresun.com/news/opinion/editorial/bs-ed-confederate-monuments-20160915-story.html, printed out 9/16/2016.

[431] Peterson, Orlando, "Slavery and Social Death: A Comparative Study," Harvard University Press, 1982. Actually the author read "Freedom: Freedom in the Making of Western Culture," Vol. 1, Basic Books, 1991 to learn the same concept.

[432] Cooper, William J., "Jefferson Davis, American," Alfred A. Knopf, 2000, page 248. Cooper tries to excuse the mortality of Davis's slaves by reporting average life spans. Reported average life spans in history are greatly influenced by infant mortality and the mortality of children. It is a common place in high school history classes for teachers to explain that just because the average life span was very low, that didn't mean there weren't old people around in the past. Even in the past, if you made it to be 15 years old you had a fairly good chance to make it to be 60 years old. To have a mortality curve truncate around the age of 40 years, is indicative of something morbid and is sinister. Cooper's rationalizations and excuses for this truncation on Brierfield are appalling. As Cooper explains in his book, Jefferson Davis was a steady purchaser of slaves, most whom would have been at least in their teenage years if not young adults. With this in mind it can be assumed that the Brierfield worked its slaves to an early death. Cooper discusses Davis' purchase of slaves on pages 248-250.

[433] I normally avoid vulgarities, but sometimes they are necessary to shout through all the chattering rationalizations.

[434] The primary reference is Am. Slave, Supp. Ser. 2 IV, 1120-21 (Mollie Dawson), I read quote on page 147, in "An Empire for Slavery: The Peculiar Institution in Texas, 1821-1865," by Randolph B. Campbell, Louisiana State University, Baton Rouge, 1991.

[435] Norris, Wesley, Interview circa 1866, in John W. Blassingame's "Slave Testimony: Two Centuries of Letters, Speeches, Interviews, and Autobiographies," Louisiana State University Press, Baton Rouge, 1977, pages 467-68.

[436] From Elliot's Debates, Vol. 5, pages 457-61, the text quoted here was modified to give Mason his full name. Also, the complete debate is online at www.confederatepastpresent.org.

[437] Quarles, Benjamin, "Allies for Freedom & Blacks on John Brown," Oxford Univ. Press, 1974, Oxford, reprinted De Capo edition, 2001.

[438] Sinha, Minisha, "The Slave's Cause: A History of Abolition," Yale University Press, 2016, New Haven, pp. 57.

[439] Sinha, Minisha, "The Slave's Cause: A History of Abolition," Yale University Press, 2016, New Haven, pp. 213.

[440] Thomas, Hugh, "The Slave Trade: The Story of the Atlantic Slave Trade: 1440-1870," Simon & Schuster, 1997, New York City, pp. 577.

[441] Sinha, Minisha, "The Slave's Cause: A History of Abolition," Yale University Press, 2016, New Haven, pp. 57.

[442] Thomas, Hugh, "The Slave Trade: The Story of the Atlantic Slave Trade: 1440-1870," Simon & Schuster, 1997, New York City, pp. 611.
[443] Thomas, Hugh, "The Slave Trade: The Story of the Atlantic Slave Trade: 1440-1870," Simon & Schuster, 1997, New York City, pp. 635.
[444] Hopefully Google translation has done a good job on the Portuguese translation of "merciless nagging."
[445] "State Documents on Federal Relations: The States and the United States," Vol. 5, "Slavery and the Constitution," edited by Herman V. Ames, published by the Dept. of History, Univ. of Pennsylvania, 1904, Pp. 16-17.
[446] Smith, H. Shelton, "In His Image, But ...: Racism in Southern Religion, 1780-1919, Duke Univ. Press, 1872, pp. 39-40.
[447] *Congressional Globe*, 31st Congress, 1st Session, Appendix, 149-157, February 13-14, 1850, page 79. I would like to thank T. Lloyd Benson in the Dept. of History at Furman Univ. for providing this text online so I didn't have to type it in from the small print of the *Congressional Globe*. http://history.furman.edu/benson/docs/davis13feb1850.html.
[448] Berlin, Ira, Fields Barbara J., Miller, Steven F., Reidy, Joseph P., Rowland, Leslie S., "Slaves No More: Three Essays on Emancipation and the Civil War," Cambridge University Press, Cambridge, 1992, pp. ix, x.
[449] Du Bois, W.E.B., "The Lie of History as It Is Taught Today," from "W.E.B. Du Bois: A Reader," edited by Andrew Paschal, Collier Books edition, New York, 1993, pp. 115-120.

Made in the USA
Columbia, SC
29 July 2023